Jim White was brought up in Manchester, educated at Manchester Grammar School and on the terraces of Old Trafford. After a degree in English at Bristol University, he became a journalist. He has worked at the *Independent*, the *Guardian* and now writes for the *Daily Telegraph*, as well as being an award-winning radio and television broadcaster. Jim White is the author of several books about football, including *You'll Win Nothing With Kids*, and the acclaimed *Are You Watching, Liverpool?*, the inside story of Manchester United's 1993–94 season.

Also by Jim White

You'll Win Nothing With Kids

MANCHESTER UNITED

UNITED

THE BIOGRAPHY

From Newton Heath to Moscow, the Complete
Story of the World's Greatest Football Club

Jim White

sphere

SPHERE

First published in Great Britain in 2008 by Sphere
This paperback edition published in 2009 by Sphere

A CIP catalogue record for this book
is available from the British Library.

ISBN 978-0-7515-3911-0

Typeset in Palatino by M Rules
Printed and bound in Great Britain by
Clays Ltd, St Ives, plc

Papers used by Sphere are natural, renewable and recyclable
products sourced from well-managed forests and certified
in accordance with the rules of the Forest Stewardship Council.

Mixed Sources
Product group from well-managed
forests and other controlled sources
www.fsc.org Cert no. SGS-COC-004081
© 1996 Forest Stewardship Council
FSC

Sphere
An imprint of
Little, Brown Book Group
100 Victoria Embankment
London EC4Y 0DY

An Hachette UK Company
www.hachette.co.uk

www.littlebrown.co.uk

To Bols, as always

CONTENTS

ACKNOWLEDGEMENTS

I've spoken to a lot of people over a couple of years in the background development of this book and I owe them all a big thank you. Without your words this book would never have happened. And some of you didn't even ask for money in return for my nosiness. I'm particularly grateful to Eric Harrison, Eric Cantona, Martin Buchan, Lou Macari, Norman Whiteside, Pat Crerand, Big Ron Atkinson, Jimmy Greenhoff, Andy Walsh and Martin Edwards (and it's not often those two names have shared a sentence), who all spent rather more time in my company than they either anticipated or would probably wish to repeat.

I read a large number of United books in my research, and I'd recommend the following as the definitive works on various aspects of the red story. Pat Crerand's combative *Never Turn the Other Cheek*; Sir Bobby Charlton's lyrical *Manchester United Years*; Michael Crick's magnificent Alex Ferguson biography *The Boss* and his angry denunciation of the Martin Edwards years *The Betrayal of a Legend*; Fergie's own book *Managing My Life*; two belters from the pen of Eamon Dunphy: his biography of Matt Busby *A Strange Kind of Glory* and the fantastic *Keane: The Autobiography*; Andy Mitten's terrific *We Are The Famous Man United*; Daniel Taylor's superb *This Is The One* which, despite being nothing more than an unabashed 328-page love letter to Sir Alex, managed to earn the author a ban from Carrington press briefings; and David Hall's compelling contemporary report of the lingering aftermath of the Munich disaster, *Manchester's Finest*. I also consulted two books called *Back From The Brink*, one by Justin Blundell centring on the wilderness years of the twenties and thirties, and the other, by Paul McGrath, centring on the wilderness years of his own alcoholism. As a guide through the financial maze that is Old Trafford, Mihir Bose is a knowledgeable torch carrier and both his books on the reds going into the red – *Manchester Unlimited* and *Manchester DisUnited* – are packed with insights, while Andy Walsh and Adam Brown's *Not For Sale* recalls the fight against the Murdoch takeover with the relish and pace of a thriller. Plus there was David Beckham's *My Side*, Tommy Docherty's *My Story*, Ron Atkinson's *Big Ron: A Different Ball Game*, Joe Lovejoy's *Bestie*, Frank Taylor's *The Day a Team Died*, *The Manchester United Opus* and Gordon Burn's *Best and Edwards*, which, to my mind, is the sharpest analysis of the many volumes dedicated to the fallen genius that was George Best.

As far as the accumulation of United facts, trivia and insights is concerned, thanks to Michael Crick, Iain McCartney and Tim Rich for their expertise and their willingness to share that knowledge. And to Chris Davies for some invaluable old material (and that's just the jokes). As far as keeping the project on track, I owe Cat Ledger a huge hug. Also a big thanks to everyone at Little, Brown: Adam Strange was a hugely encouraging editor, Iain Hunt a brilliant copy editor and Maddie Mogford a patient legal reader. You guys are a joy to work with.

Most of all, though, I'm indebted to my collaborator Andy Mitten, the man who knows more about Manchester United than any living being and without whose enthusiasm, contacts and incredibly detailed input, this book would never have existed.

Oh and cheers to John Terry: your little slip helped give the book a happier conclusion than it might otherwise have had.

INTRODUCTION

Midway through the second half of a nervy, mistake-strewn Champions League fixture at Old Trafford, the crowd has grown introspective, quiet, grumpy. Groans echo round the enormous stands. The first leg a fortnight before had been a draw and Manchester United have to win to progress to the next stage of the competition. Right now, victory appears a fading proposition; a goal about as likely as Sir Alex Ferguson joining Victoria Beckham, John Magnier and Jaap Stam as a guest on a BBC talk show hosted by Alan Green.

Sporting academics will tell you that competitive uncertainty is football's unique selling proposition. Not knowing the result before the game starts is what keeps us coming back. Except tonight, for those who have paid to watch this encounter, there is a little too much uncertainty in the chilly evening air, a few too many permutations are running through the collective mental computer. As United's expensively acquired forwards time and again fail to navigate a way through their opponents' well-corralled defence, what everyone wants is the comfort of a bit of certainty. A 4-0 certainty would be nice.

Sitting in the row in front of me, the woman who has spent much of the first half snapping the action forty yards away on a digital camera and then showing the results to her companion now has her hand in her mouth, chewing at her fingernails. The man two seats along, whose expanding frame suggests memories of his last sporting foray are buried in the thickening mists of time, is loudly complaining about his team's general uselessness. All around me, jitters are being voiced in agitated catcalls. As another move breaks down following an expansive, but doomed, attempt by United's Cristiano Ronaldo to flick the ball to a colleague with his instep, it all becomes too much for a bloke behind me. He bellows: 'Can you not just pass it, you bleedin' ponce.'

No more than a minute after the man's interjection, in a sudden blur of quick-fire exchanges, the ball makes its way out to the right-hand side of the pitch, where a player in red exploits a moment of hesitation by an opponent, advances towards the byline and spins a hard, low cross into the penalty area. After ricocheting off a couple of flailing limbs, the ball lands at the golden boots of Ronaldo himself, lurking on the edge of the box. A defender moves towards him immediately, hoping to block the route to goal. With a sway of his hips and a dip of the shoulder, the Portuguese deceives the player at the very point he lunges for the ball, leaving him marooned, embarrassed, on his backside. As Ronaldo advances goalwards, every supporter round me is up on their feet, bodies unconsciously shadowing his progress, willing him onwards, urging him towards his target. For a moment there is a shared momentum between crowd and player, an urgent, anxious forward thrust. Instantly the individual hopes of seventy-five thousand people in the stands and the eleven down on the pitch have been gathered into one irresistible whole. It is a moment of alchemy. A moment of extraordinary unity of purpose. The effort works. Ronaldo scores. After he plants the ball past the goalkeeper into the roof of the net the player stands for a second or two, eyes squeezed shut, fists clenched, chin pointing upwards towards the sky, mouth framing a guttural yell. He appears to have reached the very point of ecstasy. All around me, the joy at his goal is unrestrained. There is much hugging, much punching of the air, much relieved laughter.

'Ye-es. Ye-e-e-es. Yes, yes, yes,' shrieks the woman with the camera, like she's Meg Ryan ordering a coffee. The fat man, too, has squeezed himself from his seat and, as he bounces with joy, is giving vivid demonstration of the purpose of a sports bra. Behind me, the bloke so recently accusing the very same Ronaldo of being all mouth and no trousers, shows little shame as he celebrates the winger's goal-scoring work. As everyone jumps and shouts and bawls, it is like the lancing of a huge boil; the tension has gone, disappeared away into the ether. Everyone is smiling now. And from the vast stand to my left begins a chant, with which we all immediately join, in happy, clappy communion.

'We love United, we do. We love United, we do. We love United, we do. Oh United we love you.'

Those announcing themselves as lovers of Manchester United on that dank late winter's evening at Old Trafford are not alone in their obsession. Nor are those cramming into a pub in London in May 2009, singing out their love for the club in defiance of a humiliating defeat in the final of the Champions League by Barcelona. Being a United fan is not a unique disposition. A MORI poll commissioned by United themselves in 2005 suggested there may be as many as seventy-five million people round the world who hold some level of affection for the club. Huge numbers of those seem to fetch up at Manchester airport the morning after matches, when a teeming polyglot of support swirls through security checks and packs the airside retail experiences. United supporters come from anywhere and everywhere. A keenness for everything red is, apparently, shared by 23.6 million people in China, 5.9 million in South Africa, 3.5 million in Malaysia, 3.2 million in the USA, 3.2 million in Australia, 3.2 million in Thailand, 2.3 million in Japan, 2.2 million in Poland, 2.1 million in Singapore, 1.4 million in Canada, plus several people who live in Torquay. In Ireland, an estimated 1.3 million people support United, which – astonishingly – accounts for a third of the population of the island. With seventy-nine official supporters' branches in the country, few Irish fans have to travel far to seek out like minds. Tiny villages both north and south of the border boast clubs, which host regular meetings of members and organise excursions to matches. In Northern Ireland, affection for United is one of the few cultural indicators that cannot be used to locate someone either side of the sectarian divide: there are as many orange reds as there are green. In Scandinavia, the United supporters' branch boasts almost thirty thousand members, a figure that surged when Ole Gunnar Solskjær was signed by Alex Ferguson in 1996. Solskjær once described United as being 'the biggest club in Norway'. And that includes any of the local sides.

It is a growing worldwide congregation that has enormous financial implications. As the number of supporters grows, so does the club's bottom line. In 1980, when the owner Louis Edwards died, his son Martin had United valued for probate on his father's estate. Back then, the club was reckoned to be worth £2 million. By 1998 it was valued at £1.1 billion. In 1964 the BBC paid the Football League £5000 a year for the rights to televise highlights of League matches; the club's share of a new deal was £50. In 2007 its income from television rights topped £26 million. In 1989 it cost £4 to watch a match from the Stretford End; in 2009, it was announced that for the following season, tickets would range in price from £27 to £49 (though if you fancy a meal in the United museum thrown in, you can pay upwards of £300 for a single hospitality ticket, available just by furnishing the United website with your credit card details) . In 1985 United's highest-paid player was Bryan Robson, who earned £93,000 a year. Twenty-three years on, Ronaldo signed a contract worth £6.3 million per annum. Though even that was not enough to maintain his loyalty.

The two sets of statistics are intertwined. United's income comes from its supporters, they are its sustenance and its lifeblood; the more of them there are, the more money is generated. Some of the income comes indirectly, through subscriptions to pay television. More of it arrives directly, through match tickets or the purchase of a new replica shirt (the most popular size sold at the club's Megastore, incidentally, is XXL). Such is United's association with money, Mihir Bose, the BBC's sports editor, wrote a book about cash and the club called *Manchester DisUnited*. Every page was crammed with tales of boardroom shenanigans and share-price hikes and maximising brand value. The giddying details of United's financial success made the head swim. But through all the book's details of corporate expansion, one thing emerged about the tottering cash mountain building up inside Old Trafford: this is the fruit of a fixation. It is the pay of love.

But what is it all these millions of people love? What is it that those chanting out their affection on a cold March night find so intoxicating about United? When Ronaldo or Wayne Rooney or the much-loved Argentine Carlos Tevez score a goal, what exactly is it that they are celebrating?

If there are seventy-five million fans, there are probably seventy-five million reasons for being a supporter. For me, it was purely an accident of geography: I was raised in south Manchester and, when I became aware of football at primary school, United were the biggest story locally. In my playground, we gave each other the names of United players as we picked teams. If you were selected off the railings first, you could be Denis the King and tug your cuffs over your fist. Second, you could be Bestie and had licence to dance through the opposition defence. Third, you were Bobby and could shoot from the halfway line. I was always Tony Dunne, the left back.

From that moment on, I wore United as a badge of honour. I felt proud that people had heard of where I came from, that over the next forty years I encountered taxi drivers in Bangkok and Berlin who knew who Bobby Charlton was and always stuck their thumbs up in recognition of his name. For me, United were easily the best thing about where I lived.

And they still are. In the eyes of the many who loathe United, the club's very popularity across the globe has become a source of derision. Those who stand up if they hate Man U claim that no one within the city supports the club. It is a matter of certainty among the Arsenal fans from Banbury and Bicester that every United fan comes from anywhere and everywhere apart from Manchester. At Stamford Bridge, blues from Cornwall and Hampshire insist on United's unpopularity within their own postcode.

'You don't come from Manchester', they will sneer.

If they stood by the footbridge over the railway line behind the Stretford End on match days, those who make such comments would soon be disabused. The huge majority of fans passing by are locals, working-class Mancs, proud of the world-renowned institution in their neighbourhood. Play football in the city's vast soccer dome in Trafford Park and 90 per cent of the shirts scurrying across the many courts will be the red of United (and those that aren't will be the black of the latest away kit). Besides, why on earth would the inhabitants of Cottonopolis fail to appreciate something the rest of the world finds intoxicating simply because it is on their own doorstep? Why would Mancunians be the only ones who don't get United? The fact is, they do. And United are the thing that makes them most proud of their hometown. They have such a sense of pride in their club, they see it as something special, something apart, a regional beacon at odds with the rest of the nation. Hence the antipathy of some United fans to England. That is why they chant 'Argentina' with such relish whenever Carlos Tevez scores, or take delight in singing about Ronaldo making England 'look shite'. For them it is Manchester against the world.

And they are not alone in identifying the club with the city. It is United that Manchester's four universities use to sell themselves overseas (Umist have long used a picture of Old Trafford on the literature it sends to prospective students, while United themselves offer a Freshers day to newly arrived students, to give them a better impression of the city than that afforded by the scallies who meet them off the train at Piccadilly, looking to relive them of laptops, iPods and mobiles). It is United that the local tourist board uses to sell weekend breaks in the city. There is no question, as the banner unwittingly passed above their own heads by Manchester City fans during the last ever derby at Maine Road insisted, that 'Manchester is red'.

Still, there is no denying that many of the millions of those claimed by MORI to be United followers couldn't place Manchester on a map of the world. For them, detached from the club's geographical and emotional roots, clearly their support is nothing to do with the articulation of local identity. For many, it is largely a matter of success. And, over the past fifteen years, as United have been pre-eminent, winning more titles and trophies than anyone else in England, success has been a constant recruiting sergeant. The fact, too, that they play in an English-language environment has enhanced United's universal appeal ahead of, say, Juventus or Bayern Munich.

Identifying with success makes those doing the identifying seem successful themselves. The day United falter, many of these supporters will doubtless take their affiliation with them to Real Madrid or Barcelona or whoever it is that can provide them anew with a vicarious sense of worth.

Others, though, will be there in the stands the day United sink into the Blue Square Premier. They would much rather change their domestic arrangements, their jobs, their religion, than their football club. 'United, kids, wife: in that order' reads a banner frequently flourished at away games. It's a funny line, but those waving it are serious. For them United is woven into their very being, their attachment defining them more precisely than any other aspect of their personalities. Seventeen such fans overcame all sorts of bureaucratic obstacles to make their way to Saudi Arabia in 2008 to watch the reds play a friendly. This was the very epicentre of the hard core. Yet even here, some were anxious to be deemed more loyal supporters than others.

'I'm not sure about him,' one fan said to another. 'He wasn't at Luton away in 1984.'

And he meant it.

For sure, some supporters arrive at United intoxicated solely by the glamour, the powerful combination of wealth and fame that oozes from Old Trafford's every steel rivet. You can see them on match days standing by the players' car park, watching the boastful new examples of German and Italian machinery arrive and holding out autograph books hoping for a moment's scribbled connection with those who shimmer in the glow of renown. Sometimes they seem uncertain who it is they are celebrating. I once saw a young girl, excitement illuminating her eyes, proffering her match-day programme to a large man in a blazer who had just stepped out of a 4×4 and was making his way through a flurry of flashbulbs to the VIP entrance. It was only when she asked him to scribble his name and he nodded over his shoulder that she saw the tiny, stubby figure of Colleen McLoughlin, Wayne Rooney's partner, tottering behind him. The bloke was merely a bodyguard. After a second's hesitation, the girl asked him for his autograph anyway. His mark would do: after all, he'd been in the same car as Colleen and was thus touched by the United stardust.

Equally, there are some supporters who would rather spend time with their head in a bucket of custard than ask a player to make his mark on their programme. They loathe the circus that surrounds the team's star names, the own-label scents, the Marie Antoinette wives and girlfriends, the endless conspicuous consumption. They regard the players as dismissive, detached from reality, unwilling to acknowledge the debt they owe to the fans.

For some, United is all about now. It is about the breathless chase for the Premier League title and whether the treble will ever be achievable again. It is about sitting in the pub poring over the fixture list and worrying what will happen if Arsenal get those three points at Wigan and United lose away at Tottenham. For others, what they love is the history, the tradition, the continuity of past and present. Poring over the menu from the post-match banquet at the 1968 European Cup final is their idea of fun.

Tony Wilson, the late Mancunian music entrepreneur and lifelong red, thought it was all about history. United, he once told me, attracted such a huge following for three reasons: the Munich tragedy, the team of Law, Best and Charlton, and the hooligan support of the seventies. Wilson made a career out of shameless provocation. But on this one, he may have a point. At least in my case. The first time I went to Old Trafford in 1974 I remember looking at the fifteen thousand people occupying the Stretford End, tumbling down the terraces in a recklessly choreographed surge, chanting as one at the little knot of opposition fans at the other end of the stadium, telling them that they would be going home in an ambulance, and I thought, Blimey. From that moment, I was smitten.

Even today, in an era when CCTV cameras and insistent policing have all but eradicated such in-stadium displays of collective aggression, there are plenty who are principally attracted by the fan culture. They cannot get enough of the latest ditty about Anderson sung to the tune of 'Agadoo'. Or the one about Ji-Sung Park not being a Scouser. Or the one about how Ronaldo's 'way with a brass is class'. Their enthusiasm is for the banter in the pub, the buzz on the coach to away games, the jokes that sound so great when you hear them in the stadium, but look lame when you repeat them in print. It is about the fanzines, the fashions, the fun.

And just as there are millions who call themselves United fans who have never seen the team play in the flesh and never will, others have clocked up millions of miles following the object of their affection. Phil Holt, for instance, has been a regular home and away supporter for nearly forty seasons. And that includes the two years he was living and working in Australia.

'I moved to Sydney at the start of 2004–05 and made it to Christmas without missing a game – not bad for a 25,000-mile round trip,' recalls Holt, who hails originally from Blackpool. 'I clocked up so many air miles on my Amex card that they begged me to use them up because the amount was clogging up their system. They told me I was their second highest unused points holder after Noel Gallagher. So at least City won something that year.'

Holt has never been recognised by the club as significant to its history. There is no plaque dedicated to his efforts at Old Trafford.

There are no free tickets to the directors' box for Phil, he has to pay his way like everyone else. Yet, he is as much a part of United as many a player, shareholder or board member. Much more than many.

As it happens, the season his United obsession resulted in a carbon footprint marginally bigger than China, a bunch of Phil's long-term United-going friends decided to detach themselves from the object of their affection and create something of their own. Already wearied by the commercialisation, the financial mania, the widening chasm between their own sense of United and the way the operation was heading, divorce became the only option when the club was bought by the Glazer family. The money-making dynasty from Florida snapped up all the club shares in a hostile stock market takeover that was completed in May 2005. Many of those attending the FA Cup final that month wore black to signal their opposition to an owner who, they believed, had no interest in United beyond using the club as a vehicle to buff up his own wallet. In order to procure the investment, Malcolm Glazer had taken on humungous debt, which he transferred on to the club. To pay the interest on the purchase, ticket prices rose exponentially. While a huge number of match-going fans wouldn't care if Attila the Hun was chairman so long as the team kept winning, a significant number believed the Glazers had taken their club away from them.

Some decided to form an outfit of their own, one which could promote the aspects of United they loved and do without the bits they hated. They call it FC United of Manchester and they play in the Unibond League, in front of crowds of over two thousand former regulars at Old Trafford.

'What is it you love about United?' says Andy Walsh, one of the founding fathers of FC. 'It's not the board, it's not the money-making, it's not the whole media Man U thing. That's not United. That's not the soul of the club.'

Like all religious schisms, this one has been bitterly contested. The theological disputes have simmered across the blogosphere, the internet an apparently irresistible opportunity for United fans to bicker among themselves. There were those believers who insisted that to leave the United family was betrayal, heresy even. They reckoned the departed should have stayed on and fought the new regime from within, that it was perfectly possible – as the ever-present graffiti around Manchester declares – to love United and hate the Glazers. It is an argument you can see rehearsed in the Ken Loach movie *Looking for Eric*. And it is one that continues to rage, even as FC's march up the non-leagues has stalled somewhere south of the Blue Square Premier.

'I've never seen Manchester United as mine,' says Stephen Armstrong, a lifelong home and away supporter from Moston. 'Those that do end up bitter, twisted and evidently jealous when someone does make it theirs. I belong to United but I don't own it. Fans never have done. That is why we are called fans or supporters.'

But never mind who is in charge, never mind who is in the dugout, never mind which passing millionaire is slipping on the red shirt, Phil Holt for one will always be there. 'I have seen United play in forty-four different countries,' he says. 'The buzz that comes with travelling to see the team really can't be beaten and seeing the same old faces turning up in so many corners of the globe is an amazing thing to behold. In the remotest areas of the world you can bet your house that at the end of any given night everyone will have unwittingly been drawn together in some seedy dive singing away in remembrance of our history much to the bemusement of our American, Brazilian, Chinese or whoever hosts. It's always the same people, all from different walks of life, always the same songs, always the same hangover'

So what is about United? How did a local sports club established in the depths of the Manchester smog to stop a bunch of working men pickling themselves in booze come to play such a significant part in our culture? What is this body that is capable of inspiring such dedication, such love, such regular assaults on the credit card? Is it just about the great players? Because United have had more than their share of them – Denis Law, Duncan Edwards, George Best, Eric Cantona, Roy Keane, Cristiano Ronaldo. Or is there something more substantial? Are there characteristics identifiable across the generations that make it United? Does it have a soul? A beating heart? What makes this an entity worth fighting over? Why on earth do rational human beings come to love something as vast, something as contentious, something as disparate as United? That is what this book is attempting to discover.

1

A BUNCH OF BOUNCING HEATHENS

For a couple of years at the start of the noughties, just before the teams ran out on to the pitch at Old Trafford, out from the public address system issued seemingly the most low-key of rallying calls. Unlike the theme songs echoing round many a stadium in the country, the lyrics of this mournful ballad did not boast that we are the champions or that the team is simply the best or indeed that we will in any sense rock you. Instead it told a wistful tale of an urban romance conducted beside the entrance to the gas works, down along the towpath of the canal.

Written in the early 1960s by the folk singer Ewan MacColl, 'Dirty Old Town' is Manchester's anthem, a tune as evocative of its place of origin as any of the great works of American popular music. Covered by everyone from the Pogues to Rod Stewart, this is a song that tells as much about its writer's surroundings as 'Route 66', 'Wichita Lineman' or 'San Francisco (Be Sure to Wear Flowers in Your Hair)'.

Heard a siren call from across the docks
Saw a train set the night on fire
Smelled the spring on the Salford wind
Dirty old town
Dirty old town.

That song provides a snapshot of how Manchester has long been viewed by the artists, actors, playwrights and musicians who have found their muse in the bleakest corners of their home space. As is suggested by the pictures of L. S. Lowry, the kitchen-sink dramas of Shelagh Delaney, in Walter Greenwood's *Love on the Dole*, in the music of Joy Division and in Paul Abbott's television series *Shameless*, Manchester isn't southern California. There are no golden shores or big skies or harvest moons here. More like cranes and grey cloud and rain.

Sure, the wind emanating from Manchester's twin city of Salford has changed direction since MacColl wrote his song. The gas works have long been demolished; the factory door now leads to a development of loft apartments; instead of steam trains sparking the night air, electric trams swish through canyons of steel and scrubbed-up brick, their sheen reflected in the freshly clean water of the canal. So much has altered that were he still alive, how astonished would MacColl be to see a tourist information bureau sitting in the middle of what was once a heaving dockside, an office in which visitors from across the world seek directions for the great new sights of Salford: the Lowry Centre, the Imperial War Museum, the outlet shopping mall. And to the towering cathedral at its heart, Old Trafford, its imposing glass-clad frontage illuminated and visible right along the dual carriageway of the A56, calling the faithful to prayer.

Yet, whatever the twenty-first-century spring clean, Manchester's sense of itself is still largely of the dirty old town. And it is not hard to see why. Even now, after a dozen years of voracious urban renewal, not all is fancy in Manchester. Not every nook and cranny of this city has been touched by the busy fingers of regeneration.

There are parts where poverty is entrenched, where disappointment is written across every face, where the recent revelation that Manchester now boasts a higher concentration of millionaires in one of its suburbs than Beverly Hills would be greeted with hollow laughter. Places like Northampton Road, Monsall.

'Welcome to Manchester, European capital of umbrellas,' said the train manager as the express hauled into the city's Piccadilly station. It was a good line that, at once both mocking the grandiose boasting of Liverpool, in 2008 the European Capital of Culture, and yet accepting the national stereotype of a place where drizzle is endemic. Simultaneously chippy and self-deprecating: very Manchester. Northampton Road is no more than a mile from where the trains fetch up in a station rebuilt for the 2002 Commonwealth Games, only a ten-minute walk east of the sparkly new white footbridge that takes you through a ravine of office buildings, past a smart restaurant where a butternut squash starter costs £7.95. But it might as well be on another planet.

Walk towards Northampton Road and within moments you are strolling along a high street where the only open businesses seem to be pawn shops and post offices, where youths in black trackies hang on street corners on mini-BMXs, where the faces waiting at the bus stop are so pale and pinched, it appears as if the sun hasn't shone round here for a decade. Take a left into Northampton Road and you are in the North Manchester Business Park. And between the new pavilions of commerce is a patch of unoccupied land, strewn with the detritus of demolition. There is nothing here to indicate that this is where the world's greatest sporting institution has its roots, that it was here the Manchester United story began. Actually there was a plaque here once; at one time it was fixed to the wall of the now demolished Moston Brook High School. But it got nicked. And no one has thought to replace it.

Back in 1878, this place, now off everyone's compass, was at the very epicentre of change. A mere thirty years previously, in the middle of the nineteenth century, this part of Manchester had been open heathland stretching to the Pennines. But by the late 1870s, in the height of Victorian expansion, North Road as it was then known, made its way through the most modern of industry, running alongside newly laid railway tracks, on which steam trains hauled coal into a hectic melee of iron, steel and chemical works. Everywhere was the noise and grime of industrial wealth-generation, a thick blanket of noxious fug belched out from a forest of chimneys, punctuated by flames spitting from furnaces. So grim was the scene, one unnamed local writer imagined what the Devil might make of it if he took a detour overhead on his way home from a night behaving badly:

> *As Satan was flying over Clayton for Hell*
> *He was chained in the breeze, likewise the smell*
> *Quoth he: 'I'm not sure what country I roam*
> *But I'm sure by the smell I'm not far from home.'*

It was here, in this industrial Hades, in between the tracks and the chemical works, that the world's richest football institution took its initial wheezy breath. It was here, in a spot that knew little of a world beyond its own filth-restricted borders, that a worldwide phenomenon followed with religious devotion by millions took its first, faltering, Bambi-esque steps. No, Bambi is the wrong image: nothing in Monsall then or now has ever been cute. This is dirty old town.

What we know for sure is that there was no hint of the substance to come at the beginning. The club of Taylor, Edwards and Colman, of Law, Best and Charlton, of Cantona, Beckham and Giggs, of Rooney, Tevez and Ronaldo had an inauspicious beginning, played out in a mudbath and choked in smog.

Unlike many football clubs there was no church connection in United's start. Although the reds have frequently been identified as Manchester's Catholic club, that was a reputation which did not emerge until the 1950s when Matt Busby, the devout west of Scotland Catholic, tapped into a nationwide scouting network of priests and boys' clubs in a relentless search for footballing talent. In return for tip-offs, he would invite the churchmen to Old Trafford to watch games. By the 1960s, such was the priestly presence, one observer would speak of 'a tide of the cloth' washing through the main stand on match days. Busby's immediate successors – Wilf McGuinness, Frank O'Farrell, Tommy Docherty and Dave Sexton – were all Catholics, as was his assistant, Jimmy Murphy, and the owning Edwards dynasty, adding apparent evidence to this theory of sectarianism. But there has never been anything in United's constitution about it. And once Busby's influence began to wane in the boardroom, so did the Catholic connection. When he was appointed in 1981, Ron Atkinson was the first Protestant to manage the club since the flinty-eyed nonconformist Scott Duncan in the thirties. Not that he made much of his faith; Big Ron's religious inclination was largely restricted to self-worship. Besides, even in Busby's pomp, United never operated a selective religious policy out on the park. Ability was what mattered – the faith of football came above all else.

No, there was nothing Catholic about United back then. Indeed, far from being God-botherers, the club started out as a bunch of Heathens. It was on North Road that the Lancashire and Yorkshire Railway Company's Newton Heath carriage works established a home for its Football and Cricket Club, an operation that was almost immediately nicknamed the Heathens.

It was some company, the L&YR. There is a magnificent tiled mural on one of the interior walls of Manchester Victoria station that shows a map of the operation in its heyday. Its lines snake all over the north of England. Out of hubs in Manchester and Leeds they run, spinning laterally along the valleys of the Pennines, the Moors and the Dales. The spidery red routes reach out from Goole in the east across the tiles to Liverpool in the west, marking an expansion so rapid it makes the motorway-building programme a century later look timid and anaemic.

Within twenty years of its foundation, the L&YR was employing hundreds of men, sucked in from all over the country to service a growing need for locomotives and carriages. It wasn't a barrel of laughs working on the railways. It was dirty, dangerous and with little to entertain the working man in his brief moments of spare time, other than drink that is. In the middle of the nineteenth century the average male life expectancy in Little Ireland, the notorious part of Manchester now booted and suited and known as Castlefields (the favoured place for United's players' Christmas parties), was as low as seventeen. Booze was the principal escape from the wretchedness of industrial city life. The burghers of Manchester were so alarmed that the men whose labours had made them rich were becoming pickled in alcohol that they looked around urgently for an antidote.

In 1878 the L&YR board, in an attempt to find a solution, charged its dining room committee with organising what it termed 'classes of improvement'. Team games had recently been codified in the public schools and were being actively promoted as a muscular alternative to the many evils thought to be afflicting Victorian society, from drinking to masturbation. So the committee proposed a sports club, and the board approved, drafting in a raft of local luminaries – including C. P. Scott, founder of the *Manchester Guardian* and the local MP, and future Prime Minister A. J. Balfour – to act as the club's vice presidents.

At the time, however, rugby, with its unlimited opportunities for on-field violence, was the more popular game locally. But the committee believed that football, which enjoyed an image of Corinthian gentlemanliness, might serve as a better moral guide for the railwaymen. Thus football came to Monsall. And a patch of land just by the railway line was levelled and prepared for use.

Mind you, it wasn't much of a home. Goodness knows how the cricketers managed to play on a surface that for most of the year was ankle-deep in mud. Not that you could often see the mud for the smoggy haze oozing off the railway lines. As for the footballers, well, there wasn't even a hut in which to get changed. There were none of those little leather manbags players carry these days into the showers, there weren't even showers. Back then they were obliged to trudge after matches to the Three Crowns pub on Oldham Street, more than half a mile away, to get out of their mud-encrusted kit, leaving a trail of filth across the snug floor that drove a succession of landladies to distraction.

In those early days, kitted out in the company colours of green and yellow (a style briefly resurrected, complete with lace-up collars, as a change strip in 1993), the most bruising encounter for the Newton Heath carriage team was with Newton Heath Locomotive, the side made up of the men from the L&YR engine depot, who looked upon themselves as superior in manufacturing skills. Quite what the results were of those early meetings, we will never know. The matches, played during what passed for daylight hours in the smog-shrouded environs of the heath, may have drawn a fair crowd of fellow workers, but they were not reported by the local press and the club's early records have been lost. Probably swallowed up by the mud. We don't know who played, whether anyone trained them, indeed whether there was a selection policy beyond the requirement of belonging to a railway section. In all probability, like amateur football ever since, it was a case of desperately asking round for recruits, resorting to a plaintive cry of 'If you've got boots, you're in'. Except no one had football boots in those days. They played in their work clogs. Then, after matches, a local chimney sweep known as 'Father' Bird would invite the players back to his for a sing-song and a meal of Lancashire hot pot or potato pie. It wasn't quite the Sugar Lounge, the Cotton Tree, the Living Room or any of the other Manchester haunts the modern player goes to harvest a wag, but it filled a hole.

Under the presidency of a certain F. Attock Esq., the club was soon looking beyond simple inter-works rivalry and set up its own offices at 493 Oldham Road. The fixture list of the 1882–83 season, the earliest surviving scrap of United memorabilia now lodged in the Old Trafford museum, includes games against other works sides in St Helens, Southport and Crewe, away days which could easily be accommodated along the growing rail network, particularly as L&YR employees were eligible for concessionary train fares.

Soon the carriage men had outstripped their fellow works teams and were looking for fiercer opposition than the likes of Oughtrington Park, Bootle Wanderers or Manchester Arcadians. Attock's ambition was to take on the longer-established clubs of Lancashire, and he got his first chance to pit his wits against the best just five years after the Heathens had been founded, when they drew Blackburn Olympic, the then FA Cup holders, in the first round of the 1883–84 season's Lancashire Cup. It was the first taste of the big time and it was a chastening one: the Heathens were drubbed 7-2.

The Manchester Senior Cup, inaugurated the following season, however, proved a less daunting proposition. On 3 April 1886, Newton Heath reached the competition's first final, where, before a bustling, excited crowd of four thousand, they lost 3-0 to Hurst, a side from Ashton-under-Lyne. It was the club's only defeat of the year, but it came in their most important game. Two years later they went one better, beating Manchester FC 2-1 in a controversial, bitterly contested final (the winning Heathens goal would still be disputed five years later, the Victorian equivalent of Geoff Hurst's crossbar rattler in 1966). The Senior Cup was a trophy they admired so much, they won it four more times over the next seven seasons.

By now football was becoming part of the fabric of local life. The L&YR gained considerable prestige from the exploits of its team, and was happy to allow officials to offer jobs in the carriage works as an enticement to attract decent players from further afield. There were perks, too. Mr Sedgwick, the stationmaster at Victoria, always ensured the Heath lads travelled to away games in a reserved first-class saloon. Such enticements were particularly appealing in the ailing Welsh coalfields, and a number of Wales internationals – including Jack Powell, Tom Burke and the Doughty brothers, Jack and Roger – arrived to work for the railway, but more to the point to play for a club that was now pre-eminent in the

Manchester area. If not quite the Arsenal of the day, there were soon enough Welsh, Scots and other out-of-towners turning Heathen for the *Manchester Evening News* to report in 1886 that it 'did not recognise a local man in the team'.

Emboldened by their cosmopolitan new line-up, Newton Heath entered the FA Cup for the first time in 1886. In the first round they played Fleetwood Rangers and ended the match with a creditable 2-2 draw, both goals scored by Jack Doughty. Under the impression that a replay would be required to sort out the winners, the Newton Heath players were surprised to be told by the referee that extra time was to be played instead. Certain in their reading of the rulebook, the Heathens refused to take part, heading off the field and home. The game was awarded to the opposition. It wasn't to be the last time the club got into trouble staging a walk-out from the FA Cup.

The following season, the smart, well-funded Lancashire clubs, many of which were taking full advantage of more lenient rules on professionalism, decided to form a league. By now presiding over Manchester's most successful club, Newton Heath's committee assumed an invitation to join the elite would be forthcoming. It wasn't. Instead the club joined first the Football Combination, then the Football Alliance, short-lived attempts to rival the League. Neither provided much in the way of financial stability and for several years the Heathen committee looked at the burgeoning Football League with increasing envy. In 1891, anxious to break out of the Alliance doldrums and prove their suitability for League football, the officials went for broke. And almost found it. They used what little financial reserves they had to build two grandstands at the North Road ground, accommodating up to two thousand spectators. The committee's profligacy brought them into conflict too with the L&YR, which refused to finance the developments. In what was not to be the last row about ownership of the club, all ties with the company were cut. From now on membership was not restricted to railwaymen, anyone could become a Heathen. News of the split from its parent broke soon after tidings of a more uplifting kind: the Football League had decided to expand into two divisions. Newton Heath were asked to join. What's more, they were to be placed in the First Division. Nearby rivals Ardwick – soon to be rechristened Manchester City – were allocated a slot in the Second Division. Thus was local pecking order established early on.

2

MONEY, MONEY, MONEY

Newton Heath's first season in League football was a traumatic one. On the pitch, they finished bottom of the table and remained in the top flight only after winning a play-off against the Second Division champions Small Heath, from Birmingham. And off it, financial problems began to mount. A mooted flotation to raise £2000 in share capital was a damp squib; worse, the L&YR served an eviction notice on the freshly improved North Road ground. A desperate scramble to find a new home in time for the next Football League season was concluded when a lease was signed on a field three miles away in Clayton just days before the first fixture against Burnley. It was a heady occasion: seven thousand fans crammed into a small wooden stand running along one touchline. But an attempt to bring the two new stands across the city from North Road failed and eventually they were sold for a miserable £100.

The Bank Street ground is now the site of the car park for the Manchester Velodrome, built for the Commonwealth Games, over the road from the City of Manchester Stadium. Thunder-thighed cyclists can park their cars and take in a plaque commemorating this vital part of red history on the wall of a house opposite the entrance. Not that the new ground provided new fortune, the club was relegated in its first season. And so, after just nine months, Newton Heath's only ever stay in the top flight under that name ended. Worse, the committee risked what little money it had on an ill-advised libel case against the *Birmingham Daily Gazette*, which had remarked that the Heathens' tactics during a rare 4-1 win over West Bromwich Albion were 'simple brutality'. The presiding judge reckoned the case frivolous, and though he gave moral victory to the Heathen committee, he awarded them a mere farthing in damages and saddled them with all the legal costs. Meanwhile, if the team were hoping that the liquid mud of North Road had been left behind, they were soon to be disabused. So appalling was the condition of the new playing surface, it cost them a record. A 14-0 romp over Walsall Town Swifts on 9 March 1895 was declared void because the visiting club secretary took the precaution of lodging an official complaint about the state of the pitch before kick-off. The game was ordered to be replayed. And in the follow-up fixture, the Heathens managed only a 9-0 win.

As the century drew to a close, Newton Heath had become a decent, unspectacular Second Division side, only occasionally, such as when they beat the mighty Blackburn Rovers to win the Lancashire Cup in 1898, showing much in the way of ambition. Which was no surprise as things were decidedly rocky in the committee room. Long hamstrung by the debts associated with their move, the finances were slipping deeper into the mire. Professionalism, for several decades frowned upon, was now a reality. Income from gate-receipts, though, was not sufficient to meet existing obligations, never mind attract in the better players who might allow the Heathens to match the big Lancashire clubs with their wealthy benefactors. Hand to mouth barely describes the club's financial condition at the time. Photographs of the team invariably include a collection box at the feet of their captain Harry

Stafford. This is how they survived: through the charity of their fans, a financial plan that has been followed by many a football club ever since. Stafford was a tireless fundraiser, using his St Bernard dog, Major, to solicit cash. Major even appears in one team photo, a collecting tin on his collar where his Alpine relatives might wear their barrel of brandy.

In February 1901, with his club as usual utterly strapped for cash, Harry Stafford took it upon himself to organise a fundraising bazaar in St James's Hall in Manchester town centre. The aim was to collect enough to pay off debts of £2670 that threatened the club with bankruptcy, and Major was dispatched off round the city's pubs to pick up loose change. The day was a disaster. Not only did the bazaar fail to come up with anything like the target amount, but Major disappeared, along, more to the point, with his collecting tin. Stafford was in despair. A couple of days later, however, a team-mate spotted an advert in the local paper, a St Bernard had been found in one of the pubs belonging to the Manchester Brewery. By coincidence, the owner of the brewery, John Henry Davies, was looking for such a dog to give as a gift to his daughter and the two men turned up at the pub at the same time, both in search of the mutt. They got talking, and, in exchange for the brewing magnate agreeing to put money into the club, Stafford handed over his dog. It was the start of a beautiful relationship.

Or so the story goes. There is no documentary evidence to confirm the dog's role. But the idea of a St Bernard rescuing a football club appealed to mythology and Major has long been credited as Newton Heath's saviour.

John Davies, a well fed individual with a magnificent handlebar moustache, was a wealthy man in his own right. But he had the added blessing of being married to the heir of the Tate & Lyle group. He was consequently about as rich a benefactor as could be found in the whole north of England; Major had chosen well. Although not a football fan, Davies liked his sport – and had already donated significant sums to local cycling clubs and provided bowlers at one of his pubs with a new green. He set about

Newton Heath with relish and business acumen: he took full control of things, cleared its sizeable debts and, to declare a fresh start, suggested a change of colours – to red and white. Also, since they had not played on the heath in nearly a decade, Davies thought a new name was in order. A special meeting of fans, directors and interested parties was convened on 26 April 1902 to discuss the issue. The gathering quickly dismissed Manchester Celtic as an idea, while Manchester Central, it was thought, sounded too much like a railway station. Everyone present, however, agreed that a nineteen-year-old supporter called Louis Rocca had a good idea when he proposed Manchester United. Or at least that was the tale Rocca dined out on for the next half century. There is no documentary proof that the man who went on to do every job with the club, from chief scout to temporary manager, actually conjured up the name or merely picked up a cry from the crowd. But no matter, Manchester United it was.

There was a real buzz around Clayton in those tentative, early days of United. John Davies, after sorting out the debts, was keen to progress the club, to move it on from being merely a working man's pastime into a nationally recognised ambassador for Mancunian self-esteem. He saw an immediate financial relationship between performance on the pitch and attendances at Bank Street, and set out to ensure a benevolent circle was quickly achieved. With secretary James West and the Heathen stalwart Harry Stafford put in charge of the team, great things were anticipated locally: twenty thousand people, more than five times the size of the average crowd the previous season, turned up for United's first home game in the 1903–04 season, a 1-0 win against Burton United. But the optimism soon dissipated. Davies had provided a transfer war chest of £3000 to the management duo, but through their first season in charge, United stuttered and faltered in the mud. Injuries were commonplace, recruitment of new players erratic and they finished the season well off the pace in the Second Division.

Davies was not one to tolerate ordinariness. James West paid the penalty for failing to deliver the chairman's ambition and resigned in September of 1904. He was not out of the firing line for long. That winter an FA investigation into financial irregularity in the League – a regular occurrence at a time when much of the finances of football were distributed in a brown envelope – found him guilty of accountancy errors and he was banned for five years from any involvement in the game. The same inquiry also ruled Harry Stafford to have acted illegally during his time attempting to keep the Heath afloat on the mud. His defence, that, well yes, the books had not been entirely accurate in recent seasons, but that any cooking he might have done was not to line his own pockets, it was simply to keep the club alive, was dismissed. He was banned and never played for United again; the captain was now history. And he didn't even have Major any more to comfort him.

John Davies acted swiftly, and after taking advice from chums on the FA, invited Burnley's secretary to head to Bank Street to take charge. His name was Ernest Mangnall. In many ways the story of Manchester United is the story of three men: Matt Busby, Alex Ferguson and Ernest Mangnall. The three defining characters, between them, they accumulated all the club's League championship titles, plus eight of 11 FA Cups. A well-educated man with a fancy for cigars and a straw boater, like the two Scots, Mangnall had an eye for Europe, leading the United on their first ever continental tour to Prague, Vienna and Budapest in the summer of 1908. More importantly, though, there was something else the threesome had in common: a workaholic's energy. Mangnall was appointed club secretary, but in effect he was United's first team manager. He was by no means a tracksuit boss, in those days training was haphazard, random and largely conducted by the senior players. But he recognised fitness was key to performance – in the summer of 1904 he had cycled from John O'Groats to Land's End, and that was in the days when saddles were rock hard – and he insisted his charges made greater effort towards achieving it. He did that largely by making it clear he would find others to step into any malingerer's boots.

The momentum began to build almost immediately Mangnall arrived. In his first season in charge, United finished third in the Second Division, a point behind the runners-up Woolwich Arsenal (Preston were champions). It was a feat they repeated the following season, taking in along the way an unbeaten run from 24 September 1904 to 21 January 1905. Mangnall built his sides on sound defence rather than fluid attack. One of the first things he did was to spend £600 of Davies's money on Charlie Roberts, a muscular centre back from Grimsby Town. Roberts was to slot into the half-back line alongside Dick Duckworth and Alec Bell, a threesome that became as celebrated in their time as Law, Best and Charlton would be later. Not that Roberts, Duckworth and Bell were renowned for attacking flair. Let in fewer than you score and you win the game was one of Mangnall's favoured dictums. And behind the tightest of Edwardian defences, he stationed Harry Moger, the tallest keeper in United history until Edwin van der Sar arrived. At over six feet three inches, Moger towers over every other player in team photos of the time, looming like Lurch above the Addams Family.

It was those difficult-to-beat qualities that eventually, just as Davies began to despair his huge investment in the club would ever pay dividends, led to promotion in 1906 when fifteen thousand delirious spectators crammed into Bank Street to see the climactic 6-0 home victory over Burton United.

A bit of a Brian Clough, an early precursor of José Mourinho, Ernest Mangnall fancied himself as a sporting philosopher. As his fame grew, he was often asked for an opinion. He loved nothing more than to give it, once writing in the *Manchester Evening News* that 'a great, intricate, almost delicate and to the vast majority of the public, an incomprehensible piece of machinery is the modern up-to-date football club'. That was certainly the way he wished to portray his job: something no one else could do, something directors and committee members would do well not to enquire too deeply about.

Mangnall demanded and got total respect from his players; he ruled the club with patrician good humour that belied a fiery competitiveness, plus – just like the two great Scots who were to succeed him – he had his information. He seemed to know more about what was going on in football than anyone else. With a network of spies he got the inside line on opponents, tailoring tactics to suit the opposition in the days long before the video or the scouting report. It was this ability to keep one step ahead of the pack that enabled him to pull off his smartest coup.

Manchester City, by now the dominant local force in football, had won the FA Cup in 1904, at the time considered an achievement of far greater significance than the League championship. But the evident ease of their success had aroused suspicion from the authorities. An FA investigation found the club directors had breached rules on the maximum wage for players when they secretly handed out astronomical bonuses as high as £7 a man for winning the Cup. The board members in question were all banned from football for five seasons, while their star winger, the Welsh wizard Billy Meredith, was prevented from playing until the end of the 1907 season. In a bid to save what little assets they had remaining, the club organised an auction of their top players, inviting representatives of all the Football League teams to a fire sale at the Queen's Hotel. When the other club secretaries and chairmen arrived at the hotel they discovered they were a bit late. It transpired that a certain Ernest Mangnall had been sharper off the starting blocks. Tipped off by a City insider, he had already signed up Meredith, together with Herbert Burgess, Jimmy Bannister and the bullocking centre forward Sandy Turnbull on free transfers. Virtually the full forward line of the most attacking side in the country was grafted on to the best defence around. In what reads like an Edwardian prototype for Alex Ferguson's 2007 championship-winning side, Mangnall now had the winning formula.

Billy Meredith's arrival was particularly important. This slim, tricksy winger was the first United player to deliver a bit of glamour to the place. The precursor of Mitten and Best, Cantona and Ronaldo, a sparky, aggressive character off the pitch, aware of his own worth and determined others should be too, he was the first to characterise a trait that United fans have long sought in their heroes. With his neckerchief and toothpick, his off-field commercial activities (he had opened Manchester's leading sports shop while still in City's colours), his on-pitch bandy legged shuffle and dainty footwork, he was the maverick, the individualist, the man apart, the player who helped define the club's sense of itself. Very different. Very United.

And he was the man to kick-start the reds' first golden age. In the autumn of 1907 they raced to the top of the League after a run of ten straight wins. Fed by Billy Meredith's crosses, Sandy Turnbull scored 25 goals in 30 games, a record that stood for forty years until Jack Rowley came along. With such firepower and a parsimonious defence, United never relinquished top spot and the first title in the club's history was secured in May 1908. To celebrate the triumph, chairman Davies paid for the team to go on a tour of the Austro-Hungarian empire. It ended in mayhem. After hammering Ferencvaros 7-0 in Budapest, the United players were attacked by infuriated locals, a riot that was only broken up by the arrival of a troop of cavalrymen who laid into the crowd, swords drawn. A bruised Ernest Mangnall came away from the club's first European venture saying the team would never again play in Budapest. By chance United didn't until a European Cup tie eighty-six years later.

The big one, though, still eluded Mangnall and United – the best they had achieved in the FA Cup was a quarter-final slot. Then, in 1909, things changed. After wins against Brighton, Everton and Blackburn in the early rounds of the Cup, United played Burnley, Mangnall's old employers, in the quarter-final. With a blizzard blowing round Turf Moor, United looked to be heading out of the competition with Burnley leading and only eighteen minutes left to play. But the weather rescued the reds when the referee abandoned the game. So bad were conditions, the official was too cold to summon up the puff to blow his whistle to call the game off, and handed it to United's captain Charlie

Roberts to do it for him. In the replayed fixture, the reds won 3-2 and then dispatched the League champions-elect Newcastle in the semi-final.

Amid enormous interest in Manchester, the United team journeyed down to London to take on Bristol City in the final at Crystal Palace. Thousands of fans went with them, described by *The Times* thus: 'There are no people in the world like the northerners. They spend their money, they have their quaint ways. They bring stone jars of strong ale and sandwiches an inch thick packed in the wicker baskets which can be used for conveying carrier pigeons.'

The team were armed with a change strip of white shirts decorated with a red 'V'. Long before sponsorship deals, the shirts had been specially ordered from Billy Meredith's sports shop and were presented to the team by the music hall star George Robey. The intervention of celebrity proved lucky: Sandy Turnbull scored the only goal of the game and the oldest trophy in world football was on its way to the north-west. When presenting the cup, Lord Charles Beresford, commander-in-chief of the Channel Fleet, announced: 'I do not think I have seen finer specimens of British humanity than those who played in this game.' Manchester was delirious, more than three hundred thousand people lining the streets between Central station and the town hall as Roberts and his men paraded the Cup from a carriage pulled by six grey mares. On board, players, management and directors celebrated as one.

It was, as it turned out, a misleading show of unity. That summer, as the Cup nestled in the Bank Street offices, Charlie Roberts, Sandy Turnbull, Billy Meredith and the rest attended a meeting at the hotel opposite London Road (now Piccadilly) station that is now the Malmaison. Fed up with parsimonious employers insisting on a maximum wage, they formed the Professional Footballers' Association and sought to affiliate with the General Federation of Trades Unions (GFTU). These guys had just won football's most prestigious trophy. Yet their chances of enjoying the financial fruits of success were minimal. Meredith was the one who articulated it best. Sure, he argued, footballers were blessed to be able to spend their working lives playing a game most could only espouse in what limited spare time they had. Sure, they were lucky not to be confined to the mine or the factory like their contemporaries. But thousands of people paid hundreds of pounds in gate-receipts each and every week to watch their endeavours and they were seeing none of it. They weren't ordinary workers, they were entertainers and deserved to be rewarded as such, like the music hall heroes who commanded fees of up to £100 a performance.

It was appropriate the body was formed in Manchester, home of the co-operative and union movements, birthplace of the Chartists and the suffragettes, cradle of the *Guardian*, a town that always had at its beating heart radicalism and dissent. With Billy Meredith as its sardonic, cynical mouthpiece, the body was quick to set out an agenda: a fair distribution of football's wealth, an end to under-the-counter payments, a recognition of the players' standing within the game. Plus some sort of security of tenure. An end, in short, to the virtual slavery that had shackled the game since it was first codified. And if it didn't come, then the right to strike.

Football's plutocratic governors in London were incensed by the Manc upstarts and their Welsh mouthpiece. How they wished they had banned Meredith for life when they had the chance a couple of years previously. The FA instructed all club chairmen whose players had joined the putative union to sack them on the spot. The United team were locked out of Bank Street and Davies stopped their summer wages. A furious Sandy Turnbull led a break-in at the offices to seize property in lieu of payment; items purloined included the FA Cup itself. Rumour had it that the trophy that afternoon found itself on Turnbull's sideboard. Club captain Charlie Roberts, ever alert to the wider implications of their actions, sensed that the moral high ground had been abandoned by such theft. He organised for all the goods to be returned. Despite his efforts, the ban was upheld by an FA determined not to let power slip. Elsewhere in the country, the striking players at other clubs panicked and returned en masse to the life of near servitude. But at United there was a tougher resolve. As the start of the new season arrived, the United stars were still locked out, training in Fallowfield, calling themselves 'The Outcasts' and earning the admiration of fans everywhere.

'Manchester United Without a Team' was the bald headline in the *Manchester News Chronicle*, above a picture of the rebels, gathered round a sign declaiming their new name. Meredith, in particular, saw his status enhanced by his actions; wherever he went he was mobbed by back-slapping fans. Profits at his sports shop went into orbit. John Davies, meanwhile, was having a less happy time. Trapped between the FA and his mutinous players, the chairman tried to get the first few fixtures of the season postponed. The game's rulers refused.

By the end of September a compromise was offered: the FA was prepared to give limited recognition to the players' union, provided that it did not affiliate with the GFTU and forgot all talk of negotiating wages and the right to strike. Meredith, Roberts and the United boys argued that this would represent a pitiful climbdown. Confident in their cause, they organised a ballot of England's professionals seeking a mandate to press for affiliation to the wider union movement. They were soundly beaten, by 470 votes to 172. One by one the United players signed up to the new FA-approved way of doing things and returned to Bank Street. Billy Meredith was the last to go. He later wrote in his memoirs of the incident: 'A man said to me the other day: "ah the players did not have the pluck of the miners". He was right, of course.'

With player discontent if not dissipated then at least now accommodated, Davies continued his march for progress. If the locals had been hanging from lamp-posts to watch the Cup winners parade the trophy through the streets of Manchester, then he needed somewhere to house them all when the team played their home games. In 1910 he bought a chunk of land from the Earl of Trafford's estate over the other side of the River Irwell, in Salford. Here, without incurring any debt or mortgage, he commissioned the architect Archibald Leitch – who had recently designed the three big stadiums in Glasgow – to build a new home for his United, capable of containing up to a hundred thousand paying spectators. It took less than two years to complete. A photograph of Davies, surrounded by his manager and players in front of the new main stand at the ground, shows it was a substantial structure, with rows of wooden benches stretching out of frame. On the other side of the ground was an equally impressive enclosure, while two huge cinder banks provided standing room for nearly eighty thousand. It was, Davies boasted, the finest ground in the country, better than Crystal Palace, Stamford Bridge, the newly built Highbury or anything else in London. The press agreed. The *Sporting Chronicle* described the ground as 'the most handsomest, the most spacious and the most remarkable arena I have ever seen. As a football ground it is unrivalled anywhere in the world.' More importantly, the site had proper drainage; at last the reds had a pitch to play on, 'a lush green carpet', insisted the *Manchester Guardian*. As the locals preened themselves that this was the smartest stadium in the empire, the change of venue clearly proved inspirational to the players. They won the title again in 1911, Roberts, Turnbull, Meredith, Moger and the rest setting a pace by winning their first seven games, which no one else could match.

That was the last hurrah of Ernest Mangnall's red and white army. A side ageing together (Charlie Roberts was by now in his mid-thirties and Billy Meredith's best days were widely assumed to be behind him) needed rebuilding. But the manager clashed with his chairman over funds for the reconstruction. Not that Davies had a lot left after building Old Trafford. Mangnall, however, showed little sympathy for his well-heeled chairman's temporary embarrassment and resigned, heading off across town to the welcoming embrace of Manchester City. John Bentley was put in charge at United, but it was not a happy time. In 1913 and 1914 United were First Division also-rans and failures in the Cup. But then, minds might well have been distracted by ominous rumblings from the continent.

When war came in the summer of 1914, it cut a swathe through English football, killing off players by the dozen. Sportsmen were generally the first to volunteer, believing that taking on the Germans would be much like an away fixture against Burnley. Whole companies of footballers who stuck together in the trenches, much like the platoons of butchers, bakers and candle-stick makers, were wiped out at the Somme, Passchendaele and Ypres.

Back on the home front, things carried on as normal for a while. League football continued until 1915, when it was finally deemed a distraction from the all-consuming business of war and sus pended. In the last fixture of that final season, United needed a win against Liverpool to stay in the First Division. They got it 2-0. Which all seemed a touch too convenient, given Liverpool were patently superior opposition. It was. Knowing that the League was due to be suspended, a number of United and Liverpool play-ers saw this as their last opportunity to make a nice little earner from the game. A betting coup was organised between the two sets of players and when a letter signed by 'Football King' was printed in the *Manchester Evening News* a few days after the match alleging that the game had been fixed during a meeting at the Dog and Partridge pub just round the corner from Old Trafford, the FA launched an investigation. Four Liverpool players and three United stalwarts – Sandy Turnbull, Arthur Whalley and Enoch 'Knocker' West – were found guilty and banned for life for match-fixing. All were eventually pardoned (although it took West until 1945 before he was officially able to play again; a bit academic as he was sixty-two by then). Sandy Turnbull's ban was tragically short-lived. On 3 May 1917, the first great United centre forward, the scorer of the winning goal in the 1909 Cup final, the man who once nicked the FA Cup, was killed in action at the second battle of Arras. Football, the working man's escape, the game dreamed up as an improving moral force, suddenly did not seem quite so important anymore.

3

SO WHO OWNS THIS CLUB?

It was a Sunday morning, 9 September 1998. This was an international break, United hadn't played the day before, so for a lifelong red like Andy Walsh, it was a bit of a weekend off. Time for a lie-in. But Walsh, the chair of the Independent Manchester United Supporters' Association, was in no mood to snooze. He had just been woken by a reporter seeking a comment on the news that Rupert Murdoch had made a bid to buy the club. As he took in what he was hearing, Walsh felt as if his stomach was making a bid to evacuate his body via the soles of his feet. Through his television arm BSkyB, Murdoch, the world's most powerful media mogul, had offered almost £624 million to hoover up all the available United shares on the open market. There was nothing illegal about this: since 1991 United had been a publicly listed company, its shares freely available to anyone who wished to buy them. According to the reporter, it seemed that morning like the deal had been done. All that was left was to dot a couple of i's, cross a couple of t's. Outside Old Trafford the news cameras had already found a couple of United fans who seemed more than enthusiastic about the impending deal.

'It means we'll be able to buy Ronaldo, Zidane, anyone we want,' said one of them.

Walsh, however, was less enthused by the idea. He saw Murdoch not as a benevolent sugar daddy happy to splash his cash on whichever world-class player took the fans' fickle fancy. Rather, he believed him to be a raider whose interest in United began and ended with the further procurement of money and power.

A Ph.D. in economics was not required to work out why it was to the former Australian's advantage to buy United. As head of the company with the contract to broadcast domestic football, owning the club would give him invaluable access to both sides of any future negotiations, allow him to exercise almost total control over the game. In the vocabulary of modern marketing, he would own the content as well as the point of delivery.

Supporters like Andy Walsh had long laboured under a different belief in United's purpose: that it should be a football club, operated for the benefit of those who pay to watch, an entity owned by the membership of which the chairman was a temporary custodian. From the moment the news broke, Walsh's mobile had been bleeping. What everyone wanted to know was: what could they do about this? How could a campaign be conducted against someone as determined as Murdoch? After making a couple of phone calls, Walsh decided that he was not going to let the takeover happen unchallenged. If nothing else, it was important to let it be known that for United's hard-core support, there was a lot more to their club than a bottom line. For them, this was not a set of figures, a profit and loss account that they were fighting over. It was a living, beating entity, a thing with a heart and a soul.

'What you defended was your experience of going to United with your friends and family,' says Walsh. 'It was the sense of belonging, of being part of the Man United movement. That was United.'

It was a definition growing ever less visible. The organisation that began as a recreational outlet for working men had developed in the latter end of the 1990s into an international leisure conglomerate. The change had happened slyly, a snowballing agglomeration of hints and clues like a flotation on the Stock Exchange in 1991 and the removal of the words 'Football' and 'Club' from the club crest in 1998 (they went, incidentally, because the designers of the newly streamlined badge suggested that the international market could not understand what they meant). In less than a decade United had become an entertainment corporation, a Hollywood-style purveyor of celebrity, a production line to manufacture cash housed within the Theatre of Dreams.

'It is', according to José Angel Sanchez, director of marketing at United's rivals as the world's wealthiest football club, Real Madrid, 'a company that provides content, like Universal Studios.'

Now it seemed, as it lay prostrate at the feet of BSkyB, this institution had finally lost all contact with those whose loyalty had built it in the first place. The end of the game was in sight.

What Walsh wanted was confirmation of the definition of a football club as given by the *Athletic News*, which suggested that it must be 'sustained by the voluntary effort of a number of people resident in the locality of its headquarters and that there are many shareholders who, with separate interests, have the right to elect directors'. He would also have concurred with a directive from the Football Association which stated that 'the private proprietorship of clubs carried on for the purpose of speculation and profit' was invidious to the interests of the game as a whole. The fact that both of these statements were made in the 1930s suggest that the battle for the spirit of football clubs like Manchester United was not a new one. Indeed, Walsh and the like minds plotting resistance to Murdoch would have drawn comfort they were not the first United followers to fight over the very beating heart of the organisation. It had happened before, in 1931. Back then, the dispute was bitter and lengthy. It pitched supporter against director in a civil war that seethed with rancour. It too came from an idea of what United should be and what it could become.

The battle of 1931 was, however, a subtly different clash to the anti-Murdoch dispute nearly seven decades later. This was a row not about how the fruits of success should be divided. Rather, it was about failure. And how – in the supporters' minds – the directors and those in charge of the purse strings had brought the club to the lip of oblivion by their inertia.

Failure and Manchester United: they have not been words often seen in close proximity since Alex Ferguson began his trophy rush in 1990. But imagine how it felt for anyone attending the last Manchester United home game before the Second World War. When they opened the programme for the match against Grimsby, they would have seen that the page detailing the club's honours had not altered one jot since 1911. On the pitch, the period between the wars was the most barren in red history, two decades of under-achievement, of yo-yoing between the top two divisions, in which the highest League position was ninth and the most significant result was a defeat in the semi-final of the FA Cup. This is how bad things got: at one point during the 1934 season, as the club faced the very real possibility of sinking into the third tier of English football, they even changed strip for a couple of months, hoping a different colour of shirt might bring better luck. Though it is hard to fathom why anyone imagined fate would favour cherry and white hoops.

On the other hand – and maybe this was no coincidence – off the pitch, those twenty years were full of intrigue and infighting, of directorial wrangles and managerial sackings, of threats of foreclosure by the bank. With the action on the playing surface largely moribund, most of the excitement was in the boardroom, including the time that A. E. Thomson was forced to resign as a director after scandal erupted when one of the United players eloped with his daughter. Neil Dewar, the player concerned, took young Miss Thomson with him when he upped sticks and left for Sheffield Wednesday. He was, it seems, so desperate to be on his way from Old Trafford he didn't even delay the departure long enough to secure his future father-in-law's permission for the ensuing marriage (they were reconciled in time for a proper wedding ceremony, though judging by the tense-looking official photograph taken on the occasion, relations had yet fully to thaw between father and son-in-law).

To understand what went wrong, it is necessary to go back to the Armistice. The immediate post-Great War period should have dawned brightly for the club. Once peace had been secured, like the rest of the football world, at Old Trafford the 1919 season was greeted with a wave of optimism. Football was briefly an escape for everyone: immediately after the war, a visit to Old Trafford was something of a social occasion, a draw for the locally monied who wished to see and be seen. The *Manchester Guardian* reported of a 1919 derby that 'the approach to the ground resembled a vehicle park at a great racecourse. On either side of Warwick Road transport of every description was lined up – charabancs (extemporised and deluxe), taxis, private motors, motor cycles and even a number of horse-drawn carriages.'

Huge crowds clacked through the turnstiles for those first couple of post-war years. On 27 December 1920, for instance, 70,504 filed into Old Trafford to see United take on Aston Villa, a record for a League game at the ground that was to stand until the 2006–07 season. In the days before health and safety, however, the accommodation was clearly not up to hosting such a bustle: several crush barriers buckled under the throng. Fans complained of not being able to see anything, of being trampled. Although the sense of claustrophobia was not to last long. The team had its own solution to the issue of overcrowding in the stands. As they did quite often in those days, the reds lost that particular crowd-pulling encounter 3-1. And the following day, only three thousand turned up for a friendly against the Corinthians. Indeed, such was the team's inability to make the most of football's mini-boom, average home crowds were down to below thirty thousand by the end of the following season.

Much of the problem was to do with personnel. Of the side that had been involved in the last fixture before the wartime cessation of the League, Sandy Turnbull, the fine striker who had scored the winner in the 1909 Cup final, was killed in action in the trenches. Others had been injured in the conflict, or had grown too old or had simply been diverted by the hiatus away from the game. Billy Meredith, the Welsh Wizard who supplied the pre-war side with its box office sparkle, was still around, but he was now in his forties. Moreover, during the war he had often guested for Manchester City in unofficial fixtures and in 1919 he demanded a transfer across town, saying he wanted once more to link up with his old mentor Ernest Mangnall, now in charge of City. The two clubs agreed a fee, but Meredith refused to participate in the move, insisting, with characteristic stubbornness, that he was not a commodity to be bought and sold and that he should be allowed to go on his own terms.

'I will not', he told the board, 'be traded like a piece of horse flesh.'

He wanted a free transfer and nothing less. The board insisted on a fee. There was a lengthy stalemate, as Meredith – the wily old veteran of disputes past – stayed on with the reds for a whole season, a grumbling presence on the fringes of the dressing room, often spending entire matches standing on the touchline, barely participating, simply chewing on his toothpick. Eventually the club tired of fighting over a man in his mid-forties. Even one who – thanks, he claimed, to a regimen of herbal remedies and after-match rubdowns using a bizarre collection of unctions – boasted the fitness of many men half his age. Believing he had no remaining residual value, he was allowed away to join the blues for nothing. Little did anyone realise the crafty old curmudgeon would carry on playing until he was nearly fifty.

Just as serious an absentee from the pre-war crew was the

chairman, John Davies. Soon after the war's conclusion he decided
he too no longer wished to be involved in the club. Davies's legacy
was not just the only major silverware the club had acquired, but
also Old Trafford. Boasting only one roofed enclosure (the rest of
the ground was open terraces, with the loyalists congregating in
the popular 'Pop' Side, where the North Stand is now), its facilities
were nevertheless considered state of the art. One contemporary
report swooned about the changing rooms, which boasted 'a large
hot bath, neatly tiled, while showers and other contrivances make
for the comfort of the playing staff'.

Such attractions were noted across the country. The ground
hosted an international between England and Scotland in April
1926, which the Scots won 1-0 in front of a crowd of forty-nine
thousand. Four FA Cup semi-finals were held there in the twenties,
plus a rugby union match between Lancashire and the touring All
Blacks, the Manchester County Police annual sports day and, in
1927, a tennis exhibition featuring the Wimbledon Ladies champion Suzanne Lenglen. You imagine all concerned appreciated the
bath.

Despite such a bequest, however, Davies's successors in the
boardroom could not match his financial acumen: soon the regular
profits he turned when in charge were a thing of the past. The
inertia in the boardroom spread to the pitch. Many a visiting side
to Old Trafford found it a far from intimidating venue, generally
scuttling off home not only nicely spruced up after their ablutions
in the renowned facilities, but with two points in the bag. In 1922
the reds found themselves relegated for the first time since 1894. It
wasn't even a close-run thing: when the season ended they were
eight points adrift of Everton and safety. A measure of the gap
between United and the Merseysiders was that the reds lost 5-0 at
Goodison that year.

John Robson, who had been the club's secretary/manager since
1914, duly accepted responsibility for the decline and resigned.
Into his place came the Scotsman John Chapman. Hailing from
Glasgow, Chapman was the first of several sons of the Clyde to

occupy United's bench, the first to demonstrate what later was to become a de facto football twinning between the two grand, but rough-edged cities.

Robson arrived with something of a reputation. He had made Airdrieonians a genuine force in Scottish football and his ability to organise a defence was much admired. Such was his prestige, the United board agreed to pay him an annual salary in four figures and present him with a house.

One thing they were not buying with the new man, however, was immediate success. Chapman did not set too high a standard for his fellow Scots to follow. A dour, unsmiling Presbyterian presence around the club, his personality was reflected in the way his team played: only three times in his first two years in charge at Old Trafford did the players manage to score more than two goals in a game. Finishing so low down the Second Division they were behind Stockport County was not likely to have the locals singing from Salford's roof tops. Crowds diminished to the point where as few as eleven thousand would rattle round Old Trafford. Things were no happier among the playing staff. According to a director called George Bedford, interviewed in the *Topical Times* magazine, there was 'some chafing in the dressing room'. It sounds painful and it was. Neil McBain, the centre back, demanded a transfer then went public with stories of other players putting pressure on the management to drop him. There were tales of a split between the English and the Scots in the dressing room. There was even a theory that the new ground at Old Trafford was cursed (Joe Spence, in the intemperate language of the times, suggested the pitch be dug up to see if the remains of a 'policeman or Jew or somesuch' had been buried there to put the kibosh on the team). Meanwhile, across town, City, with Meredith, Mangnall and the rest, were kicking up a storm in the First Division; crowds, momentum and local dominance all belonged to the blues.

Dismayed by the shadow in which they were obliged to operate, supporters and shareholder groups got together in 1924 to

demand that one of their number be placed on the board of directors. It was not much of a demand. But this was the time of the
national strikes, of labour mobilisation, of revolution. Fearing that
they too were to be victims of a socialist putsch, the board resisted
all such manoeuvres. It was a decision that was not forgotten
among fans who grew ever more infuriated at the rising tide of
failure.

The board were, however, sufficiently alarmed by the unrest to
sanction a spending spree for Chapman in an attempt to invigor-
ate the United side with new signings. It didn't have much effect.
The biggest signing was when the manager paid South Shields
£1000 for the magnificently named Lancelot Holliday Richardson.
But the only ever transfer between the two clubs was not an
overnight panacea. Big Lance, as he was known, eventually tired
of picking the ball out of the net at Old Trafford and moved, via a
brief spell at Reading, to Argentina. Here, about as far from failure
as he could escape, he established a successful ranch in Cordoba,
which he worked until his death in 1958.

Much of Chapman's forays into the transfer market smacked of
desperation. Take the strange case of Albert Pape. On 7 February
1925, United were due to play Clapton Orient in a Second
Division match at Old Trafford. Pape, Orient's centre forward,
arrived with his team-mates on the train fully expecting to turn
out against United. However, just ninety minutes before kick-off
Chapman persuaded his opposite number to sell the player to
the reds. The registration details were wired to the Football
League headquarters in time for him to turn out for his new
employers in that very game. His Orient team-mates were completely unaware that he had made the switch until, just before the
game started, they saw him inspecting the pitch with the United
players. They were even more surprised when he duly scored for
his new club. The glory did not last long. Within nine months he
had been transferred to Fulham. Though, in an odd twist, he
retained the house in Wigan he had bought on his arrival up north
and for his entire time at Craven Cottage continued to train at Old

Trafford. Not a situation you imagine being tolerated by Chapman's Glaswegian successors.

At least, throughout all this, Chapman could call on the services of Joe Spence, the reds' leading goalscorer in every season in which the Scot was the manager. Known by the magnificent nickname of 'The Scotswood Whippet', Spence, a quick, skilful, wiry Northumbrian, rarely missed a chance. 'Give it to Joe' was the legend written on placards flourished in the Pop Side. It wasn't far from summing up the total extent of United's tactical plan. With him on the teamsheet, Chapman finally managed to achieve what he was being paid handsomely to do. After three long years in charge he steered United up into the First Division again. The reds finished second to Leicester City in the Second Division in 1925, their promotional charge underpinned not just by Spence's goals but also by the most parsimonious defence. They only conceded twenty-three League goals all season.

At the heart of that stone wall back line was the captain, Frank Barson, one of the hardest men ever to slip on a red shirt. A colliery blacksmith by trade, the centre back hailed from the aptly named pit village of Grimethorpe near Barnsley. He was renowned for an unsophisticated approach to the game that largely consisted of kicking them before they could kick him. Chapman paid £5000 to Aston Villa to secure his services, though Barson was as tenacious when it came to negotiating his own personal terms as he was in the tackle. He agreed to sign only after United said they would, as a bonus if promotion was secured under his captaincy, buy him a pub. In 1925 the board were as good as their word and, once the First Division beckoned, a large ale house in Ardwick Green was duly found for him. The opening night of the new landlord's tenancy, however, turned into something of a promotion party. So many fans and well-wishers poured into the premises, hoping to slap the skipper on the back – and perhaps get themselves a free drink in return – that Barson took flight. Just half an hour into his career, he told his wife the life of a licensee was not for him, chucked his keys on to the bar and never set foot in the place again.

The crowd may have warmed to him, but Frank Barson was not a popular figure in the United boardroom. Even the ebullient Louis Rocca, by now elevated from the postroom to be the club's chief fixer, was more than a little wary of his Yorkshire bluff. 'A gentleman of firm-set opinion' is what Rocca called him.

On the field, under Barson's captaincy, the reds managed a respectable fifteenth position in their first year back in the top flight. Plus they enjoyed something of a Cup run, though it was to end in ignominy for the skipper. They reached the 1926 FA Cup semi-final, which was lost in a tetchy, ill-tempered battle with their local rivals in blue. During a particularly fraught passage of play, a Barson challenge left the City captain Sam Cowan unconscious. The referee didn't see anything untoward in the incident and Barson remained on the field as Cowan was carried off. But the FA acted on complaints from the City management. Barson became the first player retrospectively to be charged with misconduct and was banned for two months. That semi-final, incidentally, was such a high point in a barren period that the match-day programme at Old Trafford was still carrying action photographs from it two years later in 1928.

Just as success looked as if it might return to Old Trafford, however, scandal broke forth. In the autumn of 1926 an investigation by the FA found John Chapman guilty of 'improper conduct in his position as secretary/manager of Manchester United'. He was suspended for the rest of the season, banned from his duties as manager. Far from standing by him, the directors immediately fired the Scotsman. The reasons for his suspension and subsequent dismissal, however, were never made public: neither the FA nor the United board would reveal what he had done. And in more deferential times, the press did not even speculate. Although it was hinted by Alf Clarke in his 1948 history of the club that Chapman was covering for a match-fixing player, Gentleman John – as he was known – never spoke about the case and carried his secret with him to the grave. Maybe it was Barson and he was simply too scared to point the finger of blame.

In October 1926, Clarence Hilditch took over as player-manager, the only one in red history. His reign was only ever meant to be brief, holding the fort until a new recruit could be signed up. And in the summer of 1927 Herbert Bamlett arrived from Middlesbrough. After the only player-manager came another unique occupant of the dug-out: Bamlett is the only qualified referee to be in charge at United. Indeed, when he turned up from the north-east he was well known to red fans with longer memories as the ref who, in 1909, called off the FA cup tie at Turf Moor between Burnley and United as a blizzard enveloped the ground. He it was who had been too cold to blow the whistle to bring the action to a conclusion and had to hand it to the United skipper Charlie Roberts to blow it for him.

Despite fielding not one but two players named James Brown, Bamlett's United very rarely demonstrated any soul, even when the Browns were joined at times by a certain Tom Jones. By the end of the season, the fans were getting restless. 'One has sentimental reasons for supporting United but sentiment dies too. The management will find this out if we are subjected to many more inept displays.' So a fan signing themselves 'Old Trafford' wrote to the AGM that year. But the board were not inclined to win popularity by buying their way out of a crisis.

Besides, they did not have the financial wherewithal for much sustained investment in players. The late twenties and early thirties were not a good time to be in Manchester. The city was in crisis. The depression was having a catastrophic effect on jobs, trade was in freefall and the cotton industry that had for so long been the wellspring of Mancunian affluence was in steep decline. Consequently there was little spare cash around to devote to watching football. As crowds tumbled, United lurched into a vicious downward spiral.

Even if there had been much in the way of spending money, not many would wish to dispose of it in the environs of Old Trafford. After two wholly forgettable seasons in charge, at the start of the 1930–31 season Herbert Bamlett's side hit rock bottom. The once parsimonious defence shipped twenty-five goals in the first five games. This was just the start of the longest sequence of defeats in red history: twelve in succession saw them nailed fast to the foot of the First Division. 'They are the worst team in senior football,' announced the *Football Chronicle*. It was hard to argue.

4

DECLINE AND STUMBLE

In the early autumn of 1930 George Greenhough was elected the secretary of the Manchester United Supporters Club and Shareholders Association, a body freshly formed by fans infuriated by endemic failure. A gruff, ill-tempered taxicab proprietor from Rusholme, whose wife ran a boarding house for music hall acts, Greenhough was in his forties when he decided that something needed to be done to alter the direction of United beyond mere grumbling at every home game (the Pop Side had the reputation at the time as being the moaniest stand in football). Acting under a democratic mandate of association members, gained at meetings in halls across the city, he issued demands that the board resign en masse and that the FA investigate the financial dealings of the club. Neither route elicited so much as a reply. As the team's slump gathered pace, Greenhough's group issued a five-point plan to the board. Their demands were: a new manager, a better scouting system, the signing of quality players, the election of new board members and a rights issue to raise more money to take the club forward. Setting a precedent that would be later followed by several United chairmen, George Lawton, John Davies's successor, refused to meet with the group, saying he did not believe that they carried a democratic mandate of all the fans.

There followed a frenzied fortnight of meetings. At one, a more radical idea than simply issuing statements was proposed: if the board refused to meet the group, or if results did not improve, the fans planned to organise a mass boycott of the Arsenal game on 18 October 1930. Arsenal were the best team in the country at the time, a glamorous opponent; in normal circumstances they would likely draw as big a crowd as anyone, maybe as many as fifty thousand. What better way to voice discontent than to hit the board where they would be most hurt: in the pocket? The idea was accepted unanimously.

Both sides attempted to seize the moral high ground via the local press. The letters pages of the *Manchester Evening News* and the *Athletic News* bubbled with intrigue and counter-argument. Some felt that while the supporters' resentments were justified, nothing could excuse a boycott: it simply wasn't sporting, concluded one correspondent to the *Athletic News*. Claim and counterclaim bucked and fizzed. Greenhough's insistence that his every approach had been rebutted by the board was denied. More revolutionary elements among the fans circulated a handbill attacking the players, which Greenhough publicly disowned: his argument, he said, was not with the lads on the pitch, it was with the management. He also, in one letter to the papers, counselled that gloating City fans keep out of the row. This was red on red violence. And, as the date of the meeting approached, with no hint of rapprochement, the mood was growing angrier by the moment.

In the two matches before the proposed boycott the team lost 4-1 to Manchester City then 5-1 at West Ham. It could hardly have been a more clear mandate for action. So, on 17 October 1930, the night before the Arsenal game, George Greenhough organised a mass meeting at Hulme Town Hall in order to discuss whether the boycott should go ahead. Reports vary on the numbers who turned up: Greenhough claimed three thousand, the *Manchester Evening News* twelve hundred. However many, there were enough to create a sense of occasion. Greenhough spoke and was given a rousing ovation. His five points were, once more, passed. And the ultimate sanction of a boycott supported. After Greenhough had spoken, the meeting chairman Mr S. Mason asked if there were any dissenting voices. A hand was raised in the crowd. It was Charlie Roberts, the former captain, founding father of the Professional Footballers' Association and a supporters' champion. Declaring himself fully in favour of the group's aims, he nonetheless had argued for the previous fortnight in the local papers against the idea of a boycott. Now, to huge applause, he made his way to the front of the meeting. In a moment of high drama, he argued vociferously that, yes, the management of the club was a shambles and, yes, the fans had every right to be shirty. But a boycott was not on. This was a time, he suggested, that fans should be getting behind the players, not undermining them with talk of splits and division. His impassioned rhetoric, though, failed to sway the meeting, which voted overwhelmingly in favour of staying away the next afternoon.

On the day of the boycott, the police presence around Old Trafford was sizeably increased. Gaggles of bobbies gathered round the turnstiles. Horses patrolled the area. But there was no sign of trouble. No pickets were placed outside the Pop Side to deter spectators; in fact, with telling precedent for the anti-Murdoch and anti-Glazer protests seventy years on, there was no match-day upset whatsoever. Soon fans were arriving in numbers. Inside the ground, the Beswick Prize Band played 'Happy Days Are Here Again' as the crowd greeted the arrival of the players with a huge ovation. In the directors' box, the board were buoyed by support from the football establishment. George Lawton flourished a telegram from the directors of Blackpool FC wishing him a 'bumper gate'. It was a typical response. In the programme notes for the trip to Portsmouth a few days later, the Pompey directors wrote of the boycott, 'anything more stupid by those styling themselves as "supporters" cannot be imagined'. In the end there were twenty-three thousand there. Not the fifty thousand there might have been in better times, but still it represented the biggest crowd of the season. The boycott was described by the *Manchester Evening News* as 'a total failure'. The *Athletic News* smirked, 'the much-discussed boycott was on, but nobody noticed it'. Greenhough's group was widely derided and its moment in the arclight of publicity had gone. All talk of future boycotts was dismissed when the idea was voted out at a public meeting in December.

Over the next couple of years, George Greenhough's name crops up occasionally in AGM reports, usually making failed attempts to move a motion of no confidence in the directors. And he and his group are entirely absent from the official history of United as demonstrated in the Old Trafford museum. Nor should they, it might be argued, take up space required for memories of triumphs and trebles. Yet Greenhough's organisation represents something important. They were the first to organise around an articulation of what they wanted United to be, the first to recognise that there was something intangible about the character of this club that was worth fighting for, something about it that was more than just the accumulation of League points or profits. They were the anti-Murdoch, anti-Glazer, IMUSA of their day.

That said, as anyone who has ever organised a fan protest knows, the easiest way of ensuring a boycott is successful is for the team to play poor football. Herbert Bamlett's United duly obliged. After the failed coup, things got steadily worse on the pitch and in the stands. For the rest of that season, as the team remained resolutely at the foot of the table, there was only one home crowd of over ten thousand. For the final game of the term, when the club was already relegated by a huge margin, only 3900 bothered to turn up at Old Trafford to see them draw 1-1 with Middlesbrough. That was what you call a boycott.

The crisis was by no means confined to the pitch. At the end of that first season of the 1930s, United stood on the cusp of bankruptcy. Although they owned the ground, tumbling crowds had completely undermined financial viability. They owed £30,000, a huge sum then, to the bank, most of it due on a loan to build the new North Stand, a structure that was now largely empty on match days. In addition to the backlog of debt, the annual report for that year showed a loss of £2509 11s 6d on day to day business, with revenue down £7500 over the previous year. Over his copy of the report, the director Herbert Davies scribbled notes of increasing desperation. He couldn't understand why 'players' outfits' had cost £46 when he thought '£5 would be more than sufficient'. A campaign of belt-tightening ensued that took almost comical dimensions when, at Christmas 1931, Walter Crickmer, the club secretary, was denied the funds to buy the players and staff their traditional Christmas turkey. Perhaps it was the lack of a decent Christmas lunch that explained the reds' dreadful form in seasonal matches at that time. They lost 7-0 to Aston Villa on Boxing Day in 1931, 7-0 to Wolves the following year and 7-3 to Grimsby the Yuletide after that.

By now time had been called on Herbert Bamlett as manager. He was not offered a new contract (though history does not record whether Charlie Roberts was called in to blow the whistle on his reign). Walter Crickmer took over on a temporary basis, aided by Louis Rocca, who had done virtually every other job at the club so it was only a matter of time before he was put in control of team matters.

A more significant change, however, occurred in the boardroom in 1932. With the team now marooned in the Second Division, United were obliged to try to survive on crowds down to well below ten thousand. They couldn't and the financial crisis reached a head. Things had been thin for a while (supporters were even washing the players' match-day kit to save on the laundry bills), but that winter it came to a crisis point: the board did not have enough money to pay the players' wages, the corporation had cut off the gas supply to Old Trafford for non-payment of bills and the bank had initiated procedures to foreclose on the mortgage debt. None of the current directors had the wherewithal to stave off disaster, their preferred business strategy had long been Micawber-like: wait and see and hope for the best. George Lawton, by now desperate, issued an appeal for anyone who might help. It was like 1902 all over again. Except United were hardly an attractive investment proposition. Ten years of systemic failure had completely changed the character of the club: this was an institution ripe with dissent and dismay, poorly run and consequently poorly supported. They were a joke, a music hall mainstay. In the playgrounds of Manchester the gag was: 'Have you heard United have signed two Chinese internationals: We Won Once and How Long Since.' George Greenhough and his fellow supporters were eventually to get what they wanted, wholesale change in the board. It might have come about through the force of economics rather than their revolutionary activity, but change came. United were a reflection of dark financial times, a wilted, emaciated shadow of the muscular sporting giant they had been under Ernest Mangnall, battered into embarrassment by inertia and incompetence in the face of the worst recession in history. Like the nine out of ten men in parts of Salford who found themselves unemployed, they were just another victim of a worldwide slump.

Step forward James Gibson, partner in a Manchester clothing manufacturer called Briggs, Jones and Gibson. It was Louis Rocca who persuaded him that the plight of Manchester United was near fatal. Not a football fan, but a loyal Mancunian and a citizen unwilling to allow such a potentially vibrant constituent of Manchester's sense of itself to disappear, Gibson stepped in with £2000 of his own money to affect a rescue, just as John Davies had done back at the turn of the century. But Gibson was not satisfied merely in a salvage operation. He wanted to develop the club, seeing it as a potential vehicle to put Manchester back not just on the map, but at the epicentre of the universe, where so many of its loyalists believed it should lie. He wanted to see a team of local youngsters, taking on the world with hearts bursting with Manc pride. He announced he would provide more money if his original injection of funds was matched by other interested parties and –

crucially – if the fans supported his vision. Four new directors came on to the board, each providing £2000. As for the fans, the first game in which Gibson was in the directors' box recorded an attendance more than twice the previous highest that season: 33,312 watched Wolves being beaten 3-2 in a Second Division game. Gibson was smitten. He remained chairman until his death in 1951. And Violet, his wife, was still the club's most significant shareholder when she died twenty years later.

Thus by the end of 1932 all five of the demands made by the fans two years earlier had been acted on: the club had a new chairman, a new board, new money, a promise of new players and a new manager. How George Greenhough must have been smiling on the Pop Side. Particularly after Gibson, cannily recognising that it is always better to have your potential enemies on the inside, had invited the fan leader for talks in the boardroom. Impressed by what he heard, the former rebel disbanded his old supporters' association, dropped all note of complaint against the board and put his weight behind a new, official supporters' club with an annual membership sub of one shilling. Publicly demonstrating that fan and director were now pulling in the same direction, a club office in a hut behind the Pop Side was opened by Gibson himself. The beers flowed that day.

But, proving that unity and solidarity alone are not enough in football, if the fans were hoping for a brighter dawn from the new regime on the pitch, the darkest hour was yet to come. True, there was a fresh face in the dug-out. Scott Duncan, another Scot, took over from the temporary Crickmer/Rocca partnership and promised a swift return to the First Division. He said he 'knew where to look' for replacements if the current United players were not up to the task. Subsequent events suggested he did not have the sharpest eye for a player. Although he did have an eye for tailoring. He used to wear spats into the club offices.

The 1933–34 season was described at the time by the *Manchester Evening News* as 'the most heart-breaking in the history of Manchester United'. Stuttering and spluttering, the side had a dire start to the Second Division campaign. It was thought that, as they lost 6-1 at Bradford Park Avenue, 5-1 at Lincoln and then 5-1 again at Bolton, things could not get worse. They did. So bad did it become, Scott Duncan attempted to change the club's luck by playing in different shirt colours. Several were used, none had the desired effect. On 5 May 1934, the last day of the season, United met Millwall at the Den. It was a game with the most stark of outcomes: both poised on the edge of the relegation zone, whoever lost would go down to the Third Division. Millwall, though, were marginally better placed: a draw would be sufficient for the hosts to stay up. United had to go to London's intimidating docklands and win to prevent a tumble into the third tier of English football for the only time in the club's history. Thirty-five thousand fans turned up in almost ghoulish fascination. United won 2-0, Tom Manley and Jack Cape the goalscorers. A gale of relief could be felt throughout Manchester as three thousand people crowded into Central station to welcome the team home. It was almost as if they had won something, rather than merely conducting a Houdini-like escape. But it indicated the depth of loyalty among the supporters. And the potential if things could be turned round.

From there things could only look up. At the end of the 1934–35 season the annual report showed a profit of £4490. This was largely achieved by James Gibson's careful stewardship. For instance, the last game of that season was away at Plymouth, a pricey journey involving hotels and rail fares, yet because of League rules, the visiting club would receive none of the gate-receipts. So Gibson and Walter Crickmer organised to play a friendly the next day at St Austell on the understanding that their hosts would split the gate money with them. It was enough to show a modest profit on the road trip.

Gibson did not entirely restrict himself to economy. In 1935 he persuaded the Midland Railway – which operated express trains from Central station out to Liverpool and Warrington on a line passing directly behind Old Trafford – to put in a halt station at the ground and to run match-day special trains. Soon fans could travel straight to the ground from Stockport, Crewe, Birmingham, even London. The idea of being a Manchester United supporter from beyond the city confines became a physical possibility.

With the purse strings loosened slightly, Scott Duncan managed to put together a team that gained promotion back to the First Division in 1936. The following season United came straight back down again. That year Duncan – the man who said he knew where to look for new talent – selected no fewer than thirty-one different players, including Walter Winterbottom, a cultured wing half who looked the part until his progress was blighted by a dangerous spinal injury. Unable to play on after the war, Winterbottom took up coaching and eventually became the longest serving England manager in history. Not to mention, along with Sir Matt, Sir Bobby and Sir Alex, one of four knights of the realm associated with United.

Some of Duncan's other signings, however, enjoyed less elevated careers. Goalkeeper Tommy Breen was signed from Irish football and his first piece of action as a United player was picking the ball out of his own net on debut against Leeds. He endured another unfortunate, long-standing record. In a Cup tie against Barnsley in 1938, he touched a long throw-in into his own net – the only occasion in Cup history a goal has been scored in that manner.

With buys like that, the self-styled wheeler-dealer of a manager hardly distinguished himself. And in the middle of 1938 Scott Duncan parted company with the reds. As was characteristic of the time, no one speculated on whether he jumped or was pushed. Whatever the cause, few were surprised: Duncan had promised much, had been given more funds than several of his predecessors, but had delivered little except a more than adequate impression of a yo-yo.

The loyal Walter Crickmer took over again and immediately changed the emphasis of the club, steering it towards youth. Together with his chairman, he had established the Manchester United Junior Athletic Club (MUJAC) in 1937. Johnny Carey,

Charlie Mitten, Johnny Aston and Stan Pearson were all blooded in its ranks. The youth team played in the Chorlton Amateur League and in its first year of competition scored an astonishing 223 goals. And now he was in charge of the first team, Crickmer brought some of the more promising young players forward. The effect was immediate. Jack Rowley (as it happened, a Duncan signing) scored four goals in only his second game, Pearson's debut was almost as dramatic, while Carey had already played internationally for Ireland before he got his chance in the Old Trafford big time. With an injection of youthful vim, United won promotion back to the First Division at a canter. What's more, the club that had so recently faced financial meltdown, had made profit for five successive seasons. At the AGM in 1939, Gibson spoke of his vision for the years ahead: 'We have no intention of buying any more mediocrities. From now on we will have a Manchester United composed of Manchester players.' This was a new aim: United the vehicle for local pride.

The future looked bright on the morning of 2 September 1939 as the young Manchester United turned out against Charlton at the Valley. At the back they included a lad called Allenby Chilton, the most coveted youth in English football, making his debut. Chilton, everyone reckoned, was at the start of a very long career. Maybe, but it was to be a suddenly truncated one. United lost 2-0 on Chilton's introduction, but the next morning the idea of brooding over defeat seemed somewhat irrelevant: Britain declared war on Germany after Hitler refused a demand to withdraw his troops from Poland. The Football League was immediately suspended. It was thought this might be a temporary measure, but the competition was not reinstated for another seven years.

For six years Old Trafford was dark. Yet, whatever the external storms, the seeds had been planted. All that was needed now was for an expert gardener to be found who might bring them to fruition once the war was finished. Now was the time for an individual who, more than any other, would impose his own personality on the place and come to define it through his very presence.

5

JUST GO OUT AND PLAY

In the 1994–95 football season, Manchester City's East German international Uwe Rösler scored twenty-two League and Cup goals. In celebration of his achievements, blues supporters – always anxious to find some way of relating anything that happens at the club to their red neighbours – sported a T-shirt bearing the legend: 'Uwe's granddad bombed Old Trafford'. Whenever he was asked about this dig at red expense, Rösler looked perplexed: none of his relatives, he insisted, had been anywhere near the Luftwaffe, let alone discharged their payloads over Old Trafford. But whoever was flying the German military's planes, the fact was, Manchester did not escape untarnished from the Blitz. Although not suffering as much as London, Plymouth or Coventry, over the winter of 1940 and spring of 1941 the damage was widespread. The Free Trade Hall, the Royal Exchange, the assize courts and Victoria station were all hit. The bombers' main target, however, was the docks of Trafford Park, where goods and materials from the United States were unloaded by the hour to keep the Manchester munitions factories stocked and rolling. In March 1941 the Luftwaffe came looking to put out of commission the likes of Metropolitan Vickers (where the Lancaster bomber was under construction) and Ford (where Spitfire engines were assembled). And the collateral damage was significant, bombs sprayed everywhere, splattering Stretford Girls High School, St Hilda's Junior School, Old Trafford baths and Lancashire's cricket headquarters. And on the night of 11 March 1941, John Davies's magnificent football ground at Old Trafford took a direct hit, bang on the main stand.

There is a picture of the stadium taken a couple of days after the raid. The spring sun pours through the newly opened-up hole in the roof, illuminating what appears to be the aftermath of a wrecking party. Rows of wooden seats lie ripped out and in disarray, charred beams hang giddily from the broken roof, a couple of ARP (Air Raid Precautions) wardens pick their way through the debris, dwarfed by the twisted girders piling up around their feet.

If a football club is about bricks and mortar then there wasn't much to Manchester United when the war came to an end in April 1945. For four years following the bombing raid, Old Trafford had stood unrepaired. The terraces were pockmarked with weeds, scraggly bushes, some as tall as six feet, had colonised the pitch, a Nissen hut served as the club office. Although the War Damages Commission had agreed to James Gibson's request that it help rebuild the ten football grounds that were damaged in the war and Walter Crickmer, the resourceful club secretary, had managed to elicit a promise of £17,478, not a penny was scheduled to be released until March 1948.

But then the soul of a football club does not lie in its real estate. And the work on restoring Manchester United had begun long before a new beam was put in place. Crickmer and his chairman James Gibson still believed that the mission they had embarked on before they were so rudely interrupted – a team of Manchester men to make Manchester proud – was a viable one. Especially since the one thing they did still have was a roster of players. It wasn't a bad one at that: Jack Rowley, for instance, had been England's chosen centre forward in several wartime internationals and the twenty-six-year-old Stan Pearson was widely respected as the canniest inside forward in the land. What's more, although most of those on the club's books before war started had seen service none had been killed or seriously hurt. True, Allenby Chilton, a volunteer in the Durham Light Infantry, was twice injured, at the Normandy landings and later at Caen, but somehow he had walked away from both. Johnny Morris, too, had some close calls in the tank corps (he had seen his best mate killed). The majority of the United staff, however, enjoyed a less traumatic war. Charlie Mitten, for instance, had volunteered for the RAF, filled with romantic notions of becoming a rear gunner. During a weekend leave from training, he was walking along the promenade in Blackpool when he bumped into Stanley Matthews, who was also in the RAF. Matthews had no intention of going anywhere near action and was astonished to hear what this fellow pro was up to. He himself was in the physical training section, was in charge of the RAF football team and needed an outside left. Mitten liked the sound of that. A transfer was initiated, and he subsequently spent his war playing on the wing, rather than being shot at over Germany.

As Mitten played all over Britain and Europe, back in Manchester, Gibson, Crickmer and Rocca were engaged in organising friendlies to boost public morale. United played all sorts during the war, and, as the usual rules on registration were lifted to allow teams to pick whoever was on leave and in the area, had all sorts playing for them. Players on the books would turn out for the reds when visiting home on leave; Johnny Carey, back from training in Lincolnshire, scored a hat-trick in the last game at Old Trafford before the bomb struck, a pasting of Bury.

As it became obvious after D-Day that things were going to end in an Allied victory, the United board members met to map out a future. It was felt by all that the club needed a serious football operator to take control of the playing side of things. Louis Rocca said he knew just the man for the job. 'Leave it me' was the gist of his contribution to a board meeting in December 1944. Of all the many things he did in a fifty-year association with United, the letter he wrote on the fifteenth of that month was without doubt the most important.

It was addressed to Company Sgt Major Alexander Matthew Busby, of the Ninth Battalion King's Liverpool Regiment, c/o The Royal Military Academy at Sandhurst. Rocca was aware that Busby's last known place of footballing employment was Anfield and that the Merseysiders had already offered him the job of assistant to the manager George Kay, hence the tone of conspiracy that infused his correspondence.

'Well Matt,' it read, 'I have been trying for the past month to find you and not having your reg. address I could not trust a letter going to Liverpool as what I have to say is so important. I don't know if you have considered what you are going to do when the war is over but I have a great job for you if you are willing to take it on. Will you get in touch with me at the above address and when you do I can explain things to you better, when I know there is no danger of interception.'

The letter was signed: 'Your old pal Louis.'

Rocca had once tried to sign Busby from Manchester City back in 1930. But United were so broke they couldn't afford the £150 transfer fee. Still, he had become friendly with the Scotsman through their mutual membership of the Manchester Catholic Sportsman's Club. Like many who came into contact with him, Rocca was immediately struck by the elegant Manchester City wing half. There was something about him, he thought. Something distinguished.

His biographer, Eamon Dunphy, describes Busby as already being regarded as the most prominent Catholic in Manchester public life as early as the mid-thirties. As a player at City, then at Liverpool, Busby stood apart. A thinker, a calm, elegant presence on the pitch, he had an air about him off it. Nothing affected, just a way, a manner. For a start he always took care how he dressed.

By his mid-twenties he had adopted a look that was to remain intact for the rest of his life: Crombie overcoat, well-cut suit or tweed sports jacket, pipe and trilby. Alongside his cloth cap-clad co-workers in their mufflers and collarless shirts, he looked already managerial, a leader of men.

The moment he signed up for war service, the Busby leadership qualities had been noted and he was fast-tracked to become a senior NCO: Sergeant Major Busby of the Army's PT section was made manager of the Army football team sent out to entertain the troops after the invasion of Italy. In his side were Joe Mercer, Tommy Lawton and Frank Swift, the Manchester City goalkeeper who, fourteen years later, would be one of the journalists killed in the Munich air crash. Here was nearly five years of managerial experience, paid for by the Army and with no pressure of results.

Busby was still in uniform when he turned up in response to Rocca's letter to see James Gibson at Cornbrook Cold Storage, on the canalside in Trafford Park, one of the United chairman's many local businesses. By now it was February 1945, but the job offer was still open and it was a substantial one: manager of Manchester United. Busby had an idea of how to operate as a boss forming in his mind. He explained to Gibson that he wanted to do things differently. He wished to go about his business on the pitch without directorial interference. He wanted to pick the team, negotiate transfers, sell on those players he no longer wanted without those who did not know the game as well as he dictating the terms. In short, he wanted total control. Plus, he told the chairman, it would take time to build the sort of club the two of them craved. Five years, he suggested, would be the minimum requirement before anyone saw any tangible results.

It was not a one-way conversation. As they talked, so the pair explored the possibility of their mutual regard. They both liked what they heard; this wasn't a job interview, it was a shared vision. Gibson reported back to the board that he was impressed by 'Mr Busby's ideas and honesty of purpose'. On 19 February

1945, the thirty-six-year-old Busby was offered the job as manager of Manchester United Football Club. He signed a five-year contract, worth a basic £750 a year, plus bonuses and perks. One of those was a club house in Wilbraham Road, Chorlton-cum-Hardy, the suburb a couple of miles south of Old Trafford that largely consists of Manchester's biggest cemetery. He arranged for his wife Jean and their two children to move in to the house immediately.

Although he was not officially due to start work until he was demobbed that autumn, Busby was fully engaged in the process of managing Manchester United from the moment he and Gibson shook hands on their deal. That spring he was in Bari, southern Italy, preparing for an Army game, when he watched a training session for NCOs taken by Jimmy Murphy, the former West Bromwich Albion half back, renowned in his playing days for the ferocity of his tackling. As the man known throughout football as 'Tapper' communicated his ideas about how the game should be played, Busby was impressed. Not so much by what he was saying – though that was intriguing enough – as by the way he said it. With all the passion of a male voice choir in full throat, the Welshman held the soldiers in his sway. Here was a born orator, and Busby recognised immediately that this would be the perfect training ground conduit for his management ideas. After a brief chat, Busby offered Murphy the job of assistant manager: Murphy would look after the reserves at the weekend and during the week the pair of them would run the first team training. Murphy said yes on the spot.

As a signing, it was inspired. There seemed to be an immediate recognition from Busby that Murphy would be his perfect foil; Murphy's passion would dovetail neatly with his control, the Welshman's emotion would counterbalance his reserve, his number-two's approachability offset his own distance. All bases would be covered between them.

Of Irish descent, Murphy, importantly to Busby, was a Catholic. He remained a regular churchgoer throughout his life, his stints in the confessional largely consisting of owning up to ripe language. Boy, could Murphy swear. Although rarely, across a quarter of a century together, did he unleash his tongue in the Boss's hearing. But then few did. It was part of Busby's presence. Pat Crerand, who was brought up barely able to string a sentence together unpunctuated by expletives, the linguistic glue of Glasgow, recalls being struck dumb in Busby's presence when he first fetched up in Manchester. Silence, he says, was the only way he could ensure nothing untoward inadvertently tripped out of his mouth. Murphy was the same. He was among the first to recognise what was soon to become a commonplace observation in football: Busby had an aura. It would soon attach itself to the football club as a whole.

Busby and Murphy took up their posts in October 1945. By the time they got to work, United were lying sixteenth in the ad hoc regional league that picked up from the hiatus of war. Training took place at the Cliff in Salford, matches at Manchester City's Maine Road, a facility that was costing United the tidy sum of £5000 a year in rent, the equivalent of about £180,000 at today's prices.

There is a picture of Busby meeting his players for the first time in 1945 on display in the club museum. The handshakes have a stiff formality about them, with the players standing in a contrived line, as if about to meet the queen. Nevertheless there is something revealing about the snap. All of the players are decked out in the training gear of the times, the roll-necked woollen sweaters and cotton shorts so voluminous they appear to have been crafted from leftover parachutes, and mud seeping up over the sides of their heavy ankle boots. The picture's uniqueness is revealed when you look to the left of frame and study the new boss. Busby is wearing the same kit. Before the war managers didn't dress like that. They were distant figures, aloof from the hurly-burly of training. In most cases their visits to the training pitch – if such a facility existed – would have been rare to the point of non-existent. Ernest Mangnall, the only man yet to have won anything as a Manchester

United manager, spent most of his time in the office or the board-room, dealing with finance; Mangnall, like all his contemporaries and those who followed, left the coach or the senior players to sort out the training, if indeed the haphazard physical jerks could be described as anything as formal as that.

But this was a different time. The war had changed everything, there was a socialist government in power and, on the Salford mud, here was a manager mucking in, kitted out, recognising that what happened on the training pitch could have a vital impact on matches. What that picture represents is the first ever photographic record of a tracksuit manager in British football. Except that Busby is wearing shorts.

One thing was clear, with Busby a regular attendee, there was to be no shirking in practice. The new boss believed that fitness was at the core of everything, so for the first hour of a morning session, players would run, lapping the pitch, varying their speed, occasionally walking, occasionally sprinting. Sometimes, to graft on added stamina, they would gallop up and down the terracing at the damaged Old Trafford. Most mornings, the manager would fall in beside a player during the jog and give him a word of encouragement or advice. Then, eschewing the bizarre received wisdom that players should be starved of the ball so that they would be more hungry for it on Saturday, there would be ball work. Busby would go through problems encountered during matches: stiffen up the defensive wall for opposition free-kicks, sort out the marking at corners, see if his goalkeeper could stop a Charlie Mitten penalty. Things would end with a free-for-all, big-sided match. When Old Trafford was back in commission in 1949, these would take place on the gravel car park behind the ground. 'Round the back' it was called, a phrase that came to have the same mythic associations as 'the Anfield bootroom'. This was a place where footballing alchemy was achieved. In games round the back, Busby and Murphy would join in on opposing teams, their role to add a bit of spike and venom to proceedings, to up the competitive stakes.

If it was a revolutionary way to conduct things, it still bore no relation whatsoever to today's scientific methodology. Some of the habits back then seem not so much of another era as from a different planet. On the Friday lunchtime before home games, for instance, the trainer Tom Curry used to inflate the match ball, lace it up and immerse it in a bucket of water, where it stayed, kept submerged by a brick, until just before kick-off. It would then be pulled out ready for action, saturated, weighing about half a ton. Jack Crompton, Busby's first keeper, recalls how once, in his eighties, he strolled across the pitch before a game at Altrincham's Moss Lane ground, where he was a director, to make a presentation. The players were kicking balls to one another, and when one flew towards him, he instinctively held up his hand to catch it.

Oh bugger, he thought as he did so, there goes three of my fingers broken.

Which would have been the case had his octogenarian's hand come into contact with a ball the weight he was used to. Instead, he could not believe how light the modern one was.

'Compared to what we kicked and headed and caught, it was like a beach ball,' says Crompton.

With or without the ball, Matt Busby had enormous work to do. The players had not played competitively for six years. And several, Charlie Mitten among them, had never played League football at all. At twenty-five Mitten might have been one of England's brightest talents – a dead-eyed Cristiano Ronaldo when it came to a free-kick or penalty, he used to practise in a blindfold and still reckon to beat the keeper every time – but he had yet to tussle for championship points. Allenby Chilton was another. To this day, he holds the distinction of experiencing the record gap in United history between debut and second game.

The only transfer James Gibson sanctioned was £4000 for Jimmy Delaney, the canny, thirtysomething Celtic winger whose proneness to injury had gifted him the nickname 'Old Brittle Bones', but who would serve Busby valiantly for three seasons. The money for his purchase came not from the United budget, but from the chairman's own pocket. As for the rest, Busby was obliged to make do with what he inherited. Although, as things turned out, he was a master at making do.

He soon revealed a knack of spotting that some players weren't up to the job (he shipped out the likes of Jack Smith and Bill Bryant within days of arriving) and that others were playing in a position that did not offer the best showcase for their talents. Henry Cockburn was one, who, within a fortnight of meeting him, Busby switched from inside forward to wing half, intuiting that a lack of sprinter's pace would be a less significant drawback in that position. Johnny Carey was another who benefited from such insight. Busby was immediately impressed by the way Carey carried himself. He was serious, old for his years, chastened by his war service. Maybe, in the way he dressed and in his refusal to engage in the earthy language of the training ground, he reminded Busby of himself (though Busby never went as far as to become, like Carey, a teetotal non-smoker). Never mind that the rest of the lads considered him stand-offish and mean with his money ('Short arms and deep pockets' was the considered opinion), for the manager, the Irishman represented perfect captaincy material.

As Busby saw it, the only problem with this model pro was that he wasn't that good out on the park. Charlie Mitten, never one to spare others from forthright judgement, reckoned him 'a bloody terrible inside forward, he was a bad player, slow and cumbersome'. Busby was less inclined to write him off. Indeed in defence of Carey he had a very public row with Harold Hardman, a long-time director who had been with United through all the lean times of the thirties. After one match Hardman loudly criticised Carey within Busby's hearing. The barb was deliberate, an attempt to put the new manager in his place. Without raising his voice, Busby made it quite clear he did not want to hear such talk again. He then placed an item headlined 'Interference by Directors' on the agenda of the next board meeting. Gibson backed the manager, Hardman backed down and the point was made.

Hardman, though, had a point and Busby knew he could get more out of Carey. So he tried the Cockburn trick and moved the player back towards his own goal. First he tried him at wing half, then put him at full back, where he blossomed into a world-class player. It was a repositioning that had repercussions for years afterwards: Carey was still club captain in 1953.

When the League reconvened in the autumn of 1946, Busby found himself in charge of a singularly determined dressing room. These were footballers who had experienced life beyond the cloistered confines of football. War had shortened their patience, made them more determined to make the most of life. This sense of urgency translated itself into performances. In that first League championship after the war, United finished second, the highest they had been in the table since they won the title under Mangnall thirty-five years before. Never mind the five years Busby had told Gibson it would take to build a decent club, here was something approaching instant gratification.

Busby, a manager who was later to become synonymous with the development of youth, first found success at United with men, not boys. And alongside a physical determination his players demonstrated they had their opinions. On one occasion in those early days, there was a heated row during a team meeting over what was reckoned to be a substandard recent effort from a couple of the regulars. Busby tried to impose order, but he was put in his place by Allenby Chilton, the Normandy veteran who had seen at close hand the consequence of lacklustre performance.

'Sit down, Matt,' Chilton ordered. 'I know these better than you.'

Busby did just that and Chilton proceeded to analyse his teammates in uncompromising fashion. The debate that followed was brusque and pointed. But effective. When the air cleared, the lean spell was over.

That Busby was prepared to stand aside and give Chilton the floor should not be construed as a sign of weakness. Nor – as others were to discover – that he ran the dressing room as a democracy. Rather, this was an early demonstration of Matt Busby's prevailing philosophy. The three most important assets in a footballer, he always said, were 'skill, flair and character'. Before adding, subconsciously aping the declaration in John's gospel about the pre-eminence of love, 'And the greatest of these is character.' He wanted characters in his dressing room, men prepared to take responsibility, strong enough to recognise where things were going wrong and flexible enough to change to put them right. In the creation of character he believed, above all, it was good to talk.

'Matt encouraged us to analyse each other's faults at straight-talking sessions with no punches pulled,' Mitten wrote in his autobiography. 'We found this honesty made us a much more formidable team.'

Busby had learned through experience in the mines and in the forces that trust was vital in the creation of teamwork; in extremis you needed to know that your mate would look out for you. And trust was arrived at through honesty. How could you trust someone who was holding something back and wasn't being truthful to you? Busby wanted proper men in his side, open, passionate in their opinions, not cowed and cliquey, talking behind each other's backs. In 1946 he found them in the Maine Road dressing room.

And when he found them, he knew how to treat them.

'Bullying can only bring instant obedience and never lasting results,' he once said.

Although, as Harold Hardman discovered in the boardroom, there was a physicality about him, a sense that he could handle himself if the situation demanded it, he never sought to dominate the players either physically or verbally. In his playing days he had seen too often the result of the heedless exploitation of power – the shattered confidence, the depression, the festering of grudges. Unlike many of his predecessors, contemporaries and indeed successors, Busby did not flaunt his control. He rarely raised his voice. Nobody got a public dressing down. Humiliation for the sake of it was anathema to him. He believed in trust.

Part of that trust could be achieved by looking after his players in all aspects of their lives. He knew from his own experience, when his wife Jean had suffered a miscarriage while he was at City and his own form had suffered, that what went on off the pitch could have a profound bearing on what happened on it. Old school managers couldn't care less about players' welfare. But Busby was not old school. He left nothing to chance. At a time when there was a national housing shortage, he ensured every married first-teamer had a club house. A decent one too, rented to them at a modest thirty shillings a week.

He looked after them in their social lives. From the early days at United, he worked to ensure the players had the best of whatever limited fun was available in the war-shattered city. Every man was given club blazer and flannels, to make them look a cut above the crowd. There were hotel stays in Blackpool, outings to the end of pier shows, free tickets arranged at the Gaiety cinema. Plus, there were the golf days at Davyhulme Golf Club. With its magnificent art deco clubhouse, Davyhulme became an integral part of Busby's routine for the next twenty-five years. Every Monday the squad would head to the course for a round or, for those who didn't play, a game of billiards in the bar. In those early days the players didn't have enough money for kit, so used to borrow what they could from the members' dressing room, often without seeking the owners' permission first. John Anderson, a stalwart of the 1948 FA Cup side, recalls once being on his way to the first tee when a member came out of the clubhouse and confronted him. Of all things, the victim of Anderson's misdemeanour was a priest.

'Great heavens, that fellow is wearing my cap,' the priest complained, pointing at Anderson's head. In the late forties the idea that a priest would be more materially blessed than a footballer did not strike anyone as odd.

It did not take long for the Busby revolution to be noted beyond the dressing room. Tom Jackson – another writer later to die at Munich – claimed this of Busby in the *Manchester Evening News* in 1947: 'He never browbeats a player for some blatant mistake on the field. He takes him to a quiet corner for a fatherly chat and a pat of encouragement. The player is refreshed and unembarrassed at being shown the right way.'

Jackson, the local man and an important link with the supporters, was clearly won over. That he knew the details of how Busby worked was early proof that the United manager was a clever manipulator of the press. Courteous, affable, apparently open, Busby was acutely aware of the fact that his players read the papers too. Thus he would never allow a bad word about them to be attributed to him. Any reporters who attempted it, or revelled in criticism, were ostracised; those who were supportive were allowed limited, distant but polite access. Busby's concern when cultivating certain writers was not to buff up his own ego. It was solely to promote his players, to let them see that he backed them publicly. It was all about maintaining confidence.

Not that everyone was instantly impressed by every aspect of the way the new manager went about his business. From the moment he met him, training on a public park in Fallowfield in the pre-season of 1946, the sharp-tongued Charlie Mitten was dismissive of Busby's grasp of tactics. And Jimmy Murphy's for that matter.

'In terms of knowledge: zero,' Mitten once said. 'Both of them. Jimmy has yet to tell me something about football that I don't already know.'

What Mitten recognised, however, was the pair's ability to forge team spirit.

'Jimmy had guts and he imparted that to the players,' the winger believed. 'Matt was the boss. He understood players and geed them up. He never just criticised and left you without an answer. He knew the cures to a hundred and one things that can go wrong in a footballer's life.'

Jack Crompton agrees: 'Those lads knew how to play, nobody showed them,' he says. 'But more than anything they knew what was important in the making of a team. They knew how valuable it was to trust each other.'

The emerging Busby philosophy can be neatly summed up in

the five-word dressing room mantra he employed across his twenty-five years at Old Trafford: 'Just go out and play'. It is possible, in these days of video analysis, pass-completion statistics and ice baths to characterise Busby's approach as hopelessly naive. It would, however, be wrong to suggest, as the Mitten view perhaps implies, that this was all he ever said.

'It's just not true to say he never went into details,' remembers John Anderson. 'Before the game he'd go right through the opposition team, starting with the keeper, giving you details like, he's not good on crosses or what was the best way of putting pressure on him.'

Such application of detail is widely forgotten by players who prefer to remember the romantic simplicity of 'Just go out and play'. The point is, Busby's apparent laissez-faire direction was the culmination of a lengthy process. Throughout the week on the training pitch he exuded a confidence in the players. What he was saying with that simple instruction was this: 'I trust you.' He did not clutter their heads with complexity or attempt to gee them up with blood-curdling calls to arms. He simply reminded them that he considered them good enough to overcome whatever obstacles were presented. And that this was essentially a simple game. 'Just go out and play'. On its own it cannot work. As the distillation of a process it built three of the greatest club teams England has ever seen.

That immediate post-war side was the first of them. In 1948 they reached the FA Cup final, then the most important trophy available in English football. They got to Wembley the hard way, with every game in essence an away fixture. Their Cup run was like a repertory company on tour of the north-west. Dependent on their landlords at City, United were obliged to look elsewhere than Maine Road if the blues were also drawn at home. Thus, after advancing via a thriller at Villa in the third round, they beat first the champions Liverpool at home at Goodison Park, then Charlton at home in Huddersfield. By the quarter-final, City were out of the Cup and Maine Road turned red for a tie against Preston. By now

United's star was in the ascendant. The team was earning a reputation for barnstorming attacking play that cut through the
post-war austerity and brought crowds scurrying in to watch. For
the match against Arsenal on 17 January 1948, 81,962 turned up at
Maine Road, to this day a record for a crowd at an English League
game. It was so packed in the ground the fans poured off the terraces and were standing in every available space. When he went
across to take a corner, Charlie Mitten had to move the spectators
back to give him room to swing his leg. Before the war United
had been a music hall joke, the material of gags and put-downs.
Now they were beginning to be regarded as not just compelling,
crowd-pulling entertainers but something else: invincible. Bill
Shankly best summed up the prevailing feeling about Busby's
team. Coming off exhausted after being hammered by the reds in
the Cup quarter-final, Shankly, then playing wing half for North
End, put his arm round Mitten, who had been magnificent, scoring
in a 4-1 romp. 'Bloody hell, Charlie,' wheezed Shankly. 'The way
you lot are playing you could win the Boat Race.'

After Stan Pearson's hat-trick had seen off Derby in the semi,
the clamour for tickets to the final against Blackpool was cacoph-
onous: thirty thousand people queued up for United's allocation of
twelve thousand. In these bleak, austere, bombsite times, the
weekend trip at the end of April to Wembley represented escapism
at its most alluring. Contemporary pictures show the United fans
on their way to London in the highest of spirits. In collars and
ties, in raincoats and waistcoats, they gurn cheerfully at the
camera, waving rattles, full of big-day-out excitement. To get there,
many had fallen back on that mainstay of the wartime economy,
the black market. Terrace tickets priced at three shillings changed
hands at as much as £1. The players were each gifted a hundred of
the pricier tickets and a Manchester businessman called Maurice
Kingsley let it be known that he could find good homes for any
spares the lads didn't want. Several players took up Kingsley's
offer. To those who were about to play at Wembley, every little
helped.

To avoid a colour clash, Blackpool wore white and United shirts of royal blue. Perhaps it was the change of colour that confused Allenby Chilton. The war hero was all kitted up, stripped and ready to go out on to the pitch when somebody pointed out he was still wearing his shoes. The tension of the afternoon certainly appeared to infect Busby. He seemed preoccupied by the reputation of Stanley Matthews. The Blackpool winger was widely regarded (without, it has to be said, much in the way of knowledge of what went on beyond the white cliffs of Dover) as the finest player in the world. Busby obsessed about stopping him. John Anderson remembers being instructed to track back and double, even treble, mark Matthews. Mitten, too, was told to keep an eye on him. 'Keep it tight' was Busby's final instruction. 'Just go out and play' was seemingly for another day.

Charlie Mitten, for one, found this new defensive responsibility a tough proposition. As Matthews and his England team-mate Stan Mortensen dominated the opening exchanges, Mitten was chasing shadows. At one point in the first half Matthews asked him what the hell he was doing: 'Charlie you'll never be a good player if you keep following me,' the Blackpool winger said. 'Now fuck off back up front.'

At the interval, with Blackpool leading 2-1, the atmosphere in the United dressing room was fractious. Several players questioned the Busby approach. 'We got here by attacking, let's attack' was the gist of their analysis. Busby, though, was more anxious to tell Henry Cockburn to close down Blackpool skipper Harry Johnston, who had been the chief supplier to Matthews. This was the tactical note that made the difference. But, as they went out for the second half, Busby's instruction was once more 'Just go out and play'.

And play they did. They blew Blackpool away, swarming to a 4-2 victory. Stanley Matthews, quoted in the *Sunday Express* the next day, was generous to a fault: 'When we were leading 2-1 I really thought it was our day. But Manchester United were inspired after their second goal. We were beaten by a great team.'

Returning home, the team found three hundred thousand Mancunians lining the streets to watch them parade the Cup from station to town hall. Later they were to take a detour via James Gibson's house, where the chairman was convalescing after an illness which had kept him away from the game. With seven men born within walking distance of Old Trafford among them, these were, as Gibson had so long dreamed, Manchester men to make Manchester proud. It was Frank Butler of the *News of the World* who was the first to articulate what was going on in the post-Cup-winning euphoria. This was a team, he said, capable of 'playing the finest football in the country'. Noting the source of the revolution, he suggested now was the time for the club to be renamed. From now on it should by rights be called: 'Matt Busby United'.

6

YOUNG GUNS GO FOR IT

Even as the crowds hung from the lamp-posts to laud their heroes' Wembley return, even as the pressmen lined up the superlatives, even as the manager himself was banking a £1750 Cup-winning bonus from a grateful, gleaming James Gibson, beneath the surface of calm camaraderie at Matt Busby United there bubbled a growling discontent. It came from a simple source: money. The players – these very same Mancunian ambassadors so fêted and adored – were paid £12 a week basic, with the maximum allowed bonus of £20 for winning the Cup. Twenty quid: you could hardly sustain a stableful of Lamborghinis, build a gated mansion or fill a boutique hotel with top-class skirt on twenty quid.

This was all the FA allowed. But football, ever since the days of Billy Meredith and Charlie Roberts, had a way round the rules. Under-the-counter cash, backhanders, bungs, brown envelopes, a decent drink: these were the game's lubricant. Everyone was at it. Football was shot through with illegal signing-on fees, illegal bonuses for victory, illegal extras for this and illegal extras for that. Everyone, that is, except Matt Busby's Manchester United. Matt valued honesty. That honesty in the dressing room, that honesty in the to-and-fro of the training pitch, that honesty in self-analysis, it had to have reciprocation in the principles of the place. How could you claim to be honest when you were dealing with illegal payments? So there was to be no culture of under-the-table payments on his watch. Players would get the maximum to which they were entitled. But no more.

The other way, however, was constantly in Busby's players' faces. When they played Derby in the FA Cup semi-final, the lads from the Baseball Ground berated the red players that United's victory had cost them a nice little earner. They were all due a bonus of £100 should they reach Wembley for the second year running. Now that was a goner. The news crackled round the United dressing room. A hundred quid? If Derby could hand out that sort of money, then what might United afford? The lads decided someone needed to say something. Johnny Morris and Henry Cockburn were deputed to go and see the manager and ask, no, demand, their cut.

Oh dear. Big mistake.

Eamon Dunphy reckons the steel in the manager's make-up was really only ever evident over issues of money. Finance was at the root of all the major fallings out with his players. Busby took it as a personal slight when someone challenged his carefully constructed wage structure. When Morris and Cockburn took along the lads' request, his reaction was like a scene from *Oliver Twist*. As he would be every time anyone approached him for more, he was incandescent. Surely he had done enough for them. What about the cinema tickets? The golf days? They had steak at Davyhulme Golf Club every Monday. And here they were asking for more. He took it as a personal slight: after all he had done for them. Getting to Wembley, the finest day out in any footballer's imagination, should be reward enough for them. The players were sent back to the dressing room with a message:

there would be no illegal money at United and if anyone didn't like the way things were done here then they could go elsewhere.

Matt Busby knew he had a strong hand. Nobody was going to rebel right now, not when they were just off to Wembley. But if the skirmish was won, it didn't stop them grumbling. The disappointed players immediately characterised the Boss as tight, mean with money, too careful by half.

There was more to it than that. Busby's anger wasn't rooted in money worries. Things were easing there, bankruptcy no longer hovered over the club, profits were now the norm. This was about power. At Busby's club things were to be done his way. Control of money was a crucial part of his insistence that his way was the only way. If everyone bought into the Busby line, they would be fine. To challenge his way of doing things, however, was to challenge him. It may not have been his money they were arguing over, but it was personal. In any battle of personalities at Matt Busby United there could only ever be one winner. Meanwhile, the players had no idea that Busby was about to put his pen to a new contract worth £3250 a year, roughly five times their basic wage, a deal that would make him the highest-paid employee in English football.

The team put its disappointment on Cup bonuses behind them and won the trophy. For a moment, in the post-Wembley euphoria, everyone forgot about money. The rewards of victory may not have been financial, but they were tangible. The lads were heroes, Busby himself was chosen to manage the Great Britain football team at the 1948 Olympic Games in London, and Johnny Carey was voted footballer of the year and selected to captain the Rest of Europe team in an international against England. On a tour to Ireland that summer the flow of Guinness was unending. And every one of the players got a free set of golf clubs from a grateful wealthy supporter. The ecclesiastical membership of Davyhulme could rest easy now that there would be no more locker room theft on Mondays.

Once the party was over and the hangover kicked in, however, the bitterness bubbled to the surface. When the players reconvened for the following season, a meeting at the training ground decided that something had to be done. Johnny Morris, the dressing room militant, was elected once more to go and see Busby. This time, to give his deputation some substance, he was to be accompanied by Carey. It made no difference. Their pleas for greater bonuses were greeted with a simple no. Back among the players, the resolve was hardening.

'We convinced ourselves we were on strike,' recalls Jack Crompton. 'We had a committee in the dressing room. We demanded a meeting with the directors, but Harold Hardman took the Matt line.'

The manager saw the problem as one of personality. And that personality was Johnny Morris. He was some player, Morris, a low-centre-of-gravity inside forward of skill and steel, the Paul Scholes of his day. You don't score 32 goals in 83 matches without being a little bit special. Plus, at twenty-four the lad from Rochdale was younger than many of the war veterans around him. He was one for the future. But as he constantly sought confrontation with his manager on the training pitch, this was the one player with whom Busby found it hard to communicate.

'I've tried every angle, I've bullied, I've used flattery. I've tried every way but I just can't get through,' Busby wrote of Morris, in a manner that had later echoes in his own relationship with George Best and Alex Ferguson's with Paul McGrath.

In March of 1949 Morris had lost his place through injury and had not recovered a starting role after returning to fitness. He wasn't happy. Busby noticed he was shirking on the training ground and berated him for it. Morris, asking what the point of training was when he was only playing the reserves, started to walk off the pitch. Busby called after him: 'If you walk off this pitch, you'll never play for this club again.' Morris carried on walking. And Busby went straight to his office to alert the Press Association that Morris was for sale. Within a week the player was on his way to Derby – where he was given a tobacconist's shop as a signing on fee – for a then world record £24,500. The reaction among those left behind was immediate: the Boss was not messing around, if Johnny the great hope was expendable, then everyone else would be. By going through with his threat, Busby had re-established the order of things. Talk of dressing room committees and strikes faded. Morris, incidentally, lived to regret his long walk. Nearly six decades on he readily admits he was a fool to leave that United team.

'Even when I went to Derby and I was on better money, I would never stop missing playing for United,' he says.

It is a lament to be heard down the generations, the one summed up best by Tommy Docherty: 'There is only one place to go when you leave Manchester United and that's down town.' Ruud van Nistelrooy and David Beckham are perhaps the only two who might disagree.

But Johnny Morris's departure sent a vital message to all the players. It was one that was a constant throughout Busby's time. 'We were never in doubt that Matt was the guardian of the club, that it was the club which was the most important thing to him,' recalls Wilf McGuinness, a Busby Babe and his successor as manager. 'Everyone learned that. Johnny Morris, Charlie Mitten, Johnny Giles, George Best, Denis Law. All fabulous players, but in his mind, none of them bigger than the club.'

Without Morris, that season concluded in the same manner as the previous two: United were runners-up. There was a solidity about them that mocked their pre-war incarnation as a yo-yo. That solidity stretched from pitch to boardroom. By the start of the 1949–50 season, with a profit of £50,000 a year, things were looking good everywhere for United, especially now they had returned to a patched-up Old Trafford, the roof back on its main stand just in time for the match on 24 August 1949 against Bolton. Content and in control, that year Busby celebrated his fortieth birthday with his pal Paddy McGrath, a Blackpool-based United fan of colourful business background. The pair were often seen patronising a

Manchester social scene that was slowly emerging from the dead hand of post-war austerity. Busby liked a steak, and he and Jean, and Paddy and his wife would most Saturdays hold court in one of the city's restaurants. Sometimes the two men would head for the dog track or the horses. Wherever they went, Busby was greeted by United fans. And there were plenty of them – attendances averaged at least three times what they had been fifteen years before. The club was a growing influence on the city and Busby its polite, smart, dignified ambassador. Indeed, with both Louis Rocca and James Gibson constrained by illness, he was its public face. The ambition he shared with his chairman five years previously was bearing fruit. This was the club he wanted. And it was now his. Almost.

In the summer of 1950 Busby took the players on a tour of North America. It was just the sort of thing he reckoned was crucial to welding team spirit: a light-hearted trip to somewhere none of the lads would ever get the chance to visit if they weren't playing for Manchester United. They went over on the *Queen Mary*, cruising with the wealthy. This was the big time.

Not that the players saw it that way. When they arrived in the States, they were each given $5 a day allowance. It had to cover everything. The lads soon discovered that in smarter places, as Jack Crompton recalls, it barely covered the tip. Fed up with the perceived parsimony, a meeting was convened and the motion was proposed that they were not going to carry on with the tour unless the allowance was upped. Like most of the dressing room rebellions of the time, this one died almost as soon as it was sparked. It was Stan Pearson, the man they all looked up to, the giant of the forward line, who talked them out of it. 'We knew what we were getting in to when we agreed to come on this tour,' he said. 'We'll tell them what we think of the allowance, but there's no way I'm going on strike. I agreed to come on those terms and I'll carry on with the job.'

Fearless on the pitch these players might have been, but it was undoubtedly the thought of getting on the wrong side of Busby that spiked their revolutionary ire. So the games went ahead, including a 9-2 drubbing of the United States national team that was later that summer to eliminate England from the World Cup in Brazil. Charlie Mitten scored a penalty in the rout, hitting the ball so firmly it bounced off the back netting out on to the pitch. One of the American players, perhaps not fully conversant with the laws of the game, complained that the goal shouldn't be allowed to stand: 'The ball's got to stay in the net for it to count,' he whined.

Quite why the likes of Mitten and Pearson weren't in Belo Horizonte with the England team is one of football's lingering mysteries. Mind you, had Mitten been selected, he wouldn't have been in his New York hotel room to take a call from Neil Franklin. Franklin was England's centre half who had absented himself from the World Cup to sign up for a new venture in Colombia, a team called Sante Fe, who were offering English pros life-changing inducements. Franklin asked Mitten if he fancied joining this growing band of English galacticos.

'Well, it depends,' said Mitten. The depends, Franklin informed him, consisted of a £5000 signing-on fee, followed by £5000 a year basic, plus win bonuses. The kind of dosh, in short, undreamt of by even the most feverish of English pros. There in New York, Mitten's reservations melted away. He went to see Busby to tell him he would not be accompanying the lads back to England on the boat, but would be flying down to Colombia to check out the Santa Fe circus. The Boss was perplexed. How could Charlie go? He was a United player. Mitten reminded Busby that his contract was up for renewal; he was, in effect a free agent. The manager asked him why he wanted to go. To which Mitten reported the salary he had been offered. Busby jokingly asked if Santa Fe needed a manager. But as Mitten left the room he told the winger, by all means go to Bogotá to see what was on offer, but he should think carefully before signing. The pair arranged to talk in a fortnight back in Manchester. There was, Mitten recalled, only a hint of frostiness in Busby's manner.

Busby remained relaxed because he was convinced he would be able to pick Mitten for the first game of the new season. If he did, it would mean the wonderfully consistent, injury-free winger would play 114 consecutive games for the reds. The manager's conviction was based on the knowledge that Mitten was wrong, there was no real freedom of contract. Players were not really able to sign with whom they liked, even if they were out of contract they needed their last club's consent to go elsewhere, and there was no way Busby was going to give that. No wonder. This is what John Arlott had just written in the *Manchester Guardian*: 'Mitten's left foot is a precision instrument as accurate as any in contemporary football.'

However, what Busby failed to recognise was that, because the country's FA was not affiliated to FIFA, Colombia was outside the feudal cabal of world football. So when Mitten returned from that initial meeting in Bogotá smitten by the Colombian cash, there was nothing Busby could do to stop him going, no hold he had over him. Charlie Mitten was on his way. Thus, following Johnny Morris, another star was walking from Busby's Mancunian firmament in pursuit of cash. And he certainly wasn't going to wave the player off. As it turned out, the only United figure to witness Mitten and his wife leaving Manchester that late summer day in 1950 was Billy Meredith. The old hero, the union stalwart, the Charlie Mitten of his era, Meredith saw him off from London Road station with a cheery cry of good luck.

'If there had been chances like this when I was playing I would have walked to Bogotá,' Meredith told a reporter from the *Manchester Evening News*. And he probably would have done, too, chewing his toothpick as he went.

Busby neither forgot nor forgave the errant winger. When Mitten came back a year later he went to see the manager in his office. Mitten explained he would love the chance to play for the reds again; he was, he said, a much-improved player. But Busby was having none of it. Even knowing that Mitten would be banned for six months by the FA for his treachery, he banished his former

favourite forthwith, refusing to allow him to train with the lads
while he served out the ban. While he played for a pub team to
keep fit before he could be transferred to new club Fulham, Mitten
reflected that Busby might have been a firm friend. But he was an
even more implacable enemy.

What's more, though many on the terraces thought it might not
be a bad idea to spend some of United's now mounting profits on
new recruits, Charlie Mitten was not replaced. 'You can call me a
canny Scotsman if you like,' Busby was quoted as saying in *All
Football* magazine, 'but I do not believe you can buy success.'

And Charlie's absence did not seem immediately to affect performance. That season, for the fourth time since the war, Busby's
team were championship runners-up, this time to Portsmouth.
Besides, the information Busby was getting from his lieutenants
about what was going on elsewhere in the club suggested there
would be no need to trouble the Gibson cheque book for a while.
After five seasons of underachievement, Jimmy Murphy's reserves
were beginning to fill with youthful talent, players like Mark Jones
and Roger Byrne. Plus, there were stirrings lower down the age
scale. It was all the result of a major change of approach initiated
by Busby.

In 1950, after a long illness, Louis Rocca, for four decades the
man who signed up talent to United, died. Busby felt it was time to
professionalise the club's scouting network. He brought in Joe
Armstrong to supervise the recruitment of youth and he immediately instituted a system that was to be followed more or less
unchanged to this day. No longer would this be about what went
on in Manchester. A network of spies across the country would
report back on the best youthful prospects, a spider's web constantly feeding information from all corners to Old Trafford. For
Armstrong, Ashington would now be as likely to yield a United
player as Altrincham, Dudley was to be as much United territory as
Davyhulme, the parks of Belfast would be as watched as those of
Belle Vue. And when his spies found him a likely lad, Armstrong
would move in, second to none at schmoozing. The man was a

world champion at buttering up over a cuppa in the kitchen. He preferred to talk to the mums, sensing that was where domestic power lay; he would usually have their consent before flattering the dads over a pint down the pub that it was their decision all along to send their lad to United. Plus, he was not shy about the odd little – let's just keep this between ourselves – incentive.

There is an inexplicable irony lurking at the heart of Busby's stewardship of United. While he railed against anything heading from under-the-counter into a first-teamer's pocket, the evidence suggests he presided over a scouting system that bent almost every rule in the FA book. When Harry Gregg was signed by United from Doncaster Rovers in the autumn of 1957 he was told there was to be no signing-on fee.

'We don't do that sort of thing at Manchester United,' Busby said.

Yet Duncan Edwards's family, for instance, were gifted a washing machine when their son decided to go with Armstrong in June 1952. Not much for the finest youth prospect of all time, maybe. But nonetheless an inducement to sign on that was against the rules. Latterly, it wasn't washing machines, it was cash. Or scouting jobs for dads who wouldn't know a footballer if he fell in a crumpled heap at their feet. Or maybe a nice holiday for mum, she deserves it after all.

Perhaps Busby didn't in those days know what his chief scout got up to. Perhaps Joe Armstrong covered his tracks with a labyrinthine accounting system. But it seems unlikely. Twenty-seven years later, in 1980, in the same Granada TV *World in Action* programme that would bring down Louis Edwards, it was alleged that Matt Busby himself was often present when cash was handed over to families.

It may have been illegal. It may have been murky. It may, given Busby's attitude to the financial aspirations of Mitten, Morris and the rest, have been the apex of hypocrisy, but what cannot be denied is that the system Armstrong instituted worked. Within twelve months of starting work for United, the new scout had signed up Dennis Viollet, Jeff Whitefoot and Jackie Blanchflower.

These young players were put in digs as soon as they arrived at Old Trafford. Armstrong recruited a mum's army of landladies such as the redoubtable Mrs Watson, who presided over two large houses knocked together in Birch Avenue, just down the road from Lancashire cricket ground. During the day the recruits were sent off to serve trade apprenticeships in Trafford Park. At night they would learn about football from Jimmy Murphy. And if they were under the impression this was just some sort of game they were about to engage in, Murphy soon disabused them. A man who looked almost permanently harassed, Busby's lieutenant took things seriously – so seriously it was almost comical. He worked his charges endlessly. Training was hard and so was Murphy. Swearing and shouting, he would drum an endless message into the recruits: pass and move, cover and mark, spread the play and attack, attack, attack. There was no place for softies: 'Get bloody stuck in,' he'd shriek. Except he didn't say 'bloody'. Bobby Charlton recalls being kicked viciously from behind during a training kickabout once and realising, as he fell to the ground clutching his ankle, that it was Murphy who had kicked him. And the ridiculous thing was, Murphy wasn't even playing. He was the referee.

'We make it out to be beautiful, looking back on it, but it was bloody awful at the time,' recalls Wilf McGuinness of youth football at the Cliff. 'The floodlights were dreadful, you could hardly see. And the training kit: Christ, it was never washed. Big heavy sweaters thick with mud. Afterwards you'd get in the bath all forty of you, or however many, and you were never clean.'

Indeed the manager of the Locarno ballroom down the road in Sale always knew when the footballers had been in: when he came to clear up after last orders, there would be a dusting of mud on his dancefloor.

But it was at the Cliff, or round the back, under Murphy's restless tutelage, that the players learned the game. Sometimes Murphy would impress upon them that they had to work hard because he was coming to watch them. The Boss. They knew when the father of the United family was there, not because he announced his presence with fanfare or fuss, but because Murphy would suddenly stop swearing. The manager would spend hours with his boys, watching them in action and then talking to them, letting it be known what it meant to represent Manchester United. Bobby Charlton, in an interview in the *Daily Telegraph*, recalled Busby saying to him soon after he arrived at United: 'All those lads you see going to the factory in Trafford Park, they come to watch you on Saturday. They have boring jobs, so you have to give them something, something they will enjoy.'

Unlike many who succeeded him at Old Trafford, Busby did not believe that football's escapist possibilities should be exploited merely in order to produce financial return. He saw entertainment as something akin to duty. The boys in his dressing room were privileged, but they also bore a responsibility. It was a matter of working-class solidarity that they gave a lift to their neighbours, that for ninety minutes on a Saturday they provide temporary relief from the shabby humdrum of ordinary workaday life.

And shabby humdrum it was. Back in the fifties Manchester wasn't a barrel of laughs, L. S. Lowry did not make it up. The place may have been the beating heart of industrial Britain, but it was dirty, damp and relentlessly ugly. Charlton, coming from a pit village, was appalled at the filth. Behind the Pop Side a small Himalaya of coal reared up over the stands, the stockpile for the Edward Wood steelworks. Every other Saturday several intrepid sherpas would hike up this mountain to watch home matches for free. That's if they could see that far through the fog. The ground was surrounded by chimneys blasting out toxic smoke, shrouding the whole city in a thick, cloying smog for much of the winter. There was a smell about the place, too, an industrial honk from the chemical works that clogged the nose and tingled in the throat. Lowry, brought up down the road in Salford, would watch people shuffling through the pea souper, their shawls and caps pulled down against the enveloping damp, scarves over their mouths against the stench, tiny in this unforgiving, monumental landscape. These were the people United served. For Busby, entertaining them was not an optional extra. It was the very purpose of his profession. It was football's unique gift. Playing for Manchester United wasn't just a job, it was a vocation.

But all that was for the future. For the post-war side that Busby inherited there was to be one last, astonishing hurrah. In 1952, without anyone expecting it, least of all the manager, United for once did not finish as League runners-up. For the first time since 1911, they finished as champions. Even shorn of Morris and Mitten, the old boys proved the finest in the land. The season began with Jack Rowley's record succession of hat-tricks, three threesomes in four games in August 1951. Bought by Walter Crickmer from Bournemouth for £3000 as long before as 1937, 'The Gunner' had an astonishing Indian summer awash with goals, thirty of them in the League, the second highest League total in United history. Busby's reds stormed to the title in a style emphasised by a 6-1 defeat of Arsenal at Old Trafford that scaled the achievement. Together with Stan Pearson, Allenby Chilton, Johnny Carey, Johnny Aston and Henry Cockburn, Rowley had been with Busby since he became manager after the war. As final acts went, this one was pretty compelling.

But if anyone watching the wartime survivors parade the trophy round an ecstatic Old Trafford were inclined to see this as a job completed and that the end of the line had come for a fine football institution, then clearly they were not following the real pattern of the season. In the January freeze, United had hit the doldrums. Apparently weary, the old lags had stumbled and slipped to seventh in the League. At that point Busby decided to inject some youthful verve into ageing limbs. Into the mix he flung Jackie Blanchflower, Jeff Whitefoot, Mark Jones and Roger Byrne. The latter in particular transformed things. His grit, his nous, his goals from the wing made him look a veteran, not a twenty-two-year-old beginner. He stayed in the side until the end of the season, scoring one of the six against Arsenal, a strong, confident, certain harbinger of things to come.

7

INTO EUROPE, IN COLOUR

Charles Buchan's Football Monthly arrived on newsagents' shelves in 1951. The idea of the former England international and BBC football commentator whose name it bore, this mass-circulation football magazine carried within its pages an innovation in its time almost as significant to the wider perception of the game as the arrival of satellite television was to be forty years later. It ran colour pictures of football or – as the magazine inevitably called them – soccer players. As it happened, these weren't produced from colour film, they were hand-tinted from standard black and white stock. But boy did they make footballers look glamorous, almost as swanky as the Hollywood stars in the pen pictures of the time, from which the Buchan style was borrowed. Suddenly, in to many a home greyed by relentless post-war austerity, came a shock of vivid blue, yellow and green. Plus red; red was everywhere in the magazine's pages. From the first days of the publication, Manchester United players were featured more than those from any other club. In Football Monthly reds were here, reds were there, reds were Buchan everywhere.

Moving away from the posed formality of traditional photography, the shots were of reds in action, reds addressing huge brown balls, reds high-kicking on impossibly verdant green pitches. Later, reds were to be seen endorsing Brylcreem and Dextrosol ('Extra energy makes the difference, says Duncan Edwards'). United players were chosen not simply because they played for one of the country's leading teams, nor was Buchan part of a secret conspiracy to promote the club. No, they were there because they were young, far younger in both chronology and outlook than anyone was used to from First Division footballers. And, by the mid-fifties, young had become the very thing.

There is, for instance, in an edition of the magazine published in the summer of 1955, a portrait of United's David Pegg, Colin Webster and Tommy Taylor playing cards in their digs. They are engaged, so the caption claims, in a game of canasta. This appears to be early evidence of media spin; their game of choice was generally poker Taylor in particular was something of a sharp, who got into trouble at his digs by once peeling too much money off the landlady's husband. But never mind the game, what is noticeable in the snap is how they are attired. Webster has his hair in a slicked-up quiff and is wearing a cap-sleeved T-shirt, Taylor a lumberjack shirt and jeans, rolled up into big fat turn-ups. They might be extras in a Marlon Brando picture, playing a hand on an upturned crate on the New Jersey shore, rather than in the drawing room of their Stretford lodgings, lace doilies protecting the surface of the sideboard. Whether they realise it or not, they are representatives of the biggest social change the country was to see in a century: its first youth awakening. Not for Pegg, Webster and Taylor the pipe and blazer look of their immediate predecessors Johnny Carey and gang. Those guys were men, middle-aged before their time, with foreheads colonising their hairline, enthusiasts for collar and tie and sensible barbering. These, the picture makes clear, are lads. Carefree, young and – for the first time the word might be applied to footballers – fashionable.

In the half century since, much of the character of Manchester

United has formed around an insistence on youth. The fans expect it, the mythology is built on it, that's what United is all about. Giggsy, Scholesy and Big Norman: our boys.

And these were the first. In the mid-fifties this was something new. Its timing could not have been better. Just as the rhythms of the slaves in the southern states of America were being repackaged for worldwide mass consumption, just as James Dean was marinating in post-adolescent angst on the cinema screen, just as boys in drainpipe trousers and girls in voluminous skirts and bobby socks were announcing down every high street that the teen age was born, so were the Busby Babes. This was a new era being delivered on the football pitch.

Like all great overnight success stories, there was a long evening before the Busby Babes emerged to be thus christened in 1954 by Tom Jackson in the *Manchester Evening News*. Their birth did not happen by chance. In 1952 Busby had won the League. Welcome as the victory was (and Busby later called it his most unexpected), he knew it was the last shout of the team he had constructed in the shattered leftovers of war. Allenby Chilton was thirty-four, Jack Rowley thirty-two, Stan Pearson thirty-three. At thirty-four Carey was almost – though not quite – as old as he looked. Busby's side needed surgery. And there was little money available to do it via the transfer market. James Gibson, the manager's supporter in the boardroom, the man who had done very nicely in the war manufacturing uniforms for the Army and had bankrolled much of the reconstruction of Old Trafford, died in 1951. His shares were kept in a draw by Violet, his widow, until she – seemingly unaware that they held much in the way of value beyond sentiment – sold them to Louis Edwards in 1971. Violet never had any interest in taking charge of her husband's train set. So, even as Gibson's son Alan was voted in as a director, control of the board passed to Harold Hardman. Though Busby and he had had their differences, there was no suggestion that the new chairman did not know his football; together with Henry Stafford, Les Olive and Bobby Charlton, he is one of only four former players to take up a seat round the United boardroom table. A diminutive but pugilistic character, the septuagenarian Hardman did not become chairman for the trappings: he used to catch a bus to and from matches and board meetings. For him a taxi would have represented needless extravagance. Which gives an indication of his attitude when it came to buying players. Conservative with his own and the club's money, while willing to back Busby on occasion (he was to fork out, for instance, a record fee for the card sharp Tommy Taylor), he had neither the inclination nor the bank balance to buy up a new side. The manager had to find the replacements from within his own resources. There was only one way he could do that: breed them from the MUJACs.

The thought did not alarm Busby. He was not one to throw money at a problem either. The idea of a team of young players, brought up in the Murphy school, appealed to him. Not least because they would be untainted by the cynicism of the older pros. Writing in *Football Monthly* in 1951, he said of the life of a professional player, 'Fresh air and physical fitness make for good health which is better than any financial fortune.' You could almost hear in his voice the tone of weariness with old lags and their constant demands for this, that and a bit of a backhander. Football, as he implied in print, was about more than just the money. He no longer wanted talk of cash souring his dressing room. With young players, that was never going to happen. Optimistic, carefree, without a thought to the future, they weren't going to worry about how much – or how little – they were getting. They would be simply thrilled to play football for a living instead of heading to the nightshift with their schoolmates. He could surround himself with boys who wanted to play for playing's sake, mould them into the kind of players he wanted: players for Matt Busby's Manchester United.

Busby's timing was impeccable: there was change afoot everywhere. The England national team's humiliating defeats by Hungary in 1953 and 1954 led to a self-flagellating examination by the more enlightened elements within the game. Sure, there were many who thought the foreigners had merely been sneaky. But Busby noted what was going on overseas. And for the modernisers, those whose head was not thrust deep into their own certainties, his way at United was soon seen as the solution: youth would save the day. Youth, furthermore, brought up to pass and move, to love the ball like those Hungarians. They started coming in quickly. They had to. In October 1952, just five months after lifting the championship trophy, an ageing, creaking United, lost 6-2 at Wolves. With playmaker Henry Cockburn sidelined with chronic bronchitis and newly signed goalkeeper Reg Allen suffering from a dressing-room breakdown, which was a legacy from his years as a prisoner of war, that result saw them sink to twenty-first place in the First Division. The surgery was immediate. Busby was not a man to stand on sentiment.

'Everyone has an image of Matt Busby as the genial godfather,' says John Doherty, a MUJAC who became a regular that season. 'Well, everyone knows he had charm, but beneath that front he was as hard as bloody nails.'

The hard man did not shirk tough decisions. Pearson, Rowley and Crompton were all sold off, Jimmy Delaney had long gone. Doherty, Pegg and Dennis Viollet all made starts in the 1953 season, joining Jones, Blanchflower and Whitefoot who were already regulars. Twenty-one-year-old Tommy Taylor was bought in from Barnsley on £29,999 of Hardman's money (the other quid going to the tea lady at Oakwell, so as not to saddle Taylor with the imposing burden of being the country's first £30,000 footballer). And when Johnny Carey retired at the end of that year to take up a post as Blackburn Rovers manager, the twenty-three-year-old Roger Byrne – the oldest of the new wave – replaced him as club captain. This despite having asked for a transfer earlier in the season. Busby forgave him that transgression largely because there wasn't a financial consideration behind the demand. Byrne was a stroppy sort, at training he would argue with anyone, regardless of age or reputation. So when he got fed up being played on the wing instead of his favoured slot at full back, he was not shy of letting the manager know. Although rebellion was always quickly stamped on, Busby rather liked a player who cared that much about his football. As soon as Carey had gone, the full-back position was offered to the pig-headed Byrne, along with the captaincy. If it seemed an unlikely indulgence, five years of superb leadership in response suggested the manager knew what he was doing.

Busby tried not to saddle the new boys with nervous expectation, making the transition to the first eleven as much a matter of fact as he could. He would issue instructions to Jimmy Murphy to send a lad over to train with the first team and then, as they became convinced they were there for a bollocking, let them find out for themselves the news that they would be playing on Saturday.

'It was dropped in so casually,' David Pegg wrote of his debut. 'It was a Friday and the teamsheet seemed to take longer than usual coming down from the office. When it was posted on the board in the dressing room I wandered over to look at it. I wasn't in the reserve side but in the same split second I noticed this, I saw I was selected for the first team. No one said anything. It just seemed a natural thing.'

History suggests, however, that the real significance of that season was not the transition unfolding at Old Trafford. It was taking place at the Cliff, where United had entered a new, midweek competition played under floodlights: the FA Youth Cup. Night-time football was such an innovation that the teamsheet for these games had a helpful tip printed at the bottom: 'To read, hold programme to light.'

If only playing the United youngsters were that simple. As the poor kids from Nantwich Town discovered. It was the Babes' second game in the competition, played on Tuesday 4 November 1952. Looking back, you couldn't consider the result a close-run thing: United beat the Nantwich crew 23-0. In the rout, there were five goals each for Pegg, Doherty and Duncan Edwards. The centre forward, Eddie Lewis, must have felt somewhat aggrieved: He only managed four.

Over the next six years, Jimmy Murphy's juniors did not stop winning. Across forty-one Youth Cup ties they were undefeated, lifting the trophy in 1953, 1954, 1955, 1956 and 1957. Their prowess caught the public mood. In the final of 1953, twenty-one thousand saw them beat Wolves 7-1 at Old Trafford in the first leg. From that moment on, youth became not simply an adjunct to the Manchester United story, it became the romantic kernel at its heart.

The Youth Cup was only the start of it. As had been proven by England's humiliation at the feet of Puskas, Kocsis and Hidegkuti, Matt Busby believed there was much to be learned from playing abroad. So that summer, he, Murphy and the first-team coach Bert Whalley, took their cup-winning youngsters to Zurich for an international youth tournament. It was a forerunner of European competition to come. They all got a taste for it: they won at the first time of asking. 'I think United broke down barriers by flying abroad,' says Wilf McGuinness. 'We travelled in planes, not many did. We learned things together, we had meals in continental restaurants where they brought a plate of salad with your main meal and you didn't know what to do with it.'

'It was a vital part of our education,' agrees Bobby Charlton. 'We played Italians, Germans and Yugoslavs and learned about their different ways of playing. The only game we lost in three years was in the final against Genoa, and they never came out of their own half, except once. It was frustrating, but the kind of amazing education we'd never have got at home.'

Jimmy Murphy's task with the youth team was made easier in those early days by the fact that he had a phenomenon in his ranks. In April 1953 George Fellows – another journalistic fan of the Babes whose infatuation was to meet its conclusion at Munich – wrote in the *Daily Herald*: 'Like the fathers of the first atom bomb, Manchester United are waiting for something tremendous to explode.' The imminent eruption to which Fellows referred was Duncan Edwards. The lad from Dudley, the half back capable of five-goal hauls, was just sixteen when Fellows wrote that eulogy.

'Compared to him, the rest of us were like pygmies,' says Bobby Charlton of his great friend. Charlton was built like Michelangelo's David, yet he felt physically inadequate in Edwards's presence. Everybody did. Everyone who met him, played alongside him, or just enjoyed a kickaround on the cobbled streets of Stretford near his digs, calls him a giant. Which is odd, as he was five feet eleven and weighed no more than thirteen stone. The thing was, that thirteen stone was made up largely of muscle. And most of it was in his thighs, which, in an early bit of footballing mind games, he exposed by hitching his shorts up way higher than was the convention, folding the waistband over several times to keep them aloft. One glimpse of those legs and the opposition was finished.

Everyone in football knew about Edwards, almost, if not quite, from the moment he emerged as an eye-watering nine-and-three-quarter-pound baby, to be fed on a diet of rusks and stout. When he played for Dudley schoolboys, the touchlines were claustrophobic with scouts. Bolton, Arsenal and Wolves were all over him and his parents like a demob suit. When he heard a rumour that the fifteen-year-old was about to sign for Bolton, Jimmy Murphy hired a car and drove from Manchester, fetching up on Sarah and Gladstone Edwards's doorstep with Joe Armstrong at two in the morning to divert the signature Unitedwards. How he did it might have had something to do with a new washing machine on order. Maybe the thought of a never-ending supply of clean laundry swung the deal. Edwards, though, later claimed his decision to join United was solely about the football, not the April freshness of his smalls. Writing in *Football Monthly*, he implied United had already established renown for the quality of their youth system: 'I thought my future would be better away from the Midlands where I lived. United had a great reputation for giving plenty of opportunities to young players and treating them in the best possible manner.'

He liked what he found as soon as he arrived: 'The first time I entered the dressing room to meet the other players I wondered if

I was in the right place. There were so many other youngsters that it seemed almost like being back at school. I found it very easy to settle down and make friends.'

Despite what might be suggested by the formality of this writing style, Edwards was not well educated. From the C stream of Dudley's least distinguished secondary modern, football saved him from the life of physical drudgery that was his caste's lot. On the pitch, however, he had a football brain even more sizeable than his thighs. Allied to work rate, a freakish muscular strength and an unquenchable will to win, from the age of fifteen he was the dominant figure in the youth team, his seventeen- and eighteen-year-old team-mates happy to take their lead from this astonishingly well-developed prodigy. So much so, that Jimmy Murphy began to worry about his prominence. Before one Youth Cup game against Chelsea, Murphy told the other players they had become too dependent on Edwards's ability to conjure victory. He wanted them, he said, for this game only, not to pass to him, just to prove to themselves they could manage if he were not around. This they duly did, only to find themselves trailing by the only goal at the interval. Murphy walked into the dressing room, his hangdog expression – if it is possible – even more forlorn than usual, and issued a simple, new tactical directive: 'Just fucking give it Duncan.' In the second half, balance restored, the United boys went on to win the game. Edwards, with the sort of inevitability that had begun to be associated with his development, scored the winner.

'Duncan was the Kohinoor diamond among our crown jewels,' Murphy was later to say. 'Whenever I heard Muhammad Ali on television say he was the greatest, I had to smile. There was only ever one greatest and that was Duncan Edwards.'

Edwards's development was stellar. In an era when physical strength was imperative, he was strong enough to command a first-team place from the age of sixteen. When he was barely seventeen Busby felt so confident in the newcomer, Henry Cockburn was sold off to Bury. Cockburn was unlucky to lose his place to

Edwards after suffering from a broken jaw. But there was little sympathy from the Boss; now Cockburn was no longer needed, he was shipped out, no sentiment involved. Edwards made his England debut at eighteen. It was said when he lined up along- side Tom Finney and Stanley Matthews in a white shirt he did not remotely appear nervous. It was as if he always knew that was where he belonged.

Unlike Norman Whiteside and Wayne Rooney, the two whose subsequent United career trajectory is the closest to the Edwards blueprint, injuries were rarely an issue. In 1957, the year Edwards did his National Service, he played ninety-five games for United, England and the Army. His fame was soon earning for United a following from far beyond the streets of Salford. Jim Holder, from Oxford, was taken by his school to a match at Bicester Barracks and remembers being astonished at the Army team's number six, a giant of a player who he couldn't take his eyes off.

'Was he any good?' says Holder. 'Best I've ever seen by a coun- try mile. I've never seen one player boss twenty-one others like that. He was only a boy really, too, not much older than us. Though he didn't look it, he looked like a man all right. I became a United fan on the spot, mainly because I became a Duncan Edwards fan.'

Matt Busby was also an Edwards fan from the first moment he caught sight of those thighs. 'We looked at Duncan right from the start and we gave up trying to find flaws in his game,' he later wrote. 'Nothing could stop him and nothing unnerved him. The bigger the occasion, the better he liked it. While other players would be pacing up and down a dressing room, rubbing their legs, doing exercises and looking for a way to pass time, Duncan was always calm. He was a good type of lad too. Duncan didn't want to know about the high life. He just wanted to play and go to his digs or go home. He lived for his football.'

When he arrived at Old Trafford Edwards was sent to a local factory to be apprenticed as a carpenter. He loathed it. So much so, he managed to wangle his way on to the ground staff ('on the brush' it was called, a reflection of the young players' endless cleaning duties), where he buffed up everything from the terraces to the lavatories, via the boots of the senior pros. Only those who had passed the eleven-plus were exempt such duties. Bobby Charlton, when he arrived from Ashington the year after Edwards, was sent to school, in order to earn the grades that would help him fulfil his ambition to be a sportswriter. Astonishingly Stretford Grammar School demanded first claim on him. If there was an SGS fixture on the same day as a United youth team game, he was expected to play for school.

'I remember writing to my mum saying, "I've come to play for United not the school",' says Charlton of those days. He wasn't to remain in the classroom much longer.

All the young United players lived within a short cycle ride of the ground and the Cliff. Indeed Duncan Edwards's sole recorded disciplinary transgression was when he was caught by a policeman riding his bike without any lights and was told by Busby that he was 'letting down everyone at the club'. Of the new kids on the block, only Roger Byrne drove a car. And he did his best to make the management consider this a form of transport not to be encouraged. He was warned constantly to slow down. He did not heed the advice, until the day he was driving through Chorlton, hit a corner too quickly for his Austin's steering and ploughed into a suburban wall. Even as he got out of the car and started to put the bricks back in place he might have got away with it. A couple of match tickets and a smile would keep his transgression from the Boss. Except the wall into which he had crashed, he realised the moment he saw Jean Busby arriving on the scene with an alarmed look on her face, belonged, by appalling coincidence, to the neighbours of his manager. The car was garaged soon afterwards.

As a married man, Byrne lived in a club house. The rest of them, living en masse in digs, would socialise together, heading for town in a big, carefree group of mates, generally corralled by the genial giant Mark Jones. They soon became known about the place.

'They were so accessible,' recalls Tom Clare, a United fan from

Stretford. 'If you waited long enough after a match, you could walk with them or travel with one of them on the bus; you would meet them in the shops, and always at the local dance halls – the Locarno in Sale, the Plaza on Oxford Street, or at Belle Vue – mostly on Saturday evenings after home games. I have a few mates in Sale who are a little older than me, but who have related to me tales of how they used to sit with them in the Locarno, and the United lads would have a lemonade on top of the table, but half of mild underneath it.'

At the Locarno, or the Plaza, where Jimmy Savile was the resident DJ, they would be the main attraction, noted and spotted by the better looking local girls. But this was in the days long before players took to harvesting the queue outside a boutique hotel in Great John Street. In the mid-fifties the pleasures were much less Roman, a bit of 'birding it' the limit of ambition. Most of the time, if they weren't having a lager and lime or a game of pool, or heading off into town, to the Gaiety or the Oxford cinemas, they would spend their spare hours joining in the games of street football with the local kids.

'I remember I must have been about eight and a mate coming round to see if I wanted to play football,' says Robert Richardson, another Stretfordian. 'Well, I'd been ill, so my mum wouldn't let me. The next day at school, he's full of it. He's only played all night long with David Pegg and Billy Whelan and, yes, Big Dunc. So that's my story: I'm the kid whose mum wouldn't let him go play with Duncan Edwards.'

Such familiarity gave extra depth to the relationship between player and supporter: these were our boys, the locals thought. When they saw them run out in Youth Cup games, or for the first team, they felt they knew them, thought of them as family. Never mind that they came from the Midlands or the north-east, they were theirs, real Mancs. Or in the case of Eddie Colman, who was born and raised in Archie Street, the very terrace that was featured in the original credit sequence of *Coronation Street*, real Salfordians.

'They were our team,' says Steve Fleet, an Odsall resident and schoolmate of Colman. 'Everyone round our way followed the reds. On Saturdays in Salford, you could hear everyone walking to the ground and to me, the sound of the shoes on the cobbles, that was like music.'

Mind you, the boys occasionally got a little too familiar with local life for Busby's tastes. Once, for instance, when Mrs Watson's old man started hitting out after being drunkenly relieved of his dosh in a card game, the boys were split up into twos and threes. Duncan Edwards moved to live with the Dorman family in Gorse Road, Stretford. Eric, the son of the household, became his best mate. Edwards won all his England caps living there. It seems beyond conception now that an established England international, the finest player of his generation, would be living in the spare room of a terraced house in Stretford, minding his Ps and Qs and observing a strict curfew about what time he came home on a Saturday night. But that was the Busby way: footballers needed looking after. And until Edwards married his sweetheart Molly, he was obliged to stay with a surrogate family, being looked after. As events turned out, he was never to get the key to his own door.

United's youth and reserve teams may have been winning most games by cricket scores, but Busby knew the gap between the juniors and the real thing was not bridgeable overnight. For two years he changed things gradually, patiently until by the end of the 1955 season, he had a team with an average age of twenty-one, the team he wanted, with competition for places among players of the highest potential. That year the reds came fifth, five points behind the champions Chelsea. As title-holders the Londoners were invited by UEFA to compete in a new competition, dreamed up by Gabriel Hanot, the football editor at *L'Equipe* newspaper. The European Champions Cup was a sort of grown-up version of those Zurich youth tournaments United had been dominating for the last few years, a chance for the best in Europe to test themselves against each other. Matches would be played midweek and under floodlights, so as not to disrupt the operation of the domestic leagues.

Chelsea and their manager Ted Drake were all for it and initially accepted the invitation. In Scotland, too, the champions Hibernian snapped up the offer. But the Football League, stuffed with little Englanders convinced there was nothing of footballing value beyond the white cliffs of Dover, declined the opportunity on Chelsea's behalf. 'Too many wogs and dagoes' was the considered view of European football as expressed by Alan Hardaker, the League's secretary.

For now, it was of no interest to United. And it seemed over the first few weeks of the following season there would be no interest in the competition for some time. United won only three of their first eight games. They were too callow, was the widespread opinion, even on the Old Trafford terraces. In the 1950s, too, it was assumed by many that you win nothing with kids. The bad start meant the crowd was also slow out of the blocks. Only twenty-two thousand turned up at Old Trafford to see Busby's United take on the champions Chelsea in November 1955. By then Tommy Taylor and more to the point Duncan Edwards were back from a month-long absence with injury (United were by no means a one-man team, but having Edwards in your line-up always helped). Plus Eddie Colman, the seventeen-year-old half back with a physique like Puskas and a touch to match, had made his debut. Duly strengthened, United won 3-0. And from there on, they never looked back. They galloped up the table, losing only one game between 31 December and the end of the season, the kind of run-in that came to characterise United sides under Alex Ferguson. For the final match of the term, 62,277 had been attracted back to Old Trafford, a post-war record. Blackpool, the eventual runners-up, were beaten 2-1 and United won the League by a massive eleven points, an astonishing margin in the days when a win was only worth two points. It was a good year for Manchester, that: as United put the championship trophy in their cabinet for the second time in four years, City won the FA Cup.

But it was the red half of town that was really humming. What a team had been created by Busby. Someone dubbed them that season the Red Devils, and he liked that epithet much more than the by now ubiquitous Busby Babes. It gave an inkling of their steel, their spark, their joie de vivre. In goal was Ray Wood, protected by captain Roger Byrne and the stout legs of Bill Foulkes, the right back whose pit-prop physique was strengthened by regular shifts underground at a colliery in his native St Helens. At half backs were Jones, Edwards and Colman. The wingers were David Pegg and Johnny Berry, while Taylor, Billy Whelan and Dennis Viollet provided the forward thrust. In reserve, if any of them faltered, or were injured, half a dozen gilded youth players stood ready, hungry and waiting. It was a team built for attack. Taylor scored twenty-five goals that year, Viollet twenty. And the first team was but the start of it; in the Youth Cup that year, United won again with a team containing the likes of Kenny Morgans, Wilf McGuinness and most exciting of all Bobby Charlton. Everywhere he looked Busby would have seen a golden harvest.

The swathe the young United team cut, however, was solely a footballing one. Despite their youth, their looks, their style, they were not a wider social phenomenon. Nobody took much interest in them beyond their ability to kick and head a football. Nobody – except anyone catching sight of them from the top deck of the last bus – was aware that Jackie Blanchflower and Tommy Taylor would sway home after last orders on a Saturday night on the town, so bladdered they could hardly stand. Nobody who saw them at it seemed to question why every Sunday they would repair to Old Trafford and do twenty-two laps of the pitch, to sweat off the night before. Nobody noticed, either, what Dennis Viollet got up to. Once he made it to the first team, Dennis was not one for joining the rest of the boys on their trips to the cinema, or their secretive halves of mild at the Locarno. Hollywood handsome, his hair slicked and quiffed, dressed in the snazziest of Italian-cut suits, he would head off to Manchester's more sophisticated spots in pursuit of his favourite leisure activity: ladies. If Busby knew – and he cannot fail to have done, night-time Manchester back then was more village than metropolis – he turned a blind eye. Dennis scored him goals and that was all that mattered.

Younger, fresher, swankier than any before them they may have been, but the fact was, these red devils were still just footballers. Their sphere of influence was prescribed by *Charles Buchan's Football Monthly* not *Heat*, the back page of the *News Chronicle*, not the front page of the *News of the World*. To play for Manchester United in 1956 was not remotely of the same order of national prominence as to play for them half a century later. Not least because Taylor, Edwards, Viollet and the rest were on a basic wage of £15, with an appearance fee of £5 and a win bonus of £3. There is nothing remotely sexy about £23 a week. And that was in a good week.

That summer of 1956 Busby got the invitation he was waiting for: would his English champions like to join the newly established European competition, the Champions Cup? He took the letter he received from UEFA to the board and Hardman gave him his unequivocal support to enter. The Football League immediately growled their disapproval, but Busby was not to be swayed. Convinced that if the FA approved he would not be in contravention of any constitutional niceties, he approached the governing body of the English game. The rather grand Stanley Rous, the head of the FA, had never got on with Hardaker or what he once called the other 'shopkeepers' of the Football League. This was a chance too good to pass up to thumb his nose at his enemy. Rous condescended to grant United FA blessing. It was all Busby and Hardman needed. So long as they fulfilled League fixtures, there was nothing the preposterous Hardaker could do about what they did with the rest of their week. United were in.

'Some people called me a visionary, others a reactionary, while a few thought me plain awkward and stubborn', Busby was later to write of his enthusiasm for Europe. 'But it has always seemed to me that you cannot make progress standing still.'

So it was that United lined up in Brussels against the Belgian champions Anderlecht in the first round of the 1956–57 European Champions Cup. It was a long journey, by train and boat, and Edwards and Charlton were both unavailable due to Army duties. But it didn't affect the result: the reds won 2-0. In the second leg – played at Maine Road because the Old Trafford floodlights had not yet been installed – Edwards returned and the game ended up like one of those romps the lads had been used to in the Youth Cup. According to the official UEFA statistics sheet of the day, Dennis Viollet scored four goals, Thomas Taylor three, William Whelan two and John James Berry one. The final score of 10-0 represented the sort of victory even the United songbook insists seldom happens. Busby described this first ever European victory on English soil as 'the finest exhibition of teamwork I have ever seen from any side at either club or international level'.

Hippolyte van den Bosch played for Anderlecht that night. Now in his mid-seventies, he still recalls the trouncing as if it were the day before yesterday: 'We were the best team in Belgium, a really great side,' he says. 'We knew very little about our opponents from Manchester. Scouting didn't exist and we had never seen any images of Manchester United before the first game in Brussels. But they were on another level; Bobby Charlton wasn't even in the starting eleven that day, just to give you an idea how strong this team really was. The two strikers [Taylor and Viollet] impressed me the most, I remember Taylor lifting his hand up and cheering before even putting the ball into the back of the net. It was just too easy for them.'

Van den Bosch and his team-mates went back across the Channel embarrassed, but aware of the significance of what had just happened to them. 'This was the best English team I've ever seen. I honestly think that the team we played in 1957 had more talent then the Rooneys and Ronaldos of today,' he says. 'We made sure that Man United's first ever appearance in a European cup was never forgotten. I just never looked at it that way until today.'

United's victory that day lit a spark: in Manchester, Euro nights became the latest thing. Under the Maine Road floodlights it was as if the whole city was illuminated, not just by the wattage beaming down from the pylons, but by the performance of Busby's players. In the next round, 76,598 poured into the ground to witness the triumph over Dortmund, victory that brought a quarter-final against the Spanish champions Athletic Bilbao.

For the first leg, United headed to the Basque country in a February blizzard. On the flight over, chairman Hardman, by now seventy-four years old, suffered from hypothermia after Bill Foulkes – stretching out his legs as he snoozed – accidentally kicked the lever controlling the plane's heating into the off position. Hardman was admitted to hospital on his arrival and, when he returned to Manchester a couple of days after the team, it was decided he should not fly abroad again. When they heard that news, several of the players secretly envied him. Indeed, in his autobiography Foulkes gives an intriguing view of how the players regarded the process of heading overseas to play. In the days before package holidays, when nobody of their age or class ventured abroad, for these lads – even those who had been to Zurich for the youth tournament – where they were going was, in Ian Rush's memorable phrase, a very foreign place. It was freezing, dark and as for what they were expected to eat . . .

'There were difficulties with food at the hotel, where we were served ham and eggs in some sort of jelly', Foulkes wrote. 'Fortunately our club secretary Walter Crickmer was a resourceful fellow and he proceeded to dispense lessons in English cooking to the kitchen staff, who mercifully proved to be quick learners.'

This was in an area of Spain that has long been famed for the magnificence of its cuisine. These days San Sebastian, just along the coast from Bilbao, has more Michelin-starred restaurants per head than any other city in the world. Yet here were visitors from a place where Spam was reckoned a culinary treat, complaining about the food. As for flying, the players regarded it as close to torture. Getting to Bilbao was not like jumping on the bus to an away game at Bolton. Mark Jones and Billy Whelan in particular were so terrified as the plane wobbled through a snowstorm on its way to Spain they both threw up.

And their nerves were hardly smoothed by the return journey. After losing 5-3 on a frozen, ploughed-field of a pitch, there was an interminable delay at Bilbao's airfield as ice was cleared from the runway and from the wings of United's Dakota aircraft. Such was Busby's anxiety to get back to England, he encouraged the players to help in the process of getting the plane ready. Whelan, a keen amateur photographer, took snaps of his team-mates, several up on the wings, joining in the brushing. The manager was asked by a pressman why the rush, why not wait until conditions had mellowed. He replied that they had to dash back to fulfil a League fixture that Saturday. He didn't want to give Hardaker and his cronies the opportunity to say 'I told you so' and slap some sort of revenge penalty on the club.

When they got home, it was a different story. Fuelled by the standard grub served up at their digs, in the second leg United produced a thriller at Maine Road. Needing to win by three goals, they did just that. The stadium throbbed that night, pulsating with noise and fervour as the new phenomenon took root: Manchester United in Europe. The point about Athletic Bilbao was that, unlike Anderlecht, they were no ingénues, blinking in the floodlights, intimidated by the cold or the size of Duncan Edwards's legs. These were hard men, Basques, used to a scrap and a kick; this team had never lost by three goals before. Yet they were outfought, outpassed, outplayed. The significance was enormous. Henry Rose, the *Daily Express* football correspondent, articulated the country's growing infatuation with this sparkling young United team: 'My hands are still trembling as I write. My heart still pounds. And a few hours have passed since, with 65,000 other lucky people, I saw the greatest soccer victory in history, ninety minutes of tremendous thrill and excitement that will live for ever in the memory. Salute the eleven red-shirted heroes of Manchester United. The whole country is proud of you.'

The year 1957 was Busby's annus mirabilis all right. In Europe his team had announced themselves with a victory so significant that later that year Real Madrid were to offer him a jaw-dropping £100,000 a year to coach at the Bernabéu. At home they dominated in a way no other team had managed since the Invincibles of Preston North End in 1897. Playing football that mixed grace with power, artistry with strength, smothering defence with breathtaking attack, they retained the League by eight points from Tottenham. They reached the final of the FA Cup after beating Birmingham City in the semi. And they were in the semi-final of the Champions Cup. Never mind the double, in itself an achievement reckoned all but impossible at the time, here were United heading for a treble.

It wasn't to be. In the Champions Cup semi-final, United went back to Spain where the holders Real Madrid, in their tight white shirts and short white shorts, outclassed them (and out-kicked them) to win 3-1. It was an eye-opening trip for the Mancunians in more ways than one. Paul Satinoff, son of Busby's great friend Willie, who travelled with the team to that game, recalls: 'I can remember the discussions afterwards with my dad and Matt about Real Madrid being a real football club. They said that they got the youth involved, the council involved, whereas United were just not involved in the local community. City were better at reaching out to the community. They had the Young Blues and they had access to the players. United turned up and played football. It was a money-making operation even then. That's not a criticism, just a fact.'

A proper football club on and off the pitch – just what Busby was trying to build in Manchester – Madrid remained unassailable. A spirited 2-2 draw in the return at an Old Trafford now fully equipped for the competition with floodlights, was not enough for Busby. Not that he was unduly unhappy in defeat. He had pitched his side against the best Europe had to offer and they were not found wanting. He had learned enough to think that next time they met in the competition, he could outflank Madrid. And if he could outflank Madrid, it meant he would win the competition.

Mind, his ebullient mood would have been tested in the FA Cup final. At Wembley, United faced Aston Villa. Almost the first significant piece of action that day was an assault so brutal were it to happen on a football field today it would provide weeks of material for newspaper opinion writers to thunder about how our national sport is leading us to hell in a handcart. The Villa player Peter McParland body-checked Manchester United's keeper Ray Wood with such force he knocked him out cold, breaking his cheekbone. It was ugly, seemingly premeditated and back then absolutely legitimate. Wood was thought to be United's weak link and McParland was not even given a talking-to by the referee for his efforts.

Watching footage of the incident fifty years on, it is surprising how inadequate the response to Wood's discomfort was. With no substitutes allowed, the first priority of the United backroom staff was to remove the stricken keeper's shirt in order to give it to Jackie Blanchflower, who had agreed to step into goal. At a moment when he should have been lying still, in a neck brace, possibly being given oxygen, a clearly groggy Wood's head lolls alarmingly even as his jersey is hauled off his ragdoll body. He is then led to the touchline from where, after about fifteen minutes and still clearly concussed, he reappears on the wing and con-tributes one run to the cause, during which his legs wobble so much he is obliged to retreat to the dressing room. That, though, is not the end of him. He emerges once more in the last twenty min-utes to take up his place in goal. That's what you did in those days: you soldiered on. Self-pity had yet to be invented.

Listening to the match commentary only adds to the sense that this is some sort of episode of the *Keystone Cops*. As the United fans boo McParland's every touch, Kenneth Wolstenholme tuts sancti-moniously. 'That's really rather silly,' he says. The assault on Wood he claims is 'just one of those things that happen in football' and McParland's later contribution to the game – the two goals that gift Villa the Cup – should be applauded, not booed.

What is clear from watching that match now, as United gamely

try to overcome the one-man deficit and lack of a proper keeper, is that this was a team who could play football. Although the pace is so slow the film appears to be running at half speed, the passing, the movement, the ball control, the tactical awareness would not have been out of place in today's Premier League. These were the very best, the new Gods of the game. As Arthur Rowe, the Spurs manager, insisted at the time, United did not succeed through individual genius. Writing in the *Encyclopaedia of Association Football*, published the following year, Rowe suggested of the League champions: 'They played to order and precision, with method and movement. Because they were fluid and not trying to do what they could not do, because they were doing things within their limits, they were successful.'

And as the forty-eight-year-old Busby looked on from the Wembley dug-out, he would have been convinced that days like this, when things conspired against his young side, were likely to become ever less frequent. From now on – particularly if he got himself a more robust keeper – his United were going to win everything in sight. Nothing could stop them. Nothing.

8

THE FLOWERS OF MANCHESTER

It is a beautiful February day for the 150th Manches
spring sun sparkles off the glass-fronted apartment
ing the Manchester Ship Canal. The game coinci
fiftieth anniversary of the Munich air crash and the
globally warmed contrast to half a century
Manchester was shrouded in freezing smog for a
many believed that the sky – leaden, grey, heavy —
in sympathy with the city. Today, few making the
lunchtime kick-off bother with coats. Most are in s
shirts, replica United jerseys of a provenance tl
decades from 1958, through 1968 to the latest Nik
number. Two lads in red tops make carefully cl
progress along Sir Matt Busby Way, celebrating as
ubiquitous attacking threat of Cristiano Ronaldo:
left has 'He plays on the left' printed on the back
boy on the right has 'He plays on the right'. A third
makes England look shite' has presumably been

try to overcome the one-man deficit and lack of a proper keeper, is that this was a team who could play football. Although the pace is so slow the film appears to be running at half speed, the passing, the movement, the ball control, the tactical awareness would not have been out of place in today's Premier League. These were the very best, the new Gods of the game. As Arthur Rowe, the Spurs manager, insisted at the time, United did not succeed through individual genius. Writing in the *Encyclopaedia of Association Football*, published the following year, Rowe suggested of the League champions: 'They played to order and precision, with method and movement. Because they were fluid and not trying to do what they could not do, because they were doing things within their limits, they were successful.'

And as the forty-eight-year-old Busby looked on from the Wembley dug-out, he would have been convinced that days like this, when things conspired against his young side, were likely to become ever less frequent. From now on – particularly if he got himself a more robust keeper – his United were going to win everything in sight. Nothing could stop them. Nothing.

8

THE FLOWERS OF MANCHESTER

It is a beautiful February day for the 150th Manchester derby, the spring sun sparkles off the glass-fronted apartment blocks framing the Manchester Ship Canal. The game coincides with the fiftieth anniversary of the Munich air crash and the weather is in globally warmed contrast to half a century before when Manchester was shrouded in freezing smog for a fortnight and many believed that the sky – leaden, grey, heavy – was mourning in sympathy with the city. Today, few making their way to this lunchtime kick-off bother with coats. Most are in sweatshirts, T-shirts, replica United jerseys of a provenance that spans the decades from 1958, through 1968 to the latest Nike third-change number. Two lads in red tops make carefully choreographed progress along Sir Matt Busby Way, celebrating as they walk the ubiquitous attacking threat of Cristiano Ronaldo: the boy on the left has 'He plays on the left' printed on the back of his shirt; the boy on the right has 'He plays on the right'. A third party with 'He makes England look shite' has presumably been held up some-

8

THE FLOWERS OF
MANCHESTER

It is a beautiful February day for the 150th Manchester derby, the spring sun sparkles off the glass-fronted apartment blocks framing the Manchester Ship Canal. The game coincides with the fiftieth anniversary of the Munich air crash and the weather is in globally warmed contrast to half a century before when Manchester was shrouded in freezing smog for a fortnight and many believed that the sky – leaden, grey, heavy – was mourning in sympathy with the city. Today, few making their way to this lunchtime kick-off bother with coats. Most are in sweatshirts, T-shirts, replica United jerseys of a provenance that spans the decades from 1958, through 1968 to the latest Nike third-change number. Two lads in red tops make carefully choreographed progress along Sir Matt Busby Way, celebrating as they walk the ubiquitous attacking threat of Cristiano Ronaldo: the boy on the left has 'He plays on the left' printed on the back of his shirt; the boy on the right has 'He plays on the right'. A third party with 'He makes England look shite' has presumably been held up some

try to overcome the one-man deficit and lack of a proper keeper, is that this was a team who could play football. Although the pace is so slow the film appears to be running at half speed, the passing, the movement, the ball control, the tactical awareness would not have been out of place in today's Premier League. These were the very best, the new Gods of the game. As Arthur Rowe, the Spurs manager, insisted at the time, United did not succeed through individual genius. Writing in the *Encyclopaedia of Association Football*, published the following year, Rowe suggested of the League champions: 'They played to order and precision, with method and movement. Because they were fluid and not trying to do what they could not do, because they were doing things within their limits, they were successful.'

And as the forty-eight-year-old Busby looked on from the Wembley dug-out, he would have been convinced that days like this, when things conspired against his young side, were likely to become ever less frequent. From now on – particularly if he got himself a more robust keeper – his United were going to win everything in sight. Nothing could stop them. Nothing.

where in the crowd. Several people take pictures with their camera phones of the pair as they walk past. The two Ronaldo fans stop over the road from the monumental glass-frontage of Old Trafford and stare up at the mural that has swathed it for the previous week. It is of an image that dates from long before either of them were born, probably before even their fathers were born. Up there is the Manchester United team, snapped lining up for the European Champions Cup quarter-final against Red Star in Belgrade on 5 February 1958. This is the last picture of that side taken together and it looks freezing where they are. The pitch is rutted and icy, pockmarked with patches of snow. It might be cold, but the players are all in short-sleeved shirts. None of them is wearing a base layer undershirt like their modern successors, none of them sports little black gloves, none bothers with lycra tights. Mark Jones, big and slope-shouldered, bites his lip against the chill. Alongside him Eddie Colman appears to be in the midst of a little jig to keep warm. Nearest the camera, Duncan Edwards is smoothing down the front of his shirt, tucking it into his shorts. He looks huge. He looks eager. He looks ready. Wow, he looks an athlete.

On the right of the picture are the lyrics to the Manchester United calypso, penned in 1957 in celebration of a bunch of bouncing Busby Babes. Beneath that are the words 'They play on in our memories', which are flanked by the logo of AIG, United's shirt sponsor. Over the ten days the mural has been in position, this logo has been paint-bombed by militant United fans furious at what they see as crass commercial exploitation of tragedy. But for today it has been cleaned up in order to provide United's leading corporate backer with the message it pays £15 million a season to convey, a link between its product – whatever that might be – and the most legendary club in world football.

To the left of the mural, under the Munich memorial that is fixed to the outside wall of the stadium, a sizeable scrum of fans has formed. At the front of the crowd, a man with a fine folk warble begins to sing:

One cold and bitter Thursday in Munich, Germany
Eight great football stalwarts conceded victory
Eight men who will never play again met destruction there
The flowers of English football, the flowers of Manchester.

This is the lament written within weeks of the disaster, first heard in the Princess Louise pub in London's Holborn on 3 March 1958. It exemplifies the depth of the fans' sorrow. Since 2001, sung in this spot on the home match nearest to the date of the crash. It is movingly done, a piece of secular worship greeted with a reverence that would not seem out of place down the road at Manchester's cathedral. Several of those watching find it hard to join in the chorus without their voice catching in their throats.

After the singing has finished, the crowd make their way into the stadium and head, for once, straight for their seats. Twenty minutes before the game is due to start the place is packed. Normally, as they make the most of the secondary spend opportunities in the stadium's below-stand retail areas, the fans at Old Trafford wait until the last moment to take up their positions. Usually it is like a vast scale conjuring trick in there, David Copperfield at his most ambitious: thirty seconds before kick-off it is half empty, then, as the referee puts the whistle to his lips to facilitate the start, seventy-five thousand seats are suddenly filled. But today everyone is in early, opening up the complimentary commemorative package that has been left on their seats, containing a scarf and a reprint of the first match-day programme after the disaster. In the City section, the visitors too have been left scarves, these in their club colours. To keep themselves occupied, the inhabitants of the Stretford End sing their songs, giving particular relish to the one that wonders why City don't fuck off home. The City fans respond with their latest favourite, a reminder of United manager Alex Ferguson's recent criticism of his own supporters: 'Fergie is right, your fans are shite,' they sing. It is boisterous in there, louder than it has been for ages.

Then, suddenly, the mood changes. From out of the tunnel to

the left of the Stretford End emerge the two teams, walking through an honour-guard of United youth players, led by a lone piper who plays 'The Flowers of Manchester'. Quiet replaces the tribal bile. Down on the pitch, the United players are dressed in shirts identical to the ones Duncan Edwards and crew are wearing in the photograph outside. There is no sponsors' marque, no manufacturer's logo, no League champions crest on the sleeve. They look, in their uncluttered retro condition, tellingly elegant. City also wear shirts without logos, instead with a small black ribbon embroidered on to one shoulder. In their attire, both clubs are keen to send out a message to their supporters that they recognise this is not a day for commercialism or marketing. It is a day for remembering.

As the two teams ring the centre circle, Ferguson and the City manager Sven-Göran Eriksson lay wreaths on the centre spot. Then comes the moment everyone has been anticipating: the minute's silence. And what a silence it is. The crowd falls utterly quiet. The only sound comes from a couple of pyrotechnical pops emanating from outside the stadium. Many people assume this to be the start of a twenty-one-gun salute, but it turns out to be fireworks set off by some freelance idiot.

Near me in the south stand as I look across from the press box, I see a man in his seventies, standing with his scarf held proudly aloft. He stares into the distance, his imagination seemingly playing through the images of Duncan, Eddie, Tommy and the rest. He appears to see them passing and moving on the pitch below him, still in their prime, undiminished, unsurpassed, unfettered. As the memories run Technicolor though his head, tears roll down his face.

Beyond him the City followers stand mute, blue and white scarves up above their heads, faces solemn. As the stadium stands in quiet, the names of the players who died at Munich are flashed on the electronic advertising hoardings fringing the pitch. Where normally Betfred and Air Asia display their logos, instead there are the memories of the great lost players: Duncan Edwards, Tommy

Taylor, Eddie Colman, Roger Byrne, Mark Jones, David Pegg, Billy Whelan, plus Geoff Bent, the young substitute who had only been taken along as a covering precaution and didn't even play in the game against Belgrade. Next are the names of Bert Whalley and Tom Curry, the club's two trainers. Then Walter Crickmer, the club secretary, the man who was an unmovable fixture in the United story for thirty-eight years. As the names snap through, the silence is profound, remarkable, it sends a small shiver up every spine in attendance. When the referee blows his whistle to mark its conclusion, there is an eruption of noise and Ferguson marches towards the City contingent, hands in front of his face applauding their contribution. The man near me wipes his face with his souvenir scarf, claps his hands vigorously together and yells 'C'mon you reds.'

'They do that sort of thing awfully well, United,' Martin Edwards, the club's former chief executive and chairman, tells me the following day. 'It's something we can be very proud of.'

It is, in truth, something few had imagined. Certainly not in the media. In the week beforehand the papers, web forums and radio phone-ins had been full of tales about how the City fans planned to disrupt what they were referring to with glee as 'The Golden Jubilee'. It was reported that someone had been spotted at a recent City home game with the words 'Headless 58' on the back of his sky-blue shirt. So certain was everyone that the silence would not be respected Kevin Parker, secretary of the official City supporters' club, wrote to United suggesting that, instead of the silence, they stage a minute's applause, the better to drown out those bent on ruining things. United's chief executive David Gill refused to change the arrangements: a minute's applause might be the thing to do to mark a life fulfilled but it would not be appropriate, he said, to commemorate lives taken away so cruelly, so prematurely. Still, in the newspaper opinion columns and on the blogs, writers had already convinced themselves the minute would not be observed properly, particularly after the one before an England match at Wembley four evenings previously had been foreshortened after the anti-United shouts threatened to turn it into a farce. What is wrong with us, they wanted to know, that we can't respect the dead? What is wrong with our football?

As it happens, on the day, the power of the memorial overwhelms any urge to disrupt. Besides, City lost one of their own in the crash: Frank Swift, their renowned keeper in the pre-war era, the man Busby referred to admiringly as 'the Big Fella', was one of eight journalists killed pursuing the greatest sports story of their time. When remembering Munich, as the two sets of fans stand in silence, scarves outstretched, Manchester becomes a city united in respect. With their dignified response, City fans emerge with the plaudits. Plus – to much red chagrin – the three points as their team proceed, deservedly, to win the game.

If it seems odd that so many assumed the commemoration would be anything other than observed as perfectly as it was, it is because in the half century since it happened, the Munich air disaster has come to mean very different things to different people. For those who love Manchester United it is a point of reverence, a sacred tenet of faith to be cherished against those who seek either to exploit or demean its memory. For those who have found commercial advantage from Manchester United, it is a unique selling proposition, the brand's marketing core from which everything else has stemmed. While in the minds of the growing numbers of those who stand up because they hate Man U it has become an unmissable opportunity for iconoclasm. In the orbit of United-haters the very word Munich has changed from one cloaked in tragedy into one of derision.

Thus, if you want to know how big a surprise it was that City fans kept so silent for that minute, there is a clue after the game. A City supporter is walking towards a minibus full of his comrades, parked on the forecourt of the United hotel, just over the road from the stadium. They watch his approach through the bus windows. As he heads in their direction he is clapping his hands in front of his chest in rhythmic appreciation of his team. Then, gradually, imperceptibly, he moves his arms out to his side so that they resemble aeroplane wings. Finally he wobbles them to imitate a plane's imminent crash and destruction. Though they have seen such a mime show many times before, in the minibus his mates laugh at his actions, enjoying them hugely.

'Fucking Munichs,' the man shouts as he climbs into the bus, pulling the door behind him. 'We did the fucking Munichs.'

Of all the many things said about the Munich disaster in the lead-up to its fiftieth anniversary, Harry Gregg said the most pertinent. United's big Irish keeper – signed only three months previously – was the reluctant hero of the crash. Though only lightly injured, in the ripping, sparking, sliding black confusion of its immediate aftermath, he was convinced he had died and was now in the other place.

'I thought, I'm dead, I'm in hell, hell fire, damnation and all that,' he says. 'I could feel the blood coming down my face. And I didn't dare put my hand up. I thought the top of my head had been taken off, like a hard boiled egg.'

Recovering his wits, he crawled from the wreckage to be confronted by one of the crew who shouted at him that if he had any brain he would run before the whole plane exploded. Instead he stood for a moment, considered the scene and then, shouting 'There's people alive in here', went back into the buckled, broken fuselage. After failing to free a couple of his dead team-mates who still sat, unblemished, in their seats, he hauled out to safety a pregnant woman and her small child.

'To me, Harry Gregg has always been Superman,' says Mrs Vera Lukic, the Yugoslav woman he rescued.

Fifty years after his moment of singular bravery, he was persuaded by a BBC documentary team to return to the scene for the first time. The result was a piece of work whose every moment was infused with melancholy. In one sequence Gregg was filmed walking around the terminal of the Munich airport as he had that February afternoon half a century before. Now disused and empty, this was the place to which the young United team had repaired while their plane was attended to on the runway.

'Because of what happened when we left this building,' said Gregg, pacing round the empty hall, an uneasy look on his face, 'Manchester United changed from a football club into an institution.'

What happened when Gregg and company left the building was that instead of taking off, the chartered Elizabethan aircraft in which they were due to fly home skidded off the end of the runway, smashed through the perimeter fencing, clipped a house and broke in half, its fractured pieces settling into marshy ground beyond the runway's end. Gregg was in the front half. Most of the twenty-one people who died instantly were in the back. Several of them had deliberately headed for the back because they thought it was safer there.

It was an avoidable crash. The plane was in Munich to refuel. The team had just completed their European Champions Cup quarter-final victory over Red Star in Belgrade and in those days it was too far to fly back in one hop. Conditions in Bavaria when they arrived were appalling, the runway was thick with melting snow. The plane should have been held back till the next day. The pilot had already aborted take off twice. But United needed to get home; the duffers at the Football League, after all, wouldn't countenance any excuse like the wrong kind of slush on the runway. As the third attempt at take-off began, as the plane shuddered and stuttered towards its end, several of the players were terrified. Many – remembering their near miss in Bilbao the previous winter – feared the worst. Gregg recalls hearing someone suggest they were all going to die and then Billy Whelan, the least confident flyer among them, saying, 'This may be death, but I'm ready.' At 3.04 p.m. on Thursday 6 February 1958, death arrived.

Even then, if the fencing had not been so close to the runway's end, if there had not been buildings in the way, if there was not a fuel dump in its path, in short if the safety precautions had been remotely like those that are standard today, the plane would have simply come to a halt in a run-off, an aborted take-off that would have resulted in nothing more than a few bruises and abrasions.

But safety is learned in the aftermath of disaster. The accident happened and the details – the roll-call of the dead, the long and difficult recuperation of Matt Busby, the eleven-year fight of the pilot to clear himself of blame – have been repeated multiple times since. They are details that lose nothing in the retelling. Details that still reverberate round Old Trafford fifty years on. It was not the accident itself that changed United, however. It was, as Gregg implied, what happened next. In his autobiography, Bobby Charlton puts it this way: 'Before Munich, United were seen as Manchester's club. Afterwards everyone felt as if they owned a little bit of it.'

There have been other football disasters, which have informed the way we think of the clubs affected. Celtic, Rangers, Bolton Wanderers, Bradford City, Juventus and Liverpool have all suffered grievously. The history of every single victim in those tragedies is charged with grief and loss, the back story shot through with scandalous neglect of stadium safety. But it is Munich whose echoes sound wider and further. And Munich wasn't even the only plane crash to affect Manchester that month. On 27 February 1958, a plane on a flight from the Isle of Man to the city's Ringway airport ploughed into Winter Hill, between Chorley and Bolton. Such was the blizzard affecting the area that night, by morning there was no sign of the crash, all traces had been smoothed out by a blanket of snow. Thirty-five people died. Their names, however, are not recorded on a plaque at the stadium of the world's most famous football club.

The thing about Munich – unlike Heysel, Hillsborough or Valley Parade – was that it involved players. And that gave it a much more intense symbolism. These were not just any players, either, but young players so chock-full of potential the pain of their loss extended out beyond a group of relatives. Everyone thought they knew the Babes, every kid who tore a colour picture of Duncan

Edwards or Eddie Colman from their *Football Monthly* and put it on their bedroom wall felt the loss. It was a shared grief, a public grief. As the *Manchester News Chronicle* put it the day after the crash: 'It is as if every family had lost a personal friend. Manchester United had become more than just a football team. To the man in the street this was a symbol of how British sportsmanship, good honest Lancashire endeavour, the boy next door could reach the top.'

This was the beginning of the legend. For the players who died, their reputation was to be forever secured, preserved as if in aspic. Actually, more than that: it was enhanced. There was to be no defeat for these lads, no descent into bitterness or booze, no career-ending injury or stroppy demands for a transfer over the paucity of their new contract. None of them ended up scraping a living guesting on a local radio late-night phone-in or selling their story of booze-raddled decline to a Sunday tabloid. They died young and carefree, about to conquer the world. And in many an imagination they would go on to do just that. In the collective mental cinema, Duncan Edwards could become the greatest player of all time, he could be the man lifting the World Cup for England in 1966, he could become Busby's successor in the Old Trafford dugout. As with James Dean or Buddy Holly or Jimi Hendrix, for whom there was never to be a crap B-movie or dodgy B-side, in death they were never to be diminished. In the memory their spirit was forever buffed and polished. They became not just a bunch of talented lads, with all the foibles that a bunch of lads might be prey to, they became gods of the game; physically, spiritually and morally they became unimpeachable.

The point about Munich, though, was not that it imbued the club with tragic resonance at such heinous loss. People do not support United across the planet, from Wythenshawe to Wagga Wagga, from Hulme to Hong Kong, from Salford to Singapore, because they feel sorry for them. Few choose their football team out of sympathy. No, what made United, what added to the poignancy of loss was the comeback. United didn't die in the slush of Munich. The institution, the loose amalgam of spirits that comes together on the pitch and in the stands, refused to be cowed by disaster. With upper lips stiffened, chins raised and backs braced they rebuilt and recovered. They were resurrected. And that was what resonated, that is what still resonates today.

As Rio Ferdinand put it after the fiftieth-anniversary match, Munich was 'the starting point, really, for the tradition, the start of setting down the standard for Manchester United Football Club'.

It didn't happen to Torino, United's precursors in tragedy. On 4 May 1949, a plane carrying the Serie A champions crashed in thick fog into a church in the Turin suburb of Superga on the way back from a friendly against Benfica in Portugal. Everyone on board was killed, including eighteen players of whom ten were Italian internationals. The sympathy for the club was huge: for the last four fixtures of the Italian league, as Torino were obliged to field their youth team, so did their opponents, with instructions to lose. Torino duly won the scudetto. But from there they never recovered their prominence. Within five years of the crash, the club was bankrupt, had been forced to sell its ground and was sharing facilities with neighbours Juventus. They didn't win the championship again until 1976 and since have sunk into Serie B more frequently than they have graced Italy's top division.

In Manchester, in the first few days after the crash, it felt as if United might follow the same path. Everywhere there was a numbed sense of loss. Jimmy Savile was due to host the annual press ball in his Plaza nightclub that evening. On hearing the news, he locked up and put up a sign on the door saying, 'Cancelled'. He simply couldn't go ahead. In his brilliant book *Manchester's Finest*, David Hall, a schoolboy at the time of the accident, tells how common this was as a reaction. Manchester was a city traumatised by Munich. Hall recounts the groups of workers gathering on street corners in the days after the crash, stunned and silent. He tells of how news was devoured by those who seemed to need confirmation that it had really happened.

Every day people rang the Manchester newspaper offices seeking forlorn assurance: 'Say it isn't true.' He also relays the pitiable tale of a United fan called John Bunn. Depressed beyond reason by the disaster, one evening at his home in Northwich Bunn took out a pocket knife and stabbed himself to death. 'Suicide when the mind was temporarily unbalanced' was the coroner's verdict. The city knew how he felt: its mind also seemed temporarily unbalanced.

And yet, running counter to that depression, almost from the moment the news of the crash first filtered through, there were those saying that disaster made no odds to the institution: United would not die. Johnny Carey, by now manager of Blackburn Rovers, set the tone when he was interviewed on the television news. 'When I first heard I was absolutely shocked to the core,' he said. 'All heads are bowed in Manchester tonight. But Manchester United will live on.'

This tallied with what was immediately cast as official club policy. There was a board meeting scheduled the day after the crash and chairman Hardman – who, after his unhappy turn on the way to Bilbao, had not flown to Belgrade – decided it must go ahead anyway. The meeting's intended purpose was to elect Louis Edwards, Busby's buddy, to the board in place of George Whitaker, the director who had died the night before the Babes' last ever game in England, against Arsenal at Highbury. Busby had wanted Edwards as a director for some time, but Whitaker had opposed him. Indeed Edwards was offered a seat on the plane to Belgrade, but because he had not been voted on the board yet, felt it might not be appropriate. His place went to Willie Satinoff, who lost his life. This time Edwards was voted on unanimously and Les Olive was appointed secretary to replace the hugely missed Crickmer.

After the formalities had been concluded, Hardman mapped out United's strategy over the next few weeks. He intended, he said, that they should fulfil all the fixtures in the three competitions in which they were still involved. 'We have a duty to the public and a duty to football,' he said. 'We shall carry on even if it means being heavily defeated.'

Apart from asking the FA to delay that Saturday's League game against Wolves and hold the FA Cup tie against Sheffield Wednesday four days later than scheduled, he was to seek no favour from authority. Red Star Belgrade had already said that United should be made that season's honorary European champions, but Hardman wanted none of that. United would survive on their own strengths, not on the charity of others. Unlike those – including the Leeds United manager Raich Carter – who felt that the League programme should be suspended for at least a week in memory of those who died, he wanted things to carry on.

'I sincerely urge all players to turn out and play the game in the normal way,' he said. 'This would be the best way of paying tribute to everyone concerned in this tragedy. I am confident our manager Mr Matt Busby and the others who lie injured in Germany would wish it so.'

This is what was done in those days: they carried on. It was only eighteen years after Dunkirk. Locked into the nation's sense of itself was the idea that in the face of extremis, you got on with things. Munich was United's Dunkirk, and Hardman refused to be defeated. His strategy for renewal, though, depended for success on one man. Hard as it might be to imagine in these days of a carefully coordinated football calendar in which European competition takes precedence, Jimmy Murphy had not flown to Belgrade because Wales had a World Cup qualifier that same evening against Israel. And in addition to his duties kicking and swearing United into shape, Murphy was Wales's manager. He had returned to Old Trafford from Cardiff on the afternoon of the crash unaware it had happened. The first person he met was Busby's secretary Alma George, who had to tell him the news three times before he took it in.

'The words seemed to ring in my head. Alma left me and I went into my office,' he later recalled. 'My head was in a state of confusion and I started to cry.'

Now he was tasked with the most significant duty of his life: he had to run Manchester United on his own. First he had to bury the team he had created. Murphy flew out to Munich the day after the crash, with the families of the injured, to organise the return of those who didn't make it. At the Rechts der Isar hospital, Dr Georg Maurer, the surgeon in charge of the medical team attending to the United party, took him to the bed of each survivor and matter-of-factly spelled out their chances. Of Big Dunc and the Boss he gave odds of fifty-fifty. Blanchflower would live, but his leg was in a bad way. Charlton, Wood, Viollet and Kenny Morgans all looked in reasonable shape and greeted Murphy with a charged mix of laughter and tears. Albert Scanlon looked astonishingly spry since he had been found unconscious in the wreckage eight hours after the crash by a couple of German newsmen looking for lost rolls of film. Gregg and Foulkes had discharged themselves the night of the crash and were ready to return home on the train. Of Johnny Berry, suffering from massive head injuries, Maurer could only say, 'I am not God.' Murphy had conversations with everyone who was conscious. Through a morphine haze, Busby issued him with the instruction he took to heart: 'Keep the flag flying, Jim, till I get back.'

Murphy's first job on his return was to find a team to play Sheffield Wednesday in the FA Cup fifth-round tie scheduled now for Wednesday 19 February. The FA waived the fourteen-day registration rule on signed players and, in the circumstances, Cup-tied players could turn out for a second club in the competition. Offers of help came in from all sides. Some were more practical than others. Three of the Magical Magyars – Zoltan Czibor, Ferenc Puskas and Sandor Kocsis – proffered their services to the reds for the rest of the season. They were living in exile in Italy, having left their homeland in the 1956 uprising. Murphy was tempted, but couldn't agree terms for them. No surprise there. All he could offer was the £18 maximum wage. In the summer of 1958 Puskas was to sign a contract at Madrid worth £800 a week. Indeed, Murphy soon found out that United were so hopelessly uninsured for player loss, he was effectively without any transfer fund, which was why an offer from Bishop Auckland, the amateur club in the Durham coal-field, to loan the reds three players was so enthusiastically grasped. Bert Hardisty, Derek Lewin and Warren Bradley filled in the gaps in United's reserve team for much of the rest of the season.

It was lucky they were amateurs: Ken Ramsden, who was work-ing in the office with the newly appointed Les Olive, recalls that there was no money for anything in the aftermath of disaster. They couldn't even afford a new typewriter to respond to the bag-loads of sympathetic correspondence daily dropping into Old Trafford. Everyone had to make do and mend. Murphy was on the phone almost continuously in those early weeks of recovery. He worked frantically, twenty hours a day. He was there too, at every funeral, comforting distraught relatives through every wake.

'Murphy was an absolute giant,' says Martin Edwards of those days. 'Without Jimmy it may well have sunk. I'm sure of that.'

Ernie Taylor was the first player to be signed, from Blackpool for £8000. Then Murphy persuaded Jack Crompton to come back to United to replace his lost friends, the coaches Bert Whalley and Tom Curry. Everything was a rush: the paperwork for Stan Crowther's transfer was completed just an hour and a quarter before kick-off in United's first game back. What an occasion that was, so charged with emotion, Old Trafford so awash with sym-pathy, Wilf McGuinness – whose recent injury had prevented him travelling to Belgrade – recalls feeling sorry for the visitors. 'It was the worst thing for Sheffield Wednesday,' he says. 'Everyone in the world wanted United to win.'

And everyone in the world appeared to want to be there to watch it happen. The black marketeers, certainly not the last to appreciate the economic possibilities of the disaster, were out in force. Not that they could accommodate the whole crowd: thirty thousand were locked out that night. A young Denis Law was one of those who made it in. He travelled over from Huddersfield, where he was an apprentice player and together with a team-mate paid £1 for two half-crown tickets.

'The emotion that night outside the ground from about four-thirty was amazing,' recounts Law, who stood at the back of the Scoreboard End.

It was emotion that did not diminish when fans bought their match-day programme, the item that was to become the most cherished piece of United memorabilia in history, pristine copies of which these days change hands for over £1000. On the front cover Hardman articulated the philosophy of renewal: 'United will go on,' he wrote. 'Although we mourn our dead and grieve for our wounded we believe that great days are not done for us. The sympathy and encouragement of the football world and particularly of our supporters will justify and inspire us. The road back may be long and hard but with the memory of those who died at Munich, of their stirring achievements and wonderful sportsmanship ever with us, Manchester United will rise again.'

Inside, on the team line-ups page, opposite the names of the Sheffield players, were eleven empty spaces. Murphy did not know who would be playing in sufficient time to alert the printers. Still, from somewhere, he managed to come up with a side. The *Manchester Evening News* called them Murphy's Chicks, an epithet that didn't catch on. In the team were his two recent signings, seven youth-team players and two Munich survivors: Harry Gregg and Bill Foulkes. Gregg, for one, was enormously relieved to be back.

'Nobody could help me but myself. I had to get out of the house and get back and kick and shout. Otherwise I believe I would have lost it up there,' he says, tapping his temple. Spurred on by a riptide of sentiment pouring down the terraces, this patchwork team won the game. There could be no other result. Many in attendance concluded there was some kind of celestial presence directing events. The sense of other-worldly contribution was enhanced when the first goal went in. Shay Brennan, a young Manc left winger of Irish extraction making his debut, took a corner. As it arced into the penalty area, nobody touched it. Yet, somehow, it swung into the net. There were plenty in attendance who thought the spirit of the Babes had intervened to alter its trajectory. Brennan himself said it was as if Tommy Taylor had risen from the penalty spot to nod it home. The game ended 4-2, a result that unified the country in celebration (well, apart from the blue bits of Sheffield).

There is a photograph taken of the makeshift United team in the dressing room after that game. You can see the sense of relief in every grin, the sense of achievement in the bottles of beer the young lads hold. But studying it again fifty years later, Harry Gregg invites you to look into his eyes as he stares past the camera into the middle distance. Like those of Foulkes alongside him, as they look vacantly apparently at nothing, the story they tell is not of triumph, but of emptiness.

'They're dead eyes, nothing there,' says Gregg. 'All we could think about that night was who wasn't there.'

No wonder: it was still not a fortnight since the pair had walked away from the shattered plane that had served as their friends' execution chamber. Foulkes had lost nearly two stone in weight since the crash. If it seems beyond any comprehension that they were expected to play so soon after the event, these were very different times. Post-traumatic stress disorder had not yet been recognised. Fifteen years before Munich tens of thousands of men had returned from war and were expected to jolly well get on with it. There was no counselling for them, even those who had been through times that would stalk their sleeping hours for the rest of their lives. Of the Munich survivors, all but Johnny Berry and Jackie Blanchflower, so seriously hurt neither would ever kick a ball again, were similarly expected to get on with it. The club's continued well-being was predicated on the assumption that they would do just that. To the outsider, United's policy of carrying on regardless may have been noble, but it brooked no accommodation for those at the tragedy's heart who found it hard to summon up the personal reserves of will required. Bill Foulkes, for instance, looks back with a degree of rancour at how little understanding he was shown.

'I played the rest of the season and it did me a lot of damage, with my head,' he says. 'I had pains and I didn't get any sort of help for it, I just carried on playing. You just got on with it in those days. But the pain lasted for a couple of seasons. I wasn't happy with the way I was treated, not happy at all.'

Kenny Morgans, the young Welsh winger who was to play for much of the rest of the season, agrees. He found it almost impossible to refocus on the business of football. To him, it seemed so trivial. 'I just didn't feel like playing. It just wasn't the same,' he says, at the time of the crash a nineteen-year-old on the verge of breaking into the big time. 'I was quite happy to go back to play in the reserves. I didn't have the appetite. What was the point?'

Jackie Blanchflower was the same. 'After I got back to England I couldn't even watch United on television. It wasn't United for me,' he once said. 'Tommy Taylor was the worst blow for me. I've never made another relationship like that.'

The idea of just getting on with it has informed United's attitude to Munich ever since, long after the consequences of trauma have been understood. Some believe it became a handy excuse for neglect of duty. Never mind that the survivors went without formal counselling at the time, they – and the victims' families – went without adequate compensation until much, much later. For some, like Scanlon, this was fair enough. 'I never felt they owed me anything,' he says of the club. 'And I'd have always preferred it if there weren't any anniversaries.'

Others were less sanguine. The family of Johnny Berry, whose story was retold by his son Neil in the book *Johnny: The Forgotten Babe*, felt particularly aggrieved that, with his career finished at Munich, it took until 1998 for the club to organise a testimonial to raise funds for his old age. And even then, although each beneficiary (either the survivors or the immediate family of those who perished) received £47,283.89 from the evening, that money came, effectively, from the pockets of the fans, not from the players' employer.

'It may be true more could have been done at the time,' says

Ken Ramsden, United's former secretary. 'But fifty years on it's a different world.'

Indeed it is. Back then, as he recovered his health and was discharged from the Munich hospital, Bobby Charlton was stricken with what we now term survivor's guilt. At the time it just seemed a horrible confusion. If he was not asking himself why he had made it when better people like Duncan had died, there was in his mind a constant nagging inquiry as to what was the purpose of carrying on. In desperation, on his return to Manchester, he sought help from his GP. The doctor talked about the war and how many men had returned with much the same feelings, and how they had recovered by focusing on the need to go on in memory of fallen comrades. That was what Charlton decided to do: play for the friends he lost. In his autobiography he writes of his subsequent gilded career: 'You were giving everything you had for Manchester United and the lads who didn't make it at Munich. In the hospital, along with the other survivors, I had asked the question: what can we do? It was simple enough, really. We could just play in a way that showed we would never forget the lads who died at Munich.'

This was the message United wanted to convey. The machinery of recovery demanded the swift return to competitive normality. That would be the great healer. Yet for every couple of steps forward in those first few weeks after the crash, there was a step back. David Hall recalls how everyone believed that if Big Dunc survived, everything would be fine. And for over a fortnight it seemed he might. For fifteen days the giant of the team hung on in the Rechts der Isar hospital, refusing to yield. News of his condition span across the city. At the funerals of those killed, the crowds lining the pavements, after bowing their heads as the hearse passed by, would exchange tales of his improvement or decline. Someone would say how they'd heard Jimmy Murphy had been to see him in hospital and Edwards had asked when kick-off was on Saturday. Someone else would talk about the state-of-the-art artificial kidney machine that would sort him out. Another mourner would point to the *News Chronicle* headline that suggested he would 'be playing again next season'.

No more than twenty-four hours after the Sheffield game came news that he wouldn't be. In the early hours of Friday 21 February, Duncan Edwards's kidneys failed and he died. He was just twenty-one. It was as if a light had gone out on United.

In Munich, lying in his hospital bed, the critically injured Matt Busby was another wrestling with a sense of hopelessness. In the accident, debris had crushed his chest, his stomach, his legs. In the first couple of days afterwards few thought he would survive; he could hardly breathe on his own accord and was lying unconscious, his leg trussed in plaster, when his son Sandy came from Manchester to see him.

'I went past his room first time, then came back and saw this grey-faced old man and thought, Oh God it's me dad,' recalls Sandy. 'I remember putting my head under this oxygen tent and saying, "You can't die, Dad".'

Slowly, agonisingly, Busby improved. But, as he lay there in the weeks after the crash, he was paralysed with guilt about what had befallen the team. It was, he reasoned, his fault those young lives had been taken. For hours on end he was afflicted with tortuous self-doubt that it was his ambition, his overarching need to prove that his methods were the most effective in world football that had conspired to end the lives of his lads. If he had stayed at home, if he had not fought the football authorities, if he had concentrated on domestic domination, they would all be alive still.

In that state of mind, he would have been forgiven if he had simply rolled over and given up. As Alex Ferguson put it in the week of the fiftieth anniversary, if Busby had walked away from football, sickened and distressed, nobody would have thought any worse of him as a man.

But he didn't. He always credited his wife Jean for helping make the decision to return and devote his energies to United again. He once put it like this: 'In the hospital in Munich the sense that everything we had tried to do had literally turned to ashes hit

me so hard. I didn't see how I could carry on. I thought that I had
done everything I could and fate had intervened and destroyed it
all. But a voice kept saying, "You can't quit, you have to go on for
so many reasons. You have to go on for the lads who died, for the
lads coming through and for the people." It was the voice of my
dear wife. She said that with the help of those lads I had built
something worth fighting for and whatever the odds against us
now, there was no alternative. We had to go on.'

Fifty years on, the story of how Jean broke the news to him that
so many of his favoured boys had died in the crash is still capable
of bringing a tear to the most jaded eye. For weeks the doctors had
kept the information about fatalities from him, fearful it might
weaken his parlous condition. Anyone coming to his bedside was
told not to say anything about the deaths.

'None of us mentioned the crash,' recalls Sandy. 'We just
couldn't. We knew it would break his heart.'

Then, one night about three weeks after it happened, Busby
asked Jean if Big Duncan had gone. She simply nodded. And he
began to spell out the names of others – Roger? Bill? Eddie?
David? As he did so it became clear to Jean that he knew. In his list
he only mentioned the names of the dead ones. Those he uttered
were the ones who had not been spoken of by anyone visiting his
bedside. Visitors had chatted about Bobby's recovery and how Bill
and Harry were back in training, or how Albert and Dennis were
doing. But nobody mentioned Roger, or Billy, or Big Dunc. So he
knew. He knew all right. And he decided then and there to come
back for them, to secure their memory.

For the sixth-round FA Cup replay on 5 March 1958, Old Trafford
was full an hour before kick-off. With sixty thousand already in the
ground, thirty thousand people were locked outside. A further
five thousand were stuck at Central station after British Railways
cancelled all the football special trains into Old Trafford station on
news of the lock-out. Nearly a hundred thousand people tried to
watch that game. The previous weekend an unprecedented fifteen

thousand away supporters had travelled to West Bromwich to see the 2-2 draw that had precipitated the replay. They had got there on special trains, by bus, by hitching a ride down the A34. No club's followers had travelled in such numbers before, but United's supporters now had a cause. There was an overwhelming sense in those few weeks after the crash that the fans could play a significant part in the club's recovery. The board acknowledged their contribution in the match-day programme. Partly it was financial. Far from deserting the club in its lowest point, they were filling its coffers as never before. Mainly, though, it was about the noise they made. It was a bit more than that normally provided at the stadium by the Beswick Prize Band and Jack Irons, the United mascot with red and white tailcoat and red and white umbrella. The emotional surge tumbling down the terraces froze the opposition and inspired Murphy's hodge-podge replacements. Chanting out the names of players, singing up for the lads was no longer an optional distraction, it became – for those few months in the spring of 1958 – a duty.

'We weren't just playing eleven men, we were playing sixty thousand fans as well,' Albert Quixall, Sheffield Wednesday's captain had said after the fifth-round game. And for the match against West Brom, United's twelfth man had even more to cheer about. On to the pitch before kick-off came the German doctors and nurses – led by Georg Maurer – who had been looking after United's injured in Munich. Many in the crowd could recall how the Germans had bombed their city. Now here were German people being cheered to the echo of the very stadium they had destroyed seventeen years before. Things had moved on indeed. And United were moving on with them.

The emotion, the surge, the sense of destiny was too much for West Brom. Colin Webster's late winner did for them. It was too much for Fulham in the semi too. In terms of talent, Jimmy Murphy's team was a mere shadow of the one that had been lost in Munich. And it was found out in the League. Of the remaining fifteen games after the crash, United won only one, drawing another four. Whereas before it happened, Busby could choose from a cornucopia of riches – Wood or Gregg in goal, Morgans swapping with Berry on the right wing, Charlton or Whelan at inside forward, Scanlon or Pegg at outside left, and always Duncan at wing half – Murphy was beyond the bare bones. He was down to very marrow.

Yet somehow in the Cup, driven by Ernie Taylor and Charlton, returning from his recuperation in Munich, it was a different matter. There was a sense on the terraces and in the press that the story would reach its logical conclusion at Wembley. For the players, this sense of duty hung heavy. The dressing room and the training grounds had become sombre places. Pranks were considered inappropriate. Everyone worked harder than ever, duty demanded it. Practically every week there would be another reason to gird their loins and up their game. None more so than when Busby, walking with the aid of a stick, returned to the Cliff to meet the players one day in April, just before the FA Cup final. He had been with Jean in Switzerland recuperating for a fortnight since he left hospital in Munich. As he came into the dressing room he looked about fifteen years older than the last time anyone had seen him in there. His flaxen hair had greyed, his face had lined, his eyes had dulled almost beyond recognition. Flanked by Murphy and Jack Crompton, he attempted to say a few words. He couldn't. Faced for the first time with the enormity of such profound change in the very heart of his territory, he broke down. They knew, the players, as they watched him being led away by his able lieutenant, what they had to do. And if they didn't, Murphy quickly let them know. They had to bloody win it for the Boss. Except, as always, Murphy didn't say bloody.

United's players, led out on to the Wembley turf by Murphy, with Busby watching from the bench, wore for the FA Cup final special shirts. On the chest they had embroidered a club badge incorporating a phoenix. It was a brilliant graphic image, the earliest demonstration that those in charge of the club were more

The Newton Heath team that beat Walsall 14-0 in 1895. The result was chalked off because of a muddy pitch. The Heathens won the replay only 9-0 (Getty Images).

Right: United's first trophy-winning manager, Ernest Mangnall, 1903–12 (Colorsport).

Far right: The man who did everything: Louis Rocca, one time manager, coach, scout, club secretary and chief bottle washer. Oh, and he claimed to have invented the name Manchester United (Colorsport).

Master of all he surveyed, Matt Busby, 1945–69, 1970–1 (TopFoto).

A fine day for an execution:
Frank O'Farrell, 1971–2
(Colorsport).

A brief and unhappy marriage: Pat Crerand (left)
assists Tommy Docherty (1972–7) (Colorsport).

Dave Sexton, the quiet man,
1977–81 (Colorsport).

Ron Atkinson, the man with the
tan, 1981–6 (Colorsport).

Sir Alex Ferguson, nobody
does it better, 1986–present
(Colorsport).

Billy Meredith, for once pictured without his toothpick, at Old Trafford in 1909 (Colorsport)

John Davies, brewery magnate, facial hair enthusiast and saviour of Manchester United, photographed at his new stadium, 1909 (Colorsport).

Reds in Piccadilly Circus before the 1948 Cup final: a pulse of colour in austere times (TopFoto).

Jack Rowley demonstrates his head for heights at Wembley in the 1948 Cup final against Blackpool (TopFoto).

Old Trafford in the winter of 1950: executive seating area not in picture (Colorsport).

The world's most complete player, Duncan Edwards, takes on Aston Villa on his own during the 1957 FA Cup final (Colorsport).

Tommy Taylor ignores the local smoke and dances across the Old Trafford mud, August 1957 (PA Photos/TopFoto).

The Babes take to the field before their last ever game together, 5 February 1958, Belgrade (TopFoto).

The remains of United's chartered aircraft lie on the runway of Munich airport, 6 February 1958 (Ullstein Bild/TopFoto).

Matt Busby alongside Jimmy Murphy, the man who played a blinder after Munich, at the FA Cup final, May 1958 (Colorsport).

Two thirds of the way to
the golden trinity: Denis
and Bobby in July 1962
(AP/TopFoto).

Getting up close and personal in the aftermath of winning the League title in 1965
(TopFoto).

The madness of King George: football's first superstar and his staff, 1966 (Ullstein Bild/TopFoto).

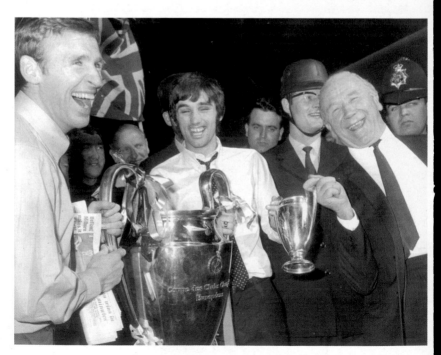

It's a wonderful world: Pat Crerand, George Best and Matt Busby can't stop smiling as they bring the European Cup back to Manchester. The cop behind Busby was clearly a City fan (PA Photos/TopFoto).

than aware of the symbolic power of the crash. United had risen from the ashes of Munich and the sympathies of the country, maybe the world watching on television, were with them. Surely, to mark their rebirth they would win the Cup. They had to win the Cup.

Bolton Wanderers, however, were too canny to be disturbed from their own ambition by sentiment. Unlike Sheffield Wednesday, West Brom and Fulham, hardened old pros like Nat Lofthouse were not to be intimidated by destiny. Or by the noise reverberating from the United sections of the ground. Bolton's rugged, physical victory that day did not go down well with certain sections of the United support. On the way back from Wembley, their team bus was stoned as it made its way through Salford.

'It was like going through Cheyenne country' was how one Bolton player described the experience.

Bolton was about the only place that celebrated the victory. It still does. It is commemorated by a T-shirt on sale outside the club's Reebok Stadium. '03.05.58, Wembley Stadium,' it says. 'Bolton Wanderers 2 Munichs 0.' Semantics again.

For Harry Gregg in particular, the end of that season could not come soon enough. For him, Foulkes, Charlton, Viollet, Morgans, the survivors who played in that final, the ghosts of their lost comrades were everywhere, stalking every blade of the Wembley grass they had graced but a year before. 'Playing football after Munich was a saviour of your sanity, getting involved, letting off steam. But the games themselves were an anti-climax,' Gregg says. 'Right through the Cup run the games meant nothing. It was empty. Even the final, it was cold, cold.'

But that was not yet the end for United that season. There was still the small matter of the European Champions Cup semi-final, the very game the team had been playing for back in February when disaster had struck. Four days after defeat at Wembley, at an Old Trafford once again crackling and pulsing with emotion, Bobby Charlton, by now playing every game as if his life depended on it, was not available for selection. He was required for England duty in a friendly international against Portugal. Somehow, even without him, a mentally shattered United won the first leg against Milan 2-1, the estimable Ernie Taylor scoring the winner. Charlton was similarly obliged to be elsewhere for the second leg the following week. While United travelled to Milan by train, only to be defeated 4-0 in the San Siro, their best remaining player, the man on whom the rebirth of the club was to centre, was turning out for his country against Scotland in a home international at Wembley. Incredibly the FA refused Murphy's entreaty that he not be picked. Thus did the season that had begun in such optimism back in September with a 9-2 thrashing of Shamrock Rovers in the first round of the European Champions Cup before tragedy intervened, fizzle out in wistful fantasies about what might have been. Fantasies that were still being played out in the imagination of some supporters fifty years on.

Mind, there was time for one last moment of official pig-headedness. That summer UEFA invited United to compete in the following season's European Cup, along with Wolves, the Football League champions. It was a noble gesture, an offer that Hardman, Murphy and Busby, now back at work, were keen to take up. They sought the permission of the FA, which initially gave its blessing. But at the Football League, Alan Hardaker saw his chance for revenge. He refused to accept the FA's conciliatory attitude and insisted on a joint FA/Football League inquiry into the offer. All parties agreed to accept the outcome, which Hardaker ensured went his way after privately leaning on the investigating committee members. A joint FA/FL communiqué was issued, which read: 'The committee is of the opinion that, as by its name, this is a competition of Champion clubs, Manchester United FC does not qualify to take part in this season's competition. Consent is therefore denied.'

Two years after claiming the competition had no part in the football calendar, suddenly here was Hardaker defending its integrity. Never mind the hypocrisy, the upshot was, there would be no immediate return for United to Europe. The chance for catharsis would be put on hold. Hardman was right: like the survivors, like the victims' families, United would have to recover from Munich on their own, without any outside help. And on the terraces at Old Trafford, the sense of isolation, the idea of an authority unyielding in its anti-United instincts began to harden. From now on, it was us against them.

9

THE LONG (AND WINDING)
ROAD BACK

One Monday afternoon in the autumn of 1958 the Manchester United players were at Davyhulme Golf Club enjoying their usual collective rest and recuperation. Stan Crowther, the emergency recruit signed by Jimmy Murphy from Aston Villa just minutes before the first game after Munich, was not a golfer. Shouty and sweary, prone to face-offs and fisticuffs on the training ground, he really didn't have the patience for the game. So he was in the snooker room, playing billiards instead. Not that he was particularly good at that either. That afternoon he kept missing easy shots. Then he failed to sink the simplest of pots. Exploding with fury, he whacked his cue on the side of the table before breaking it into several small pieces over his knee. After he had finished raging, there was a quiet in the room. Everyone there knew the significance of what they had just seen. From that point on mad Stan was finished at Old Trafford. This was a representative of Manchester United – the man who wore the number-six shirt – behaving in a public place like a street hoodlum. As soon as Matt

Busby heard what had happened, Crowther was on his way to Chelsea. After all, that number six was a bit special. It was Big Dunc's shirt.

Eamon Dunphy recalls that Munich was never mentioned around Old Trafford when he joined United as a teenager in 1960. A commemorative clock was attached to the outside wall of the Scoreboard End in a special ceremony on 25 February that year. But Munich was not a topic of conversation. In fact nobody, but nobody uttered the word. Especially not in the manager's hearing.

Unspoken it might have been, yet Munich was already woven into the fabric of the place. Like the local smog, it hung heavy in the atmosphere. Every player on the staff knew they were treading in the footsteps of lost giants. And for some, like angry Stan Crowther, their shoe size was never going to be substantial enough to fit.

If anyone thought they might escape the comparison, there were plenty prepared to point out the inadequacies of those tasked with replacing the irreplaceable. In those early aftermath days the press, for a start, was never shy of sitting in evaluative judgement. Mark Pearson was the first to suffer from the contrast. A raw-boned, sharp-elbowed eighteen-year-old youth product, he was sent off against Burnley just a month or so after the crash. Bob Lord, the mouthy Burnley chairman, started it. In many ways Lord was the first to find derogatory meaning in the word Munich. Eager to articulate an annoyance at the huge attention that had come United's way following the crash, he was quoted in the papers the day after that game describing Jimmy Murphy's team as a bunch of Teddy boys. It was about as disparaging a remark as could be made at the time, what with the draped-coated, drainpipe-trousered, crêpe-soled fans of Bill Haley slashing up the cinema seats of the nation even as he spoke.

'There is too much sentiment about Manchester United,' added Lord. 'All the talk about Munich seems to have gone to the heads of the young players.'

Pearson, the centre forward with the slicked DA and chunky sideboards, was the main focus of such disdain. And the young lad hardly helped dispel the image when he was sent off again the following October. Pearson was immediately informed by half a dozen editorials that he was tarnishing the memory of the departed.

'Living Down the Teddy Boy Bogy' was the headline in *Football Monthly*. And that was above a sympathetic piece about the player. Such shadows were too long for him to escape from under. He was sold to Sheffield Wednesday in 1963.

The unspoken responsibility was way beyond the capacity of Albert Quixall, too. The Wednesday captain that first game back after Munich, he was Busby's first signing on his return to work. He cost a record fee – £45,000, a sum Harold Hardman was reluctant to part with. The United chairman was born a mere four years after his club. When he became acquainted with the red cheque book following the Great War, players cost a couple of hundred quid. He was finding it hard to accommodate to the new ways. As it happened, Busby also fretted at the cost. Wednesday were aware of United's plight and were not going to part with their best player without exploiting the moment financially. At one point in the tortuous negotiations, Busby was going to back out of the deal. But he had a new confidant in the boardroom. And over one of their regular Saturday-night steaks, Louis Edwards encouraged him to go for it: you have to speculate to accumulate, he told him and he travelled to Sheffield with the Boss to complete the deal.

It was, however, Hardman's instincts that proved to be the more accurate about Quixall. For a time the most expensive player in British history, the plume-haired inside forward proved himself to be what his fellow Yorkshireman Geoff Boycott would call 'a show pony'. Busby had been alerted to Quixall's talent by his son-in-law Don Gibson, who played with him at Hillsborough. When Don came to Chorlton with his wife Sheena to visit the Busbys in their new semi in King's Road, he would regale his host with tales of the man they called Quickie's skill on the training park. And indeed, he proved to be pretty good there, as he was when applying the finishing touches to a seven-goal rout (he once scored a hat-trick in a 5 0 shoeing of Wolves). It was during a full-on scrap on a muddy field in Bolton on a Tuesday evening that he was less effective. There he went missing. As his sometime colleague Dunphy, in a cruelly dismissive turn of phrase, suggests: 'Albert Quixall could do anything with a football, until you put an opposition on the field.'

He was a joker, mind, Quickie. Once, as the United players inspected the pitch in a freezing fog at White Hart Lane, they heard an odd drumming noise emanating from the murk. Peering through it, they could just about make out Quickie relieving himself on the centre spot. 'I've always wanted to piss all over Spurs,' he said.

That was one of his more sophisticated gags. There was something desperate about the practical jokes he inflicted on the dressing room. He was particularly fond of one involving a turd wrapped in fancy paper, which he would leave in a colleague's locker along with a note alleging it was a gift from a female admirer. The likes of Harry Gregg and Bill Foulkes were not often amused. The increasingly manic comedy turn was but a thin cover: Quixall was shot through with nerves almost from the moment he arrived at Old Trafford, gripped with a terror at the enormity of the task of replacing the fallen.

'He used to come out in big red blotches before games and was very agitated,' says Pat Crerand, who played with him for a season. 'We didn't realise at the time that he'd had a mental breakdown.'

But then, even if they had diagnosed the cause of his distress, who is to say anyone would have thought to intervene. This was, after all, the football club where you simply got on with it.

There was a giddying through-put of players in the couple of years after Munich who, in their different ways, failed to live up to requirements. Busby had never been much of a dealer in the transfer market. Between buying Tommy Taylor in March 1953 and recruiting Harry Gregg in December 1957, he had not troubled Hardman's sense of propriety once. But needs must. Any plans he might initially have had to shore things up with his own resources were hardly helped when, in December 1959, Wilf McGuinness, the youth-team player for whom he had such high hopes, shattered a leg in a game and was obliged to retire. Wilf became first-team coach, but it wasn't quite what Busby needed: he needed quality players. And he needed them fast. In a busy few months, he bought Noel Cantwell from West Ham, Maurice Setters from West Brom, Graham Moore from Chelsea, David Herd from Arsenal and Tony Dunne from Shelbourne. Not all of them settled in happily. Or quietly.

In his book *A Strange Kind of Glory*, Eamon Dunphy describes Old Trafford as a bitter, riven, unhappy place in those early sixties seasons. There were rows on the training ground, divisions in the dressing room, factions everywhere. For the younger players, Foulkes was a particular object of disdain. Sarcastically, they called him PB: Popular Bill. On one occasion there was a clear-the-air meeting in which senior players and Jack Crompton, the first-team coach, accused each other of letting down the United tradition. And Busby just stood by and let them get on with it. To the unschooled eye, he appeared to be doing little to address the problems. By the time Dunphy arrived he seemed peripheral. The original tracksuit manager was rarely seen on the training ground, leaving that sort of work to Murphy, McGuinness and Crompton. Instead he was ensconced in his office at Old Trafford, a distant, unapproachable figure.

The fact was, though he wouldn't admit to it or allow it to be known, Busby was still suffering the after-effects of Munich. Physically, the crash left him with a residue of problems in his leg and back. He was in pain much of the time. Mentally, he found it harder going than he ever imagined when he told Jean he would carry on in memory of the fallen. He looked haggard. The spry, trim, elegant figure pre-Munich was now universally referred to as 'the Old Man'. As the sixties began to roll, he had difficulty summoning up the reserves of energy to counter the drift.

Worse, his methodology seemed suddenly old-fashioned. Like the wider world, football took to the sixties looking to the white heat of technology. Modernism was everywhere. New methodology was being applied by a vibrant younger generation of managers and coaches, people like Alf Ramsey, Don Revie and Joe Mercer. Busby thought that playing the game was the best way to learn it. These new boys believed in lots of pre-prepared drills, teaching how to play to patterns and formulae. The trouble with bringing outsiders into Busby's closed world was that they weren't schooled in his philosophy. To incomers his 'Just go out and play' seemed trite. Cantwell was particularly dismissive. He told Dunphy he couldn't believe how lax and unfocused training was.

'Give it to a red shirt?' Cantwell raged, quoting one of the Old Man's favourite instructions. 'You don't need a fucking manager for that.'

And he was the club captain.

It hardly helped that Busby seemed to make some eccentric decisions. If buying Quixall appeared understandable at the time, getting rid of Dennis Viollet didn't. Electric-heeled and predatory, in the 1959–60 season Viollet scored thirty-two League goals. It remains a club record to this day. Nobody, not the Lawman, not Ruud, not Ronaldo, has matched him since. Moreover, those sharp-shooters played in good teams: Viollet did it in a season of shift and lack of focus.

His downfall was that he rubbed up against Busby's old Achilles heel: money. In 1961 a spirited campaign against football's maximum wage was launched by Jimmy Hill and the PFA, the body founded by Billy Meredith (who had died shamefully unnoticed by United in the autumn of 1958). After much lobbying the then ceiling – £20 a week – was abolished. At Fulham, Johnny Haynes was immediately gifted £100. Busby marked football's financial freedom by offering his senior players £25. Still, they

talked. Not just to each other, they talked to international colleagues, they talked to old muckers at other clubs. And they
discovered they were being left behind. As the new era dawned,
United were the worst payers in the First Division. Dennis
wanted more than that. He had a lifestyle to finance. He determined after Munich to celebrate his survival by making the
acquaintance of every single woman in Manchester (and quite a
few of the married ones as well). Busby didn't mind that so much:
it was what he perceived as greed he couldn't take. He suggested
if it was money that motivated him, then Dennis should look
elsewhere. So the record breaker was on his way to Stoke. Sure,
his subsequent career did not suggest Busby had made a mistake.
But who is to say what Viollet might have become had he stayed
at United.

John Giles, however, did not slip into quiet obscurity when
Busby decided to remove him. Giles was an inventive, aggressive,
intelligent midfielder, who became a fixture in the United side
from 1961. His problem was not so much financial as one of self-
worth: he thought himself better than Busby gave him credit for.
He wanted to play inside forward, not out on the wing as the
manager insisted. Unlike Bobby Charlton who was similarly cast
out to the periphery in those days, he did not keep his counsel. He
complained. Busby thought Giles was wrong. With unhappy
timing, for a couple of months following their discussions, Giles
was afflicted with an undiagnosed virus. Instead of seeking help
he did what Manchester United players were expected to do post-
Munich: he just got on with it. Watching his undistinguished
performances with greater scrutiny, Busby thought him expendable. He was sold to Leeds United, then languishing in the Second
Division. As he went on to become the fulcrum of Don Revie's all-
conquering side, Busby later admitted letting Giles go was the
biggest mistake of his career.

'I wanted to prove Matt wrong when I left Old Trafford,' reveals
Giles. 'And I think I did. I've great admiration for Matt Busby.
He's one of the great football men of all time and United wouldn't

be what they are today without him. My episode was merely a blip
on his career.'

That it happened in those unhappy post-Munich times was perhaps no coincidence.

As United bumbled along in mid-table mediocrity the crowd
showed its impatience. Numbers tailed off alarmingly from the
months after the crash when thousands had come to show their
solidarity. In the spring of 1962, when United sat at fifteenth in the
First Division, only 20,807 people turned up for the home match
against Aston Villa. Sentiment had by now largely dissipated.
What the fans wanted was proof of recovery. They wanted entertainment. And frankly, they were more likely to get that from Cliff
Richard and the Shadows playing at Belle Vue than they were
from watching the reds.

It was not a happy period.

That summer, however, something happened that spoke of ren-
aissance. Busby bought Denis Law. Such was the inflation
afflicting football's finances as the sixties kicked in, the sum
Torino wanted to send their homesick Scot back to Britain was
more than twice the record amount Busby had forked out for
Albert Quixall just three years before. He must have known
Hardman would not be happy. The chairman pointed out that he
had stumped for Cantwell, Setters, Quixall and the rest without
apparent return and here was the manager wanting to pay an
unheard-of £115,000. Such a sum would push the club into the red
and Hardman had been around in the thirties: he knew what it
was like to be saddled with debt. All too fresh in his memory
were images of Walter Crickmer forestalling a closure order. He
couldn't countenance such outlay. It was out of the question:
owing money, he counselled, should never be the way at Old
Trafford. The manager, however, had seen Law in action. He
knew what the boy who had come across the Pennines to watch
the first game after Munich could do on a football pitch.
Supported by Louis Edwards and Alan Gibson he got his way.

And every United fan who ever saw Law play will be forever thankful he did.

'Matt always said of all the players he had, the greatest was Law,' recalls Martin Edwards. 'I'd have to agree with that. I was a teenager in those days, going along to watch matches with Father. To me, Denis from 1963 to '67 was unbelievable. In the same way you could say Paul Scholes and Ruud van Nistelrooy did in 2003, or Cantona did in '96, he won the League for us in '65. He was just outstanding.'

Edwards was not the only young man who found Law compulsive viewing. It wasn't just the quicksilver finishing or the way he could seemingly hang in the air before applying his head to a cross that made him stand out. It wasn't even the manner he acknowledged a goal, arm raised, finger pointed skywards, the cuff of his shirt tugged over his fist, a trademark celebration copied in playgrounds across Manchester and beyond. There was something else about him, something edgy. He was always in his opponents' faces, full of sardonic wit. Gordon Banks remembers diving into the fray during an England–Scotland match to grab the ball. As he lay there for a moment, eyes tight shut, collecting his thoughts, the great keeper could feel someone standing over him. He glanced up and saw Law there, looking down, grinning. 'Aye, Gordy,' the Scot said. 'And I'll always be here. Waiting.'

Law had a poor image among commentators and pressmen, his frequent outbursts of sharp temper regarded as evidence of football's wider decline. When he was sent off – and it was often in those early days – the tutted comparisons with the Munich lost were implicit.

'Black Saturday' was the headline in *Football Monthly*. 'Saturday November 16th 1963 was a black day for the so-called sporting spirit of English football when Denis Law, Britain's most expensive and talented player, was sent off ... When will they ever learn? When will they ever learn?'

For the teenagers filling the Stretford End this was precisely what made Denis the King. Just as Peter Cook and his Fringe

chums were announcing the end of deference to politicians, Law
was a harbinger of a new era on the football field in which tugging
the forelock – to the referee or anyone else – was no longer an
instinct. He was anti-establishment, he was the outlaw. To the lads
on the terraces here was someone who fitted the image of what a
United player should be. Here was their new hero. And he was a
hero to plenty of others too. Unless they were employed as football
journalists. Law won the *Football Monthly* readers' vote for player
of the year three times in the sixties. He never won the Football
Writers' award.

In his early days at Old Trafford, the Lawman was everywhere
on the pitch, coming deep to fetch the ball, tackling back, buzzing
across the turf. But Busby saw his future as a poacher, using his
malevolent streak to maximum effect in the opposition penalty
box. In order to push him forward, Busby bought Pat Crerand
from Celtic to supply the long balls from the back that would set
him free. It was an inspired piece of casting. Crerand was the
player who most reminded the manager of his own way with a
ball: not blessed with pace – all right, he was slow – but with an
ability to pass that had few peers. Plus – and this fact was not lost
on Busby – this fiery Catholic brought up in the Gorbals could
look after both himself and those around him. Never mind what
Bob Lord might say, a decent football team needs a bit of the Teddy
boy. Particularly in the sixties, when hard men lurked in ambush
in every defence in the land.

Crerand was a man with opinions. He could pick an argument
with a cardboard box, more so if the cardboard box gave hint of
any Loyalist tendencies. With a temper that made Stan Crowther
look like the secretary-general of the United Nations, he had fallen
out with virtually everyone at his beloved Celtic, despairing at
what he saw as a total lack of direction there. But unlike Noel
Cantwell, on arrival at United he found Busby an immediately
impressive figure. A man who would in later life chase half a
dozen trouble-seeking Manchester City fans out of his pub with a
baseball bat, Crerand was not easily intimidated. Busby, though,

could reduce him to a wobble with just a sigh of disapproval. Crerand – never the most organised of individuals – remembers arriving late for a bus to an away game at Stoke. Without raising his voice, Busby gave him a mother and father of a dressing-down: 'Patrick, you must be a very important person. You have kept the directors of Manchester United waiting. You have kept your team-mates waiting. You have kept the press waiting. And you have kept me waiting. It must be wonderful to be as important as you are.'

Crerand was devastated and recalls sitting in gloomy intro-spection for the rest of the journey south to the game. That, he says forty years later, is the respect that built United. And by the time Crerand appeared, the Old Man's managerial aura was back in full working operation.

When he arrived, Crerand found an Old Trafford looking a tasty bet for relegation. Through the frozen winter of 1963 they barely accumulated a League point, ending up only two places off the trapdoor. In the FA Cup, though, things began to thaw. After not playing a single game between Boxing Day and March due to the weather, the Cup run came in a mad rush of rearrangements. Huddersfield, Aston Villa, Chelsea, Coventry and then South-ampton in the semi-finals were beaten. At Wembley in the final United overwhelmed Leicester City with a display of attacking football that reminded everyone of the old Matt Busby magic, the one that for a time appeared to have been mislaid in the Munich snow. Law was astonishing, Crerand and Charlton leather-lunged in the cause, even Quixall had a good game. Cantwell was so excited by victory, as he made the lap of honour, he chucked the Cup high into the air, only to get a bollocking from a Wembley commissionaire.

'That's the FA Cup, Mr Cantwell,' the jobsworth tutted. 'I think you should treat it with more respect.'

'Don't worry, I knew I was going to catch it,' the red captain replied. 'I played cricket for Ireland.'

It was fifteen years since Busby last won the Cup. It was five years since Munich. There was something symmetrical about his way with an anniversary. What pleased the manager more than any neat tying of historical strands, however, was that with Crerand and Law added to a core of Charlton, Gregg, Foulkes, Herd, Dunne and the young half back Nobby Stiles, United were beginning to resemble a team. What's more, as Crerand recalls, it gave them an injection of confidence. 'After winning the Cup, we realised that we could then win anything,' he says. 'It was the start of our good run in the 1960s, much like Alex Ferguson's success in 1990 was the start of what has become the greatest era in United's history.'

More than that, though, as the summer began, Busby knew what lay around the corner. He knew that lurking in the background, banging in the goals for Jimmy Murphy's youth team, scaring every poor full back in the reserve league, was a talent that he suspected from the first moment he clapped eyes on him would count as his finest ever discovery, a talent to outshine even the lost Babes. His surname summed him up. It was Best, George Best.

It is possible for one player to define a football club. Thirty-five years on from his heyday, when we think of Ajax, we still imagine a sophisticated, clever operation, innovators at the application of science to the game. We think, in short, of Johan Cruyff. Bayern Munich, too, are still the side of Franz Beckenbauer, haughty, elegant, just a touch pleased with themselves. While Milan are Paolo Maldini: unruffled, unflappable, the essence of cool.

Manchester United, however, present a more complicated face to the world. This is a club whose character can be said to derive from the combination of three extraordinary men. From 1963, by one of those pieces of football serendipity that generally occur only in the most fevered imagination during the sleeping hours, the three of them played in the same football team. They were never close, indeed at times they hated each other; I was once witness to Best publicly shredding the reputation of Charlton in the most vituperative, inelegant terms. As people they trod very different paths. One was spiky and rebellious, anti-establishment and ironic. Another was the establishment's athletic face, noble and upright, shot through with a sense of duty, the last Corinthian. The third was a mercurial gadfly, hedonistic, self-absorbed and self-destructive. Together, however, they made something that had never been seen before. Together their disparate talents dovetailed to create football from another orbit. Together Law, Charlton and Best – Old Trafford's golden trinity – made Manchester United.

Best was the last to arrive: the other two were both internationals before he had celebrated his sixteenth birthday. For all the brilliance of his nature, there was nurture involved in his story. Bob Bishop, Joe Armstrong's man in Northern Ireland, was absolutely right when he sent a scouting report to Busby informing him that he had discovered a genius. Genius he might have been, but he was also tiny, a frail, spindly fifteen-year-old when he arrived in Manchester from the Protestant east of Belfast. Jimmy Murphy set about toughening him up. He was dispatched to digs in Chorlton with a certain Mrs Fullaway. The first of many hundreds of women in Manchester and beyond to fall head over heels in love with this gentle, soft-voiced, blue-eyed boy, Mrs Fullaway was charged with giving him some beef. As she shovelled in the stodge, Murphy worked him round the back. He knew the shin saboteurs of the First Division would be waiting to take the young lad apart. So he got Foulkes and Gregg and the old hackers to have a go at him in the kickarounds. Murphy himself would go in there, try to slam him up against the concrete wall at the back of the stand. Best would dance through the tackles, his balance something that had to be seen to be believed. He'd nutmeg one, skip past another, swivel past a third. As he watched him dance, Murphy would shout at him to provide the end-product, get a cross in, look, just pass the fucking thing. And the kid would merely dip his shoulder, beat another man and bend the ball between the two iron posts that served as a goal round the back.

Then, after the game, he'd smile diffidently as Murphy ruffled his hair, and go off and work on his own. He wasn't hungry for self-improvement, he was ravenous. He trained himself to be as strong with his left foot as he was with his right. He hung a tennis ball from a door frame just out of his reach then leapt and leapt again until he could reach it with his forehead, at which point he would strap it up higher and start again. Busby watched it all. When the kid shot home to Belfast, hamstrung with homesickness, it was Busby who persuaded him back. When the kid made his debut in the Youth Cup, Busby was there on the touchline. He was always there, Busby. He knew what he had here and he was not going to lose this one. Not like he'd lost the others.

And, from the start, the affection was mutual. 'If we were playing a Youth Cup game and he was there, I could feel his presence in the stands,' Best once said. 'I played for him.'

Best was still a work in progress when he made his first-team debut against West Brom in the autumn of 1963. He didn't play again in the first team for four months, before returning in a Boxing Day fixture away at Burnley when he destroyed the full back John Angus, leaving him, in Pat Crerand's memorable phrase, suffering from 'twisted blood'. That was the game, incidentally, in which was observed for the first time a new phenomenon. The United fans turning up to Turf Moor celebrated Best's arrival by fighting with the locals before, during and after the game. They remembered Bob Lord's remarks about Munich – how everyone made too much of a fuss about a few dead footballers – and they looked for someone to pay for the insult. As they threw their punches, they reckoned they were justified. They reckoned they were defending United's honour.

Not that anyone at the club saw it like that. An embarrassed board hoped it was a one-off. They insisted that the 'punch-up youths' – as *Football Monthly* coyly referred to them – were not representative of the vast majority of United's supporters. Busby just sighed and got on with it. Besides, he had real work to do. As

Best continued to give full backs hernias, the manager knew the time was right. Now he knew he could play the new lad on the wing, move Charlton inside and with Law up front, he'd have a triangular heart to his team that would be unstoppable. Just thinking about it was therapy. Suddenly the pains in the back and legs began to ease. Now he had something.

Mind you, the Lawman didn't seem to need anyone else that season. In 1963–64, he scored forty-six goals in all competitions, still a club record. He did it, as the slashing, scything tackles flew in around his ankles, without any protection from referees. In fact, what with his habit of getting his retaliation in first, the officials largely sided with the ankle assassins trying to kick him into the Manchester Royal Infirmary. But Law was brave. And he was spiteful. He knew the best route to revenge against those who hacked at his hamstrings was to score. So score he did, just to hurt them. With Law slamming them in, suddenly United – the team that had been facing relegation twelve months previously, the team that Cantwell had so recently complained were a shambles – were contenders everywhere. For the first time since the pre-Munich days, they were up there in the League, were in the last stages of the FA Cup and – more to the point – were back in Europe. Sure, it was the lesser competition, the newly introduced European Cup Winners' Cup. But it was still Europe. And when they cruised past Wilhelm 11 and then the holders Spurs, they looked good for the semis after beating Sporting Club of Portugal 4-1 at home in the first leg of the quarter-finals. But the confidence that Crerand saw seeping into the team on the Wembley turf the previous May was in danger of turning into cockiness. In Lisbon, Sporting won 5-0, the worst defeat in United's European history. It was hard to know who had played worse: the hapless David Gaskell replacing the injured Gregg in goal, the useless defence, the spineless midfield or the toothless attack. In *The Times*, Geoffrey Green reported that 'Law and Charlton were reduced to nonentities'.

Pat Crerand still finds it embarrassing to talk of the game now, not least because it was the first and only time that he saw Busby lose it completely in the dressing room. 'He ranted and raged at us,' he recalls. 'What Matt was going to do to us was nobody's business. Murder was the least of it. He said our performance was an insult to the people of Manchester and that we had let him down badly.'

Busby didn't mention Munich – he never did – but everyone present knew it was there, lurking at the back of his complaint. They had thrown it away, his chance for everything he was working for. To compound their misdemeanour, a bunch of them went out in Lisbon that night and royally drowned their sorrows. The youth-team graduate Phil Chisnall and old timer Maurice Setters, two of the drinkers and two whose reputation had been least enhanced by their performance in Portugal, were to be the example. Both were quickly transferred, with Chisnall heading west along the East Lancs Road to become the last player ever to move between United and Liverpool.

If the manager's ruthless streak was back in full working order, so was his youth system. For the first time since 1956, that year United won the Youth Cup, with Best the shining light of a team that also included David Sadler, Bobby Noble and John Fitzpatrick. As reward for their success Busby took Murphy and his boys to Zurich in the summer, to compete in the annual youth tournament. One night the lads went out on the town, where, for the first time in his life, Best had a drink. He only had three pints of lager, but he was trolleyed, throwing up out of the window of the cab on the way back to the hotel. It was, as he recalled years later, the start of something.

Back in Manchester Old Trafford was selected to be one of the grounds to host games in the 1966 World Cup. Louis Edwards had become chairman on Hardman's death . He decided to mark his elevation by making a statement of intent about United's future direction. He was going to rebuild the Pop Side for the World Cup. But in its place was not going to be any old football stand. Busby and Edwards had enjoyed themselves on many a night in the private boxes incorporated in the new grandstand at Manchester's racecourse (these days the building is the centre-piece of Salford University's student village). They believed that by offering a similar service at Old Trafford they could attract some of Manchester's big-spending monied types, the sort they saw flashing the cash at the track or at the dogs or at the Cromford Club on a Saturday night. There were plenty around. In the sixties employment was high in Manchester; the factories still churned out tons of goods, the deindustrialisation that was to hit the city so hard was a good decade away. For now, there was money to be taken in town. So they commissioned Atherden Fuller, the same architects who had just spruced up the racecourse, to come up with a design for a £300,000 cantilever structure incorporating thirty-four executive boxes. These were the first in the country at football. And the prospectus was effusive about the facilities: 'There will be waiter-service available for refreshments, and a private lift will transfer spectators from ground level to the boxes, which will be approached by a luxuriously carpeted lounge. The boxes will be heated and high-class refreshment bars will be installed.'

Les Olive, writing in *Football Monthly*, explained that the boxes 'have been taken up by business houses in the city to entertain their clients in the best possible surroundings – a sort of Soccer-Ascot if you like'.

The first person to sign up for a lease was Paddy McGrath, Busby's good friend, owner of the Cromford Club. No one would ever suggest Paddy was a gangster, though he did once turn up armed to a meeting with the Kray twins at the Midland Hotel. He was just a businessman, a leading member of Manchester's spend-ing classes, a guy who liked a good night out in good company. Now he could have a good afternoon out in good company at the football. It was an important moment in the making of Manchester United, the opening of that stand. No longer would this be a club belonging exclusively to Manchester's working class. Those with a bit of cash, those with aspirations, the fancy dans, from within the city's boundaries and from beyond, were being invited to join the party.

And what a party it was promising to be. Before the very eyes of the cloth-capped Lowry figures in the Scoreboard paddock, of the boisterous young lads in the Stretford End, of the swanks and sophisticates in the North Stand boxes, of Manchester's disparate clans, gangs and classes, Busby's third great team was taking shape.

They won the League in 1965: Bobby, George and Denis. They took turns to dazzle – Bobby bamboozled Blackburn away, George gorged on Chelsea, Denis did for Everton – and sometimes they'd do it together.

'We were the Englishman, the Irishman and the Scotsman,' says Law. Except they weren't a joke. 'Sometimes we played as if we were one person.'

And if they didn't click, then Pat Crerand would do it, or David Herd. Or John Connelly, the pacy winger bought from Burnley who patrolled the opposite wing to Best and contributed fifteen goals that year. They weren't afraid of a barney, either. In a drawn FA Cup semi-final against Leeds that was universally condemned in the press as a landmark in football's shameful decline into thuggery, Law ended up with his shirt half off his back after fighting with Bobby's brother Jack. Crerand, meanwhile, was wrestling with Billy Bremner: a fight waiting to happen. Taking its lead from the scrapping on the pitch, the fighting on the terraces and afterwards on the streets of Sheffield was no less intense. It was worse in the replay at Nottingham. A United fan ran on the pitch and tried to punch the referee. And a couple of Leeds supporters ended up chucked in the River Trent behind the City ground's main stand. From which it might be deduced that United lost the replay, just as they lost in the replayed European Fairs Cup semi against Ferencvaros. But they beat Leeds to the League title. Which, in Busby's mind, was more than adequate recompense.

Nobby Stiles reckons that the most enjoyable season of his

career. Pat Crerand calls it the best team he ever played in. There may be a hint of nostalgia in their memories: in many ways that was the last season of the old United, the last year they were a mere provincial football club, the last year their foibles and fancies could remain outside the wider public gaze. In 1964 the BBC had begun broadcasting *Match of the Day*. It was television's first foray into League football. With television came exposure. And, just as United's position at the top of the pile in 1993 allowed them to exploit the arrival of satellite coverage in a way that eclipsed their rivals, so here they were in 1965, at the precise moment television's unblinking eye was first focused on its weekly rhythms, at the head of the game. Into every living room in the country every Saturday night of the season came the glories of Law, Charlton and, more to the point, Best. Now you could enjoy United if you lived in Devizes as much as you could if you hailed from Denton. The secret was out. And the corporations of the growing service economy were soon alerted to the potential benefit of connecting their brand to football's surging public prominence.

Best celebrated his nineteenth birthday on 22 May 1965. He was still lodging, along with David Sadler, at Mrs Fullaway's. His life was simply about football: training, playing, resting. Plus improving, always looking to improve. Week nights he'd be at Mrs F's playing crib for a few pennies with his fellow lodgers. Only on Saturdays would he go out, and then it was a modest expedition, perhaps culminating in a couple of pints and a discreet bit of birding it. He never had a moment's trouble in that department. He was different, Bestie. A gentle sort, not brash or brazen, he was neatly dressed, liked his clothes, always tried to keep in touch with the latest mod trends seeping up the newly opened motorway from London. There was a fragility about him; girls found something irresistible in his vulnerability. According to Crerand, the other players soon became fascinated with how he did it. After he was the first to introduce shampoo to the dressing room they all began to bring in their own bottles, thinking that might do the trick. Before that the players had scrubbed their scalps in carbolic soap, which may well explain the rapid disappearance of Bobby Charlton's hair. Yet despite all this, Best was still merely a footballer. A great one in the making, but just a kid footballer.

What changed everything was Wednesday 9 March 1966. United were back in the European Champions Cup. There was no Football League obfuscation this time; by now Europe was a significant part of English football's season. After easy strolls in the early rounds in Helsinki and East Berlin, for the quarter-finals they were drawn against Benfica. It was not an easy prospect, at the time only Madrid were more decorated in European competition. Benfica had in their ranks Eusébio, just named European Player of the Year and reckoned by most commentators to be closing in on Pelé as the world's best. United won the first leg at home 3-2 taking, according to *The Times*, 'a precarious lead' to Portugal for the return. Their last trip to Lisbon had left Busby incandescent. This one would leave him glowing. He issued instructions in the changing room to keep things tight. Best, he said afterwards, must have had cotton wool in his ears. Within a quarter-hour, United were three up. Best scored twice and laid on the third for Connelly. They ended up winning 5-1, Benfica's heaviest home defeat in their European history. Law thought it the finest team performance of his career. That night Best was just extraordinary. He played as he did round the back, a carefree, happy-go-lucky sprite, entirely unconcerned by reputation. His second goal, darting through the middle of the Portuguese defence as if it were constructed of traffic cones, leaving rivals dazed and dazzled in his wash, prompted Kenneth Wolstenholme on the television commentary to ask the question: 'What more can you say about this boy?' Plenty, as it turned out.

The next morning Best went walking along Estoril beach, near the United team's hotel. As he himself explained in one of his many autobiographies: 'Every bikini on the beach wanted my autograph, some wanted a snip of my hair. The men were just as bad. I was having my first taste of adulation and I'd be a liar if I said I didn't enjoy it.'

On a stall along the promenade he bought a broad-brimmed sombrero as a souvenir. And, as the team stepped off the plane on their return to Ringway, Best popped the hat on his head. According to David Meek, the *Manchester Evening News*'s United correspondent, he did it self-consciously. He knew what he was doing. He had a canny eye for publicity and he was about to open a boutique, which could do with a bit of press. A bit of press was an understatement. The next morning, on the front page of the *Daily Mirror*, there was a picture of Best, hat atop his thick head of hair, smiling broadly. The caption read: 'El Beatle'.

That was it. One word made the connection. The Beatles were tearing up the script on a daily basis. They made up the rules. As the four working-class lads from Liverpool went about their business, the sixties were forming around them, the entrenched barriers of class and status collapsing in their tread. Wherever they went, the air was thick with pheromones. Screaming became a national pastime. And here in football was their spiritual confrère. When he first appeared in United's team, there were lookalike pictures in *Football Monthly* pointing up his uncanny resemblance to Gene Pitney. A year or two later, never mind old-style American crooners, now his hair had grown and his jacket turned to leather, Bestie was being associated with the most fashionable, dynamic and above all talented group of young people the country had ever produced. Now he was the fifth Beatle.

As the Beatles had made the country hungry for the new, styles changed with breakneck speed. George Best helped satisfy the craving, he was one of those filling in the gap the moptops created. Youth had been at the core of the United story for over a decade. But this was youth of a different kind. This was youth in the ascendant, upward mobility at its most intoxicating. The fifth Beatle was instantly elevated. Overnight he broke beyond football's restricted boundaries. He was wanted by fashion houses, by women's magazines for clothes shoots, by sausage manufacturers to promote their bangers. Everyone craved connection with him: they named potato crisps after him, they got his endorsement on cologne, his signature Stylo Matchmaker football boots with the laces to the side became the must-have for every schoolboy aspirant in the country. It helped, naturally, that he was the most handsome young man of his time. It helped that the camera could not get enough of his vulnerability. More than anything it helped that he was talented beyond precedent at his chosen calling. Style and substance: what was there not to like?

And Manchester United could jog along in his wake. There was nothing remotely modern about Matt Busby or Bobby Charlton or Louis Edwards. But because they were connected to Bestie, they became modern by association. United were football's fashion leaders. Mind you, they didn't know what to do about it. Nobody did. There was no route map for the direction Bestie was heading.

'I was in an incredible situation,' Best told Eamon Dunphy. 'I was getting ten thousand letters a week so I had to employ three girls just to answer the mail. I was driving a Rolls-Royce, I was going out with Miss England, but I was living in digs.'

That was the club rule: single players lived in digs. And Bestie was definitely, defiantly single. He was soon playing a field far wider than could ever be accommodated at Mrs Fullaway's. He needed out, he needed space. But he didn't argue with the club rules, he just rented a flat in Manchester with his City chum Mike Summerbee and there he would entertain the fruits of his fame, before heading back to Mrs F's for form's sake. Busby, who prided himself on knowing everything his players got up to, who could track Dennis Viollet's every liaison on a Manchester street map, hadn't a clue. Why? Because this was something new, moving at a pace he could not comprehend. He didn't so much take his eye off the ball as never saw it coming.

Besides, why should he worry? Where it mattered, Best was more than doing the business for him. He was a ferocious trainer, he was always there in matches, bravery personified. He didn't even argue about money, unlike so many others. There was no need. He was earning so much from his off-field activities, he treated his United earnings as little more than a bit of spare change and never asked for more. So integral had he become to United's progress that when he went down with cartilage problems before the emotional return to Belgrade for a European Cup semi against Partisan, Busby ordered he be strapped up and play anyway. He could barely run and United were out.

Denis Law can hardly believe even now what an opportunity was missed that year. Here was the team who had destroyed Benfica, battered them, failing to overcome very modest opposition. 'Sometimes you look back with regret and that was a big regret,' he says. 'We should have won the European Cup that year. We should have been the first British club to do it. We should have beaten Celtic to it. But we played too many games, too many heavy pitches.'

Busby was distraught after the game. 'We'll never win the European Cup now,' he said to Pat Crerand. And Crerand thought he saw, for the first time in the Old Man's face, a look of defeat.

That summer England won the World Cup, a victory achieved with three United players, Charlton, Stiles and Connelly playing a part. And the following season it all came right for a Scotsman. Wherever Busby took his boys to play, people came out to watch; United attracted over a million paying customers to grounds around the country in 1966–67. The average gate at Old Trafford was 53,800. Entertainment was on the menu and people went to great lengths to ensure they were there to experience it at first hand.

'We used to catch the bus from Woodsend about twelve o'clock for a three o'clock kick-off,' recalls Michael Webster, then a young teenager mainlining on the adrenalin of United. 'Even when we arrived, the queues were vast and would snake right down the United Road. The turnstiles would open two hours before kick-off and we'd rush in and stand on the left side [of the Stretford End] with all the other Woodsend lads, about twenty of us. It was the highlight of your week, no question.'

Woodsend, near Urmston, is only about five miles from Old Trafford. But the fame of Busby's boys meant there were people coming from much further away to witness it in person. The buses lined up outside Old Trafford cricket ground ready to take fans back to Oxfordshire, Birmingham, Herefordshire, Cornwall even. Dozens came up on the trains to support United from London, the cockney reds. Andy Walsh recalls a man from Hertfordshire, a regular in the Stretford End paddock, berating him once for missing a home game.

'I had to get up at six this morning to get here, you only live about five minutes' walk away,' the man said to Walsh. 'You've no idea how lucky you are.'

United were now the nation's team. Those without familial attachment to their local club could find in United glamour by association. Munich, Law, Best and Charlton: no other operation in England had a mythology as potent. If they couldn't get to matches they could watch on telly, or ogle Bestie in the fashion pages. Entertainment was what the crowds wanted and there was plenty of it about. Football in the mid-sixties had become an adjunct of showbiz. Every team had its teasers and jugglers. There were great sides everywhere: Bill Shankly was building Liverpool into a supreme sporting engine, Don Revie's Leeds were methodical and scientific, Joe Mercer's Manchester City had a trio of fliers of their own in Summerbee, Bell and Lee.

None of those, however, were capable of doing what the United of Denis, George and Bobby could do. That season, after losing on Boxing Day, United did not lose another game in the League. The denouement of their year, the game they were crowned champions, was the moment that sealed the myth. At Upton Park they beat West Ham 6-1. This was the side containing three of England's World Cup winners, Bobby Moore, Geoff Hurst and Martin Peters. But whereas West Ham relied disproportionately on the Jules Rimet contingent, United could back up their gilded trio with

competitors of the tenacity of Stiles, Crerand, Foulkes and the new
keeper Alex Stepney, brought in to replace the frequently injured
Gregg. This was a team all right. Everyone took note. Particularly
the cheeky cockney scamps who followed West Ham and gave a
traditional East-End welcome to the visiting hordes by chucking
bricks at them through the game.

Busby, though, didn't dwell on that. He had other things on his
mind: the glorious nature of his creation. 'There are times when all
the uncertainties of football disappear,' he said after the game.
'You have a sense that your players can do anything. That is the
most wonderful sensation for a manager.'

It was, he added, his finest hour.

But even in victory, even in glory, there was, unrecognised at
the time, a poignant hint of decay to come. There is a photograph
of the United side in the dressing room afterwards, toasting their
championship in champagne (Best, interestingly, is the only one
without a glass in his hand). Ten of them – Stepney, Brennan,
Dunne, Foulkes, Crerand, Stiles, Aston, Best, Charlton and Sadler – were to taste even further glory a year hence. The odd one
out, the one who was to miss the pinnacle of Busby's achievement, is Law. His reserves of good fortune in staying one step
ahead of those out to do him damage were on the point of exhaustion. The broad grin filling his face in the Upton Park dressing
room that day was about the last he would wear as a United
player. Injured midway through the following season, the King
was to spend much of his next six years at United in the treatment
room, his talent snagged on the studs of those not fit to tie the
cords on his regal robes. You wouldn't know it at the time that
picture was taken, but, after a mere three years of untrammelled
glory together, United's golden trinity were effectively about to be
shorn of a limb.

It was then that Best upped his game. Both on and off the park.
In every respect, in every moment of his life, in 1968 George Best
was living it. Stuart Hall, later the cackling master of ceremonies of
It's a Knockout, was a television reporter in Manchester at the time.

He recalls how Best became the epicentre of the city's social scene; in the sixties Manchester swung round Georgie. Wherever he went he made the place buzz. Socially, he didn't mix that much with his fellow players. This wasn't out of snobbery – he had a lot of time for Paddy and Fitz and big Dave Sadler – it was curiosity. A lively, eager, searching mind, he found company with lawyers (George Carman, the noted libel brief, was a big drinking buddy), with writers, with television folk (Michael Parkinson was a producer at Granada and became a close confidant). Germaine Greer was a young researcher at the television company in those days and remembers thinking Bestie the most gorgeous thing she had ever seen. He became the ultimate prize for every woman in town. At times it got silly. At times the only place he could escape was the football pitch.

But there was much on offer there. The year United won the title, Celtic won the European Cup, beating Internazionale in Lisbon with a team made up of players who hailed from within twelve miles of Celtic Park. It was a Glasgow team of Glasgow men. The challenge was now there for Busby: if Jock Stein could do it, he must. Everything in 1968 was about Europe. Sure, United ran their neighbours City close for the title, only losing out to them on the last day. But that was just a footnote to their ambition.

It began in straightforward fashion, a victory over the Maltese champions Hibernians, a tie that split loyalties on the island down the middle. For many Maltese, since Munich United had been their club. There was a prospering supporters' club on the island, whose clubhouse amounted to a shrine to the reds. They threw a big party for the visitors, a reception committee whose warmth brought a tear to many a visiting eye. After the tricky, dirty Yugoslav champions Sarajevo (Pat Crerand inevitably had a fight in the tunnel at their place, incensed by the violent treatment of Law and Best), it was the Poles of Górnick Zabrze. Górnick were no pushovers. In the previous round they beat Dynamo Kiev, who had previously dispatched the holders Celtic. United's 2-1 victory over the two legs was less about the glories of Law, Best and

Charlton and more about the qualities of rugged determination personified by Crerand, Foulkes and Stiles. It brought them into confrontation in the semi-final with Real Madrid, the one team in world football more exalted than United. Back in the fifties Busby had reckoned that if his Babes beat Madrid they would win the Cup. It was an assessment no less valid ten years on. In the time since Munich, while United had been in one Champions Cup semi, Madrid had been in the final five times, winning three. These were the real deal.

In the home leg Bestie scored the only goal. It was a tense, technical game, largely dominated by Madrid's back line. Many of the 63,000 crowd went home nervy, not convinced that what they had seen was enough. The referee enjoyed it, mind. Mr Yashvili, from the Russian Federation, was afterwards effusive in his assessment of one of the participants. 'The number one gentleman on the field was Bobby Charlton,' he said. 'I have never had such pleasure in taking a match.'

At the Bernabéu stadium, United were in the big time. Around 110,000 fans packed its steepling stands. By now Law was crocked, facing an appointment with the surgeon's knife that ultimately never quite sorted his troubled knee. In his stead came Brian Kidd, an eighteen-year-old from Nobby Stiles's old school in Collyhurst. Twenty-one-year-old Johnny Aston, son of the 1948 regular and one-time United coach, had also established himself on the left wing: in the most demanding of circumstances Busby's faith in youth was undimmed. Madrid took an easy, early 2-0 lead, and even when Kidd's harrying forced a defender to turn the ball into his own net, they didn't look troubled and extended their lead further to 3-1 at the interval.

It was the most vital half-time of Busby's career. Initially it seemed he could not rise to it. Bobby Charlton recalls in the break's first few minutes he looked beaten. Shattered. He said nothing. No one did. Not even Jimmy Murphy. There was silence in the dressing room. It was as if they were at a funeral for the Old Man's ambitions. Then someone piped up that they were only one behind on aggregate. It seemed to break the spell. Busby became animated instantly. He told Aston and Best to move out wider, he told Kidd to push on, he instructed Sadler to move up from the back, squeeze down the space.

'We can do it,' he said as they went out.

And do it they did. Sadler did as he was told and got up to score a second. In those days away goals didn't count double, but it was still enough to ensure United of a replay. They weren't to need it. With twelve minutes to go, Best went on a mazy run and, after beating his full back, popped the ball into the area after catching a glimpse of a red shirt in there. It belonged, to Best's evident astonishment, to Bill Foulkes. The Munich survivor side-footed the ball into the net.

'If I'd known it was Bill, I'd never have passed it,' Best was to say later. 'He always blasted them over the bar.'

Busby cried in the dressing room afterwards. Unashamed and unabashed. Charlton, too, was overwhelmed. He sensed destiny at work. Bill Foulkes scoring was just too much for it to be coincidence: this was all about Munich. Others were less spiritual in their analysis. Geoffrey Green in *The Times* suggested that 'in the end it was English temperament, fibre and morale that won through'.

That combination of Best and Foulkes responsible for the final goal, the new and the old, the dashing and the grounded, the gilded and the workaday: that was Busby's United writ large.

The final at Wembley on 29 May 1968 saw the biggest exodus from Manchester to London in history. United were to take on Benfica, a side bent on revenge for the humiliation they had suffered at red hands three seasons before. Nearly eighty thousand United fans filled the stadium, hoovering up the neutral tickets on the black market in a manner that was to become familiar over the next forty years. The crowd that evening was in marked contrast to the last time United had been at Wembley, only five years previously. Then, for the FA Cup in 1963, it was still old-style football: collars and ties, rattles, the odd rosette. Now it was younger, so much younger. Reflecting the rising tide of youth everywhere from San Francisco to the Paris streets, these were kids on the Wembley terraces. In parkas and Harrington jackets and suede desert boots. There were scarves everywhere, hats with Best and Law's names painted on, banners reading 'United Kings of Football' and 'Man United Champions of Europe'. This was not the club's official merchandise: they didn't run to that sort of thing back then. It was all home-made, messy, amateurish, but it was work shot through with affection and pride. They were noisy too, these fans, full of the exuberance of youth, raucous with their chants and cat calls. They adopted the Beatles song 'Hello, Goodbye' in honour of the young local boy at the heart of United's effort, Brian Kidd. 'Eusébio, and I say Kiddo' it ran.

'As a Mancunian and a red, you can imagine how proud that made me feel,' says Kidd now.

The fans were rude at times. Earthy and funny. With their kinship and war stories, they thought of themselves as a second United team, complimentary to the lads on the pitch. But just as much a part of the story. 'There was definitely a sense of destiny,' says Jon Shine, a lifelong cockney red who was seventeen that night and got a ticket outside Wembley from a member of the Maltese Supporters' Club who had a spare. 'I've never known a manager as truly loved as Busby was. Everyone wanted it to happen for him. There are certain nights when you know it's written. And this was one of them.'

The moment Shine knew it was to be United's night came almost at the end of the ninety minutes. United in blue, as they had been twenty years before to win Busby's first trophy, had ridden their luck. After a cagey, undistinguished ninety minutes, with the score at 1-1, Eusébio – for once escaping the terrier-like attentions of Stiles – stood about six yards out from the United goal with the ball at his feet. He blasted at it with all his dwindling reserves of energy. From the moment he applied his foot to the ball, he seemed certain to be sending the Cup back to Portugal. But somehow Stepney got in the way of the fusillade. He even managed to keep hold of it. That was the moment fate kept her eye on Busby and United. Eusébio, in one of the great moments of sportsmanship, acknowledged it by shaking Stepney's hand in congratulation.

As the final whistle went announcing extra time, Ken Jones in the *Daily Mirror* reported that 'United were stretched like blue shadows on the green of Wembley's turf, sucking at the night air, desperately trying to slap life back into weary legs. Busby hovered over them hen-like – encouraging, anxious and fearing, perhaps, that the worst was to come.'

However knackered United were, Charlton noticed the Portuguese were worse. 'They looked terrible,' he recalls. 'If we were tired they looked close to collapse.'

Sensing victory, United went for it. Bestie, Kidd and – fittingly, exhilaratingly, wonderfully – Charlton himself, all scored. Afterwards it was harder to find someone who wasn't in tears. Even now Wilf McGuinness appears on the point of choking when he talks about it.

'You kept thinking the Old Man has had his dream, it had happened,' says McGuinness, who sat on the bench alongside his mentor throughout the game. 'Nothing could wipe away the nightmare of Munich, nothing could justify it but still in our different ways we had to try to make it good, we hadn't forgotten the lads, and here was the greatest possible tribute to the memory of them'.

That was the thing. Munich was still there. But now it could be mentioned, now it could be addressed. Now, with the giant trophy in his hands, everything made sense for Busby. He needed sixty-eight to give if not a purpose to fifty-eight, then at least to give it vindication. He had done it for them. The team he sent out on to the Wembley park was made up of three bought players and eight homegrown, exactly the same proportion as the team that played in Belgrade ten and a half years before. He had not only done it for them, he had done it in the same way. And, in those photos of celebration, hugging Bobby and George and grumpy old Bill in the delirium of victory, you can see the meaning in his eyes. As he stood up and sang Louis Armstrong's 'It's a Wonderful World' at the after-match celebratory banquet, it was there in the catch in his voice. He had done what he set out to do as he lay under an oxygen tent in Munich. He had done it for the boys. His lost, lost boys.

Forty years on Charlton, who could not join in the celebrations that night after running himself into a state of utter exhaustion, puts it like this: 'We had kept the faith.'

The faith in United. Matt Busby United.

10

LEAR LEAVES THE STAGE

In late 1969 George Best featured on a tea-time children's television programme, in which he gave youthful aspirants coaching tips. Some of them I've never forgotten, such as 'If you don't go into a tackle as hard as you can, you'll get hurt.' Until that point I thought everyone else on the team did the tackling, leaving Bestie to do the dazzling. One evening, as I watched the slo-mo footage of him skipping past a defender, leaving the bloke confused, dazzled, not sure of his own post code, my mum, watching as she served up tea, said: 'Well, I don't care what they say about him, he's still a marvellous footballer.'

And, me young, unaware of such things, I thought, What do they say about him?

I hadn't a clue, but at the time a lot was said about Bestie. A lot was said about Manchester United, too. And it was roughly the same stuff. There was a growing sense abroad that things were in decline. The genius was still there – innate, inarguable – but it was fighting a rearguard action. Everyone seemed to agree that a peak had been reached and the descent was getting ever more tricky by the day.

Bestie may have been the club's public face – the one in every magazine, the one dressed in a tie-dye T-shirt, pouring champagne down a fountain of glasses in his new nightclub. But he had problems. Mountainous problems. And they were his to face alone, the club were clueless about helping him. The attention he first sought when he popped that sombrero on his head on the way home from Lisbon was corroding his spirit. Now there was no escape. Around that time he had a house built in Bramhall, south of Manchester. This was a pad for the times, full of swanky bachelor devices like curtains that cou:d be closed at the touch of a button and a telly that rose up electronically from a cabinet at the end of his giant bed. It was a James Bond lair for a modern hero. I thought it looked great as he showed us round his lovely home on the local television news. According to my mum, from the outside his gaff looked like a public lavatory, all white tiles and what appeared to be porcelain finishings round the front door. She said this one Sunday afternoon when we drove out to see it. We weren't the only ones. There was a traffic jam in the street outside it, cars reversing in his driveway, a whole convoy of people hoping for a glimpse of the inmate. He said the place made him feel like a prisoner. If that was the case, he was in a very open prison. Never mind security, there wasn't even a hedge. Fans would picnic on his lawn (which didn't please his gardener who was also the Old Trafford groundsman). One time someone nicked all the goldfish from his ornamental pond. In the end he only stayed in what he called his 'Saturn Five space station house' three nights.

His life was bonkers. And he was trying to block out the madness by drinking more and more. Alcohol's grip was tightening round his throat. He was gambling, too, huge amounts in ever more reckless forays. Mind you, on the park, for much of the time, the theory that he was out of kilter seemed completely irrational. There he still was doing it: leading United's goalscoring charts, putting his shins on the line for the cause, bravery personified. The two images – of celebrity wastrel and professional footballer – seemed to be running in parallel. For now.

What everybody thought about United when they won the European Cup was that it marked an end. This was catharsis, redemption and lots of other things that normally come at a drama's conclusion. The assumption was the manager felt things were over too. He was nearly sixty, had been made a freeman of Manchester, had gone down on bended knee before the Queen: what was there left for Sir Matt? Many assumed he would go after that night in May, once the tears had subsided and the quarter of a million people who packed into Albert Square to watch the trophy's arrival in Manchester had gone home.

Received wisdom also suggests he had on his hands an ageing team, one that needed complete rebuilding. The facts speak otherwise. Sure, the old Busby Babes were approaching the end of their time: that May evening in Wembley Foulkes was thirty-six, Charlton and Brennan both thirty-one. But Nobby, Paddy, Tony Dunne and big Alex were in their prime, mid to late twenties. And there were four players – Best, Aston, Kidd and Sadler – all under twenty-two. The average age was in fact identical to that of the team that started the game the next time the reds reached the European Cup final in 1999: twenty-six. This wasn't a side ready for its pension. What it wanted was a nip here and a tuck there. Cosmetic, not major, surgery.

Perhaps Busby realised that. Which is why he decided to stay on, give it another crack defending the Cup. And, immediately after the biggest of all football trophies was popped into the Old Trafford cabinet, he started the process, buying the tricky winger Willie Morgan from Burnley.

Morgan settled in immediately, scoring United's only goal in their bruising World Club Championship defeat by Argentina's Estudiantes. He was no Albert Quixall, terrified by Old Trafford or what it required to be a Manchester United player. He got on well with the Boss. He played golf with the Boss. He went out to dinner with the Boss. He soon had the Boss's ear. Some reckoned he thought he was the new George Best. No, that isn't fair. I think what he actually thought was that George Best was the new Willie Morgan.

'I was the first footballer to have an official fan club,' he says. 'Two girls produced newsletters, badges and a photograph. The fans used to copy my hair and my clothes.'

Well, that's true. In 1974 I tore a picture of Willie Morgan from the United programme, took it into the barber's and asked for my barnet to be cut in the same way. This was a towering, tottering three-tiered confection, with all sorts of complex side bits that required endless under-combing to keep in position, a wedding cake bouffant that was not hugely practical in a Mancunian squall. Also, such was the investment in blow-drying, this was not a style that stuck around long. Though its progenitor stayed loyal: Willie still favours it three decades on.

Morgan apart, Busby's slight adjustments did not do the trick. He knew he needed some fresh legs and he tried plenty of them. There was a steady through-put of lads from the United youth teams. But never mind not being in the same class as the Busby Babes, some of them appeared not even to have attended the same school. Carlo Sartori, Steve James, Jimmy Ryan, Francis Burns, Don Givens: they weren't Charlton, Stiles or Best. And Paul Edwards was clearly not Duncan Edwards. The old Busby certainty – that Manchester United could regenerate from its own resources – seemed no longer to obtain. It was going to be a harder task than he initially believed. Too hard, Jean thought. He had done enough. She thought it was time to go.

Thus it was that in January 1969 Busby delivered the least surprising piece of football news in a decade: he was to retire from the dug-out at the end of the season. This wasn't farewell, more of an announcement of a rearrangement in the furniture. He was to remain at the club – it was effectively his now, after all – as the generously remunerated general manager. But he would no longer be in control of team matters. Critically, no announcement as to the identity of a successor was made. Busby thought it would be the wrong thing to do while United suffered in the League. He wanted his bequest to be something a bit more vibrant than that. As it turned out, as with much of his thinking about the succession, it was precisely the wrong thing to do.

As United pulled themselves back from the sixteenth place they occupied when he made his news public, however, there was even suggestion that he might go out on the most glorious of top notes. Denis Law, back briefly between ever lengthening absences with his knee injury, was convinced he had scored a late, late equaliser in the semi-final of the European Cup against Milan. Unlike Geoff Hurst's World Cup-winning effort three years previously, this was so far over the line when the Milan defender cleared it, you could see it was a goal from as far away as Rochdale. The scorer wheeled away, finger in the air, the Lawman of old. But the referee wasn't in Rochdale. He was officiating apparently on a different planet and the goal was ruled out.

The day Busby retired, the press tributes were rightly effusive. That day he was asked to nominate his best ever team. He thought about it for a while, then came up with this one: Stepney; Carey, Chilton, Edwards, Byrne; Best, Crerand, Charlton, Mitten; Taylor, Law. It was the most pertinent epitaph of the lot.

The speculation had been endless as to who would follow him. The bookies favoured Jock Stein, Brian Clough, Don Revie and Noel Cantwell. Busby wanted none of that. He wanted someone from within the family, someone who understood, above all he wanted someone United. In Busby's mind there was only one candidate. After making the decision, he didn't tell the favoured one for three months. Though he did tell so many other people that word leaked to Wilf McGuinness and the youth-team coach had enough time to alert a couple of mates to put some money on him at 6-1. It was the last clever move he was to make as a United employee.

'You'd better wear a tie in the morning,' Wilf was told the day before his appointment was to be revealed to the press. Like he was a schoolboy going up to see the headmaster. And in a way he was, that was how he was treated. At thirty-one years old, he was trusted with virtually nothing. Busby was to be general manager: he would be in charge of transfers, dealing with the board, talking to the press. You could see Busby's thinking here: Wilf had no experience, he needed help, a shoulder to lean on. It was the Continental way, after all. But that wasn't explained to Wilf. He was just told this is what would happen. For his troubles he was to get £80 a week. Busby had just retired on £200. No one asked him what approach he might bring to the job, or which players he might like to sign. No one asked him whether he was happy with the terms or conditions. No one asked him if he even wanted it. In the United way, he was expected just to get on with it.

Eamon Dunphy, brilliantly, puts it like this: 'The torch had been passed on. Wilf grabbed the lighted end.' Willie Morgan is no less scathing about McGuinness's tenure, blaming the appointee for the subsequent failures, never those who made the appointment: 'Matt had tremendous vision appointing someone from within the club, that hadn't been done before. The idea was right, but it just didn't work out. Wilf's a great bloke now, but he was just too immature, too petty and he messed up.'

In his first season he took United to eighth place in the League and to the FA Cup semi-final. It was at the latter that things started to unravel. Before a Monday-night semi replay against Leeds at Villa Park, the team were staying at a hotel in Worcester. The idea was the players would have lunch, then an afternoon nap, before the pre-match tactical meeting. Bestie's idea of snacking was more idiosyncratic. He spotted a woman at the bar. Next thing, when all the other lads were in their rooms, resting quietly, Bestie was in her room, coupling noisily. Wilf knew. He was incandescent. He got the hotel manager to open up the room and caught them at it. He should have disciplined Best there and then, banned him from playing. But Wilf needed him. He was his get out of jail card. He didn't know what to do, so he asked Busby. Busby said he'd sort it.

Best played, but missed the game's only real chance. And Leeds went on to win the second replay.

There was a furious reaction in the dressing room. Senior players turned on Best, berating him for his lack of professionalism. 'The trouble was, he just agreed with you and said he'd change, he'd learned his lesson and it would all be different,' says Pat Crerand. 'It never was.'

Everyone blamed Wilf. The players blamed him for playing Bestie when he was in flagrant breach of the rules. The press blamed Wilf because Bestie looked so sluggish. The fans blamed Wilf because it was yet another bloody semi they'd lost to Leeds. And Busby? Busby merely sighed his exasperated sigh.

The incident was Wilf's tenure in microcosm. He had responsibility without power. When he tried to assert himself he just put everyone's nose out of joint. He introduced complex coaching ideas, a blackboard in team talks. The senior pros watched and shook their heads. 'Just go out and play' was how they'd won the European Cup, now here was one of their own telling them to track back and mark and pick up the opposition. McGuinness infuriated Paddy, he annoyed the Lawman, he didn't half piss off Morgan when he threw his cards in the player's face after losing a round of poker on the bus back from a match. Which irritated everyone else. What, they wondered, was the manager of Manchester United doing playing cards with one of the lads on the way back from a match in the first place?

Except Wilf was never really the manager of Manchester United. Not really. Sure, he had ideas. He knew just a couple of new players would reinvigorate the squad nicely for the new season. He knew who he wanted: Malcolm Macdonald, Colin Todd and Mick Mills. Who knows whether they would have come. Certainly Wilf never found out. His request to approach them never reached the board. Instead, Busby bought him Ian Ure. Wilf never wanted him.

Frustrated, the new man took it out on the wrong people. He embarrassed Bobby Charlton when he made him do press-ups in front of the squad. Charlton now says it was just banter, a bit of a laugh, not a big issue at all. But those who were witness to the event recall the tingle that went down every spine. This was serious.

Thrashing around to impose his authority, Wilf took it out on Jimmy Murphy. Murphy was retired with Matt. No one asked. He was just retired. And Wilf wouldn't help him, didn't consult his old mentor, wouldn't give him a job to do. The man who, according to Martin Edwards 'had played a blinder after Munich' was moved along without a thank you, obliged to sit in Joe Armstrong's office and occasionally scout for young players for £25 a week. He had never learned to drive a car, but the club had always paid for a taxi to bring him from his home to the Cliff. That was cut – unnecessary expense, the board thought. Jimmy knew it was over when he was obliged to catch a bus to work. Jimmy Murphy: the giant of Munich became its final victim.

But worst of all, Wilf didn't have George Best. After doing it for him at first, Best began to despair of what he saw all around him. Now in thrall to his addictions, he convinced himself they were the symptom not the cause of his malaise. In Wilf's second season United were awful, woeful, full of holes and Wilf without sufficient fingers to plug them. There were stories in the papers about Best. Endless stories. One told – in a flurry of unhappy headlines – of how Paddy Crerand was arrested after an altercation at a nightclub. He'd smacked someone who'd had a go at George and broke his jaw. The cops were involved. At Manchester United, it just wasn't on.

In a pattern that was to become familiar over the years, faced with a crisis, Best hid. He ran away from Old Trafford. He was discovered in hiding at the actress Sinead Cusack's flat in London. Within an hour, half of Fleet Street was camped outside. Manchester United's story was no longer being played out on the football pitch. It was unfolding on the front page of the tabloids. And Wilf took the blame.

After defeat to Third Division Aston Villa in the League Cup, it was decided that the experiment was a failure. On Boxing Day 1970 Busby returned full time to the job. Best heard the news in Camden, hiding with his actress. But he was happy now to talk to the Old Man. Busby fined him and banned him: order seemed to have been restored. Best seemed pleased and came back, promising it wouldn't happen again. Perhaps he believed it wouldn't. He scored fourteen goals in the second half of the season. The Lawman, too, got off the physio's table and scored fifteen. Sanity returned.

As for Wilf, he was told to take charge of the reserves with Bill Foulkes. Nobody asked him, he was just told. These days Wilf buzzes round the Old Trafford press facilities, chatty and friendly, always there with a joke and laugh, a United stalwart. 'Cut me and I bleed red,' he chuckles.

But in 1970 he was shattered. He did as he was told for a couple of weeks, then realised his pride was being trampled on. He resigned and went to coach in Greece, where his hair fell out one night. 'He came to United a boy and left an old man' was how Tony Dunne put it. He was just thirty-three. It was shock that put paid to his hair.

'I felt desperately sorry for Wilf,' says Crerand. 'But football can be a cruel game.'

Football, note. Not Manchester United. Not Matt Busby. Yet McGuinness's humiliation was the result of a succession about as cack-handed as can be imagined. It was a misjudgement that was to inform the mythology of Manchester United for decades to come.

Not for the last time in United history, it was now decided to do the precise opposite of the previous managerial appointment. This time it was thought a big man with experience was required to do the job. Busby wanted Jock Stein and dispatched Pat Crerand up to Glasgow to try to convince the Celtic manager to head south. During their discussions, Stein's wife came into the room and said she wasn't going anywhere. She supported Celtic and that was it. 'It probably wasn't a good sign,' says the would-be headhunter now.

That – much to Stein's subsequent regret – was that. Instead United recruited Frank O'Farrell, the quietly spoken, serious-minded Dubliner doing a reasonable job with Leicester City. O'Farrell did precisely what Busby had sought to do two years previously. He brought in a couple of youngsters – Alan Gowling and Sammy McIlroy – refreshed the set-up with his intelligent, thoughtful, methodical approach and was top of the League at Christmas. Busby was quoted in the papers saying the Irishman was his finest ever signing. Everyone knew it was an illusion. O'Farrell most of all. It was down to Best, settled into a brief period of work-obsessed sobriety, who had scored three hat-tricks by the end of November.

'Every night I'd say one simple prayer,' says O'Farrell. 'I'd thank God for George.'

As the results started to turn, O'Farrell wanted to make big changes. He thought Crerand, Charlton and Law were finished, he didn't rate Stepney and thought Morgan a choker ('He would duck out from crosses at the far post,' O'Farrell says: maybe it was something to do with the hair). He needed, desperately, a decent keeper and a fiery midfielder. He went with a shopping list to the board: top were Peter Shilton and Alan Ball. Neither idea went down well. It was, O'Farrell believes, Busby who wouldn't sanction their purchase. It didn't help O'Farrell's plans that Busby's favourite golfing partners were Morgan, Crerand and Stepney. But then Ball was a big drinking pal of Best's (they owned a racehorse together), so maybe Busby had other reasons for not inviting him to a party he later confessed he'd have crawled on his knees to join.

Pointedly, when the board did sanction spending, it wasn't in areas currently occupied by the golfers. Martin Buchan came in from Aberdeen and immediately brought some authority to the defence. Ian Storey-Moore arrived as cover for Best, but was almost immediately injured. As for Wyn Davies and Ted MacDougall, they almost immediately established that they weren't United players.

O'Farrell, hard-working, quietly determined, soon realised he had a fight on his hands. Manchester United, the great entity, the most romantic football club in the country, was in a sorry mess. The biggest mess was that the work that was required would not be contemplated. The atmosphere had soured into one in which favoured cliques protected their own positions. This was a family all right, a family at Christmas in the midst of a bitter Boxing Day row. But worse – worst of all – Best had given up sobriety and once more sought escape in the bottle and the casino. O'Farrell tried to sort things. He was full of kindness, understanding, sympathy. The player was sent to live with Crerand, he was sent back to Mrs Fullaway's. By now, however, he had become a master of escape. And, finally, inevitably, the booze was beginning to have a bearing on his performances.

So this was the condition of Manchester United three years after winning the European Cup. It was a club shot through with problems. But no one could agree what they were. Some thought it was Best: he had been overindulged. Best thought it was the fact that there was no investment in quality to support him. Others thought it a lack of professionalism. Some thought it over-professionalism: what was wrong with 'Just go out and play'? There were cliques and rivalries, hierarchies and jealousies. O'Farrell became convinced that the problem was one of power. Namely he didn't have enough of it because of the blockage in the system immediately above his head.

'At one club function,' he recalls, 'Matt said to my wife after a few drinks, "Your husband is an independent sod, why don't you get him to talk to me?" I invited Matt for a coffee in my office the following Monday, as I did most Mondays. I told him what he had said to my wife. Matt mumbled on before saying, "I didn't think you should have dropped Bobby Charlton." With that Matt was interfering with my team. He also said, "I don't think Martin Buchan is playing so well." He was picking on Martin Buchan who wasn't playing badly at all. From then on it was only a matter of time before the situation disintegrated. He shouldn't have gone to my wife.'

It is significant Busby made mention of Buchan. The young Scotsman was viewed with huge suspicion when he arrived by Morgan and the golfing boys. They thought him O'Farrell's spy in the camp. They sneered at his professionalism, interpreting it as goody-two-shoes behaviour. On one occasion, Best asked if he could borrow 2p off someone to make a phone call from a pay box. Buchan handed over the coin. Later he asked for the money back. He says now it was a joke. But it was taken by those who observed it as evidence of his Aberdonian meanness. They didn't like him and they relayed their misgivings to a higher authority. And at Old Trafford that was the one that mattered.

11

SACKED FOR FALLING IN LOVE

As Scotland's international manager in the early seventies, Tommy Docherty watched a lot of English football, checking on the Tartan Army's Anglos. So nobody seemed too surprised to see him in the directors' box at Selhurst Park on the afternoon of Saturday 16 December 1972, as Crystal Palace took on Manchester United. As events turned out, Docherty cannot have been too impressed by the fate of the four Scots in the United line-up; Willie Morgan, Martin Buchan, Denis Law and Ted MacDougall were on the wrong end of a 5-0 hammering. It was a wretched mauling that spoke of morale in pieces and a club mired in self-destruction. On his return to Manchester, Law said to his old mate Pat Crerand, 'Palace were awful. And they beat us 5-0. What does that say about us?'

Docherty, however, was the one Scot who left the scene of the crime looking like a man who had just scooped the lottery. On his way out he had been stopped by a clearly dispirited Matt Busby. 'If anything happens over the weekend,' Busby said, 'would you be interested in coming to Old Trafford?'

Once Busby had lost faith in him, Frank O'Farrell was finished at Old Trafford. Subsequently both Pat Crerand and Bobby Charlton have insisted that Sir Matt was not the driving force behind the manager's departure. But there he was offering O'Farrell's job to someone else even as the Irishman was standing in the away dressing room at Selhurst failing to shift a few chins in an upwardly direction.

When he ceased to be manager, Busby might have promised himself not to step in. But United's guiding spirit could not stand by and watch while everything he had built was falling apart so quickly. By early December 1972 he had become convinced O'Farrell was a busted flush. Rumours reached him constantly via his golfing sources that the Irishman had abdicated responsibility, ducked the difficult issues. The dressing room resembled the plot-line of a sitcom: Martin hated Willie, Willie mocked Bobby, Bobby was sunk in depression, and everyone had had enough of George. Except O'Farrell, who seemed to indulge his every misdemeanour. It was the manager's fault, Busby reasoned, and he had to be let go. Not to interfere, he told himself, was worse than interfering. Not to interfere would be to commit the sin of omission.

To replace O'Farrell, United needed someone with vision and mental strength. Busby saw in Tommy Docherty a figure sufficiently expansive to succeed. What's more, this was a man who shared his West of Scotland Catholic background and footballing values: the Scotland/Manchester twinning experiment that had worked so well for the twenty-five years of his reign was surely worth another try.

Busby gave his recommendation to the rest of the United board. The Tuesday after the Selhurst debacle, Frank O'Farrell was called from the Cliff to a meeting with Louis Edwards. He had more than an inkling of what was about to happen. It was unseasonably warm on 19 December 1972 and as he, his assistant manager Malcolm Musgrove and the chief scout John Aston arrived at Old Trafford, one of the press men hovering by the stadium's directors' entrance commented on how pleasant the weather was.

'Aye,' said O'Farrell as he walked through the double oak doors. 'It's a nice day for an execution.'

It was a good line, perhaps the only memorable one he uttered in eighteen months as United boss. He was going to use it as the title of his autobiography, a contract for which he signed soon after he was sacked that mild December day. He went so far as to recruit a ghost writer, then turned cold on the project. Instead, exhausted by failure at United, he planned to retreat back to Torquay.

'I had to sue United for breach of contract as I had three and a half years left,' he recalls. 'I had to sign on the dole at Salford Labour Exchange for the first time in my life too. That felt embarrassing, humiliating almost, as I'd never been on the dole in my life. The manager of the Labour Exchange could see my embarrassment and used to let me in the back door. United took nine months to pay up my contract. I had to get a solicitor and then a QC. I'd seen the judges' influence on the Manchester United board and I was worried if I came up against one of them in court. I said to my QC, "What chance have we got if I come up against one of them?" The QC said, "I wouldn't worry as I'm a Manchester City supporter and if I get Busby in the witness box I'll be able to cross examine him." Just as the case was coming to court, United settled. They didn't need to put me through that though.'

Three days before Christmas 1972 it was announced that Thomas Henderson Docherty had accepted the board's offer of £15,000 a year to become manager of Manchester United. The news fizzed through the Old Trafford dressing room: a hand grenade was about to be placed under a few backsides. And for the likes of Willie Morgan, it couldn't go off soon enough. Busby's instructions to the new man were plain enough: do whatever is necessary to restore this club to its rightful position. Although just to keep an eye on things, Busby insisted that Crerand, always his favourite, become assistant manager, with a view to one day taking over as the boss. Docherty happily agreed (he had, after all, a respect for Crerand having tried to sign him as a player from

Celtic when he was Chelsea boss). That was the thing about the new man: in contrast to O'Farrell and McGuinness, Docherty seemed comfortable taking advice from Busby. Far from worrying about the Old Man's presence, he made much play of welcoming it.

'I've got the greatest manager in the world in an office down the corridor,' he said as he took up residence. 'Of course I'll talk to him. You'd be mad not to.'

But if the Doc regarded United as his dream job, the reality of New Year 1973 was that he had arrived to find the club looking a likely candidate for relegation. The condition of United reflected the wider world. These were bleak economic times. Like United, the once vigorous British economy was in shabby decline. There were three-day weeks, a stock market collapse, a balance of payments crisis. Inflation was rampant, uncontrolled and everywhere. Everywhere, that is, except in United's goals-for column. That was looking shrivelled and decrepit; here deflation ruled and United were bottom of the First Division table

Docherty had seen enough in his scouting for Scotland to know that the battle ahead would be a tough one. He reckoned, even as he swished into the club for the first time, that the current United team was lacking in three rather fundamental areas: defence, midfield and attack. And the goalie wasn't that great either. Plus there was the George Best question. How he came to deal with the player, some predicted, would be the first big test of Docherty's management.

For the moment, though, Best was not an issue. When Docherty showed up at Old Trafford, the winger had already been in self-imposed exile for more than a month, preferring a regime of drink and birds to one of keepy-uppies and five-a-sides. Latterly he had eschewed the glamorous orbit that once span round him, and spent much of his time in the company of the alcoholic regulars at the Brown Bull, the shabby drinking dive that became his head-quarters. Many a night he slept on a filthy mattress in an upstairs room at the pub. The new boss would have to cope without him for some time. And the way he set about his task, it did not seem as though Docherty was prepared to wait around long for the Belfast Boy to get his head back together.

Within six months of arriving in Manchester, Docherty had completely refashioned the team by buying in six players. This was as many as the three previous managers had bought between them in six years. It showed that Docherty had not only Busby's trust, but that of chairman Edwards, who, following a recent failed takeover bid by a consortium of Manchester businessmen, had managed to manoeuvre himself into almost complete ownership of the club. Edwards took to Docherty. The big man always felt a little small in Busby's presence. But the Doc was different. In contrast to Busby's patrician hauteur, he was deferential, full of 'Mr Chairman this' and 'Mr Chairman that'. A canny operator, the Doc knew precisely how to flatter. Flatter, some might say, in order to deceive.

'Oh aye,' recalls Pat Crerand. 'He made sure he had the chairman on side. He was a wily character all right.'

But if there was duplicity at work, Edwards didn't see it. He just laughed at the Doc's jokes and opened up his cheque book. All of Docherty's new boys were Scots, players he had worked with in the national first team, or whose potential he had spotted in the under-23s. His first four signings arrived within a month of him. George Graham, Alex Forsyth, Lou Macari and Jim Holton were immediately pitched into a full-on relegation struggle. Macari was the big-money buy, £200,000 from Celtic, which looked something of a snip as he tore around full of energy and buzz, scoring five goals. It was a morale-boosting coup for Docherty to sign him, snapping him up from under the noses of a then-ascendant Liverpool. Macari had been about to sign for Bill Shankly. Crerand, though, had spotted him in the crowd at Anfield and alerted Docherty of his presence. The manager had moved fast to hijack the deal.

'I felt straight away that United were the team for me,' recalls Macari. 'I had a nagging doubt in the back of my mind that I wouldn't get in the Liverpool team because they were flying. I rang Bill Shankly and told him I wasn't going to Liverpool. He wasn't happy, but he said, "It's your decision." He then joked to the press that he had only wanted to sign me to play in Liverpool's reserves. I thought that was quite witty.'

For every arrival, there was a departure. The day he set foot in the place, Docherty appeared to have revolving doors installed at the entrance to Old Trafford. There was a quite dizzying traffic in players. First out were Ted MacDougall and Wyn Davies, O'Farrell's misfiring forwards. MacDougall went with the new manager's scorn ringing in his ears: not fit to wear the shirt, was his observation. And this, despite the fact that the centre forward scored the first goal of Docherty's regime, the equaliser in a 1-1 home draw against Leeds. Soon joining them in the out-tray were the European Cup-winning heroes Tony Dunne, David Sadler and Brian Kidd. Also on his way, though this was not of Docherty's choosing, was Ian Storey-Moore. He turned his ankle in the gym at the Cliff two months after the new boss arrived. It seemed an innocuous enough accident, but he never recovered and was obliged to retire from the game aged twenty-eight.

It was hard to argue against Docherty's transfer policy in those early days. With a flourish in the spring of 1973, in which the team won five and drew two games, the drop was easily avoided. 'When he came in he was a breath of fresh air after Frank,' remembers Willie Morgan. 'Very outgoing, very positive. He was wonderful. I think his attitude alone saved us from relegation that year.'

Attitude was the Docherty hallmark. He was not a man for a dossier.

'The Doc a planner? That's so far from the truth it's almost a joke,' says Macari. 'The discipline was far more lax than it was at Celtic, the quality of training much poorer. Docherty's strength as a manager was creating an atmosphere that was very, very positive.'

Following from the quiet, self-contained O'Farrell, the corridors

of Old Trafford felt a sudden upsurge in energy as the ebullient
Doc, full of schemes and plans, bundled about the place. With a
wink for the ladies in the canteen, a joke for the commissionaires
on the reception desk, he infected the club with optimism and
cheer once more. Suddenly there was a lightness abroad, the celtic
charm that Busby brought again in evidence, albeit with a riper,
rougher, more abrasive edge. Where Busby was all paternalistic,
avuncular, redolent of pipe-smoking benevolence, Docherty could
be so sharp he was in perpetual danger of cutting himself.

To hear the Doc speak about his career now, it all sounds a bit of
joke. Indeed since he left football management after being sacked
for the last time, he has spent two decades in demand at dinners,
testimonials, corporate golf days. And no wonder, he is a terrific
public orator. To watch him at his prime was to observe a master of
the art, charismatic, not fearing of reputation or personal feeling.
The Doc coined many a modern football epithet and none of them
could be considered kindly. You can't imagine Busby ever saying
that 'Carlton Palmer can trap the ball further than George Best
could kick it' or that 'Elton John decided he wanted to rename
Watford, call it Queen of the South'.

As he talks his way through his career or makes gags about
football's problems of the moment, you begin to see what he must
have been like in the Old Trafford dressing room. How his ability
with words could lift the spirit. Or just as easily cut to the quick.
Take the case of Paddy Roche. Roche was bought from Shelbourne
for £25,000 in 1973, as a replacement for Alex Stepney. But his confidence had been damaged from the start of his first-team career
when, playing against Liverpool at Anfield in November 1973, he
had a shocker.

'It was an easy cross and I jumped high to collect it, so high that
my foot collided with the defender's shoulder,' he recalls.
'Unfortunately, that knocked me off balance and the ball spilled
from my grasp. Steve Heighway scored. A soft goal. The papers
crucified me. I found it very difficult because I'd never experienced a downer as a player before. It was hard. I retreated into my

shell and stopped answering the phone. Tommy Docherty could have provided a lot more support.'

Indeed he could. Almost from that moment the Doc's sharp tongue reduced him to comedy dust: 'Paddy Roche was known as Dracula because he was scared of crosses,' he said soon after the Liverpool game. Then he repeated it on many, many occasions.

'I felt down and it didn't help that I didn't have the confidence of the supporters,' says Roche. 'They used to boo me when I came on.'

That was Docherty's way from the start: there was no middle path. You either laughed at his gags or were the butt of them. You were either on his side or you weren't. And those who weren't shuddered at the brutality of their exclusion.

From the moment he arrived at Old Trafford, much of Docherty's drive was directed at removing what he characterised as 'the cancer' at the club. He had heard about the way player power had destroyed the reigns of McGuinness and O'Farrell and determined it wasn't going to happen to him. In his mind, if he was going to survive the most difficult posting in his career, he would have to build a team that was loyal to him and him only. That, he decided, meant an end to the old guard. His first priority, he reckoned, was to face up to the three greatest heroes in United history. The nettle had to be seized, and seized quickly.

Of the trio, Bobby Charlton had the most dignified send-off. Mind you, there are some, even Charlton himself, who say he went too soon. Lou Macari remembers that when he arrived from Celtic he was stunned at how fit the Munich survivor was. 'I thought, Yeah, well, so you won the World Cup and the European Cup, but that was then, let's just see what you've got now,' Macari recalls. 'And you know what? He had everything. He was in magnificent condition and his attitude was always first class. Personally, I felt he could have carried on for another couple of years at least.'

Initially Tommy Docherty seemed to share the view, and picked Charlton in every game for the rest of his first season in charge. But the club captain's problem wasn't physical, it was mental: he was a great athlete, but an unhappy man. He had become exhausted by the attitude of those around him in the dressing room who were not worthy successors to the lads who died at Munich. He worried that he might not have the mental strength to ride out the upheavals he saw ahead. Some of the players sensed his scorn and sneered back. Morgan in particular was scathing about the old man with the comedy comb-over who seemed to belong to another era. Ostracised and alone, Bobby, a man who believed that football was a calling, was rapidly falling out of love with the game that had given him everything. He had survived the Munich crash, but he did not have the will to survive this.

Once relegation was no longer a mathematical possibility, he sought out Busby and told him he planned to retire. Docherty, his first tough decision made for him, was effusive in his press eulogies. And rightly so: Charlton was as responsible for United's wider image as anybody. The final, visible, playing bridge to the Babes who had perished fifteen years before, he was utterly professional to the end, never once going public with his worries about United's decline. He stepped off the stage to huge acclaim after the final game of the season, a 1-0 defeat to Chelsea at Stamford Bridge.

'Sir Bobby Charlton,' chanted the crowd, with some prescience, as he departed for the last time. Even the Chelsea fans joined in.

'I grew up on a council estate in Chelsea and used to bunk into Stamford Bridge whenever Manchester United played there,' says blues fan Jimmy Byrne. 'Why? Bobby Charlton. In five decades of watching football, nobody has mesmerised me like Charlton.'

Mr Manchester United was heading to the exit. The most dignified player ever to wear red would never slip on the shirt again. The torch carrier was gone. Denis Law was not so lucky, he never had the send off he deserved. Injury had restricted him to just nine appearances in the season. Nevertheless, Law felt this was a manager he could do business with. After all, the Doc was responsible for his recall to the national squad the previous summer. Besides conversations he had with the new man involved talk of a new contract, of a testimonial, of a coaching future if he wanted one. Yet at the same time the minutes of board meetings reveal that Docherty had informed directors that Law had put in a transfer request. His recommendation was that it should be accepted. Initially the directors declined to back the gaffer on this one. Law, like Charlton, they insisted, had earned the right to retire as a red.

The gap between what Docherty said to Law and reality turned out to be as wide as the Manchester Ship Canal. Despite private assurances at the start of the summer break that a new contract was being prepared, despite the board's initial scepticism, in July 1973 Docherty insisted Law must go. Louis Edwards agreed, Busby didn't interfere and he was given a free transfer to Manchester City. To his great distress, Law learned that he was to be a blue on the television news. The testimonial never materialised. And that was a real blow. He had never been a big earner: cowed by Busby's lofty disapproval of players motivated by money he had hardly dared to ask for a rise and had spent his career at Old Trafford under-rewarded. The King of the Stretford End was on not much more than £200 a week when he left for Maine Road.

There was better news for United fans, however, about the third member of the champion triumvirate. George Best had been in hospital in the spring of 1973 suffering from a thrombosis in his leg. Busby had been to visit him and suggested it was time he was back in training. Best agreed, and that summer returned to the Cliff. 'I've missed the game more than I thought I would,' he said. 'I would like to think that the drinking problems I had and the depressions they caused are behind me.'

Docherty proclaimed himself 'delighted' at the news and hired a specialist fitness coach to work with the returning hero.

'He still had the best touch of any player I had ever encountered,' recalls Macari of that last hurrah of Best. 'Even at the end, you could see him do things in training that just made you stop and applaud.'

But as the manager must have suspected, it was the most false of new dawns. Best played in twelve successive games the following autumn, and scored a couple of goals, but he looked bloated, off the pace, a depressing parody of his former self. Fans went home after an awful 3-0 defeat at QPR on New Year's Day 1974 asking each other why he bothered. As for the drink problem being consigned to the past, sadly it was all too much a thing of the present: that day at Loftus Road he was clearly suffering after a monumental New Year's Eve. When he turned up late for a Cup tie against Plymouth four days later, his breath reeking of the Brown Bull, Docherty sent him home. He never returned. Finally, depressingly, it was over. This time he really was gone. The greatest player in United history was so enslaved to alcohol he could no longer function as a footballer. Actually, he could no longer function as a human being. A bright man, he had first taken to drink as a means of escape from the growing absurdity of his life. But it quickly held him in its sway, dominating not just his own life, but those of so many who loved him. It may have taken another thirty-two years for the booze finally to consume him, but in many ways he died the day he left Old Trafford in his sports car, a few dozen kids in parkas trotting along beside him, hoping for an autograph. What those lads were witnessing that festive afternoon in 1974 was a dead man driving.

Best lived on for another three decades in an odd kind of limbo. When challenged about the way his life had turned out in subsequent times, he would always use the same defence: he hadn't done too badly, he flew everywhere first class and stayed in the finest hotels. That he marked his life in the trappings of transience was significant; for everyone else hotels and aeroplanes were things you used occasionally, when you are heading somewhere else; for Best they were everything. From the moment he walked out of Old Trafford, he seemed forever to be searching for something, for the kind of fulfilment football once gave him. In an interview in 2000, the *Guardian*'s Sabine Durrant noted that he seemed to be permanently waiting for something else to come along, something better. Stuart Hall once told me that Best's end-less restlessness had a fundamental cause: he was, Hall believed, gay and his inability to come to terms with his sexuality infused him with an eternal dissatisfaction and self-loathing. It is a bold analysis of the world's foremost swordsman – a man who once slept with seven women in twenty-four hours. But there was something inexplicable at the root of the genius's decline.

On the terraces the fans were having difficulty digesting the news: in the space of six months they had lost the three men who had been the inspiration for nearly a decade of glory, the men whose names had become synonymous with the club, the men whose very presence on a teamsheet elevated United above any other club side in the world. Best, Law and Charlton, the holy trin-ity of Old Trafford, had gone.

A new era had begun. And it was not an auspicious start. While Docherty's defence, with Jim Holton and Martin Buchan an impenetrable heart, leaked fewer goals than any since the title was won in 1967, it was up front that his new look team struggled. At Christmas 1973 his goalkeeper Alex Stepney was joint leading scorer with just two goals, both from penalties. Perhaps through lack of striking options, Docherty played much of that winter with an unexpansive, frightened-looking 4-5-1 formation, the diminu-tive Macari obliged to spend his time haring after the forlorn long balls that were the team's one attacking tactic. Out on the pitch, the one place where United had always sought to be a cut above the rest, they looked like losers.

Up in the directors' box, Busby could see the direction the reds were heading and he despaired of the manner in which they were facing their fate. That spring, knowing that Law, Best and Charlton could no longer ride to the rescue, he took Docherty aside and said to him, 'Tom, if we are to go down, let's do it with dignity.'

It was an important word to Busby, dignity. For him United were always something more than an agglomeration of results. They were a moral force. Docherty took the remark as permission to unleash the unrestrained side of his footballing philosophy. He introduced an expansive 4-2-4 formation. Up front, the former prodigy Sammy McIlroy, whose progress after making his debut as a seventeen-year-old had been stalled by a car accident, was selected alongside Macari. On the wings were Willie Morgan and Gerry Daly, a teenager recently signed from the Irish club Bohemians. In central midfield the ponderous George Graham was axed, replaced by the busy Scot Jim McCalliog, playing alongside Brian Greenhoff, the third youthful new arrival. At the back Stepney was instructed no longer to hoof the ball forward, but to bowl the ball to his full backs, Alex Forsyth and the left back bought in from Brentford, Stewart Houston. The new boy was, it goes without saying, yet another Scot. The reds now boasted more tartan than Rod Stewart's wardrobe.

As a ploy, the switch to expansive wing play almost worked. Rock bottom in the division at the end of March, over April there was breathless revival. Four wins and a draw pulled Birmingham City and Southampton, the two teams sitting above the drop zone, within catching distance. The Stretford End began to dream of an imminent miracle.

Instead, they witnessed a nightmare. It was 27 April 1974, United's penultimate game of the season, the Manchester derby. After losing away to Everton, Docherty's team had to win and hope that other results conspired in their favour to have any chance of staying up. From the off, United attacked relentlessly. But, in a dramatic distillation of their whole season, they simply could not score. With eighty-one minutes gone, the awful *coup de grâce* came. Denis Law was City's captain that day, but that did not stop his former worshippers around Old Trafford cheering his every touch. Except the last one. Law found himself in the United box, unmarked, apparently unnoticed. A cross came in from Francis Lee, which initially he appeared to try to avoid. But his striker's instinct could not be snuffed out. Completely wrong-footing the United defence, he back-heeled the ball goalwards. It took an age to trickle over the line.

'Law!' yelled Gerald Sinstadt on the television commentary, as if scarcely able to believe the script had taken such a dramatic turn. 'It's Law!'

It was almost Greek in its resolution, the victim of treachery returning to apply the ultimate act of revenge. Not that Law seemed to enjoy sticking the knife into Docherty's ribcage. 'I'll never forget the look on Denis's face,' says Buchan. 'I thought you were meant to be happy when you score a goal.'

If there was any sense of getting his own back for the manner of his removal from Old Trafford, nobody could discern it in Law's face. His team-mates tried to make him smile to no avail. He looked shattered, dead-eyed, as if he were the member of a firing squad that had just shot his best friend. It turned out to be the last kick he ever made in League football. He retired after that summer's World Cup in Germany.

'Law's Last Sad Word' was the *Guardian*'s headline the next day. Willie Morgan recalls his former colleague's reaction was one of utter dismay. 'Denis looked so shocked,' he says. 'But it wasn't Denis who sent us down. We knew we were going down from Christmas, we just couldn't put the ball in the net. But when it finally happened, when he back-heeled the ball in, it was numb, it was an awful feeling.'

Law himself has hardly spoken about his derby moment since, even in his several autobiographies he devotes less than a page to the incident. I once tried to get him to talk us through the goal for a television documentary. He merely smiled back, the sort of smile that was born not of amusement, the sort of smile that suggested we move the subject on quickly.

As the goal went in, on the Old Trafford terraces a rumour quickly spread that the game would be abandoned in the event of a pitch invasion. It would then have to be replayed, giving United a second chance to escape the drop. After a huge surge down the Stretford End thousands of reds poured on to the playing surface, chanting their defiant pride in a side heading for Division Two. The players and match officials ran for the safety of the dressing room, Docherty and Busby pleaded over the public address system for order to be restored, but they were ignored. Then the referee, hearing that wins for both Birmingham and Southampton had made the result irrelevant, blew the whistle on the game. There would be no restaging. For the first time in thirty-seven years, United had been relegated.

It is hard to overstate the sense of shock that permeated Manchester on the realisation that the most famous club in the land had gone down. The self-image of the town, already damaged by the seventies economic depression, was further wounded. United were Manchester's crowning glory. Now they were a laughing stock. Granada TV broadcast a rundown of the season called 'United They Fall', which attempted to pin the blame for decline on everyone from Edwards and Busby to Best and the growing hooligan element among the fans. Docherty himself seemed convinced that he would be the one found culpable. Soon after relegation was confirmed, he approached Busby to ask when he would be sacked. Instead, he was told to go back to the Cliff and finish the job he had started.

'This club belongs in the First Division,' Busby told him. 'Make sure you get us back there.'

United's first Second Division campaign since the 1930s began on 17 August 1974 away at Leyton Orient. Docherty's team won 2-0, with a headed goal from Stewart Houston and an adept chip from Willie Morgan. But it was not the action on the pitch that concerned the headline writers. The next day's papers were filled with reports of United's fans storming Brisbane Road. More than ten thousand reds were estimated to have turned up for the game, flooding the tight terraced streets round the ground, a boisterous, noisy, effervescent presence. And when half of them were unable to gain legitimate access to the ground, there was a minor riot of pushing and shoving, totally overwhelming the few police and stewards. Gates were removed from their hinges, doors battered down, trees uprooted. Inside the ground there was another pitch invasion and one of the linesmen had to be replaced after being hit by a missile thrown from the visiting contingent.

'Animals,' declared the *News of the World* the next morning.

So it continued for the rest of the year. Through the sleepier backwaters of English football visits from Doc's Red Army were greeted almost as if it were their Soviet namesakes parachuting into town. Into Oxford, Bristol and York the army marched, its numbers swelled by thrill-seekers attracted by its notoriety. In Portsmouth, Sunderland and Cardiff they were met by determined local resistance and the resulting fighting was as bad as had ever been seen at British football grounds. At Sheffield Wednesday the scrapping spread to the pitch, there was another invasion and 105 visiting fans were arrested. Matt Busby was mortified, United's directors embarrassed beyond words. Though Docherty, typically, found a few.

'What can we do?' he said after the Hillsborough riot. 'We have a minority of fans who are a disgrace. Every club has one or two troublemakers among their supporters, but because of the size of our following the problem is bigger for us than any other club.'

This was indeed the issue. United may have been in the Second Division, but the combination of a fresh, exciting young team to follow and the intoxicating possibility of trouble meant that Old Trafford regularly hosted the largest crowd anywhere. And what a crowd: fifty-five thousand, of which at least half were on the terraces, singing. It is hard to imagine, in these days when seventy-five thousand can fill Old Trafford with almost total silence, what a noise emanated from the Stretford End. And what commitment was required from those who wished to be part of it.

'We used to get there early so we could be first in the ground,' recalls Andy Walsh. 'We'd walk round the ground before the queues started to build. It was called "Doing the United". There were always loads of lads trying to get in as soon as the gates opened at one o'clock, two hours before kick-off. There'd be a mad dash, up the steps to be the first, you'd look across to see the people going up the other step. And the prize was to be the first to shout "United" in the ground that day.'

The crowd was all part of the experience: the surges, the songs, the camaraderie combined into a thrilling sense of empowerment. For away matches, thousands arrived at places that had no experience of dealing with such crowds. At Norwich the invading army burned down the main stand. At Millwall there were only sixteen thousand people present, of whom about 15,999 seemed to join in a riot. It was an outbreak of anarchy without any identifiable political purpose, in marked contrast to the student riots of the late sixties, and it precipitated nearly two decades of hand-wringing among politicians, policemen and football officials about what could be done to eradicate hooliganism from the game. For those taking part, however, it was all about being part of a club, part of being United. Thirty-five years on, Michael Webster, a regular Stretford Ender in the seventies, recalls it as a time of adventure and comradeship.

'The season spent in the Second Division was brilliant,' he says. 'The buzz was in travelling to see United and we had great trips, I was so proud to be part of the Red Army. We'd get to town centres early and people would just stare at us like we had two heads. There were some who caused real trouble, but I bet they didn't have as good a time as we did. We used to drink with home fans a lot of times and, after being initially fearful, they were usually friendly football people.'

For lads working in dead-end jobs, on the production line or behind the shop counter, United was what made the week worthwhile. Following the reds offered a whole weekend of escapism to be seized with wild eyed enthusiasm. 'The more adventurous the way of travel, the better it was,' recalls Webster. 'We went to Derby once on a Friday night and got there about 8.30 p.m., sleeping under a tarpaulin in a cattle market near the rail station. Locals would ask us if many United fans were coming and I'd be really proud as I said, "Thousands, absolutely thousands".'

Coaches would line up at Gorse Hill in Stretford, ready to take the fans on their away days. For games at places like Ipswich and Norwich they would leave at midnight. Stacked with crates of beer, the coaches were a moving nightclub, their occupants United on the road.

'We'd get back to Manchester twenty-four hours later, exhausted, but still high on adrenalin. People used to love hearing stories about what had gone on and I felt part of it,' says Webster. 'It was so easy to watch United because games were pay on the gate. It wasn't expensive and you could stand with your mates. You can't do that now. I'd say that other than the birth of my kids, United have given me the greatest moments in my life.'

As Webster's memories suggest, there was a reckless glamour that attached itself to the Red Army's rampages. And if nothing else, they ensured United were the biggest story in football, even in their condition of temporary embarrassment. In that one season in the then Second Division, those wrapping red and white nylon scarves round their wrists, sewing embroidered badges to their denim jackets and embracing the full Bay City Roller baggy-trousered, big-booted chic, had plenty to shout about. Unbeaten in their first nine games, Docherty's team marched to the top of the table and stayed up there for the rest of the season. Where once goals were a rarity, now they came in a flood. The previous season the top scorer in the League was Sammy McIlroy with six. Now Gerry Daly had scored six in the first five games. The biggest difference was at centre forward. Stuart Pearson, bought in from Hull City for £200,000 was a revelation. Pearson, intriguingly, had not been Docherty's first choice. He had wanted to sign his old Chelsea sparring partner Peter Osgood, but had been rebuffed. But the second choice made an immediate impact. The *Daily Telegraph*'s report of his first game tells us that 'Pearson lit up the United front line like a beacon: mobile, quick, dangerous, everything their forwards had not been last season.'

To make way for Pearson, Lou Macari was moved back into midfield, where his industry proved more than effective. His change of position precipitated the departure of Jim McCalliog to

Southampton. At the same time Jimmy Nicholl, the youth-team full back, came in to replace Alex Forsyth. Doc's team was taking shape as one of the most vibrant in the country, built in the custom of United on youth, the average age just twenty-two.

It wasn't only the Second Division that was taken by storm either. Doc's youthful side progressed to the semi-final of the League Cup, defeating First Division Burnley and – to the huge delight of a packed Old Trafford – Manchester City along the way. In the semi, however, they were derailed by another old Docherty ghost coming back to haunt him. It was not quite as dramatic as Law's back-heeled winner, but how Ted MacDougall, the man who the Doc had reckoned a slap in the face of United's tradition, enjoyed scoring twice for Norwich as they knocked United out over two legs.

Not that ultimately it mattered. All that concerned Docherty was getting back into the top division. And when things stuttered and stalled, he was not afraid to enter the transfer market. His most significant purchase that year was an unusual one. As a boy Steve Coppell had attended John Lennon's old school in Liverpool, Quarry Bank, where he had played in the same team as Brian Barwick, the future chief executive of the Football Association. By 1974 he was an economics undergraduate studying at his home-town university and supplementing his grant turning out for Tranmere Rovers at the weekends. It was at Prenton Park that he caught the eye of Bill Shankly, who had recently been squeezed out of Liverpool. Shanks was electrified by what he saw and informed his old colleagues at Anfield that he had unearthed a gem on their doorstep. Maybe they felt they were well covered on the right wing, maybe they thought Shankly was trying to interfere, but for whatever reason, Bob Paisley and his bootroom colleagues told the old boy they would pass on his recommendation. A furious Shankly immediately contacted Docherty to tell him about his find. Docherty didn't even bother having Coppell watched; if Shanks said he was a diamond, then that was good enough for him. He quickly travelled to the Wirral and snapped up the young winger for £40,000, plus another £20,000 if he made twenty first-team appearances. It was some deal: he made more than four hundred. To Coppell's great surprise, Docherty bought him on the proviso that he continue with his studies. The manager was firm on that: 'You never know what might happen, son, and an education is a great thing to fall back on.' So Coppell was allowed to train with the university side and travel over to Manchester on Friday nights. He even continued to turn out for a student team, once playing in a university inter-departmental cup final on a college pitch in Anfield four days before stepping out for United at Anfield itself. Despite a lengthy career as a manager, Coppell still regards his debut at Old Trafford as his most vivid moment in football.

'I came on as a sub for Willie Morgan against Cardiff. It was 0-0 and I was so frightened the first time I got the ball that I just crossed it. Stuart Pearson – who had lent me some boots – scored. I had a hand in another goal and we won 4-0. It was beyond a fairy tale. My heart was jumping out of my chest and I've never had another experience like it. I wasn't running; I was floating across the grass. Words do not do the experience justice; it was a drug-like euphoric trance. I've had a few operations, and it was like that little pleasant stage after the anaesthetic. Only multiplied by a hundred.'

Coppell's arrival on 1 March 1975 provided an injection of momentum into the team, which had been faltering in early spring. With the newcomer tearing down the right wing, United remained undefeated for the rest of the season, walking away with the championship. A crowd of 58,769 turned up to see the final game of the season, at home to Blackpool. The Second Division trophy was paraded in front of an ecstatic Old Trafford, who chanted their own version of the recent Gary Glitter hit: 'Hello, hello, United are back, United are back.'

The players, though, if anything looked shame-faced as they made their lap of honour. Buchan in particular, barely cracked a smile. 'Macari reckons the Second Division was a cake walk,' he says. 'But it was never as easy as he says it was. He might have had an easy time up front, but as a defender you still have forwards to mark. The one good thing was it got us used to winning, which was rather nice and important the next year. But even so it was embarrassing to collect Second Division medals. We felt we and the club should never be in that position.'

That summer was one of eager anticipation. The players could not wait to get back to training. But on their return they found two fixtures of the dressing room had gone. Jim Holton had broken his leg playing against Sheffield Wednesday in the December of the previous season, then had shattered it again in the spring making his comeback in the reserves. By the time he had recovered, Brian Greenhoff had moved back from midfield to provide a more mobile, if less aggressive, partner for Buchan. Holton went to Sunderland, before eventually reacquainting himself with United fans as the landlord of a pub near Coventry City's Highfield Road ground. For many seasons, once a year, when United came to visit, the pub was awash with nostalgia as hundreds of reds poured in to announce that 'Six feet two, eyes of blue, big Jim Holton's after you'. His untimely death at the age of forty-two in 1993 was greeted with disbelief by United followers of a certain age; here was a man so apparently full of life, cut down in his prime.

Willie Morgan, too, left Old Trafford that summer. Steve Coppell's arrival had signalled the end for the last Busby favourite. But Docherty had been keen to let him go for a while. He was convinced Morgan was undermining him by feeding information back to the old boss over their regular rounds of golf.

'It just wasn't true,' Morgan now says. 'Believe it or not, the thing we talked about most often on the course, me and Matt, was whether he would sink that five-foot putt.'

Morgan left with an unenviable United record, that of the longest serving player never to have won a trophy. 'I did play in about twenty semi-finals,' he says, 'and even though I didn't win a trophy in seven years and nearly three hundred games at United,

I've no regrets. I had a great affinity with the supporters. I'll never forget running out in a United shirt with the Stretford End singing my name. That was some buzz, I can tell you.'

Docherty never needed any prompting to remove a player from the team. Especially one who, like Morgan, had an opinion. 'Your biggest enemy as a manager is an old pro in the dressing room, poisoning the young minds, spreading the gospel – the wrong gospel I might add,' the Doc once told me. 'The best thing is to get them on their bikes as quickly as possible.'

Morgan was put on his bike to Bolton. Docherty claimed that an eye injury, sustained when he was hit in the face playing tennis, had finished him as a top-flight footballer. An interesting diagnosis: Morgan was still playing in the First Division five years later. His departure meant that only Stepney, Buchan and McIlroy remained of the squad Docherty had inherited from Frank O'Farrell. Now this was unquestionably his United, filled with players he had brought to the club, players who owed him a debt, players loyal to him.

Behind the scenes, though they might have appreciated that surgery was necessary, a growing body of opinion felt that it would have been better if anaesthetic had been applied first. Docherty, they felt, was just plain brutal in his firing. Pat Crerand, for instance, was brushed aside with a haste that might be considered indecent.

'Pat is a man I can trust,' Docherty had said as the Glaswegian was installed alongside him in the dug-out when he first arrived. But the reality was at odds with the words. Docherty regarded Crerand as Busby's man, and was soon manoeuvring to have him sacked. A passionate, open character, Crerand was no match for Docherty's political nous. The Doc eased him out with a series of tricks a schoolboy might have seen coming. One involved giving him the wrong time for a rendezvous, then complaining to Busby about his time-keeping. Another was to take unfounded allegations of drinking upstairs.

'Pat, I hear you're late and drunk,' Busby said to his old favourite one day. 'What's going on?'

Within a year, Docherty had crowbarred his fellow Scot out of the dug-out, Crerand resigning in anger and heading off for a brief spell in charge of Northampton. He was replaced by Tommy Cavanagh, Docherty's old Preston team-mate, who had latterly been a coach at Nottingham Forest.

'Tommy Doc?' says Crerand when asked for his views about his former managerial partner. 'Come on. I'd rather go to the dentist than talk about Tommy Doc.'

For the fans on the terraces, however, everything appeared to be sweet. Doc's flying reds won five of their first six games back in the top division and Old Trafford was crowing. In their opinion, the Doc was a manager who, like Busby, could do no wrong. Everything he tried seemed to work. In November 1975 he paid £70,000 to Millwall for the services of a left winger called Gordon Hill. The new boy was, in many ways, the final proof that Docherty had shed all vestiges of the defensive carapace worn in his early days at United. Now, as the fans demanded, he was totally dedicated to 'attack, attack, attack'.

Doc's flying team caught the wider imagination. There was something carefree, optimistic, invigorating about them as they tore up the First Division table. In the era of Don Revie, they were refreshing in their lack of cynicism. Most importantly for Busby, they were shot through with the imprimatur he had worked so hard to maintain: youth, adventure and bravery. This was a proper United team again. Out on the pitch, the place it mattered, United were restored.

It was also a team very much under Docherty's control. There were no cliques or dissident voices, there weren't even any seventies-style maverick bad boys. In the era of Frank Worthington, Alan Hudson and Rodney Marsh, it was a professional, focused, dedicated bunch of players he corralled. Sure, the dressing room had its standard complement of ladies' men, drinkers and gamblers. But none of them allowed their interests to interfere with their football. Docherty introduced the Italian idea of putting the players in a hotel the night before home games, where they could rest up without distraction. According to Lou Macari, on those Fridays when the team would repair to Mottram Hall, a golf hotel near Macclesfield, most of the players simply used it as an opportunity for an early night. Macari himself would head up there after training, and get four hours kip before the evening team meeting. The Doc was the noisiest member of the party, enjoying a Scotch, a sing-song and endless banter. Macari recalls laughing more than he ever had in his career.

'Sure, he said the most outrageous things,' he says. 'He would tell you one thing and someone else another to the point where much of the time he confused himself. But that was the Doc. You just took it with a pinch of salt and laughed it off.'

There was plenty of laughter, but little bad behaviour. Even on pre-season overseas tours, there were no antics beyond Macari's schoolboy pranks. 'I once locked Paddy Roche and Gerry Daly in their hotel room in Belgrade for a day and a half,' he told the fanzine *United We Stand*. 'Somebody said to me, "If you take the key and telephone from a hotel room here, it's impossible for the people in the room to have any communication with anybody." I thought, I've got to get Gerry and Paddy. I went straight to their room and they were both laying on their beds. Gerry got up to go to the bog. The phone was between the two beds. I unplugged it and hid the phone under my jumper. Paddy Roche didn't realise what was going on because he was in a trance reading a magazine. I left the room and locked the door. I heard Gerry, who was in the toilet, shout: "Paddy, that little fucker's locked the door. I just heard him lock it. Ring down to reception and tell them to open our door."

'Then I heard Paddy shout, "But Gerry, he's stolen the phone".'

For the Doc, management was easy that season. In a remarkable turnaround from the days of Best, this was a time unsullied by dressing room scandal. It was a feat of team-building.

'The years I was there,' recalls Hill, 'there was this sense of invincibility about Old Trafford; you just thought no one could touch us and anything you did would come off. It was a lovely feeling.'

Though Hill had his own explanation for it: 'Things weren't as plush at Old Trafford in them days,' he suggests. 'Even the smell. It was not your Imperial Leather, it was rough, like your liniment. Blimey, it stank. We had this rubbing oil that Laurie [Brown, the club physio] used to put on us. What a stench. But it was a warning stench. It would linger. And if we went somewhere, taking the kit with us, the smell came as well. People knew we were coming. They'd know who they were playing and they'd be frightened. They could smell us. And once they smelled us, they were gone.'

Martin Buchan, by now club captain, and Lou Macari have a different reading. For them, it was all about Docherty. Sure, he was capricious and skittish, but he presided over a dressing room atmosphere that was electric. As the manager picked the same side for eighteen successive First Division games, characters as diverse as Stepney, Pearson, Houston and Coppell were united. Though what they were usually united in doing was winding up Gordon Hill, the butt of many a dressing room prank. On one occasion the team travelled to Middlesbrough on a Friday night for a League game. Macari – it was always Macari – persuaded Hill that he was wanted on local telly to do his Norman Wisdom impression.

'We used to piss ourselves at his impressions,' recalls Stepney. 'He thought we were laughing with him. We weren't. We were laughing at him. His impressions were awful.'

Macari lured a cab to pick him up and take him to the television studios. It was 10 o'clock at night and Macari was certain Hill would be greeted by a closed building and no chance of getting back to the hotel. The cab arrived and Hill, to much tittering from the lads gathered by reception, went to the studios. Once there he was sent by a confused security guard round to the radio studios next door. Seeing a professional footballer walk in looking to do impressions, the on-air DJ couldn't believe it. Hill was put on mike immediately and was up much of the night keeping Teesside entertained with his John Wayne, his Max Bygraves and his Bruce Forsyth.

'They thought they could get one over on me,' says Hill. 'But the thing was, at that time, whatever I did, I came up smelling of roses.'

When he wasn't smelling of liniment, that is.

By early spring United – who, at the start of the season, Docherty thought would do well to remain out of the bottom three – had so impressed on their return to the top table that on the terraces there was premature talk of the unthinkable: the double. Jostling for position with Liverpool and QPR, several times they led the division. And in the FA Cup they skipped past Oxford, Peterborough and Leicester before meeting Wolves in the quarter-final. After drawing 1-1 at Old Trafford, United were 2-0 down at half-time in the replay at Molineux. Worse, Macari had been injured and Greenhoff was obliged to play in his position. Yet from the lip of defeat they engineered a stirring comeback, capped by Sammy McIlroy scoring the winner in extra time. Once more there was a pitch invasion. But this time it was of joyous, bouncing fans celebrating the most improbable of victories. Many of them assumed United's name was on the trophy.

The feeling grew after the semi-final. United's opponents were Derby, a side that had won the title two years previously. And Docherty, never afraid to be disparaging about any other team, declared this was the real final. 'It is the first time the Cup final has been staged at Hillsborough,' he said at the time. 'The other semi-final is a bit of a joke.'

Many a red seemed to agree. The other tie was between Second Division Southampton and Third Division Crystal Palace. Get past Derby and surely the club's first trophy since 1968 was a formality. Managed by Dave Mackay, Derby were a team full of grizzled campaigners like Bruce Rioch and Colin Todd and for a while it seemed like men against boys at Hillsborough. But the boys' effervescence proved victorious. Gordon Hill was magnificent, scoring twice and sending the United fans in the Leppings Lane Stand into dancing, delighted, delirium. Twelve years before disaster struck that same stretch of terrace, it was so ram-packed in there sardines would have complained about the conditions. When the first goal went in, I lost my footing and was carried by the surge a good twenty yards. It didn't stop the singing, mind. To the theme of 'Save Your Kisses For Me', the 1976 Eurovision winner by Brotherhood of Man, the following ditty rang out across Sheffield:

> *Kisses for me, save all your kisses for me,*
> *Bye, bye Derby, bye Derby,*
> *Why don't you fuck off Dave Mackay?*
> *Because we beat you 2-0,*
> *With two goals from Gordon Hill*

Thirty years on, Hill reveals the pre-match ritual that helped him reach such heights. 'Before every game I used to get in my kit and sit on the toilet,' he remembers. 'And I'd look at the shirt, it was a lovely shirt then, a different red from now, a deeper more pure red. And I'd almost have to pinch myself that it was true. And I'd say to myself: "This is real, this is you, you're playing in George Best's shirt. Go out and play like George."'

Perhaps it was the nervous exhaustion expended that day, but the semi against Derby marked United's high point that season. Entering April a point behind QPR at the top with a game in hand, they seemed poised to snatch the title. But injuries to Coppell and Pearson exposed the squad's lack of depth and a defeat at home to Stoke allowed Liverpool through on the rails to grab the title. United finished third, four points behind the Merseyside club.

Still, at least there was the Cup. United's young players headed for Wembley with gusto. Hill was particularly busy: on the back pages of the tabloids, on the telly doing his impressions, filming an advert for Gillette. In that, he was seen with Coppell and Docherty sharing a manly shave: 'Give your beard the old one-two' was the tagline.

Maybe the United players had too great a faith in relative

League positions. Maybe Southampton's team had been so riled by Docherty's suggestion that their chances were a joke they played out of their skin. Or maybe Lawrie McMenemy, the Saints' wise head of a manager, had done more homework on his opponents than Docherty had on his. Whatever the reason, the final did not go according to the script. A seasoned, experienced Southampton shackled the reds at every turn. Hill was woeful, Coppell intermittent, Macari and Daly simply could not get hold of midfield. And though McIlroy hit the bar, there was an inevitability when Southampton broke and scored. Yet again Docherty's past had come back to bloody his nose. It was Jim McCalliog who supplied the killer pass for Bobby Stokes to convert.

'I was so disappointed that I didn't shake hands with a Southampton player,' recalls Brian Greenhoff. 'I don't regret it because that's how I felt. I couldn't even watch them receive the Cup. After the match I returned to the Russell Hotel and threw my losers' medal across the room. I said to my wife, "You can have that. I'll wait for a winners' medal next year." It was the end to a bad day. I'd not even been able to say sorry to the fans because we'd been given orders not to.'

The United players, shattered by ending a season that had promised so much with nothing, were honest in their analysis of what went wrong. 'I think it would be a lot better if players' pools were banned and they let the players concentrate on the job in hand,' says Buchan. 'It's amazing how many of our players saw pound signs in front of their eyes the first time there was mere mention of Wembley. In the end players made very little out of it once they'd paid tax. So it was much ado about nothing. On the day too many of the players were distracted by the peripheries. Too many thought all we had to do was turn up and we'd go home with medals. And they were right, we did go home with medals. Losers' medals.'

Thousands turned up to see the losers return to Manchester. In defeat Docherty did his best to lift the collective morale. 'We'll be back next year,' he said from the balcony of the town hall. 'And we'll win it.'

Compared to previous summers in the career of Tommy Docherty, the long hot drought of 1976 was a time of peace and tranquillity. There were no rows with senior players, no fallings-out with directors; he spent much of the month of June in Portugal, staying with his wife Agnes at a house rented for him by Louis Edwards. Indeed, there was a distinct new note to proceedings when United's new season kicked off in baking August sunshine: stability. For the first eight games of the term the Doc fielded the team that had played in the Cup final the previous May. Consistency, continuity, uniformity: this was a new Doc indeed. It was only when his skipper suffered a thigh injury during a 2-0 win over Leeds United at Elland Road that things began to unravel. And rapidly.

Everyone in the Stretford End knew that Martin Buchan was pivotal to the team's success, but they had no inkling quite how vital he was. In his absence United played eight League matches of which they lost five and drew three. Worse, to Busby's great disappointment, Juventus unceremoniously dumped them out of the UEFA Cup, the club's first venture into Europe since 1969. Maybe the Italians were motivated by revenge at a Macari jape. During a game between the visiting pressmen and their English counterparts at the Cliff on the morning of the tie, Macari went into the Italian dressing room and cut the toes off all the socks.

But without Buchan, the back line had looked not so much lightweight as anorexic. First the former Burnley centre back Colin Waldron was drafted in. But he had a woeful time in a 4-0 away defeat at West Bromwich Albion. Then Stewart Houston moved across to centre back, with a nineteen-year-old full back from the youth team called Arthur Albiston coming in to replace him. This was not a time to expect a young player to sort things out. Especially a young full back obliged to play behind Gordon Hill, a winger who seemed to avoid tackling back like it were a contagious disease. Pundits and newspaper columnists queued up to tell the Doc what he was doing wrong: he needed defensive rein-forcements and he needed them quick.

Docherty responded by going back to the transfer market once more. But in a magnificent restatement of United's innate attacking philosophy, he emerged not with a defender, but a striker. Jimmy Greenhoff was a United fan from Barnsley who had been sold by Don Revie from Leeds to Birmingham, before arriving at Stoke City, where he had turned into a local hero. When Docherty called to see if he might be interested in coming to Old Trafford, there was no hesitation.

'I'd been to see them as often as I could to watch my brother Brian and I just loved their style,' he recalls. 'I'd watch with envy, wishing I'd been out there, it was just my way of playing football. Trouble was, I was thirty. I thought my chance had gone.'

At Stoke there was fury at his defection. But at the Cliff, the players knew immediately what they had in their midst. 'Quality,' says Lou Macari. 'Simple as that.'

It was a mark of United's cagey wage structure that Greenhoff had to take a £50 a week pay cut to sign for the reds. From Stoke. He might have been lighter of pocket, but Greenhoff fitted in straight away. He made his debut in mid-November and scored his first goal in a 4-0 away win at Everton on Boxing Day, which suggested the team were back on track.

'I'd been at a big club at Leeds, then gone to a small family club at Stoke, and I thought I'd be going back to a big club at United. Well, obviously it was massive, but what struck me was how friendly it was, how brilliant the atmosphere in the dressing room was. It was like a family. And that was down to the Doc,' he says. Mind you, not everyone would agree. To make way for Greenhoff, Docherty pushed Sammy McIlroy back into midfield, axing Gerry Daly. As seemed to be his way, he couldn't simply drop Daly, he had to foment a row with him. A bemused Daly was almost imme-diately sold to Derby. His sale was not only unnecessary, it deprived United of a more than capable squad player. But that was the way Docherty worked: you were either in, or you were out.

Results, though, suggested Docherty knew what he was doing. Over the New Year and into the early spring United were on a roll: they won eight League games out of nine, the only blip on the record a 0-0 draw with Liverpool. The catalyst was J. Greenhoff, who formed a partnership with Stuart Pearson that electrified Old Trafford. Two intelligent, cunning, mobile forwards, they clearly relished playing alongside each other. But they were as often provider as scorer: Hill and McIlroy both netted fifteen League goals that season.

The League, though, appeared not to be the Doc's priority. It was in the FA Cup that his team really sang. After beating Walsall and QPR, they gained revenge over Southampton in the fifth round, before beating Villa to set up a semi-final against Leeds. That afternoon at Hillsborough was an emotional one for any United fan with memories long enough to recall the number of times the Yorkshire club had stymied red dreams in the Cup in the past. This time they made no mistake. Inside the ground United fans were so dominant that the report in the *Observer* the following day described the stands as looking like a boiled egg drowned in tomato ketchup, the red smothering the yellow and white at every corner. On the pitch, too, United never looked like losing. Jimmy Greenhoff paid off a chunk of his transfer fee by scoring the first in a 2-1 win. Steve Coppell got the winner. This time, said Docherty as the team prepared to meet Liverpool in the final, there would be no slip-ups.

Liverpool were at the peak of their Bob Paisley-created powers, the English game's premier force. Sure, United had the glamour, the history, the hoolies. But along the East Lancs Road they were never shy of reminding the cocky Mancs that it was Liverpool who had the trophies. They had already won the League that season. And never mind the double, they were heading for the treble: they were due in Rome for the European Cup final against Borussia Mönchengladbach four days after their Wembley appointment. With Kevin Keegan, John Toshack, Emlyn Hughes, Ray Clemence, Tommy Smith and Steve Heighway, most pundits saw them as just too powerful for United. Indeed, given what had happened earlier in the season in his absence, Docherty must have shuddered when Buchan hobbled off the pitch during the last League game of the season at West Ham on the Monday of Cup final week.

'I'd opened up my knee ligaments falling over that fine athletic specimen Trevor Brooking,' Buchan recalls. 'On the Tuesday morning I couldn't walk. On the Friday I could just about hobble. On Saturday morning I had a fitness test which consisted of me standing there, static, kicking balls back to Tommy Cav. There is no way I was fit.'

If Docherty was panicking, however, at the condition of his skipper, he wasn't showing it. He was in ebullient mood in the lead-up, finding himself on chat shows, at gala dinners, on the back page of every paper. He invited the BBC cameras into the team hotel the night before the match, where they caught Hill lying on the treatment table being given a massage by physio Laurie Brown. Hill is seen reading of Docherty's exploits in a tabloid and with astonishing foresight given the events that were to unfold, he turns to Brown and says, 'Blimey, Lol, the gaffer gets absolutely everywhere, dunee.'

Whereas the previous year's final had been a dull anticlimax, this was a cracker. Whatever his fitness problems, Buchan played the game of his life, shackling Keegan. Alongside him young Albiston, brought in after Houston broke his leg in the run-in, was terrific. Up front Greenhoff and Pearson caused Smith and Hughes endless problems. After a goalless, cagey first half, the drama began in the fiftieth minute. Greenhoff beat Smith to a header and the ball fell nicely for Pearson: 1-0 screamed John Motson, commentating on his first Cup final. Three minutes later Jimmy Case equalised for Liverpool and the treble was back on track. But then a bizarre turn of events. Two minutes on, as the ball pinballed around the Liverpool area, Lou Macari smacked a shot that was going well wide. Or at least it was until it hit Jimmy Greenhoff in the chest and ballooned into the goal. Doc was right: United had come back a year later and won it.

Undertaking their lap of honour, the players were ecstatic. There was Alex Stepney, setting a trend among United players of winning FA Cup, League championship and European Cup medals that was to be followed twenty-two years later by Beckham, Butt, Sheringham and the rest. There was Albiston, trying to press his winners' medal on the unlucky Houston. There were the Greenhoff brothers, apparently inseparable, though sadly in later life they would turn out to be anything but, falling out as they did and not speaking for nearly fifteen years. And there was Docherty himself, dancing round with the lid of the Cup on his head. More than twelve hours later he was strolling across Hyde Park, still in his Cup final suit, with Steve Coppell, Brian Greenhoff and a bottle of champagne. None of them had been to bed. In that moment, as he wandered across the grass in the early morning sun, he must have felt utterly unassailable as Manchester United manager.

A month later Docherty called the press to a house in Mottram. He was not there to reveal a new signing, but to announce that he had left his wife to set up home with Mary, the wife of Laurie Brown. They had been conducting an affair for three years and had now decided that their future was together. The collected pressmen were flabbergasted. In Manchester media circles there was not even a hint of a rumour about the relationship. It was the same in the dressing room.

'If anyone tells you they knew what was going on they are a liar,' says Buchan. 'None of us knew. Not even me, and I prided myself on knowing what was going on round the club.'

Though Martin Edwards claims the boardroom was well aware of events. 'We all knew of the rumours,' he recalls. 'And the story was he was sending Laurie away on scouting missions so he could spend afternoons with Mary.'

The gathered media representatives quickly recovered their poise. 'How will that affect your position as United manager?' was the question they all wanted answered.

'You'll have to ask the chairman,' came the reply.

In fact Docherty had already consulted Louis Edwards and was confident of his backing. They had talked about it at the Cup winners' banquet and Edwards had told him not to worry. They were good friends, not just colleagues. They went racing together, had dinner together, where there was talk of a new contract. Doc was already thinking about the new season ahead: he reckoned he had a championship-winning team as long as the chairman would give him the money to sign Peter Shilton, to give him the goalie he craved who had refused to come the previous season because United would not offer him more than £350 a week.

But at a full board meeting ten days after the Doc's announcement, it appeared that only the chairman and his son Martin felt moved to stand by the manager. The other directors voted that he should be sacked. He was invited to Edwards's house to be given the news. He appeared shell-shocked.

'I have been punished for falling in love,' he said as he left. 'This has nothing to do with my track record as a manager.' The Doc blamed the directors' wives for campaigning against him to save their social positions. As implausible as it sounds, there may be something in that.

According to Eamon Dunphy, the directors' first instinct had been to stand by Docherty and ask Brown to leave. It was clear Brown could not work alongside Docherty, whom he had given an almighty shiner on the day his wife walked out. Now he was to be sacked as well as cuckolded. Brown, though, went into a meeting with the board shrewdly prepared. Fair enough, he told the directors, ease me out if you like, but I've got some evidence of other marital dalliances at this supposedly morally upright club and I'll go to the papers with them. Suddenly alarmed at exposure, the directors performed what is known in tabloid circles as a reverse ferret. Brown was retained, even given a rise for his troubles. Then Docherty was summoned and – much to his amazement given assurances he had received from Edwards father and son – sacked.

What infuriated Docherty most of all, as he claimed in his autobiography, was that he had been led to believe Busby had kept a mistress in London for years. But because she remained a secret, it was never an issue. Docherty had stood by his lover and he was out. He was – he says now – ankle deep in the hypocrisy oozing out of the club. But the real problem for Docherty was that just when he needed them, big Louis apart, he had very few friends at United. As he himself said at the time: 'A manager of any football club is a lonely individual. He has many associates but very few friends. At least we know where we stand.'

And where he stood was with Mary, who was to remain by his side for the next thirty-plus years. But they were alone. His ruthless methods of getting rid of those he no longer considered first-team material had built up resentment. The whispering in the corridors against him was intense, the queue to apply the knife in his back stretching halfway to Yorkshire.

Everybody, no matter how highly placed they are, needs allies. Docherty, in his time of crisis in June 1977, discovered that outside the dressing room he was alone. Willie Morgan, for instance, was asked on to the Granada Television programme *Kick Off* to comment on the Doc's affair. He responded with relish. 'Tommy Docherty is the worst manager there has ever been,' he said. 'Nearly all the Manchester United supporters will be glad when he goes. Only then will United be a good club again.'

Watching at home, Docherty was outraged and instructed his solicitor to issue libel proceedings. In doing so he unleashed on himself forces that almost destroyed him. From that joyous moment of dancing round Wembley with the lid of the Cup on his head, a man happy in work and in love, he entered a giddying downward spiral. After he was sacked by United, he fell out with his new employers at Derby and the libel case in November 1978 turned into a personal disaster. Morgan's evidence filled several box files, the line of witnesses stretched round the block. Pat Crerand, Alex Stepney and many others, all were willing to add evidential weight to Morgan's assessment that Docherty was the worst manager around. There were affidavits about touts in the manager's office being supplied with Cup final tickets, and demands for personal payment for public appearances by players. There was the story of the barman in the United directors' lounge who had been so appalled when he saw Docherty entertain a leading tout, he took a swing at him. There was a tale, too, of Docherty punching a young fan who had pestered him for an autograph, an assault the club must have been obliged to cover up as no one had ever come to hear about it. In the end none of it needed to be revealed in the witness box. Football's trial of the century ended almost as soon as it had begun. It was during one of the first pieces of evidence to be heard, about the transfer of Law, that Docherty admitted what he had said under oath was in fact wrong. The case collapsed and he was charged and later tried for perjury. That charge was dismissed after the judge seemed to take the Macari line: the Doc didn't deliberately lie, he just had difficulty distinguishing truth from fiction.

Docherty's was an ignominious departure from Old Trafford, not one that reflected how much he had done to revive the place. His problem was that those he hurt, those he dismissed, those he trod on, took their complaints upstairs. Busby was constantly kept up to date with the Doc's schemes and scams, his double-dealing and half truths. It was Crerand who informed Busby about the affair with Mary Brown.

'You know what he said when he came to the phone?' says Crerand of Busby. 'He said, "What's he done this time?"'

A man who believed that Manchester United Football Club must always occupy the most elevated section of moral ground, Busby found much of Docherty's activity contrary to the Old Trafford tradition he had done so much to establish. It is unclear when exactly it happened – when he cut Law, when he cut Crerand or when he cut Morgan – but once he lost Busby's support, Docherty was finished at United. Even the patronage of chairman Edwards could not save him.

'There's a hell of a lot of politics in football,' Docherty said later. 'I don't think Henry Kissinger would have lasted forty-eight hours at Old Trafford.'

On the terraces, mind, nobody could believe it. All the foot soldiers of Doc's Red Army saw was a team playing with verve, skill and a complete lack of fear. They had no idea what was going on behind the scenes and frankly few cared. But Busby did. And what he now believed was that since much of the dirty work had been done in reviving the club, the time had come for a clean pair of hands.

12

SACKED FOR BEING TOO DULL

There was a strange symmetry at work in David Sexton's career. Almost exactly ten years to the day after he had replaced Tommy Docherty as manager of Chelsea, he was offered the opportunity to step into the Scot's shoes once more. Sexton had just taken his Queen's Park Rangers side to second in the League table, an achievement that had made him much coveted in the game; Arsenal had asked him to move across London to become head coach at Highbury. United, though, had more pressing need; their players were about to report back for pre-season training and there was no one in charge.

As it happens Sexton had been offered the Old Trafford job once before. It was in the spring of 1971, he was in Manchester leading his Chelsea side in the semi-final of the European Cup Winners' Cup against City when Matt Busby asked him if he would consider taking over. To his almost immediate regret, the ever-polite Sexton said no thanks. Not many get a second chance. And sensing he would certainly not get a third, Sexton

admitted later that he took all of twenty seconds to agree when
Louis Edwards rang to offer him the post of Manchester United
manager at a salary of £20,000 a year. It was a figure considerably
less, it turned out, than Sexton's predecessor had negotiated for
himself in the wake of that Cup triumph. But Sexton was in no
mind to prevaricate. All that the Londoner needed to do was to
extricate himself from his contract at QPR and he would be in
Manchester forthwith. He told Edwards he would walk there if
necessary.

Thus, on 14 July 1977, barely a fortnight after Tommy Docherty
had gone, United had a new manager. And rarely in sport can
there have been a bigger contrast between two men as there
was between Sexton and the man he replaced. They may have
been both Catholics but there the cultural similarity ended. The
Doc was all spontaneity and instinct; Sexton was a planner and
a reader. One was carefree and careless, an artist; the other cautious and careful, a man who thought of his calling as a science.
Docherty was loud and mouthy, a joker, he seemed to suck up
all the available oxygen in a room the moment he walked into
it; his successor was shy, not social, someone who could pass
completely unnoticed on an empty train. As a keen student of
philosophy and psychiatry (he surprised his players by reading
Wittgenstein and John Stuart Mill, as well as the poet Robert Frost
on foreign trips), Sexton would no doubt sum up the difference
between him and his predecessor thus: if Doc was the ego, he
was the id.

'How I ever became a manager I'll never know,' Sexton once
said. 'Standing in front of people, spouting. It isn't me.'

Quiet as he was, the one thing that immediately struck the players at Old Trafford about the new man was the depth of his
knowledge. He had travelled widely throughout the football
world to increase his understanding of coaching. The first thing
Sexton did when he arrived in Manchester was to buy a video
camera and screen. He then recorded training sessions and played
them back to the players, analysing everything in great detail. If

the Doc had invested in such equipment, it would have been to screen adult movies.

As befits a cautious man, there was no immediate revolution when Sexton took over. He maintained the entire backroom staff, including Tommy Cavanagh and the by now unsackable Laurie Brown. And in Sexton's first League game in charge on 1 August 1977, he fielded the same team that had won the Cup three months previously, except with David McCreery in for Jimmy Greenhoff, who had been injured in the Charity Shield. Indeed, for United fans it looked as though there would be no change from the Doc's day: the team, playing fluid, fast and fun football, won 4-1 away at Birmingham.

'Tommy Cav had been Doc's man on the training pitch so things didn't change when Dave came in,' recalls Martin Buchan. 'You didn't really notice there was much different day to day. It was just on match days that there was a change. Dave liked his tactics in a team talk whereas I'm not sure Tommy Doc ever used that word in my hearing.'

In September hundreds of red fans flocked to the industrial heart of France to see United played St Etienne in the European Cup Winners' Cup. Oddly, given United followers' reputation at the time, there was no segregation inside the ground and the visitors were given tickets in the French end. Before the game had kicked off, some pushing and shoving behind the goal developed into a ruck and the French riot police – who seemed to be itching for action – weighed in. They were indiscriminate about whose heads they cracked: thirty-seven United fans ended up in hospital. Louis Edwards, who had never shied from criticising the hooligan element in his fan base, was quick to point out that this was different: the United followers had been victim of some heavy-handed policing, he said. If his sudden urge to defend his club's followers was born of a keenness to avoid official sanction, it didn't work. UEFA chucked United out of the competition. On appeal this was commuted to a hefty fine, plus the demand that the return leg take place at a venue a minimum of 125 miles from

Manchester. The game was played at Home Park, Plymouth, and was won by United 2-0. In the next round the reds produced a horribly limp performance in Porto, and were beaten 4-0. Then, in an amazing second leg at Old Trafford, in front of fifty-eight thousand United followers, Sexton's men almost turned round the deficit, winning 5-2.

By now the new manager had sized up the task in front of him. First off, injuries had revealed quite what a shallow squad he had inherited; at different times missing Buchan, Macari, Pearson and Jimmy Greenhoff for lengthy spells, defeats in the League came as if by conveyor belt. Plus, even at full strength, the Doc's team could be easily bullied off the ball. Sexton felt he needed a bit of muscle. And he got it with his first signing, Joe Jordan, bought from Leeds for £325,000 in January 1978. Jordan had been looking to move to the Continent, but Sexton persuaded him to travel no further than forty miles west along the M62. He proved a shrewd investment. Though infamously tooth free, he added bite to the forward line. The United fans were immediately taken by his aggression. But there was also subtlety in his approach. Jimmy Greenhoff, for one, loved playing alongside him.

'Me and Stuart [Pearson] formed a great partnership, but we were very similar. Joe offered something different. Steve [Coppell] and Gordon [Hill] could bang in a high ball and know Joe would get it. When he did, he had great vision, he'd always look to play someone else in.'

More a facilitator than a prolific scorer, Jordan nonetheless managed 41 goals in 125 appearances in a red shirt and never gave less than his full commitment. His assimilation into the United set-up was greatly eased by what his new manager did next. Just a week after stealing Leeds's main forward, Sexton went shopping in Yorkshire again. This time it was for the towering centre back Gordon McQueen. If United fans were inclined to feel any animosity towards another Leeds man joining the reds, McQueen dismissed it the moment he put pen to paper. At the press conference to announce his signing, McQueen was asked how he felt. He said he was thrilled. 'Ninety-nine per cent of footballers will tell you they want to join Man United,' he added. 'And the other one per cent are liars.'

McQueen – a busy dressing room presence capable of astonishing feats of horseplay, generally involving the less elegant bodily functions – was to prove a fine foil for Buchan. As he was later to prove in Sexton's most famous game in charge at United, he also had a real eye for goal.

Not that everything was rosy about United. McQueen quickly found himself at odds with Sexton's abrasive number two. While Jimmy Murphy had been the players' friend, Tommy Cavanagh took a very different approach. Sensing Sexton's kindness, he toughened up, acting aggressively on the training field. 'He said publicly that he didn't like me and I didn't like him,' says McQueen. 'And he was a Scouser.'

But it wasn't just in personnel that Sexton was gradually evolving the side he inherited from the Doc. Training sessions became ever more tactically based. While the Doc would throw the players a ball and tell them to enjoy some five-a-side, with Sexton, there were pre-planned, pre-set moves worked out on the Cliff pitch. It wasn't to everyone's taste. Hill, who had flourished under the old regime, wilted once Sexton arrived.

'I never got on with his tactics,' he recalls. 'He was too – what's the word? – deep.'

If Hill was exasperated by the new boss, the feeling was mutual. Sexton had subtly changed the shape of Docherty's team from 4-2-4 to a more cautious 4-4-2. Coppell, whose work rate made a butcher's dog look lacklustre, adapted quickly, dropping back on the right-hand side to make Jimmy Nicholl's life easy. Arthur Albiston, the full back on the other flank, however, rarely had such luxury. Hill, never one to cover or help his full back, was bemused and befuddled by Sexton's instructions to do just that. In one game Buchan, angry at the way Hill had simply stood and watched an opposing player drift into attacking space, clipped the winger round the ear and told him to wake up. But that was Hill: a live wire in the opponents' half; dozy in his own. Despite scoring seventeen League goals – easily the most of any player – in Sexton's first season, the little magician of the Doc era found himself by its end a peripheral figure.

'Me and Sexton, we had a bit of a dispute,' Hill says. 'He told me to defend, but I couldn't do it. It just wasn't in my nature. I got dropped, we had talks, I told him I couldn't do what he wanted me to do and he said he had no plans for me in the first team. I was absolutely sick. I don't mind admitting I cried when he told me. On the way home from being told, I passed a wall with this graffiti on it saying, 'Hill in, Sexton out'. So the crowd knew what was what. They knew what was going on.'

That summer Hill was reunited with Docherty at Derby, sold for £300,000. In his place, Sexton bought Mickey Thomas from Wrexham for £50,000 more. After crashing his car through nerves on the way to his first training session, Thomas managed just 11 goals in 90 United games; Hill got 51 in 133. But at least, playing behind Thomas, Albiston did not leave the pitch after every game in a state of utter exhaustion.

Hill was not alone in exiting that summer. It was also the end for Alex Stepney. The long-standing keeper's last game was United's centenary match at Old Trafford against Real Madrid. Fittingly he saved a penalty. Paddy Roche came in for a bit to replace him. It was a brave move by Sexton. After a couple more errors, the manager became convinced they were endemic in Roche's play. He quietly dropped him, promoting the much more solid Gary Bailey in his stead. Keepers are creatures of confidence and Roche never recovered his. Ever. Thirty years on, living in Sale, he is still a nervy man, sensitive to mockery, haunted by his failure. Public humiliation at Old Trafford is no easy curse to lift.

It was not only in the team, though, that things were changing. And it wasn't all for the better. Where once there had been real optimism, up in the Old Trafford stands there was a growing sense of despondency. Docherty's team had always been greater than the sum of its parts; somehow Sexton's seemed less. The unease was shared in the boardroom. Chairman Louis Edwards promised the manager £1 million for team rebuilding, telling him that winning the League was an absolute priority. But in Sexton's second season in charge that seemed a very distant possibility. His team were first booed off the Old Trafford pitch in November 1978, following a tepid home draw with Southampton. The noise became ever more familiar as a horrible winter followed, including four successive League defeats, which left United so far off the pace they needed binoculars to spot the leaders.

There was, however, one bright spot: the FA Cup. A run including wins over Chelsea, Fulham, Colchester and Spurs took Sexton's team to a semi-final against Liverpool. The Merseysiders were already champions yet again by the time the game took place, and were overwhelming favourites. United, however, rose to the occasion and had the better of a 2-2 draw at Maine Road. The replay at Goodison Park was won by a diving header from Jimmy Greenhoff, playing his first game after a long absence with a groin problem. For Sexton it seemed that there might be salvation in the Cup. And maybe Lou Macari's contention was right.

'Whatever our struggles in the League, we always fancied ourselves in the Cup. In a way you could say that was our problem, we had become a Cup team.'

To be a true Cup team, however, Sexton's soldiers (as their tune-free FA Cup final song dubbed them) first needed to win a cup. In the final United faced their fourth London side in the competition. Arsenal, like the reds, were not the power they subsequently became. They, too, were fitful League performers and finished a disappointing season only three points ahead of United. But in the final's first half, the gulf between the two sides looked more like three divisions. First Brian Talbot, then Frank Stapleton scored for the Gunners. United looked woeful, and there seemed to be no way back; Arsenal were cruising to one of the easiest wins in Cup final history.

'It was a dream Cup final for most people – a big southern team against a big northern team and two great Cup sides,' recalls Frank Stapleton. 'Individual on individual, we felt that we had a slightly better team. We felt that Pat Rice and David O'Leary could deal with Mickey Thomas, for example.'

That was United then: everybody thought they had a chance. Then suddenly, inexplicably, with just four minutes remaining and the London fans already celebrating victory, the game burst into life. Gordon McQueen stuck out a telescopic leg in a goalmouth scramble to score for the reds. The United fans in the stadium barely had time to consider whether this might be mere compensation before Sammy McIlroy danced past three yellow-shirted defenders to claim the most improbable of equalisers. Cue utter mayhem in the stands. But even as United's fans made plans to marry the stranger they were embracing, almost from the restart Arsenal's Liam Brady slung a wide ball to Graham Rix, who slipped unchallenged to the United byline. From there he crossed to the far post where, evading the tired attempted interventions from Buchan and Bailey, Alan Sunderland squeezed in the winner. There was barely time for United to kick off again.

'It was the worst moment of my football career,' says Lou Macari. 'We thought we had it won. There was no more than a minute when Big Gordon scored till full time. And they were finished. You could tell that by their eyes. We knew we'd have them in extra time.' There was to be no extra time. Terry Neill's men had recovered from a position they had threatened to throw away. In the stands Matt Busby was seen in tears. It was cruel. And for Sexton there was to be no Cup redemption for a miserable League showing. He knew things must improve all round.

To that end that summer he entered the transfer market with intent. He sold the old Docherty stalwarts Brian Greenhoff to Leeds for £350,000, Stuart Pearson to West Ham for £220,000 and

David McCreery to QPR for £200,000. He used the money to pay a club record £825,000 for the wiles and guile of Ray Wilkins. Sexton had signed the young boy then universally known as Butch as a fifteen-year-old when he was at Chelsea. Mature beyond his age, Wilkins had been the blues' club captain at the age of eighteen. Wilkins, though, was a cockney. And that meant he was regarded as flash and unreliable by the Manc crowd. His passing was phenomenal, he was a player of huge quality, he brought calm and patience to a midfield which at times under Docherty had given new definition to the term frenetic. But it took him nearly four years to win the crowd over. Yet, as a bit of transfer business it seemed to pay off almost immediately. United hit the top of table in November 1979 with a 5-0 win over Norwich that their manager described as 'football as it should be played'.

Meanwhile, as Sexton's team challenged for honours on the pitch, off it things were less rosy. Louis Edwards's butchery business was floundering. He had been expending most of his energy on football and the local authority contracts that were his company lifeblood had slipped off to the big conglomerates. Despite his position as chairman of the city's most renowned institution, despite the outward show of champagne bonhomie and long nights at the Cromford Club, the chairman was nowhere near wealthy enough to sustain losses like he was now suffering. He sought a rights issue at Old Trafford in order to release some cash into his company coffers. United, too, were hardly printing money. In 1978 the club made a loss of £134,000, and turnover had fallen to £1.7 million from just over £2 million the previous year. Far from getting rich from football, wherever Edwards looked, he was in trouble. He needed funds.

But the board were split; Les Olive was against the plan and a Manchester businessman and lifelong fan called John Fletcher started an action group to oppose it. Busby had recently learned that his son Sandy would not be getting the permanent seat at the boardroom table he had frequently been promised. Which seemed odd as Edwards's own sons Roger and Martin had long since been invited aboard. He was thus in no mood to support Edwards's financial manoeuvrings and voted against them. Nor did he want the power at Old Trafford heading off via a rights issue into the hands of those he could not control, those who weren't part of the family. A frost developed in the relationship between the club's chairman and its public face. It was no more than that, but it was enough.

Someone tipped off researchers at Granada TV, then the other great Manchester organisation of international renown, that all was not well between Busby and Edwards. It set them thinking. And, in January 1980, after months of digging, Granada's current affairs show, *World in Action*, broadcast a piece alleging that Edwards had built an empire on bribing local council officials in order to flog his meat. Immediately the police announced that they were to initiate inquiries. The strain of such attention proved too much for the eighteen-stone bon viveur. Though the police action came to nothing, he died of a heart attack just ten days after the programme was first aired.

It was Martin Edwards and not Matt or Sandy Busby who replaced the old man as chairman of the club. Sir Matt remained on the board, but his influence had been fatally undermined. He did not have the shareholding to back his position. And Edwards Junior could not forgive him for refusing to support the old man's rights issue and gradually, if politely, eased him to the sidelines.

'I have always felt a hurt at the way my father was treated,' says Edwards. 'Many on the board wanted Matt as chairman, with me alongside him learning the business. But I was thirty-four, I felt it was now or never. Plus, though Matt was in his seventies, he might stick around for years. So I insisted on becoming chairman, I felt it was my time.'

Busby was given a title: Club President. But it was a title only. No longer was he the most powerful figure at the club. The stiff-backed, pipe-smoking force that had directed United for thirty-five years was heading for the exit. The great survivor had lost his last battle: the one of succession.

The new man was keen on making United a much more business-like operation and sought to expand operations, soon launching a weekly United newspaper and – aping Barcelona – a basketball division. He cut back, too, on what he saw as unnecessary expense.

'I introduced a budget,' he says. 'Astonishingly they didn't have one. Les Olive used to jot figures on the back of an envelope.'

To the players' dismay, one of the first items to go was nights at Mottram Hall before home games. There was a nice irony in that. It was at this very hotel that, twenty years later, Edwards was caught going off piste into the ladies lavatory, a misdemeanour that contributed to his departure from the Old Trafford board.

That was for the future. For now, when he first took over as chairman and chief executive, Edwards absorbed many of the duties formerly handled by the secretary Olive. And he relieved the manager of much of the drudgery in terms of negotiating contracts with players and transfers. Not that his business nous was entirely in evidence in the first signing of his chairmanship. In February 1980 he sanctioned the purchase of United's first ever overseas player, the Yugoslav international centre back Nikola Jovanovic. This was a player Edwards later described as pound for pound the worst buy in his time as chairman. Not least because when he returned to Belgrade a year and just twenty-five games after signing, the homesick Jovanovic took his club BMW with him. Jovanovic later claimed that his time at United exposed him to the least professional operation he had encountered in his career. In particular he was astonished by the level of casual drinking in the squad. He was not the last to be thus perturbed.

With the new man in charge in the boardroom, though, in the spring of 1980 United had a great run-in towards the championship. After winning six games in April, they finished the month level on points with Liverpool at the top. For a moment the fans could dream that the title was to be theirs. But then came crushing disappointment: Sexton's team lost the final game of season, 4-1 at

Leeds, while Liverpool won; they were second by just two points. It was the closest they had been to the title in thirteen years. Edwards seemed pleased. He gave Sexton a new three-year contract, doubled his money and promised him the full backing of the board in transfer dealings.

As the 1980–81 season got underway, however, Edwards's faith seemed a little misplaced. United were knocked out of the UEFA Cup in the first round by the unfancied Polish side, Widzew Łódź. They fell at the first hurdle in both the League and FA Cups as well; so much for Macari's contention that they were a Cup team. Sexton's real problem was that these weren't even heroic failures. The football his team played was, frankly, pedestrian. In attempting to translate those prearranged training ground moves on to the pitch rather than playing with the spontaneity of the Doc era, they appeared mechanical, cautious, lacking in sparkle. Eighteen League matches were drawn that season, eleven at home; there were no fewer than eight no-score draws. This was not football in the United tradition and the crowds responded with their feet. Fewer than thirty-eight thousand attended home games against Wolves and Palace in the days when Old Trafford's capacity was over sixty thousand. Nobody turned up two hours before kick-off to ensure their place to watch Dave Sexton's team. Nobody charged up the steps to be the first to shout 'United'. You could understand why there was such an exodus. For a club whose fans have long chanted about sometimes scoring ten, the goals-for column was an emaciated thing. Sexton's team scored a dispiriting twenty-one fewer goals than the champions Villa, and only four more than bottom club Palace. Their top scorer in the League was Joe Jordan with fifteen. No one else even reached double figures.

Worst of all for Sexton, his new signing Garry Birtles scored none at all, not a single goal, sparking endless gleeful jokes among rival fans. At the time a number of American citizens were being held hostage by radical Islamist students in Tehran. On their release after nearly six months' incarceration, a gag did the rounds. What, it wanted to know, was the first thing the hostages asked when they walked free? And the answer? Has Garry Birtles scored yet?

Birtles's failure became the manager's albatross. Sexton had paid a record £1.25 million for a man who had looked a world beater as he won the European Cup at Nottingham Forest. To make way for the newcomer, Sexton sold the youth-team prospect Andy Ritchie to Brighton for £500,000. The Stretford End was exasperated: Ritchie was a local lad, one of them, a proper United player. Besides, he had scored two hat-tricks for the first team when deputising for Jordan in the past couple of seasons and looked the business. It was a bit of transfer dealing that must have haunted the manager. While Birtles couldn't find the net at all, Ritchie scored four playing against United alone.

But Sexton's biggest problem was not who was there. It was who wasn't. So huge a presence was his predecessor that he seemed somehow still to be there, in spirit, haunting Sexton's every move. Sometimes Tommy Docherty was there in fact, lurking on the airwaves, making disparaging remarks about his successor, telling the world that Sexton had made medical history as the only living patient to survive a total personality bypass operation. The comparisons between the two men were constant. On the terraces the fans found it hard to relate to a touchline presence as lacking in animation as Sexton. Whereas the Doc had raged and stalked and punched the air whenever the Stretford End demanded he give it a wave, Sexton sat on the bench looking anxious, swallowing frequently, barely looking at the crowd as he gave them a perfunctory signal.

That said, Sexton was never quite as humourless as some of his press detractors implied.

'Dave did like a joke,' recalls Macari. 'We used to sit around sometimes after training, talking and he'd say, "Got any jokes?" Or he'd ask if you'd heard any good jokes when you were away on international duty. And he'd laugh away when you told them. But it was always you telling the jokes. Not like when the Doc was there, when you were lucky to get a word in edgeways.'

Nowhere, however, was the difference between the two more obvious than in the press room. None of the Manchester press corps would suggest for a moment that Sexton did not take his media duties seriously. That was just the problem: he took them too seriously. There was no banter, no gags, no gossip as there had been with the Doc. Just straight information, delivered in a manner that suggested permanent stage fright.

'With Tommy Doc, the press would go round on a Friday, he'd take them up to his office, open a couple of bottles of wine and hold court,' remembers Martin Buchan. 'On the way back to their offices, they wouldn't know what to leave out. He did their job for them. Dave was never like that, he was very uneasy with them, never gave them anything. They'd go back with precious little, no stories, no fun. And the press didn't like Dave as a result.'

Macari, too, recalls that Sexton was by no means a natural media performer. 'I saw him once in the corridor the day before a derby. He looked like he'd just seen a ghost I said, "What's the matter?" He said, "I've got to meet the press about the City game and I don't know what to say." I said, "Hey, it's easy, tell 'em we're going to stuff them 4-0." He seemed genuinely affronted: "Oh no, I couldn't possibly say that."'

Ever cautious, he was so anxious not to favour one paper over another that he decided not to give his home phone number to any of them. Spurned pressmen, used to ringing the Doc whenever they had a blank page to fill, soon nicknamed him 'Whispering Dave' and held a little competition following after-match press conferences to see who could best mimic his nervous habit of swallowing hard before he said anything.

Among the media corps, Docherty's time quickly became cast as some sort of lost golden era, a reign in which the quotes flowed like good wine, a cornucopia of copy. Sexton's was dismissed as the barren years. It did not help Sexton's cause that down the road at Manchester City first Malcolm Allison then John Bond behaved very much in the Docherty mould, enjoying the company of journalists and providing them with a bottomless well of useable material. Sexton was losing the PR battle at every turn. Martin Edwards, acutely aware of the diminishing scale of his bottom line, took note.

For the players, too, though they liked the manager and admired his knowledge of the game, there was a sense of anti-climax, a feeling that somehow the voltage about the place had been reduced. Training became less like playtime and more like being back in the classroom. Lou Macari recalls one session in which Sexton spent an age explaining a complex choreographed move he wanted to put into effect at corners. After failing to enthuse his enervated players into the routine, Sexton looked despairing.

'We're all shaking our heads at this point,' recalls Macari. 'Then big Gordon [McQueen] pipes up, "I've got an idea, Dave. It's not as clever as yours, but you never know it might work. Why doesn't someone cross the ball, I get my big stupid head on it and put it in the back of the net then we can all fuck off home."'

Unable to match him as a character, there was only one way Sexton was going to step away from the shadow of the previous occupant of the dug-out: by winning things. To that end he was backed in the transfer market by the United board. But as the pressure began to build he seemed to go for players in a random, panicky fashion without any coherent strategy. He had a habit of putting in bids for those who had performed well against him, regardless of whether they were the sort who might have cut it as United players. He tried to sign the Coventry keeper Jim Blyth, offering a world record fee for a goalie; given his subsequent decline into obscurity, it was probably fortunate for the reds that Blyth failed the medical. Immediately after Kevin Mabbutt scored a hat-trick for Bristol City at Old Trafford, Sexton put in a bid for him, too. Mabbutt turned him down, telling the press that he was on better money at Ashton Gate. But was Mabbutt really a United player? His downward spiral of a career would suggest other-wise. True, Sexton clearly spotted something when he tried to buy West Bromwich Albion's Bryan Robson after seeing the young midfielder mastermind several wins over his team, but frankly to miss Robson's potential was impossible.

And those Sexton actually managed to buy latterly hardly helped his cause. Jovanovic was riven with homesickness, Thomas used to get so uptight before big games he would calm his nerves with several pints of Guinness, while poor Birtles arrived with a fanfare but quickly became a national joke. There are those who say that Sexton was simply unlucky with Birtles. But it does not take the benefits of hindsight to spot that the Nottingham Forest man would find it hard at Old Trafford. He was signed to link up with Joe Jordan, but both were so left-footed, they were constantly filling the same areas of the pitch. Far from complementing one another, they got in each other's path. Some might think a man as tactically astute as Sexton should have foreseen that happening.

After a run of five League matches in which not just Birtles but the whole team did not trouble the scoreboard once, Sexton was summoned to a board meeting and asked to explain the lack of entertainment. An exasperated Edwards showed him letters from despondent fans who had been deserting the club in droves (average attendances were seven thousand down on the previous season, ten thousand on the Doc's best figures). Edwards had quickly learned that the United way of pacy, enthralling football was not just grand tradition, it had serious box office implications. There was profit in the Busby way of entertainment, cash in goals. Sexton argued that he had been without his main creative force, Wilkins, for several months following an injury on England duty, and he would soon be back; he pleaded to be judged on what happened at the season's end. Buoyed by Wilkins's return, Sexton's team won their last eight League games. It was not to be enough.

The United board minutes record that the directors had already sealed the manager's fate as early as the beginning of February 1981. However, there was a gentleman's agreement at work in the Football League to prevent chairmen from poaching managers from other clubs. There was no point in sacking him if he could not be replaced. Thus when his team finally began to play expansive football and won those last eight games, it was way too little way too late. In May of that season, instead of the new contract he hoped to sign, Sexton was presented with his P45. At an emergency board meeting in May 1981, only Busby of the directors voted against his dismissal. And, now that Martin Edwards was in charge, Busby's voice hardly counted any more.

'It was very hard to do it, it really was, because Dave was such a very, very nice man and a man full of integrity,' says Edwards. 'But it wasn't really happening, we weren't progressing and the crowd was getting restless. They were. But mostly I didn't feel the tradition was being upheld. There is such a thing as the United way. That is the character of the club. And the supporters demand it.'

After four years the cerebral, introverted, deeply shy Sexton was gone. McQueen for one feels he got a raw deal: 'There's a myth attached to the football Sexton played,' he says. 'People said that his football was negative but he didn't have a negative thought in his head when it came to attacking. I cannot tell you how strongly I feel about that, because it was totally unfair. Dave's man management was first class. He didn't have a selfish bone in his body. He wanted to improve players, improve Manchester United and he couldn't give a hoot about himself. Defensive? He used to say, "Get the ball forward", and yet he got the sack because people said he was defensive.'

But it didn't matter what the players felt. The new power at the club was Edwards. He recognised that United were in the entertainment business. He needed to make a statement. To declare a new direction. To set the company value in an upwards trajectory by returning to the club's attacking instinct. Unthinkable in the Ferguson era, United were about to engage the services of a sixth manager in less than a decade. Across those ten years, each appointment had been a reaction to the previous one. McGuinness was too inexperienced, so old stager O'Farrell was brought in to bring some gravitas. He proved dull so Docherty was brought in to gee things up. The Doc proved a loose cannon, so Sexton, a man more likely to elope with a football than the physio's wife, was appointed to steady the ship. But when falling gates suggested that fans need more than expertise on the chalk board to inspire them, Edwards decreed that what was needed was a big character in charge again. He was soon to get one. And Manchester's tanning salons would be in for a bonanza.

13

SACKED FOR BEING TOO ORANGE

Ron Atkinson is invariably known as Big Ron, as if the epithet were an official title, bestowed on him by the Queen. It is not his physical size, he can be no more than five feet ten inches. It is his presence, his personality, his spark that speak of substance. And when he strode into Old Trafford in the summer of 1981, even the most somnolent corner of the old stadium must have woken up with a start. Here was a very different proposition to the previous manager. His first discussion at United was with chairman Martin Edwards about what motor he should be given to drive.

'Mr Sexton had a Rover,' Edwards told him.

'Well, I've got a dog called Charlie, Mr Chairman,' said Ron. 'But with all due respect, I thought we were discussing cars here.'

So Ron negotiated himself a top-of-the-range Mercedes coupe. Its colour? Champagne, obviously.

On the afternoon of 2 June 1981, the man whose favoured nickname was Mr Bojangles held his first press conference as United's new manager at the Millionaires' Club, at the time the moneyed

Mancs' chosen night spot, the place the local talent went to mine for gold in the pockets of those pretending they had it. Here he was photographed behind the bar, helping himself to a bottle of bubbly, his wrists and fingers tinkling with bling. The message was clear. This was a man who put fun high on the agenda. You could tell by the colour of his suit that day that he meant show business: it was custard.

Atkinson's was some entrance. But he wasn't necessarily the man the board had wanted to walk through the door. After Dave Sexton's departure in May, United engaged in an increasingly desperate search for a new manager. As had been the case when looking for a successor to Matt Busby, Edwards found the United name was not the draw it might be assumed. Lawrie McMenemy at Southampton was first approached, then when he turned the job down, an attempt to prise Bobby Robson away from Ipswich failed. Ron Saunders was sounded out at the then League champions Aston Villa, but he wanted to stay on and make an attempt at the European Cup (not that he got one, he resigned soon afterwards following a row with the board).

'I went on tour to Florida with West Brom that May convinced Lawrie'd got the job,' Atkinson himself recalls. 'There we were in a bar in Fort Lauderdale and Frank Worthington, who was playing out there, came up to me and said, "I know who the next United manager is." I said, "Yeah, Lawrie." He said, "No." So I said, "Go on then, Elvis, surprise me." He said, "OK then. It's you." I had a right laugh with him: "Oh aye, me." But it was.'

Even then, when the approach came, he was initially hesitant, not sure whether he wanted to leave his team at West Bromwich Albion. United's fans knew all about Atkinson's Albion. They always seemed to get one over on the reds. Particularly one snowy New Year encounter in the 1978–79 season, when the Baggies had come to Old Trafford and destroyed United in a thrilling display of pace, power and panache; how United fans wished their own side was that adventurous. Long before such language was deemed insensitive, the match-day programme for that game had informed us that 'a feature of the Throstles' play has been the exciting, attacking skills of their coloured players'. And, yes, Lawrie Cunningham, Cyrille Regis and Brendan Batson enjoyed themselves that afternoon. But in among that talent, the man who really shone was a slight, bandy-legged, pigeon-toed figure in midfield who halted United's attacks with sublime tackling. He could pass, too, and shoot. In fact the only thing obviously wrong with Bryan Robson as he took United apart was the Harpo Marx bubble perm he was wearing.

That Albion team was a terrific side all right. But ultimately Atkinson's ambition overcame his sentiment and he agreed to relocate his sunbed up to the Cliff, in part because he was impressed by his new boss.

'I know he took a lot of stick off the fans and that,' says Atkinson. 'But I don't care what anyone says, Martin Edwards is still the best chairman I've worked with. His knowledge was good, his interest was high, I thought he knew the game. He said you'll only see me when you want to see me. But you could bounce ideas off him, he was good company, loved a quiz. Yeah, I thought he'd do for me.'

The feeling was mutual. Edwards felt Atkinson would have no problem dealing with the media or the other pressures of the job. Plus, flash as he may have been, his footballing philosophy was one which dovetailed with the way United ought to play. He didn't overcomplicate things, his training sessions were crisp and to the point, in his own words, he 'liked good players who could play a bit'.

His first task was to bring a few of them into the club. On arrival he took one look at the squad he had inherited and didn't think much of it. Apart from Steve Coppell and Ray Wilkins, he felt the main men were all coming to the end of their careers. Sexton's captain Martin Buchan remembers his new boss going through the squad's birth certificates almost on day one.

'Mine read 6.3.49 so I was buggered,' says Buchan. 'He wasn't going to build a team round me, was he?'

What's more, Sexton's centre forward Joe Jordan had decamped to Milan that spring and his new striking partner Garry Birtles had yet to score a goal. This was a side in need of instant work. Particularly in midfield, where Sexton had been using Kevin Moran as his holding player.

'Lovely bloke, Kevin, always did the job at centre back. But a central midfielder? Do me a favour,' says Atkinson. 'I said to the chairman, we've got to make United into a European team again. They were part of the history of what Europe was about. But I think since they won the European Cup they'd only qualified maybe twice. At West Brom we qualified every year. Well, that wasn't good enough. Everyone said from the moment I got there, we haven't won the League in fifteen years. I used to say, hang on, I've only just got here. First off, let's get back into Europe. Which we did.'

Atkinson brought with him an impressive shopping list of talent. He wanted Glenn Hoddle, he wanted Terry Butcher and he wanted Mark Lawrenson from Brighton. 'I thought I had him,' says Atkinson. 'We agreed a deal with their manager Mike Bailey where he was going to get Jimmy Nicholl and Ashley Grimes plus I think £400,000 and we'd get Lawrenson. It was all agreed on the phone, then I had to attend a function, came out and Mike rang me and said, "Are we still on for Grimes and Nicholl, then?" I said, "Sure, when can I speak to Lawrenson?" He said, "Haven't you heard? He's signed for Liverpool." They'd only nipped in while I was at the function. So I said to Bailey, "You can fuck off and all."'

He may not have got those players, but even so the Edwards cheque book was in constant use in the first few weeks of the new reign. Almost immediately in came Frank Stapleton from Arsenal and John Gidman from Everton, who was swapped for Mickey Thomas. Gidman was a hard-drinking, hard-swearing, hard-tackling former Liverpool youth-team player. He fitted in immediately with the new Atkinson way.

'The day Ron signed me, I remember driving back to Liverpool with six bottles of Manchester United champagne in the car. I said to my wife, "I've just signed for the biggest club in the world. This is a dream." And despite not having won the League, I really believed United were the biggest club. When I was at Everton and Villa all the players talked about United. And I used to get mithered more for tickets when United came to play than any other match.'

Two months into Atkinson's first season, after much negotiation, the one he really wanted was prised from West Brom for a then record £1.5 million.

'Soon as I took the job I wanted Robson,' he admits. 'When I was at West Brom, he'd put in a transfer request, slipped a letter in my office when he'd come back from being away for England. So I called him in and he said, "Well, Man United are after me." I said, "I tell you now for nothing, the only way you'll go to Man United is if I go there before you." The day I got the United job, he's out in Switzerland with the England team and he's on the phone: "Gaffer, remember what you said." Talk about managers tapping players up, he was tapping me.'

It was a transfer that had one historic and significant side effect: Matt Busby resigned from the board over it. He could not believe United were prepared to spend such sums on a player. He thought it reckless beyond imagining. Not that Atkinson regarded it as in any way reckless. He insisted the fee wasn't a bet, Robson was a surefire, copper-bottomed investment. The man himself is not so sure.

'It was a big gamble for Ron to pay that much money for me,' Robson says. 'I think a number of people in the Old Trafford boardroom must have gone: "Bryan who?"'

If they didn't know who he was, the directors were soon acquainted. In a carefully stage-managed bit of theatre, Bryan Robson signed his contract on the pitch at Old Trafford before a game against Wolves. As if the scale of his fee did not apply sufficient pressure on its own, here was the far from flamboyant Robson obliged to put pen to paper in front of forty-six thousand people, and then go and sit in the stands where he had to watch the man he was expected to replace, Sammy McIlroy, hit a hat-trick. Robson need not have worried: however many Supersam had scored that day, it wasn't going to sway Atkinson. The next week the man he describes as the most complete player in history was in the team, was named captain and McIlroy was on his way to Stoke.

Robson was not the only former player Atkinson pinched from the Albion. Remi Moses came up from the Midlands to join him, too, at a cost of £500,000. And whatever Tommy Docherty said at the time – 'Half a million for Moses? You should get the original Moses for that price and they ought to chuck the tablets of stone in for nothing' – the twenty year old United fan from Moss Side was some prospect.

Meanwhile, off the pitch, Atkinson's application of the scalpel was if anything even more radical. 'I changed the backroom staff completely,' he remembers. 'One or two of the existing staff might have been unlucky, but I'd heard so many mutterings about people stabbing Dave in the back, I thought it was important to get in there clean, get our own people in.'

One of those people was Eric Harrison, then working at Everton, who was invited by Atkinson to take control of the youth system. The pair had known each other from their days together in the RAF doing national service, and Harrison was thrilled to rejoin his old mate, especially when he discovered the likes of Mark Hughes, Norman Whiteside and Clayton Blackmore in the youth team.

'Maybe,' says Atkinson, 'the way things turned out, Eric was the best signing I ever made for United.'

The one man the new boss had wanted to keep, however, was not going to stay.

'I wish I could've kept Dave. For me, Dave Sexton is still the best coach I've ever seen, so inventive, his training sessions were a work of art. The ways things worked out for him, it was never going to happen. A shame, the two of us would have ripped up trees together. But hey.'

It had taken him six months, but by October 1981 it was very much Big Ron's United stepping out on to the Old Trafford turf. Even Garry Birtles seemed to be a new man. 'In training, Garry used to score all the time and his play really flowed,' says Frank Stapleton. 'He was a good player with a good engine, but he used to tense up in matches. I told him to relax. He used to wander and drop back deep. I'd say to him, "Where the fuck are you going? Let the midfield do their job, get up here. People are criticising you for not scoring, you are not going to score any goals from midfield." I told him to stay up with me, which he did. He broke his duck and scored eleven goals that season.'

Despite that Atkinson recouped some of Sexton's outlay by selling Birtles back whence he had come, to Forest. 'He was a good player, I'd have kept him,' says Atkinson. 'But Cloughie had been into his ear from day one of him joining. He'd go play squash with him and Cloughie was in there giving it plenty. He was gone.'

The jigsaw was almost complete, except for one vital area. 'What we lacked was width and penetration on the left,' Atkinson recalls. 'Then I heard that Arnold Muhren would be available on a free from Ipswich. Problem solved. What a player he was.'

Things began to gel almost immediately for Atkinson. Although with that financial outlay they had to. United qualified for the UEFA Cup in his first season in charge, which had been his minimum requirement. More to the point, while Sexton's team had often seemed lightweight, Atkinson's was rugged, tough, full of collective resolve. This was something he worked at on the training ground. Here he was very different from his predecessor. There were no lectures or professorial interjections or lengthy perambulations over the tactics board. Atkinson put on his tracksuit and got in there with the lads. He concentrated his energies on what he called the 'golden circle', the first-team core with whom he would play five-a-side and engage in endless banter.

'Have the crack, a little razz or two, keep things buoyant' is how he describes his approach. He loved a nickname, called Ray

Wilkins 'The Crab', after his habit of passing sideways, and christened the emerging Mark Hughes 'Sparky'. It wasn't because he thought Hughes a livewire, quite the opposite. This was an ironic term to take the mickey out of the shy, diffident lad from Ruabon.

At the core of Atkinson's side was Robson. He was the leader on the park and off it, dispensing help and advice, putting an arm round the shoulder, assimilating newcomers into the dressing room. When there were problems, poor performances, inexplicable defeats, Robson would not wait for Atkinson's intervention. He would call a team meeting and over a few drinks try to sort things out. His was an ethos shaped in the saloon bar: the team that drinks together plays together.

Two years after parking his Merc at the Cliff, Atkinson was competing for the trophies in a manner that was, he suggested, a minimum requirement for the job. In March 1983 his team lost to Liverpool 2-1 in the League Cup final, a game that marked the arrival on the big time of a sixteen-year-old phenomenon called Norman Whiteside. There had been many new George Bests since the Belfast Boy had made his mark on the United consciousness. There was Trevor Anderson, Sammy McIlroy, even, ludicrously, Mickey Thomas, once promoted as 'the Welsh George Best' (about as close to the mark as the description which once insisted that Cliff Richard was the British Elvis). Though about twice his size and with hair cropped so short no one could ever mistake him for a Beatle, Whiteside shared enough of his illustrious predecessor's background for the title to have legitimacy. They both came from Protestant East Belfast, they were both discovered by Bob Bishop, they both had magic in their boots. If anything, unlike the frail Best, at seventeen Whiteside, the man child, looked more of a footballer. He certainly did when he blasted a thirty-yard shot past Ray Clemence to put United on their way to their first ever win in the League Cup. It wasn't to be, as Atkinson recalls: 'I finished up with Macari and Stapleton at centre half. Moran had gone off injured – again – and McQueen was knackered and playing centre forward. We were winning 1-0, Norman put us in lead, I'm looking at their bench with ten minutes to go and they were beat. Then Kennedy hit that long shot which Gary made a rick of and Whelan got the winner in the last moment.'

There was a chance for redemption two months later when United made it to the FA Cup final. In the build-up Atkinson was beset with injuries. Steve Coppell, after setting a club record for consecutive performances, was forced to retire following an injury sustained playing for England. In the final his place was taken by a youth-team product called Alan Davies (who was sadly to take his own life just seven years later). Relegated that year, without their talismanic centre back Steve Foster, Brighton should have been dispatched easily. In fact they ought to have won it. With only a few moments left, and the scores level, Gordon Smith was clear through on the United goal.

. 'And Smith must score,' yelled Brian Moore on the television commentary as the future chief executive of the Scottish Football Association homed in on goal.

He didn't. Gary Bailey – blamed by Atkinson for the 'rick' that lost him the League Cup a couple of months before – saved from improbably close range.

'That was a huge moment for me psychologically,' says Bailey. 'I just kept my eye on the ball and came flying out. What made it a good save was that a lot of goalkeepers close their eyes when they come out. I've done it myself. But this time I kept them open and I was able to get there before Gordon Smith or Michael Robinson. When the whistle went, I walked off thinking, You've just saved United. You've made one or two errors but you've paid them back.'

Atkinson, too, remembers the moment: 'There's footage of me standing up looking as if my head's about to blow,' he says. 'I'm thinking, I cannot believe this, we've lost the League Cup in the last minute, now we're going to lose the bloody Cup final in the last minute. I thought we were done. And then Gary Bailey went and saved it. Sat on the ball. And we won the replay. Funnily enough, he came to live behind me, Gordon Smith, later on when he played for City and I tell you what, he could always borrow a bottle of milk.'

The replayed match was a trademark Atkinson display, a one-off of devastating power. Brighton, even with Steve Foster restored to their defence, were simply swept aside. The Seagulls never had a chance. Some observers put that down to Bryan Robson's performance in midfield. Though Gary Bailey offers his own interpretation.

'My dad had come over from South Africa for the replay. They are big into witchcraft there and he had seen goalkeepers use a lock and key. My mates had said, "Gary, you're a nightmare at Wembley; you've conceded seven goals in three games." Dad gave me the lock and key with a red and white ribbon on. I was to lock the goal before I played in it and then unlock it at half-time otherwise my team wouldn't have scored in the second half. I said, "Yeah, yeah, bullshit." But I went with it and kept a clean sheet against Brighton, then another one against Liverpool in the Charity Shield and another against Everton in the 1985 final. So draw your own conclusions. The other players had their own superstitions. Whether it got me focused or not, it was worth doing.'

One of the goalscorers that night was, inevitably, Norman Whiteside. After the victory Atkinson suggested to the youngster that he have a beer to celebrate his goal: he was just old enough to buy one. Whiteside liked that idea.

In the stands, meanwhile, United fans threatened the Wembley roof with a lengthy rendition of 'You'll Never Walk Alone'. That's right, the song that is regarded at Old Trafford these days as an item of deliberate provocation and is routinely booed whether it be sung by visiting Liverpool, Celtic or Sunderland supporters, was a regular part of the United song book in those days. In fact there are those who claim it was first sung on a football terrace at Old Trafford, brought there by members of the Chorlton Amateur

Operatic Society who were rehearsing *Carousel* in 1961. This is unlikely. More probable is that it was picked up in Liverpool from the Gerry and the Pacemakers version in 1963. Whatever the truth, United fans had no problem with the anthem until the late eighties, when it came to be seen as a musical symbol of Scouseness.

With their supporters given a voice once more that had been missing since the days of the Doc's Red Army, by now United were going places. And their progress was noted off the pitch, too. Soon after the Cup win the publisher Robert Maxwell made a bid for the club, offering Martin Edwards £10 million for his shares. Edwards was anxious to realise his asset and was initially forthcoming to Maxwell's approach. Many United fans, however, were alarmed at the prospect. Andy Walsh remembers an impromptu demonstration that took place in the Scoreboard End.

'A couple of lads climbed on to the roof of the first aid hut and told everyone to sit down against Maxwell,' he recalls. 'We all did and were buzzing off the fact the cops and stewards had a hell of a time getting us all to stand up again. That's an irony now, isn't it? A sit-down strike in Old Trafford. I don't remember whether the reasons why we were against Maxwell were all that carefully articulated. He was just seen as a dodgy bastard.'

The publisher had earned himself a bullying reputation in business and United fans feared his ownership, particularly after he tried to amalgamate the club he then owned, Oxford United, with Reading to form Thames Valley Royals, a horrible-sounding confection. Edwards was persuaded by advisors to seek reassurances on Maxwell's intentions for the club and also to raise the selling price by £5 million. After a lengthy negotiation largely conducted in the pages of Maxwell's paper the *Daily Mirror*, the bouncing Czech pulled out and concentrated his attentions once more on Oxford. With the club now in the Blue Square Conference and only recently emerging from beneath the mountain of legal problems he saddled it with on his death, it was a lucky escape for the reds.

*

The following season was the one Atkinson was convinced would land the holy grail of the title. From the turn of the year in 1984 his team embarked on a sixteen-match unbeaten run in the League that took them three points clear at the top. Things were going equally well in Europe, culminating in the European Cup Winners' Cup quarter-final at home to Barcelona. That night, 21 March 1984, is for many a red the finest moment in Atkinson's tenure. Barca, boasting names like Maradona and Schuster, were winning 2-0 from the first leg. It seemed an impossible task to turn that over at Old Trafford. Not so for Bryan Robson. That night he played as if from another planet. He brushed aside the Catalans in their primrose yellow shirts, oozing a fearsome drive that infected his team-mates. He scored the first with a header, diving full length to meet the young centre back Graeme Hogg's flick-on from a near-post corner. He scored the second, scooping up when the Barca keeper dropped a shot. 'Come on,' you could see him yelling from the centre circle after that goal, 'we can do these.' Then, as if to prove the point, he helped Frank Stapleton to the third, at which the 58,547 people inside Old Trafford went delirious, there were complaints about the noise in Rochdale and Bobby Charlton danced in the directors' box.

'The immense joy resulting from that victory surpassed anything I have ever experienced in the game,' Charlton said after the game. Praise indeed.

The whole footballing world realised they had witnessed something special that night. And Juventus were the first out of the blocks, putting in a world record transfer bid of nearly £3 million for Robson the next morning.

'Skipper, there's no way I'm letting you go if they offer the Bank of England,' Atkinson informed him.

But then, as so often seemed the way, soon after that titanic game, Robson was injured on England duty, missed the next half a dozen matches – including the Cup Winners' Cup semi – the momentum was dissipated and United ended up a full six points behind the eventual champions Liverpool. Too often for United in the mid-eighties there was a sense of 'If only Robbo were playing' or 'It'll be all right when Robbo gets back'. It begs the central question of Atkinson: was his a one-man team?

'We weren't a one-man team, definitely not,' he says. 'But when you've got an absolute world-class player, well he could get people through. We had good players without him. But I'd go so far as to say if he'd stayed fit, we'd have won the League a couple of times.'

Gordon McQueen puts it this way: 'Sometimes with him you could say, "Come on, skip, win this for us." There's not many you can say that of.'

Robson himself is too modest to comment directly on the idea. But he believes that Atkinson's methodology militated against the easy assimilation of replacements into the team when injuries struck. 'The way Ron worked,' Robson explains, 'he had this circle he was interested in, that he devoted all his energies to. Which worked well for the players in it. But the fringe players felt left out a bit and Ron's banter sometimes wasn't best for them. And when you got injuries, that's when it showed, because the fringe players always felt, well, I'm coming in for a couple of games, it doesn't matter how well I do, when they get fit again I'll be left out.'

In an attempt to buff up his squad, that summer Atkinson effectively swapped one player for three. United were now seen as a recruiting ground for the top European teams and, after being watched on many occasions by the club's chief scout, the future England coach Fabio Capello, Ray Wilkins followed Joe Jordan to Milan for £1.2 million. It was money that Atkinson spent on Gordon Strachan, Jesper Olsen and Alan Brazil. The latter – now a hugely successful broadcaster and after-dinner wit – has come to be seen as a telling mistake. He had an unhappy time at Old Trafford. So nervous he would vomit in the dressing room before games, Brazil's confidence was hardly helped when a couple of fans spat at him as he walked up the tunnel after one failed appearance. Atkinson, though, does not believe the fault lay with the player.

'I bought Brazil because he had that great link up with Muhren at Ipswich,' he says. 'The thing about Alan was, although his record is far better at Man U than he is given credit for, all of a sudden Sparky was put in and took off. I couldn't hold Sparky back. He was on fire for us.'

Indeed, the young Hughes, playing alongside Stapleton, could not stop scoring. Together with the newly signed Paul McGrath and Whiteside, who had developed into a brilliant midfielder after moving back to cover for the crocked Remi Moses, Atkinson now had a team of youth and power, as strong mentally as they were physically. Although, in retrospect, he no doubt regards it as a poor decision to suggest to McGrath that on his arrival in Manchester from Dublin he should share digs with Whiteside.

Characteristically of his teams, this side of Atkinson's was capable of magnificent one-off performances while failing to sustain a run on the League. They were particularly capable of raising their game against Liverpool. So much so that the locals grew to loathe the slick Atkinson's very presence. His arrival at Anfield was, for one game in 1986, the catalyst for a substantial upturn in the hooligan arms race between the two sets of supporters: he was tear-gassed as he entered the ground.

'We got off the coach and all of a sudden something hit us, everyone's eyes went,' he remembers. 'I thought it was fumes off new paint or something, but it's bloody tear gas. Prior to the game in our dressing room there were a lot of fans, Liverpool fans, too, kids, all sorts, eyes streaming. Clayton Blackmore was so bad he wasn't able to play. Me, I was in an awful state, I'd run in and there'd been two blokes standing in front of the dressing room door, couldn't see who they were, I was blinded and I'd pushed one of them up against the wall. Then afterwards Mick Brown, my assistant, says, "What you done to Johnny Sivebæk?" I says, "What you on about?" Turns out Sivebæk, well, we'd signed him the week before, he doesn't speak much English, his first game is against the European champions, he gets gassed as he gets off the coach and then as he's making his way to the dressing room, he gets hurled against the wall by his new team manager. It was only one of my own players I'd gone and hammered wasn't it? No wonder he didn't perform that day.'

The problem was, while they could on their day beat Arsenal, Chelsea and the champions Liverpool, they could easily lose to Luton, Watford and Stoke, or Sheffield Wednesday, who did the double over them in 1984. That season in the FA Cup, though, they were unassailable, memorably defeating Liverpool in the semi-final before meeting Everton in the final. The Merseysiders had won the championship (winning 5-0 over United at Goodison) and were set to win the Cup Winners' Cup. And United's chances of preventing a treble looked highly unlikely when Kevin Moran became the first player ever to be sent off in an FA Cup final. Seizing on a poor square ball from McGrath, Peter Reid was bearing down on the United goal. Moran lunged in and sent the Everton midfielder tumbling across Wembley. To Moran's evident distress, the referee, Peter Willis, showed him the way to the dressing room. For what seemed an age, the Irishman refused to go, pleading with Willis who towered over him like a schoolmaster dealing with a particularly irritating fourth-former. Eventually Moran left the field, but instead of going to the dressing room as the law dictates, took up a position on the bench. He was the first up when Whiteside skipped down the right wing, bamboozled Pat van der Hauwe with a Ronaldo-style set of stepovers (no doubt described by his manager as giving it the full lollipop) and bent with precision a twenty-yard shot into the one area of the Everton goal Neville Southall had no chance of covering. The first person to reach Whiteside to celebrate was John Gidman.

'If there weren't a hundred thousand people here, Norm, I'd fuck you,' he said.

Everton could not respond. The Cup was United's. The television pictures of the after-match celebration caught Whiteside, McGrath, Hughes, Gidman and Robson, mullets flapping in the breeze, in an ecstatic embrace with the hugely relieved Moran.

Their favourite watering holes would see some action over the next few days.

'People used to say we drank like a pop group: INXS,' recalls Whiteside of that era. 'Robbo, myself, Big Paul, Gordon McQueen and Kevin we were the big-hitters if you like. Though we never went near a golf course.'

Robson was the team leader of the drinking squad, a captain who found that alcohol was the best way to wind down, relax after the fray, and to bond the boys together. A loosener could get rid of inhibitions, allow a shy person to pipe up and make their point. He would often get the lads together and thrash out issues, with him and McQueen acting as agents provocateurs, encouraging the airing of grudges. Robson regarded his habits as entirely healthy.

'We enjoyed a drink, just like anybody else,' he says of a pattern of behaviour that would be totally impossible for today's players. 'I could drink loads of pints without falling over and making myself look stupid. It didn't take the edge off my game because if I'd had a session on the Monday, I wouldn't have another drop for the rest of the week. The morning after I'd train hard and sweat it out. When you are comparatively young and fit, you can cope with it. I always made sure the drink didn't affect my work.'

Atkinson himself refuses to accept that the drinking was beginning to get out of control: 'I never wanted training to be a prisoner of war camp. I wanted to see players with a bit of bounce, a bit of zip. I don't see it that if someone's having a laugh or a joke they're not switched on. I don't see that. For me, the best players are always cracking jokes. I like players to have enthusiasm. I took a relaxed attitude.'

Not everyone in the dressing room agreed that this was the right approach. The drinkers were becoming a law unto themselves. 'It was the same set of guys who used to go out all the time,' says Stapleton. 'I couldn't drink like they could at all. We would train on Tuesday morning and then be off until Thursday.

The lads would go out after training and would turn in at all hours of the morning. It wasn't for me. I'd have a few beers and then be off home. Certain lads could drink a lot more than I did. I believe that if they had done it less than we could have achieved more with the quality of players that we had. People talked about the Liverpool lads being big drinkers. I simply don't believe that Kenny Dalglish and Graeme Souness went on heavy boozing sessions. Hansen or Lawrenson were not in that group either. They worked very hard at what they did and were together a lot socially but I don't think they overstepped the mark. Whereas our lads often went too far.'

Particularly Paul McGrath who was once resuscitated by an ambulance crew after crashing through the windscreen of his car. There were extenuating circumstances for the accident: McGrath was bladdered. He had driven home several units over the limit from a session with Whiteside at the Four Seasons Hotel in Hale Barns and instead of following the road as it bent round a couple of houses, drove straight on, through a gate, across a lawn before his car ended up wrapped around a tree, with him draped across its bonnet like a glamour model at the motor show.

'We told no one,' McGrath writes in his autobiography of the incident. 'I went back to playing football again, being normal. I was like someone who had done something indiscreet at a party. It was a closed book. A family secret.'

Hangovers, secrets and drinking lies, though, were not in evidence at the start of the 1985–86 season. United embarked on a run that insisted they would surely deliver the one trophy everyone at Old Trafford craved. They started the League campaign with a record gallop of ten wins. A dispute between the League authorities and ITV meant there were no pictures on the nation's televisions of the football that autumn. But those who turned out in increasing numbers to see the reds knew what they were witnessing. Successive 3-0 victories over Newcastle, Oxford and Manchester City were followed by a 5-1 away win at West Brom. With a ten-point lead at the top of the table, there was no question the reds were champions-elect; crowds of over fifty thousand were flocking into Old Trafford to witness the anointment procession.

But then Atkinson's luck changed. Never mind running over a black cat on his way to work, he must have flattened an entire cattery. First John Gidman broke his leg, then Gordon Strachan, Jesper Olsen and inevitably the skipper himself sustained long-term injuries, as did Nicky Wood, a youth-team centre forward Atkinson believed would be the next Hughes or Whiteside. Even Arthur Albiston, the seemingly indestructible left back, missed five successive games with a hamstring tear. As his treatment room filled up, the manager simply could not find adequate replacements. The teamsheet that read at the start of the season Bailey, Gidman, Albiston, McGrath, Hogg, Strachan, Whiteside, Robson, Olsen, Stapleton and Hughes by the end of it included Turner, Garton, Higgins, Sivebæk, Davenport and Terry Gibson. Worse, Hughes, the Stretford End's favourite, was sold to Barcelona in early January, hardly the mark of an organisation prepared to do whatever was necessary in its ambition to win the title.

The Hughes sale was made all the more dispiriting by how easily avoidable it was. In the 1984–85 season Hughes had scored twenty-five goals. At the time he was still on the £200 a week he was earning when he first signed. This was not a time of big salaries – United's 1985 accounts reveal that Bryan Robson was the highest earner at the club on £93,000. That's a year, not a week. But Hughes was well down the pecking order. And when he was offered a barely improved deal (£100 a week extra, rising by £100 per week each year for seven years), he refused to sign it. Instead of negotiating, Atkinson took this as a sign that the boy wished to leave. Realising that he would get no money at all for him when his existing contract ran out the following summer, in January 1986 he sold him to Barcelona for £1.8 million, where he was paid ten times what United had offered.

'Maybe if he'd offered to put me on a par with some of the more senior players I'd have signed the contract and not left,' says Hughes. 'But he didn't and I went.'

Encouraged on his way by Edwards, who had a clause in his contract that entitled him to a percentage of any outward transfer fees. It was a clause so counter-productive to the well-being of the club (how can a chairman benefit from selling the talent?), that, when he discovered its provenance, the television journalist Michael Crick was so outraged he changed the direction of a book he was writing. Initially he had approached Edwards to write a social history of United. Instead, he centred on Edwards's stewardship and called it *The Betrayal of a Legend*.

Crick's book was the first to articulate a case that became a given among United fans: that the Martin Edwards way of doing things was counter to United's spirit. His elevation marked the start of a process of change in the way those who followed the club perceived it. Edwards's father was seen as Busby's man and thus the club was still thought to reflect the Busby philosophy. When Edwards Junior took over, and Busby was sidelined to a back-room office at Old Trafford, not overnight, but subtly, slowly, things began to change. Money became the principal goal.

As it happens, at the time of Hughes's transfer, Barcelona's internal politics were as Byzantine as United's. Thus the terms of the deal became infinitely more complex than they need have been. Because they already had three foreign players on their staff, which was then the maximum allowed in the Spanish League, Barca had to release one before Hughes could arrive. So they struck a deal with United to allow him to remain at Old Trafford until the end of the season. Everyone, though, had to keep quiet about it. But word leaked – Hughes was constantly badgered by pressmen for information and cracked under the strain. He took to lengthy drink binges back home in North Wales and his form collapsed. After apparently exiting through the door with George Best ten years before, drink was once more returning as an influence at Old Trafford. And it was not a benevolent one.

After winning thirteen of their first fifteen League matches, United lost six of the next ten, crumbled out of both domestic cups and

Europe and ended up fourth, a full twelve points behind the champions Liverpool, with home crowds slumping to under thirty five thousand.

It was a depressing season for Atkinson, who could not be blamed for the horrific catalogue of injuries. That said, his touch in the transfer market seemed to desert him. In came John Sivebæk, Colin Gibson, Peter Davenport and Peter Barnes, while, as well as Hughes, fringe players like Peter Beardsley and David Platt – who both went on to be England stalwarts over the next seven or eight years – were let go.

'People say to me what's your biggest mistake at Old Trafford, expecting me to say Beardsley and Platt,' says Atkinson. 'But hand on heart, we looked at both players very carefully. Beardsley came in on loan from Vancouver, but he hadn't really done more than OK in the reserves, he'd never suggested even in training that he'd got the ability that he ultimately came out with. Platt was the same. Even Eric Harrison was surprised by what he became. He was the classic late developer.'

At the end of the season Atkinson tendered his resignation to Edwards. He felt he had taken the club as far as he could. The chairman persuaded him to stay on, but clearly the magic had gone. Of the seven players who went to the World Cup finals in Mexico in the summer of 1986, five returned to pre-season training needing operations. Shorn of his internationals, Atkinson presided over a dreadful start to the season: of the thirteen League games played that autumn under his control, seven were lost. Why things had slipped so rapidly from the glorious peaks of 1985 it is hard to fathom. In retrospect, many suggested that discipline had gone at the club, that drinking was endemic and training shoddy. Others point to the inadequacy of some of the squad players. Norman Whiteside gives voice to the common belief that Atkinson had become distracted by his own personal life. When the manager missed the groundstaff's annual party claiming to be ill, only to be seen the same night in a Bowdon restaurant with a dining companion who was not his wife, it hardly helped dispel the sense that he had taken his eye off the ball. Whatever the reason, he had lost the confidence of the board, in particular Bobby Charlton. Now a director, the former Busby Babe had succeeded his mentor as the voice of United's conscience and argued vociferously that Atkinson should not be allowed the funds to buy any more players after the World Cup.

'When the end came at United, I was surprised, I wasn't expecting it to be fair,' Atkinson says. 'I thought with the relationship I had with Martin Edwards, he'd have warned me: "Look you've got to do this and that." But que sera sera. Maybe I should have gone. Maybe I should've realised the writing was on the wall that September when they wouldn't let me sign Terry Butcher, who I'd agreed a deal with. Perhaps I should've thought, Aye aye, something's gone on here, when I was told Bobby'd been chatting with Alex Ferguson during the World Cup. But there you go.'

He was sacked the night before bonfire night, 1986, after his team lost 4-1 away at Southampton in the League Cup.

'Correct, Ron was never out of the top four,' says Edwards of Atkinson. 'But in those days fourth was not what it is now. Back then it wasn't enough. And we were going backwards. We felt we had reached the end of the road with him.'

Atkinson is not a man to dwell long on defeat or brood over failure. His reign ended as it had begun, with the popping of corks. As Whiteside remembers: 'I was in the physio's room as usual at the Cliff when he called me into his office and said, you know, it's over. I was the one who broke the news to the rest of the lads. Then he came in, told us all and said, "Back to my office for a party." Ron's the only man I know who could throw a party the day he was sacked. We all ended up back at his place. It was a Thursday; I think it was one of those Thursday nights when I broke the rules and had a little drink. The next morning Fergie arrived and we all met him down at the Cliff and he gave us a pep talk and I don't think me and Big Paul were fully concentrating, shall we say.'

Atkinson went on to a lengthy career in management and then television punditry, which came to a shuddering halt in April 2004 when he was recorded making racist remarks about Marcel Desailly when he thought he was off air. These days he looks back on his time at United with characteristic ebullience, happy to post-rationalise his era there as being almost as golden as his skin colour: 'We were always in the frame, which we hadn't been before. And remember, the five years I was at United, in four of them the English champions were also champions of Europe: Forest, Villa, Liverpool twice. And Everton became a very good side. We were up against it. But I loved it there. People say: what about the pressure? But I had three years in a factory before I got into football full time. I know what I'd sooner be doing. I didn't find it hard to turn up at ten in the morning, nice car, put your tracksuit on and have a nice kickabout. You try clocking on at eight in the morning, half hour for lunch and the highlight of your day is banging on the lead with a hammer every time a bird from the office walks past. That's hard work, that's pressure. Managing Man U? Hey, that'll do for me.'

At Old Trafford, meanwhile, a new chapter was about to be written. And for some the party was over.

14

THREE YEARS OF EXCUSES: TA-RA FERGIE

Martin Edwards is very proud of the view from the window of his office. And no wonder. The Cheshire countryside stretches as far as you can see, unsullied by the determined march of Manchester's suburban sprawl. Verdant, undulating, unchanging, there is no hint of Dirty Old Town out where Martin Edwards lives.

'We're the last house from here to Alderley Edge,' he says, pointing westwards across endless rolling loveliness. 'And nobody's going to be building on that field there, because I bought it.'

His office is in the converted outbuildings of the farmhouse in which he has lived since 1990. There's a boardroom table in there, a couple of expansive sofas, a bar where he makes his guest a cup of tea. A fax machine spews out some legal-looking documentation. His desk is the size of Norfolk. These are the fruits of success. And Edwards has been very successful. It is a success chronicled everywhere you look in his enormous work space. The walls are

dotted with framed photographs of the seven championship-winning teams when he was chairman of Manchester United. He sits
in the middle of the front row of each of the pictures, smiling
benevolently, his staff gathered round him, like he's the proprietor
of a nineteenth-century Lancashire cotton mill. Between the snaps
are shelves groaning with medals, miniature Premiership trophies,
scale models of the FA Cup. An obsessive collector of all things
United, he has cabinets filled with videos and DVDs called things
like *United in Victory* and *Champions!* Others are crammed with
newspaper cuttings, board-meeting minute books, everything
meticulously ranked and ordered.

'My grandson plays with the keys,' he says, struggling to unlock
the door of a cupboard full of neatly filed paperwork. 'But this is
what I want to show you. There: all the annual reports since I
became a director. Let's have a look, shall we?'

That's not all. On his bookshelves sit copies of almost every
book ever published about the reds. There are encyclopedias and
autobiographies of players, histories and list books. The titles are
full of words like 'Glory' and 'Triumph'. Except for one. At the
front of the shelves is a well-thumbed copy of Michael Crick's
1989 critique of Edwards, *The Betrayal of a Legend*. You imagine the
subject of this unabashed denunciation takes the volume out now
and again just to remind himself how things turned out. As he
flicks through the pessimistic predictions the author made back in
the gloom-filled days of underachievement and failure, the ones
about how United would never win anything under Edwards's
money-obsessed leadership, how he must chuckle. Win nothing
under Edwards? United won the lot.

And, though fiercely protective of his own role in those years of
expansive success, the former chairman and chief executive, now
the club's life president, accepts that an appointment he made in
the autumn of 1986 had something to do with that.

'Do you mean players?' he says when he is asked who was the
best signing in his time at the club. 'Because if you mean of
anyone, I suppose you'd have to say it was Alex Ferguson.'

And it is not just this room, either, that was transformed as a result of that little bit of business. Edwards's place is to be found in the heart of the corridor of wealth that skirts Manchester's southern fringes. Round here they don't have houses, they have mansions. Behind electric gates and CCTV turrets, 4×4s and Bentleys purr on brick-clad driveways. As I near Edwards's place, a car decorated with the logo of a personal trainer pulls into a drive nearby, its occupant steps out in his kit, ready to give the woman of the house a thorough workout. This, there is no mistaking, is moneyland. This is Manchester's Beverly Hills.

They all live round here, red heroes past and present. Cristiano Ronaldo's bought an enormous new property just round the corner, perfect for entertaining. Rio Ferdinand has the kind of place you could lose yourself in, forget the time of day. Wayne Rooney had a house built for himself and Colleen in nearby Prestbury. Mark Hughes's gaffe is just along the way. Down the road in Hale, you might catch Roy Keane taking his retriever Triggs for a paparazzi-pursued ramble. There's an Aston Martin dealership in Wilmslow whose clientele is overwhelmingly United. There are clothes shops hereabouts that get by solely by selling £1000 frocks to wags and wannabes. Every estate agent, every taxi driver, every waiter in every Alderley Edge eaterie can give you a verbal A–Z of which players live where and how much their place is worth. The area seems to exist largely on cash generated by Manchester United's fifteen-year domination of English football. In many ways this is the neighbourhood Sir Alex built.

Not that it started like that. The thought that anything of significant value would flow from Ferguson's management was to take a long, long time to establish itself in the consciousness of United's following. When he first arrived from Aberdeen on 6 November 1986 he landed in a very different part of town from the Alderley swish in which Edwards moves. As his wife Cathy initially stayed back in Scotland to supervise the continued schooling of their teenaged twins, Ferguson lived for a while with his assistant

Archie Knox in a rented semi in Timperley, a Mancunian suburb that only the very confused could mistake for Beverly Hills.

There are some who suggest that the new man had known for a while that he would be heading south. Big Ron himself was tipped off that Bobby Charlton had been offering his job to Ferguson a good three months before he was issued with a P45. Plenty of time to fix up somewhere a bit more swanky than Timperley, you might have thought.

But that couldn't have been the case, because that would have meant United had engaged in illegal contact of another football club's employee. And tapping up has never happened at Old Trafford, certainly not – heaven forfend – under Fergie's watch. Clearly it was just a matter of admirably swift business that Edwards, who had by his own admission suffered no end through a failure to land a speedy replacement for Dave Sexton, was not caught out again. There was nothing covert in the signing, nothing surreptitious, nothing that rubbed against established rules and guidelines. Installing the man he wanted the day after Big Ron was shown the door – Edwards, Ferguson and everyone else at United have always insisted – was merely the result of speedy decision-making and the rapid tying of loose ends. Though there is an alternative theory, espoused by some well-known sports journalists, which has it that Ferguson's agreement to come to United was secured at a clandestine meeting at a motorway service station between the Aberdeen man and Edwards, Charlton and the club's legal man Maurice Watkins even as Ron believed he was still in charge. No one knows if this is true but ask Edwards these days whether Ferguson had in fact been lined up before Atkinson went and he merely smiles and moves the subject on.

'Have you seen this book?'

If there was any surprise among the players about the turn of events that autumn at Old Trafford, it was largely caused by the demeanour of the new man. The moment he heard who was to be Ron's replacement, Gordon Strachan, who had played under Fergie at Aberdeen, who had been with him as he accumulated ten trophies and shattered the age-long dominance of Scottish football by the Glasgow clubs, warned his colleagues that a hurricane was about to blow through the dressing room. This, he told them, was the most aggressive manager in planet football, determined, single-minded, shot through with a will to win. This was the manager, Strachan reminded them, who had fulminated to the television cameras about his Aberdeen team's performance immediately following a Cup final. After they had won the game. If he's like that in a moment of triumph, Strachan warned them, imagine what he's like when you lose.

'The first thing Gordon did when he heard Alex had been made manager was to shake everyone by the hand and say, "Bye bye, I'm outta here",' recalls Peter Davenport.

Reflecting over a pint or three after their first meeting, however, Whiteside, Robson, Moran, McGrath, Stapleton and the rest agreed Strachan must be off his little red-headed trolley. Instead of chewing at the wainscot and spitting nails, Ferguson presented a subdued, careful face to them. As he told them this was a new start and everyone would have a chance to prove themselves part of the future, he was, if anything, a little nervy. This wasn't Attila the Hun it was a Caledonian Mr Pooter.

'He was in awe of the place when he first arrived,' says Norman Whiteside. 'He kept coming up to Robbo and me in training and saying, "Big place this, big place".'

In one team meeting, as he read out the names of who was about to play in the match, he caused temporary confusion by calling Peter Davenport 'Nigel', like the actor.

'He was nervous, like a kitten,' says Davenport. That's Peter, not Nigel.

If Fergie was feeling a little on edge, what he discovered over the next few weeks was hardly likely to suppress his discomfort. He had taken the job because of what he described as 'the tradition, the history, the romance of the place; I couldn't refuse'. A voracious reader, a student of the game, a man immersed in its folklore, he understood from afar what United meant. He knew this wasn't just a job, it was an opportunity to leave his mark on football's most expansive stage. Driven throughout his life by an ambition to prove himself, this was the ultimate challenge. But as soon as he started digging a little, what he found was something about as romantic as rotting tripe. Although he said all the right things – 'My first priority is to bring back the League title to Old Trafford for the first time in twenty years,' he told the *Manchester Evening News* in his first interview – what he discovered suggested he had little hope that he would soon be able to deliver his promises.

Arriving at the Cliff at 7.30 every morning, Ferguson spent much of those first few weeks absorbing the club history. He read every account he could find, spoke to those who were part of the furniture, sought out Sir Matt and Jimmy Murphy, keen to establish what it was that made United tick, anxious to locate its heart, its soul, what he would later call its conscience. He would talk to fans, journalists, the staff at the canteen, the ladies in the laundry, the bloke who cleaned the windows: everyone and anyone who might have something to tell him about the place. The more he learned, the more he realised that the gap between expectation and delivery at Old Trafford was enormous. This was a club that thought of itself as the world's grandest, that projected a self-image as the most glamorous, storied football institution around. Yet it had not won the competition that most mattered, the one that had once defined it, since 1967. Here was a sporting entity that talked big, yet delivered small. Its lingua franca was groundless bravado, its principal currency self-delusion. The place was a con. And it was down to him to change it. It was a big job indeed.

The sense of detachment from reality was reflected in United's processes, the facilities, the infrastructure. They were in a state close to shambolic. Atkinson may have been good for a quote in the papers, he may have been up for a laugh on the five-a-side pitch, but his legacy was thin, emaciated, a patient in need of significant surgery. Faced with a problem, Ferguson's primary instinct had always been to work at it. That was his way, as manager of East Stirling, St Mirren and Aberdeen. He was renowned for his extraordinary effort; at times he would be doing the work of five men, and still be prepared to take on more. If he was to be defeated by Manchester United it would not be through lack of trying.

His commitment was immediate and obvious. Under Atkinson training was scheduled to begin at ten-thirty, but since the boss himself invariably meandered in late, things usually didn't get underway till eleven. After a quick game of five-a-side, it was usually done and dusted by twelve. The lads were left to amuse themselves, while the boss headed off to pursue his own personal agenda. No wonder Ferguson found the squad he inherited to be unfit, wheezing, blunted. The new man had the players report by nine-thirty. When they turned up, he was waiting for them. He worked them, pushing them for a good couple of hours in a regime of tough exercise. Then he called them back after lunch for more. His team meetings were longer, more detailed, more analytical than anything they were used to. Though he had spent his entire career in Scotland, it seemed he knew far more about other English sides than Ron. While his predecessor would claim 'there's nothing to worry about this lot', Ferguson would provide a detailed breakdown of an opponent's every strength and weakness. He was a detail man, not one given to dressing-room eloquence or soap-box oratory (just as well, as the players found his accent impenetrable for much of the time). It was, he insisted, all about getting the small things right. He made sure everyone bought into an image of professionalism and graft. The players were told to sport short hair and clean shaves, on club duty they were to wear blazer and flannels in a manner unseen round the place since the days of Matt Busby. Porridge and vegetables became the staples at the training ground canteen. Everything was being chivvied, there was a quickening in every step, no stone was going to remain unturned for long.

But, even as he tried to instill a bit of urgency round the place, there was a paradox at the heart of Ferguson's endeavours. It all pointed in one direction, suggesting that he was a man in a hurry. Yet there was to be no rapid fix at United.

Especially not where it mattered most. After watching them carefully over the first couple of months of his stewardship, he reckoned that only six of his first-team pool had what he believed it took to be a United player. At Old Trafford, he reasoned, the demands were different from elsewhere. It needed a special sort to thrive here. As Busby had once discovered, players required a depth of character capable of responding to the enormity of the challenge. They had to have, in short, a little bit more than Peter Barnes could offer.

Barnes was Manchester City's great hope in the mid-seventies. The son of the club's chief scout, Ken, in 1976 he won the PFA's Young Player of the Year. At the awards ceremony he was so traumatised by the idea of giving an acceptance speech that he had stammered hopelessly, 'I'd like . . . but . . . I would but . . .' The Stretford End, shot through with human sympathy, mocked him savagely at the next Manchester derby.

'Barnesy, Barnsey, give us a speech,' they chanted. Then responded to their own demand with a group imitation: 'I would but, I would but, I would but. . .'

By the time Ferguson met him in the United dressing room ten years later, Barnes, after drifting around never quite being the matchwinner he threatened once to be, seemed to be no more self-confident. Several weeks into the manager's reign, the reds played Wimbledon at Plough Lane. In those days of Fash, Big Lawrie and Harry Bassett, visitors were treated to the full Crazy Gang welcome: no hot water in their dressing room, cold tea in the urn and a good kicking out on the park. Half the United team went missing. After the inevitable defeat Ferguson finally showed the face to the players that Strachan had warned them about. He was incandescent at the tameness of surrender. But Peter Barnes was the one he was angriest about. The winger had been substituted with half an hour to go (an hour too late for some red tastes) and the manager was anxious to involve him in the full and frank exchange of views in the dressing room that followed the match. He was very keen he should be part of the debate.

'Where's fucking Barnes?' he shouted as he looked everywhere for the player. When he couldn't find him, he yelled at everyone else instead, then stormed out to fulfil his post-match press duties, slamming the door so hard he almost predated the ground's demolition by about three years. A couple of minutes later the door from the showers opened and a head appeared. It was Barnes.

'Has he gone?' he wanted to know of those standing around looking at their feet in silence.

Unaware that the water was cold, Barnes had been running a bath in the far corner of the shower room when he heard Fergie start his rampage and he had jumped in, ducking under the surface every time the manager came in the room looking for him. He stayed in there till the verbal storm had abated, for half an hour in the freezing water and was by now blue with the chill.

'They thought I was lying,' says Strachan. 'I'd made him out to be Hannibal Lecter or something and he'd been like a pussy cat. I told them to wait and see. It would come. When it did, he didn't disappoint.'

Wimbledon was the first time they had seen him like that. But once he had started, once he began to see quite what a shambles he had inherited, the rows became medieval. Ferguson hated losing, loathed it in a manner few of his players had ever encountered before.

'Alec is a terrible loser. Terrible,' says Mark McGhee, now Motherwell manager and one of his stars at Aberdeen. 'Whether at cards, a trivia quiz, at football, it hurts him physically to lose. And he makes sure you know how much it hurts him.'

At any hint of what he regarded as shirking or cowardice, Ferguson exploded with barely articulated rage. Crockery went flying, tea urns kicked into next week, skips of kit flung about the place. At times like these, he was consumed with such fury, his accent became impenetrable; no one could understand what he was yelling about.

Peter Barnes, mind, was not to spend much longer trying to decipher the bollockings. Ferguson soon shifted him off to Manchester City. He said a quick goodbye, too, to Ron favourites like Arthur Albiston, Frank Stapleton, John Gidman, Kevin Moran and Graeme Hogg. A bitter, disappointed Hogg sold a story to the *News of the World* that depicted Ferguson as a bully, out of his depth in England and resorting to shouting to cover his own inadequacies. Hogg's description of the manner in which the manager would stand within an inch of a player's nose and unleash a tirade of abuse so vigorous it would part the hair became immediately enmeshed in English football folklore. The hairdryer was born, though it was Mark Hughes who first used the phrase, a couple of years after he left United.

Bryan Robson reckons that the anger was partly a psychological ploy: he was testing which of his team had the mentality to take it. But then Robson never was subjected to it. 'No, I never got the hairdryer,' he says. 'But I saw people who did. I was close to them at the time. And I was happy to remain goody two shoes.'

The fact was, of all those he encountered in the United dressing room in those early days, Captain Marvel was about the only one Ferguson felt he could trust. The new Boss found empathy in Robson's desire and commitment. This, he recognised, was a like mind.

'You only have to study Bryan Robson to discover the right attitude,' Ferguson wrote in his book *Six Years at United*. 'Isn't he a joy to behold? How he bursts himself to win games.'

He loved the fact that when he made the lads lap the training pitch to check out how fit they were, Robson was invariably at the front. No, Robbo wasn't a problem. It was the ones at the back that worried him. By the end of his first season in charge, after lots of tests both physical and mental, Ferguson told the chairman that nine new players were needed to reinvigorate the squad. Edwards, however, insisted that after the transfer failings in the tail-end of Ron's regime, there was nothing like enough in the coffers to affect that sort of change. One or two – like Brian McClair from Celtic and Viv Anderson from Arsenal – was the limit.

'I told him,' recalls Edwards, 'if we go on buying players we will be forever in the financial mire.'

Even without much investment, all the hard work, extra fitness, plus the arrival of McClair made an initial difference. With the maths graduate rattling in the goals, becoming the first United player to score more than twenty in the League in a season since George Best, Fergie's United finished runners-up behind Liverpool in his first full year in charge. A bit of fear in the dressing room seemed to work.

But if that makes it sound as if they were contenders for the title, the fact was they were eleven points behind the champions Liverpool, so far off the pace they might as well have come fifteenth. There was not even the consolation of a UEFA Cup place for Ferguson. After Liverpool fans had run amok in the Heysel Stadium in Brussels before the 1985 European Cup final and sixty-five Juventus supporters were crushed to death in a vain attempt to escape the charge, English clubs had been barred from European competition. The ban was the least of it. Lives had been lost and the trauma ran deep. The casual gallop across the terrace that precipitated the disaster was familiar to anyone who went to games in the eighties; kick and run was the rhythm of the match-day experience. When it was combined with a crumbling stadium, however, the result was catastrophic. Football was suddenly a lethal pursuit. The certainties of fan life over the previous fifteen years were put into damning perspective. What once had been a bit of laugh, an opportunity to bond with your mates, suddenly looked altogether different. Many fans recognised that the game needed to sort itself out. It needed to provide facilities that were not death traps, an environment suitable for paying customers not cattle. Not that the government was prepared to leave it to fans to solve the problems of the game. As far as the Prime Minister Mrs Thatcher was concerned they were the problem. Humiliated by Heysel, she promised that something would be done. All sorts of solutions were suggested – from ID cards to playing matches behind closed doors. Football, it was widely agreed, was a pariah pursuit. In the aftermath of Heysel you kept quiet that you went to the match. And that – sadly – was not to be the end of things.

For Ferguson the European ban was added to a lengthening list of crimes perpetrated by his pet hate. Another entry was his attempt to sign Peter Beardsley from Newcastle. Though Ron had not thought much of him in his brief time at United, Beardsley was just the sort of player Ferguson admired: brave, clever, a match-winner. He thought he had secured his signature, too, only to discover the Newcastle board had sold the pocket Quasimodo to Liverpool instead. Cue another explosion.

Liverpool: it was a word that would come to dominate his thoughts, a word that seemed to sum up how the odds were stacked against him, a word that fuelled his fury. At Aberdeen Ferguson had constantly moaned that everything was constructed to favour Rangers and Celtic. Match officials, newspapers, the draws in Cup competitions: everything conspired to gift them success. It was us against them, he told his players. At Pittodrie only they stood against the forces of evil. He never let up, never relented in communicating his insistence of ingrained Glaswegian bias, in every press conference, every interview he would make mention of it. As a motivational tool it worked brilliantly, uniting everyone at Aberdeen behind his crusade, pushing them on to break – for the only time in living memory – the Old Firm cartel. It wasn't a simple football rivalry he was presiding over at Aberdeen, it was something much more. It became an ethos. A cause.

Now he was trying the same trick down south. Liverpool, the masters of English football at the time, were in his crosshairs. His single ambition, he said, on arriving at Old Trafford was 'to knock Liverpool off their fucking perch'. He saw bias everywhere. In immediate post-match interviews in the corridors at Anfield he talked about 'choking back his vomit' because of the institutional bias of referees towards the home club. He claimed *Match of the Day* continually favoured the reds because its then editor – Brian

Barwick – was a Liverpool fan. His interventions were angry, insistent, nagging.

The purpose was clear, but it had an immediate, unforeseen side-effect: it created a new image for United. Instead of rising above such things, instead of being graceful in defeat and magnanimous in victory as Busby – its most renowned public face – had been, suddenly here was the manager of the world's largest club getting all chippy and aggressive about a rival, his mouth tightening at the mere mention of the word. In the eyes of many without affection for the club, his aggressive ill-temper in defeat allowed United to be instantly cast as sore and sour.

'United were bad losers, simple as that, bad losers,' says Peter Hooten, a lifelong Liverpool fan. 'And, even worse, bad winners. Liverpool may have had an air of superiority, but they were never as universally despised as United. And that's why.'

For his anti-Liverpool policy to work, however, Ferguson needed his players to buy into it. And in 1988 not many of them took the game as seriously as he did. Indeed many of them seemed to have other priorities: namely when they might get their next pint. 'There is no denying the drinking was a serious problem but we never realised it at the time because everyone did it,' Gordon McQueen told Andy Mitten in the book *We Are the Famous Man United*, which chronicles the drinking team of the eighties.

McQueen, who had been a leading component of Big Ron's red and white boozers, is right. The sense of denial about alcohol's pernicious effects on United was routine. Robson, the champion drinker, saw it as a vehicle for team bonding, a tool for relaxation, a necessary escape. Like Tommy Taylor and Jackie Blanchflower in the fifties, he believed a night on the bevvy could be run off with a bit of extra effort on the training field. Never once did he concede that its malevolent grip might have been responsible for his catalogue of injuries, numbing the recovery process. Booze, in his mind, was the player's ally.

In the late eighties it was possible to encounter United players in many of south Manchester's hostelries. The Griffin in Bowdon, the Little B in Brooklands, the Four Seasons Hotel in Hale Barns, there they would be, slightly apart, aware of their own renown, as if standing in a forcefield of their own celebrity. But the place they went to drink seriously was the Park, the pub in Altrincham run by Paddy Crerand.

'We'd all meet in Paddy's pub,' recalls McQueen. 'It was a place ahead of its time. They had Continental hours there long before twenty-four-hour licensing.'

Crerand opened for business at the start of the 1982 World Cup finals. On the first night he had fought with a customer who had been giving him terrible sectarian abuse. There was only going to be one winner in a scrap like that. Later in the evening the man's wife came in to the pub. Not to remonstrate with the landlord for beating up her husband but to collect his false teeth that had fallen out in the altercation. It was not, then, a glamorous spot. But here the players could drink, unchallenged and unmolested, in lengthy sessions lasting hours, sometimes days. Here some home truths were relayed.

'I remember one where Colin Gibson had been told by Fergie he could play for England and he was going on and on about it,' recalls Clayton Blackmore. 'And Robbo told him there was no way he'd play for England. Poor Gibbo burst into tears.'

Yes, here things were sorted out all right.

Immediately after retiring from Rangers as a player, Ferguson had run a pub. He was no Presbyterian sneering at the sauce. A bottle of claret in his office at Old Trafford was to become a part of his managerial style in later times, its quality indicative of how well he gets on with a visiting manager. Yet those sessions at the Park were anathema to his idea of how to prepare for the challenges ahead. To him, supporting the cause – overhauling Liverpool – was all. Frankly, he regarded football as something a touch more elevated than a drinking matter.

'I don't mind drink in celebration of a great result,' he once said. 'But it had become woven into the fabric of United.' He called the players together and asked them whether anyone could name a single physical benefit to be derived from all this boozing. When it was agreed they couldn't, he instituted a new club rule. Whereas in the past alcohol was not to be consumed later than forty-eight hours before a game, now there was to be no drinking at all while players were 'in training'.

His first substantial test of the new rule involved two of his biggest stars. As far as the lads on the terraces were concerned, Paul McGrath and Norman Whiteside were unimpeachable. They were the kind of heroes United followers regarded as uniquely theirs: hard, skilful, above all good lads. To this day Whiteside is still eulogised among red followers not so much for those goals he scored in Cup finals under Big Ron, but for a performance he gave in a game at Anfield in April 1988. United were 3-1 down when he came off the subs' bench midway through the second half. His first action was to tread on Steve McMahon, putting him out of the game. His next was to seek out Ronnie Whelan, who was similarly neutralised. After he had stamped holes in the Liverpool midfield, United surged through them, roared on by their supporters in the Anfield Road stand. First Bryan Robson scored, then Gordon Strachan netted the equaliser, miming the smoking of a big cigar under the noses of the Kop.

'Funnily enough, people often remind me of that game,' says Whiteside. He's right. Almost exactly nineteen years after it, he was giving an after-dinner speech following which someone came up to him and talked about precisely that game. It was me.

Ferguson, too, was initially a big fan of the pair, calling Whiteside his Kenny Dalglish and McGrath the best player he had ever worked with. But booze came between them, booze shattered the relationship, booze precipitated the divorce. McGrath went through eight knee operations, his recovery, the manager was convinced, compromised by alcohol. As for Whiteside, at twenty-three he seemed to be getting slower and less mobile by the month.

After endless rows, confrontations, a threat to make McGrath retire, by January 1989 the pair were hardly ever available and had become a two-man drinking team within a drinking team.

Something had to be done. When they both seemed plastered on Granada's *Kick Off* football show the night before an FA Cup tie against QPR (they insisted they weren't), Ferguson found the necessary excuse to make the toughest cut. Both were put on the transfer list. Later that summer McGrath was sold to Aston Villa, where he flourished under Graham Taylor, winning the PFA Player of the Year award in 1993. He and Ferguson had suffered a painful, prickly separation. The manager found it hard to communicate with him, at one point claiming he had called in the player's parish priest to act as a conduit. McGrath was later to mock this claim. Why would he want to see a priest? He wasn't a churchgoer, he was usually too busy on a Sunday at the Park to pray. His parting sting at Ferguson was an assault in the *News of the World* that introduced to us all the idea of Ferguson's network of spies, keeping account of his players' foibles.

'I can just imagine him now,' McGrath said, 'sitting at his desk with a map of Greater Manchester, plotting our drinking route, putting in pins wherever we'd been spotted.' After United complained to the FA, his description of Fergie's cartography landed him with the then largest ever fine for bringing the game into disrepute.

Norman Whiteside's departure, however, was very different. To this day, despite the invitation to indiscretion that is every after dinner speech he makes, he will not speak ill of the manager. His memory is of a man who gave it to him straight and was solicitous for his welfare.

'He said to me, "Look, here's what you could get, go to Everton and earn a few quid".'

His departure from United, Whiteside insists two decades on, could not have been handled with more sensitivity. For those who counted themselves among Whiteside's worshippers on the terraces, however, the news of his sale was about as bad as it could be. Gates were averaging 36,500, the lowest since 1962, as many thousands of fans turned their backs on the Ferguson regime, disillusioned and dismayed. There seemed to be no progress, no hope.

And the sense of dismay was hardly helped by a dismal home defeat to Nottingham Forest in the quarter-final of the FA Cup in the spring of 1989. If United had won that game, they would have gone on to face Liverpool in the semi at Hillsborough. A tie that – in United's absence – was to mark football's arrival at rock bottom. Ninety-six Liverpool fans were killed in a ghastly crush in the Leppings Lane End. The fans were victims of crumbling infrastructure and above all shambolic organisation. But that's not how the *Sun* saw it. They blamed Liverpool's own supporters for the disaster.

'The Truth' was the headline on a front-page exposé of supporters' alleged transgressions that was wrong in every single regard.

Across the country, fans, fed up with the way they were represented in the mainstream media, began to publish their own magazines. At Old Trafford three – *Red News, United We Stand* and *Red Issue* – appeared, giving new opportunity for supporters to raise issues that concerned them.

'Clubs were extracting the urine and fans didn't have a voice,' says Andy Mitten, who was a fifteen-year-old schoolboy when he founded *United We Stand*. 'There were no radio phone-ins, internet or fan comments in newspapers. The only outlet seemed to be the letters page in the *Pink Final*, yet to me it was filled with the thoughts of the same five or six men complaining that the world was better in the 1950s and that Johnny Carey would never have stood for whatever the problem of the day was.'

Unable to afford one of the new home computers that were making desk-top publishing a reality, Mitten produced early editions on his aunt's typewriter, using letraset and scissors. The first batch went on sale at a home game against Chelsea and sold out. A new and vital forum for fan opinion was born. And, as the fanzines began to disseminate the views of the terraces, there was plenty to be opinionated about. To the new media, Ferguson didn't seem to move in mysterious ways so much as bizarre ones. He had got rid of the terrace favourites Whiteside, McGrath and little Strachan. The latter two went on to great things – Strachan captaining Leeds to the title, McGrath being voted one of the best players at the 1990 World Cup. Compared with those talents, the players he had brought in – Anderson, Mal Donaghy, his old goalkeeper from Aberdeen Jim Leighton – seemed backward steps. Sure, Steve Bruce had been bought from Norwich and Mark Hughes bought back from Barcelona, a popular purchase lauded in the stands. But even the great Hughsie had struggled in Fergie's set-up, not dovetailing with Brian McClair up front, looking at times lost and depressed. No wonder, when much of the service was supposed to be provided by Ralph Milne. Milne was a Scottish winger who seemed to have inherited none of the traditional traits of the breed: in eighteen months at the club no one could remember him beating his man once. There was nothing jinky about Milne's jinks. Yet Ferguson had insisted on playing him long after it was clear he wasn't a United player.

Hidden shallows was the view on the terraces of Fergie. He claimed to have a master plan – knocking Liverpool off their perch – but all the fans could see was a Scottish whinger with an inflated reputation for doing things in the small pond north of the border, a man who had got rid of the talent and was going nowhere. He was nothing but a shouter, everyone agreed.

'He did a lot of shouting in those days,' recalls Mark Hughes. 'You used to make sure you weren't the man with the ball as halftime approached. He seemed always to pick on the last mistake before the whistle and explode at that person. It used to scare the living daylights out of us, but it was only because of the tremendous will to win he had.'

But the shouting didn't seem to help. And the embarrassment at the time was unending, relentless. Before the first home game of the 1989 season, for instance, a small tubby bloke with a moustache, the sort of chap you might mistake for a commissionaire, was seen juggling a football on the pitch while dressed in full United kit. Over the public address system he was announced as the new owner of Manchester United. His name was Michael Knighton. Largely because he wasn't Martin Edwards, the crowd applauded his bit of keepy-uppy. Once more, after his attempts to sell to Robert Maxwell, here was Edwards, the crowd believed, trying to cash in his inheritance by selling the club to whoever happened to be passing. Looking back, Edwards does not see it like that. The Taylor Report that followed the Hillsborough disaster was about to insist on all-seater stadiums – he needed a serious investment in the club in order to finance the redevelopment and in addition to the £10 million for his shares, Knighton had promised £10 million for ground improvements.

'That was my reasoning,' says Edwards. 'We had to rebuild the stadium.'

Knighton had put a bet on with Ladbrokes that he would play for Manchester United by the time he was fifty and the first thing he planned to do as chairman was to insist that Ferguson put him on during a game, thus earning him £10,000. After a couple of months desperately trying to shore up backers for his takeover, Knighton withdrew his offer, settling for a seat on the board. Although it was later claimed he had been a long way from raising the £20 million required to buy the club, Knighton, after doing a deal with Stanley Cohen, the man behind the Betterware group, was in fact shy of only £1 million. Incredible as it might seem now, when hedge funds fall over themselves to finance football club takeovers, in those days the game was regarded as such a financial disaster zone that Knighton's bank would not countenance such a loan. So he failed to buy Manchester United for want of a sum that these days would barely cover the annual valeting bill in the players' car park.

One thing about Knighton's intervention, however: it concentrated Edwards's mind on the potential value of his asset. The would-be chairman suggested that United had systematically failed to appreciate the money that could be made from their brand.

'United have a major pulling power that is not being exploited,' said Knighton at the time. And that set Edwards thinking. First, though, he realised that in order to maximise the club's money-making opportunities the team needed to start winning things. He agreed to release funds to Ferguson for a rebuilding exercise that the manager had thought vital for some time.

Ferguson had not had much luck in the transfer market in his early days at United. He'd failed to land Beardsley; he'd tried to buy Paul Gascoigne from Newcastle, but was outflanked by Terry Venables and Spurs; he'd tried to buy Stuart Pearce – 'This is a club built for heroes like him,' he said at the time – but was outmanoeuvred by Brian Clough, who wouldn't entertain the idea of selling him and refused to see Ferguson when he turned up in person at the City Ground. So when Edwards opened up his cheque book that summer the manager was determined to land his men. Even if it cost him far more than he initially assumed. In came Gary Pallister for £2.3 million, the most the club had ever paid for a player. With him were Paul Ince, Neil Webb, Mike Phelan and Danny Wallace. This flourish of transfers represented half a team. Of the side that lost his first game in charge of United at Oxford three years earlier only one player – Clayton Blackmore – still remained at Old Trafford. This was now Ferguson's United.

Which was a bit of a problem for the manager as the new era stuttered and stalled: there was no one else to blame but the current incumbent. Neil Webb was injured playing for England, Ince looked at sea, Wallace never looked a United player. As for Pallister, so nerve-strewn and error-prone were his early appearances, George Best gave damning denunciation in the *Manchester Evening News*: 'Pallister is the biggest mistake that United have made,' he claimed.

Even in the dressing room there were doubts about the giant centre back's substance. 'Pallister was a lightweight,' recalls Blackmore. Although his evidence was based more on the player's performance in the annual Christmas party rather than on the pitch. 'He drank Malibu and Coke, a woman's drink. Once he went outside for a bit of fresh air and collapsed, passed out. I thought he was dead.'

The evening of 23 September 1989, Pallister was in need of more than a consoling Malibu or two. Fergie's expensively assembled new look United travelled across town to Maine Road where they lost to a Manchester City side so ordinary, a month later their manager was fired. In fact the 5-1 scoreline flattered United: they were flattened that day, embarrassed, humiliated. When he arrived back at his new house in Macclesfield, Ferguson told his wife he was going straight to bed. Here, he pulled a pillow over his head and groaned. The next week was the most uncomfortable in his managerial career.

'Every time somebody looks at me I feel as if I have betrayed that man,' he told Hugh McIlvanney, who came to interview him for a piece in the *Sunday Times*. 'After such a result you feel you have to creep around corners, feel as if you are some kind of criminal. But that's only because you care, care deeply about the people who support you. At Manchester United you become one of them, you think like a supporter, suffer like a supporter.'

There was no doubt the supporters were suffering, though few would admit to thinking like Fergie. He was widely distrusted on the terraces. They had grown weary of underachievement, had little faith in his team, were bored by his propensity in after-match interviews always to seek some outside agency to blame – the referee, the pitch, the television cameras. Both on the pitch and off it, United, once the nation's team, were an unattractive, moaning, whingeing proposition with a manager who didn't so much have a chip on his shoulder as a lump of Aberdonian granite. As United lost four and drew two of their League fixtures that December, the fanzines reflected nothing but dismay. In *Red News*, the editorial tone was typical: 'What really hurts, Alex, is that under you we've had shit football, shit atmosphere, shit boardroom shenanigans and our support is drifting away.'

Red Issue preferred mockery, assailing Ferguson's perceived favourite Jim Leighton, depicting him as a condom: 'Clean sheets cannot be guaranteed'. The publication was not the last to be subsequently banned from the premises by Ferguson. Pundits old and new queued up in the newspapers to belittle his efforts. 'The club and the job are too big for him,' said Brian Clough. Emlyn Hughes called him Fergie OBE, 'Out Before Easter', George Best said he wouldn't walk round the corner to watch United play, while Willie Morgan weighed in with a brusque dismissal.

'As a fan,' the *Manchester Evening News* quoted him as saying, 'I don't want to watch United again in a very long time.'

There could be only one conclusion. And there was a growing certainty that change was imminent. Jim Leighton, for instance, claims Ferguson 'had lost the dressing room'. And Clayton Blackmore recalls: 'The players thought the manager would be on his way. Manchester United need to be challenging for the League. And we just weren't.'

On 9 December 1989 the frustration washing round Old Trafford found stark articulation. During a 2-1 home defeat by Crystal Palace, a game to which only 33,514 paid to go through the turnstiles, a fan called Pete Molyneaux unfurled a homemade banner as he stood on the sparsely populated Scoreboard End terrace. On it he had painted a message that summed up the mood of the moment: '3 years of excuses and it's still crap . . . ta-ra Fergie.'

15

SQUEAKY BUM TIME

They may have been close to the point of despair at the shoddy football served up to them on a regular basis. They may have lost patience with Alex Ferguson, the man responsible for it. They may have wanted him out and someone else in to replace him (Howard Kendall was the name most frequently mentioned). But when five thousand United followers travelled to Nottingham for a third round FA Cup tie against Forest on 10 January 1990, they were going eastwards to demonstrate their solidarity with something much more significant than any one individual. They were going to support United. And on that day United, the entity that loomed so large in their emotional landscape, needed all the support it could get. This was a tough – some thought impossible – tie. Forest were a fine side at the time, manipulated by a manager who, though staggering towards alcohol-induced incapacity, still had enough about him to be a canny operator. The Nottingham players had won everything for Brian Clough except the FA Cup and as the nineties began they were presented with an open invitation to progress in their quest to do it for Cloughie: a home tie against a weak, stuttering Manchester United and Alex Ferguson, the dead manager walking.

The game was live on the BBC and the *Sun* ran a full spread of features a couple of days before, fulminating against the Scot's tenure. Under the headline 'Troubled Boss Ferguson Reconciled to Trial by TV as Another Crisis Grips Old Trafford', a string of pundits lined up to apply their shoe leather to his apparently departing backside.

'Fergie's wasted £13 million on untried, inexperienced players like Gary Pallister who are not up to the job,' said Willie Morgan, now a full-time Fergie and Pally-basher. If the game was lost, it was reckoned an absolute certainty that Ferguson would be gone. In the papers there was no doubt about it.

Television, too, didn't fancy his chances of still being at Old Trafford by the end of the week. Before kick-off at the City Ground the BBC's Jimmy Hill noted that the United players looked 'beaten in the warm-up'. It was a remark Ferguson caught on a monitor at the ground. A man who remembers things elephants long ago forgot, it was one he was to commit to memory.

Not for the last time in his broadcasting career, the redoubtable Hill was proven wrong. Entirely wrong. Far from being cowed, United showed a level of resolve that spoke of real character. Driven by an unending noise from the self-styled 'Bryan Robson's red and white army' in the Trent End, they harried Forest's elegant midfield. In the fifty-seventh minute the young full back Lee Martin – who had made his debut the season before after graduating through the youth system – chased an apparent lost cause to keep the ball in play and prevent a Forest throw. He passed it on to Mark Hughes, whose first-time ball through the home defence was headed into the net by a stooping Mark Robins. The United supporters responded as if the Cup itself had been won. And they didn't relent until the final whistle.

'I think we did it that day with defiance', Ferguson was to write later. 'Defiance from the supporters and the players responded to the supporters' promptings. Right from the word go they were on song, our support. They were not going to lose that game.'

For those supporters, sticking together, showing a unified face to adversity, this was a triumph based on United values. Martin and Robins, the key contributors to the victory were both products of the youth system. Not bought, but reared, heirs to the tradition. As had been proven by the Babes, by Best and Charlton, by Hughes and Whiteside, real heroes came from within the family. The young pair had only played because of Ferguson's crippling injury list: Neil Webb, Paul Ince, Danny Wallace, Mal Donaghy, Colin Gibson and – naturally – Bryan Robson were all unavailable for the tie. But it was the manager's response to the crisis that struck a chord on the City Ground terraces that afternoon. He had done the United thing. He had given youth a chance.

The victory over Forest is entrenched in red folklore as the game that saved Ferguson's job and thus precipitated nearly two decades of unsullied glory. Read any history of the club and that is how it is presented. It is how the fans think of it, too. Never a day goes by without Robins being stopped in the street and thanked by a United follower for his vital contribution to the cause. He was the man who turned the corner.

But if this was the start of something big it didn't feel like it at the time. Glorious, life-enhancing football did not spring from every boot from the moment the team coach left the City Ground car park. United lost their next two games to Derby and Norwich. It didn't get much better in the League for the rest of the season: only 29,281 could be bothered turning up for a boring goalless draw at home against Wimbledon that April. Here's how little immediate effect that game had. In the later League fixture at Forest, United lost 4-0.

Even in the Cup Ferguson's team were more lucky than convincing. In the next round they faced Hereford United, then struggling in the Fourth Division. At one point someone in the crowd blew a whistle. Thinking the blast came from the referee, everyone on the pitch stopped. Except Hereford's centre forward who galloped through the statuesque United defence in the direction of the goal. It was only a heroic save by Jim Leighton that kept Ferguson's ambition on track.

'We didn't play well in the League, we didn't play well in the Cup, to be honest. It was narrow margins,' says Clayton Blackmore, who scored the only goal in the Hereford game five minutes from time. 'The difference between winning that season and disaster was nothing.'

But there is a more obvious reason why the encounter at the City Ground could not have been the determining factor in Ferguson keeping his job. It was the fact that – despite what was widely thought certain truth – his job was not in danger. These days, when even winning back to back titles does not guarantee security for a manager, no operation with Manchester United's financial requirements could afford to remain out of money-spinning contention for three whole seasons. But back then it was different. Back when United's annual turnover was less than £10 million, patience was still a commodity available to chairmen, even if they only occasionally chose to exercise it.

Among the has-beens and never-weres who lined up to savage the United manager in the *Sun* before the Forest game, there was one intriguing viewpoint. It came from Terry Gibson, the misfiring striker signed by Big Ron. Although Ferguson had shown him the door almost as soon as he arrived, Gibson was around long enough to see what was happening at the club and thus gave this revealing insight.

'One thing's for sure, whoever takes over', he wrote, assuming the deed was already done, 'will be the luckiest boss in the land. How would you like to take over that group of players? There is so much talent there that one day they could be a real force.'

Surprisingly, despite the universally negative tone of the papers, the diminutive forward was not alone in seeing things like that. Before that Cup tie a worried Ferguson – who has never felt as secure about his position at United as his record suggests he ought – had separately consulted Matt Busby, Bobby Charlton and Martin Edwards, the three men who represented the club's inner core. All of them had made supportive noises. Busby told him to stick to his convictions, it would come good. As the man who had headhunted him from Aberdeen, Charlton was equally unequivocal.

'During that time we never, ever discussed Ferguson's position,' he says. 'Because we knew what he was doing was right.'

The most important reassurance, however, came from Edwards. This, remember, was the man who had already sacked two managers in his time in charge at Old Trafford. On this occasion, although he did not want to give Ferguson the curse of a public vote of confidence, privately he told him there was nothing to fear.

'We knew how hard he was working,' says Edwards now. 'You cannot believe how hard he was working. You just knew it would come right. And you knew it would come right in the right way, the United way.'

If you knew where to look, the appearance of Martin and Robins at Forest was the clue. It spoke of revival in the most vital part of the club. They were the green shoots of recovery. Youth was supposed to be United's strength. Yet when he first arrived in Manchester Ferguson could barely believe what had been going on under Ron Atkinson. Once again United were living on reputation not reality. Scouting was minimal, City absorbed all the better players locally and instead of giving them the belief that they could graduate to the first team, the youngsters were routinely ignored. The new man immediately set about changing that.

'Ron never had any time for us,' recalls Russell Beardsmore, one of United's young shavers at the time. 'I spoke to Alex more in his first three or four days at the club than I spoke to Ron in his entire time.'

As for those working with the young players, they were left in no doubt as to what was now expected. 'Alex Ferguson had me in within the first week he was there,' says Eric Harrison. 'He said to me, "I'm not happy with the youth system." I thought he was having a go at me personally, so I got a bit prickly and said, "What do you mean? We've had Mark Hughes through, Norman Whiteside, Graeme Hogg." He said, "Well, that's OK but I want more." I said, "Get me more good young players into the system and I'll get them into the first team for you." He said, "It's done." And it started from there. The number of scouts increased dramatically. All over Britain, we swamped the place. Plus – and this was really important – he brought Brian Kidd in to sort things out locally.'

Harrison soon found that once he trusted them the manager was willing to back a colleague. 'I admit the structure wasn't too clever,' he says. 'For instance, we trained in the gym at the Cliff and I remember counting one day and there were forty-eight boys in there and there was just myself and Brian to organise them. Crazy. Brian and I looked at each other and were flabbergasted. I said to him, we've no chance. So I said to Alex, "What do you expect us to do here?" He just said to us, "Whatever you need, whatever it takes." He made sure we got it. From the word go.'

And the pair did their best to encourage local boys. Like James Gibson, they wanted a United team of Manchester men. 'There was great local talent which needed nurturing,' says Kidd. 'There was a perception that somehow a player not from Manchester was better. That didn't wash with me. I felt it's important for Mancunians to play for United. We as fans can relate to Mancunians and so can their local community. Imagine how proud Langley people are seeing Paul Scholes. One of their own doing what we'd all love to do.'

Mark Robins, who hailed from Ashton, was typical. He was given his first professional contract only a few weeks after Ferguson arrived; he was, in effect, the new boss's first signing. A lynx-eyed finisher, he scored over a hundred goals in the youth teams.

'He was a fantastic lad,' says Harrison. 'And the only thing that stopped him being top class was a lack of pace. He had everything else. Especially the temperament. He was cool as ice. I wasn't the least surprised when he scored at Nottingham.'

A youth-team product of character: very Manchester United.

It became clear to Edwards, Busby and Charlton that what Ferguson was doing as he set to work was restoring the ethos of the place, returning it to what it should be.

'Sir Matt lost and rebuilt a team, rebuilding it the right way, in the fashion of what he thought Manchester United should be. My job, really, was to regain that,' Ferguson told the *Daily Telegraph* on the twenty-first anniversary of his United arrival.

In retrospect, the evidence was there as early as New Year's Day 1989, when he had fielded a team that beat Liverpool which included four youth-team players: Robins, Beardsmore, Martin and Lee Sharpe, a pacy winger he had bought as a seventeen-year-old from Torquay. Guiliano Maiorana and Deiniol Graham were on the bench. The press labelled them 'Fergie's Fledglings'. It turned out the fledglings' appearance – a bit like Murphy's Chicks thirty years before – was fleeting. But it sent out an important message: this was a manager prepared to play young players. It was a message directed at ambitious talent that might otherwise be tempted to go elsewhere. Talent like a schoolboy called Ryan Wilson. The son of Swinton's Welsh rugby league player Danny, he was on City's books when Ferguson first arrived. But once the manager put the word out to the scouts that he wanted no stone unturned in the search for the best, Wilson was invited to the Cliff for a trial. His performance stopped the watching coaches in their tracks. It was so good it might actually have stopped the coaches' watches.

'First time I saw him play he took my breath away,' recalls Harrison. 'Dear me, I couldn't believe what I was seeing. He was so quick, so graceful, so skilful. You just knew you were in the presence of something special.'

Once he caught sight of him, the new manager determined to have Wilson on his staff. The boy's parents were in the midst of an unhappy divorce at the time. He was very close to his mother, whose maiden name he was soon to adopt. Ferguson worked tirelessly to persuade Lynne Giggs that her boy's best interests lay at

Old Trafford. There he would flourish. There he would get his chance.

'We got a great piece of luck when we took Ryan Giggs from Manchester City,' Ferguson told the *Daily Telegraph*. 'If I hadn't have come to the club when I did, he would have ended up playing for them, no question. My first real challenge was to get Ryan signed up on schoolboy forms and we worked hard at that. We were up at Ryan's door every night until he signed.'

For Giggs, Ferguson's arrival on the doorstep of his mum's neat little cottage in Swinton the evening after he had been for a trial was the clincher.

'If you're fourteen years old and the manager of Manchester United turns up at your house, you tend to be a bit flattered,' Giggs once told me. 'It's a nice feeling and not something you turn down. I said yes straight away. But my mum said we'd let him know. Because City had been good to me, she wanted to give them first refusal. So she went to see Ken Barnes [City's chief scout] and asked if he was going to sign me on as an apprentice and he said no, he wasn't. Not interested. So the next time Fergie came round, she said yes.'

Signing fourteen-year-old schoolboys is not the kind of news that fills papers. Nor was a lot of the other work Ferguson was engaged in. Insiders could see it, even if to outsiders things looked depressingly unfocused and messy. That was the way of Ferguson's priorities: family first, wider world a distant second. It didn't help his image, but he wasn't interested in public relations. Whereas other managers worry themselves to distraction about how they are perceived (when he became England coach Steve McClaren, for instance, hired the PR supremo Max Clifford to buff up his public persona), Ferguson had more important matters on his mind. His priority was getting everyone to buy into the idea that knocking Liverpool off their fucking perch was the most important thing in the world. The cause was what mattered. He wasn't going to win many headlines that way, but he was convinced it would win him a lot of trophies.

Those who met him privately at the time, who witnessed at close quarters the charm he exuded when representing the club's charitable efforts, could hardly reconcile his avuncular presence with the purple-faced, tight-lipped whinger moaning about referees to the *Match of the Day* cameras. Though he claimed to share so many of his values, Ferguson seemed to be the opposite of Busby. The Old Man disguised a steel core beneath a carapace of gentleness; the new man hid his sweetness behind a bucket load of sour. At points of crisis – and there were to be many over the years he was in office – this was invariably to prove an issue. It has always been easier to kick Alex Ferguson than to love him. And the build-up to the Forest Cup tie was but the first occasion of many in which his many enemies have mistaken wish fulfilment for fact, speculation for certainty. The point is, in those few days in January 1990, nobody outside really knew what was going on at United. Which was just how Ferguson has always liked it.

'Fergie's strong,' says Clayton Blackmore. 'He never showed he was under pressure. But there was pressure. There was pressure all right.'

Two more pressured victories over Newcastle and Sheffield United, brought Ferguson to an FA Cup semi-final against neighbours Oldham Athletic. An ambitious club managed by Joe Royle, Oldham had already reached that year's League Cup final and had knocked Arsenal, Villa and Everton out of cup competitions. With a certain Denis Irwin at left back, they made life tough for Ferguson, forcing a replay when their United old boy Andy Ritchie scored the equaliser in a harem-scarem 3-3 draw. It was a Robins goal in the second game that finally earned Ferguson his first trip to Wembley as United manager.

Here United met Crystal Palace, managed by another former red hero Steve Coppell. The encounter is less remembered for the stirring 3-3 draw in the first game than for Ferguson's team selection for the replay. Between matches he dropped his keeper Jim Leighton, the man whose save at Hereford had got them to Wembley in the first place. Leighton's form had been wobbly in the League and Ferguson had considered not picking him for the first match. Loyalty to a man who had been by his side through all his Aberdonian triumphs – the three titles, the four Scottish Cups, the European Cup Winners' Cup win – prevailed. But Leighton had a poor game, culpable for a couple of the Palace goals. He looked edgy. He looked vulnerable. After a sleepless night Ferguson took the player aside the morning of the replay and told him he was dropped. Ferguson's assistant Archie Knox thought the decision harsh and counselled that it would not only destroy Leighton's confidence, it would undermine team morale. But the manager was determined.

'The easy decision was to play him,' he wrote later. 'The hard decision won us the trophy.'

Leighton was distraught. He played only once more for United – a League Cup tie at Halifax – before heading back to Scotland. He never spoke to Ferguson again. But by wielding the selectorial knife, the boss had proven his single-mindedness. he was prepared to do anything, even compromise personal loyalty, in order to further the interests of Manchester United.

'It was animal instinct. I smelled danger after the first Wembley game. I knew Jim had to be dropped,' Ferguson was quoted as saying in the *Sun*.

In Leighton's place came Les Sealey, a loanee from Luton who had only played once for United that season. A loud and lary cockney, Sealey was the nervy Leighton's temperamental opposite. Awash with self-confidence he was a solid presence in the red goal in the replay and celebrated Lee Martin's winner as if he had been born on the very cobbles of Salford. The win made Ferguson the only manager to lift the Cup on both sides of the border, a distinction he still maintains. The first man he raced to congratulate at the final whistle was the ebullient Sealey.

'The last and bravest decision of Alex Ferguson's tormented season brought historic vindication,' wrote Jeff Powell in the *Daily Mail*.

Sealey turned out to be something of a talisman for Ferguson.

Over a sporadic, five-year career at Old Trafford, he played just fifty-five times, but that included four finals.

'Yeah, I think I was the manager's lucky mascot,' Sealey once told me. 'I believe in all that, superstitions. I've got my own way of doing things. I had this accident on my way to a game once, bumper ripped off the front of the car. I played a blinder that day and didn't want to get it repaired. I got slaughtered, all the lads saying, "Look at the state of your car". But I wouldn't get it repaired.'

Sadly Sealey's reserves of good luck turned out to be limited. Aged forty-three, in 2001 he died after a heart attack while working as West Ham's goalkeeping coach. Stephen Bywater, the Derby County keeper, was Sealey's protégé at the time and wears the number 43 as a memorial to his mentor.

Though he would always claim to be a believer in the philosophy of Gary Player – the harder I work the luckier I get – that Wembley final signalled the start of Alex Ferguson's lucky streak. Once the blockage had been removed preventing him from winning his first trophy, the prizes came in an incontinent rush. The following season saw the lifting of the ban on English clubs in European competition imposed after Heysel. After sprucing up the youth system, here was his opportunity to engage with another facet of United legend: Europe. Sure, the Cup Winners' Cup was the most junior of European trophies, one that was to wither away altogether when it was absorbed into the UEFA Cup in 1999. But it was one that had emotional resonance for the manager: he had won it in 1983, his unfancied Aberdeen beating Real Madrid in the final. Besides, for a club that regarded overseas competition as an essential part of its annual calendar, just to be there once more was enough. The paucity of opponents on the route to the final suggests this was not the toughest of examinations for Ferguson's emerging side. Pesci Munkas, Wrexham, Montpellier and Legia Warsaw were less elevated opposition than the sides faced in that year's gallop to the League Cup final. In one early round of the domestic competition they had played Arsenal, then pursuing the title, and beat them 6-2 on their own turf, with Lee Sharpe scoring an exuberantly celebrated hat-trick. But to underline the lack of consistency of Ferguson's side, they lost at Wembley to Big Ron's Sheffield Wednesday. And how the man with the tan relished getting one over on the man with the plan.

United's nervy showing at Wembley hardly filled United fans with much optimism ahead of the Cup Winners' Cup final against Barcelona. As fanzine founder Andy Mitten, back then a seventeen-year-old traveling to his first European game, puts it: 'Barca had Michael Laudrup, Alexanco, Ronald Koeman and Johann Cruyff as coach. United had Clayton Blackmore. Barca had just won the Spanish League and they would win their first European Cup a year later. United had finished sixth in the League and only four days before Crystal Palace had beaten us 3-0 with Paul Wratten coming off the bench.'

The game in Rotterdam represented the first appearance of English supporters in a European final since the awfulness of Heysel and there was much trepidation about how the visiting hordes would behave. But the English fans were changing. England's relative success at Italia 90 had made the game fashionable. A new type of fan was being attracted to matches. The Taylor Report had insisted that stadiums be updated, all-seater venues were to become compulsory. The game was being culturally cleansed, hooliganism marginalised, pushed to the boundaries, no longer an ingrained part of the match-going experience. What's more, Manchester was in the grip of its own youth phenomenon, recognised on the front cover of *Time* magazine, a baggy-trousered, ecstasy-fuelled love-in. For United's Madchester followers, in their fishing hats and flares, the final was less an opportunity to fight than to, in the words of Mitten's travelling companions, 'get blissed up and pissed up'.

'It was also a chance', says Mitten, 'to show the Scousers that unlike them we could behave.'

And behave they did. It may have been loud, it was certainly ramshackle, but United's presence in Rotterdam was not remotely threatening. Eighteen months earlier they had been singing for the club's future in Nottingham. Now twenty-one thousand United fans stood in the pouring rain in Feyenoord's open stands yelling out the anthems of Madchester, particularly James's 'Sit Down'.

'The final meant more to United and United fans [than to Barcelona],' says Mitten. 'We'd been fed on scraps. Now we had a chance to sit at the top table.'

Ferguson and United relished it. They won 2-1. Two goals by Mark Hughes cemented his place in red hearts, while a goal-line clearance by Clayton Blackmore from Michael Laudrup did as much to secure the trophy. Afterwards on the pitch a drenched Ferguson, the man whose mouth had been in a tight knot of fury for so much of his time at Old Trafford, beamed hugely as he became only the second manager to win the Cup with two different clubs. As he stood there, the United fans in the stands who had so recently called for his sacking chanted his name to the echoes. They had warmed to the man. He understood their values. He wanted exactly what they wanted: success, dominance, knocking Liverpool off their perch. And now he was beginning to deliver. He would do for them.

Ferguson, too, was thrilled by Rotterdam because he knew what it meant. He was beginning to shape a team in his image, determined, characterful, pathologically averse to defeat. A team the manager – now released by victory from speculation about his future – reckoned capable of the most important challenge he had set himself: winning the League title.

Between Ferguson's two cup finals that year, Martin Edwards floated the club on the London Stock Exchange. He had got the idea from his friend Irving Scholar at Tottenham, then regarded as the most sophisticated money-making operation in football. Edwards needed money, both to clear the personal mortgage he had taken out to support his father's rights issue and to rebuild

Old Trafford. He had tried to sell to individuals twice but this seemed a much more sensible way of doing things, especially as he stood to gain £6 million, enough to buy outright his office with a view. As Mihir Bose puts it in his book *Manchester DisUnited*: 'He could sell off some shares, pay off his bank manager, make vast sums on a scale no previous director of a football club had ever made and still remain in control. He had at last squared the circle.'

There were those, like Ferguson, who were against the idea, believing it was more for the chairman's benefit than the club's. He believed that a plc and a football club could never be compatible: the need to pay a dividend to shareholders would prevent profits being recycled back into the playing staff. He was worried that too many layers of management would be put between him and the financial decision-making. To show his concern, he decided not to take up the club's offer of share options. Although that might have had something to do with discovering that the finance director had been allocated three times as many as him.

Others thought it a good idea. By giving ordinary United fans a chance to buy into the club, it would, they thought, prevent a single predator taking control. Never again would a chairman be able to sell the club's soul to the first bloke passing with a sizeable wallet. I was one of the optimists. I bought 150 shares and gloried in the thought that I now owned a bit of the club, even if it was little more than a rivet in the scaffolding shrouding the new, all-seater stand where the Stretford End used to be. As it happens, most of the shares went in this way, in small parcels. The flotation was under-subscribed. It valued the club at just £47 million. City institutions paid no heed to the opportunity; they had yet to be convinced that there was money to be made in football. For the small shareholder the returns were never vast – £8 was the largest dividend payment I ever received – but there were certain privileges. Such as turning up to the AGM, where you could ask questions of the board and watch the plc chairman Sir Roland Smith make fun of Martin Edwards. We enjoyed that, we small shareholders. It was our little moment of victory over the boss classes.

And at first the worry that the plc would stymie investment did not seem valid. In the summer after the flotation, Ferguson made three significant purchases: Andrei Kanchelskis, Paul Parker and Peter Schmeichel. After some of his earlier wobbly buys, these were three unarguable crackers. Indeed, along with Denis Irwin, bought the previous year, Edwards reckons Schmeichel the best buy he ever made. How he enjoyed bringing the finest keeper in United history to the club for just over £500,000. Landing Schmeichel for half the sum Brondby originally wanted was his equivalent of winning the double.

'What an incredible buy,' he says. 'They wanted a million, because he was at the end of his contract. We argued all day, sticking and holding. I knew Alex was desperate for him, but I wasn't going to let on.'

These were not the only new faces in the United first-team dressing room. Archie Knox had decided in April 1991 to return to Scotland to join Walter Smith at Rangers. Ferguson was hurt by his assistant's move and didn't speak to Knox for years afterwards. In his place he brought Brian Kidd. For the fans, this was a masterstroke: Kiddo was one of theirs, a Busby Babe, a European Cup hero, a man with the words Manchester and United tattooed on his soul. But Kidd wasn't just window-dressing. He brought a new dimension to the dressing room. A keen student of coaching, he travelled all over seeking inspiration and tips from those involved in rugby league, American gridiron, anything that might have something to teach football. The players immediately responded to his ideas. Training became challenging, exciting, innovative; something different every day. Everywhere things were coming good. Everywhere, that is, except in the League table.

Ferguson thought he had the team to do it. With Schmeichel in goal, Parker and Irwin at full back, the hugely improved Pallister and Bruce forming a rock-like centre-back pairing, with Ince and Robson flanked by Kanchelskis and either Sharpe or the young flyer Giggs, and with Hughes and McClair up front, no one could argue he had balance, strength and – above all – sheer, counter-attacking pace. What's more, symmetry, if not destiny, suggested that around twenty-five years after Busby won the club's last title, this would be the perfect season to do it again. Everything seemed to be going well when he won the League Cup in March 1992, his third knock-out trophy in three seasons. Ferguson had worked doggedly to shape the club in his own likeness: resolute, determined, single-minded. And now the reward was there for the taking.

The trouble with bending the whole enterprise to your will is that sometimes your bad habits rub off with the good. In 1992 all was going efficiently and effectively until the last. Ferguson has subsequently referred to the title run-in as 'squeaky bum time'. It is an apposite image, one that speaks of the gut-churning tension shared by dressing room and terrace. This was the first time in a generation that United had got anywhere near having a problem with their digestive process. And with six games to go, all was solid and regular. United were ahead, in cruise control. Leeds, doggedly pursuing in their wash, could not win it unless United slipped up. The championship, the thing everyone craved, the thing Ferguson had been brought in to deliver, was United's to lose. Which is exactly what they proceeded to do. During the final six games of the 1991–92 season, United went from racing certainties to dead beats. They lost at home to Forest, drew at Luton, lost away at West Ham and away at Liverpool. How the rival fans relished United's discomfort. West Ham were already relegated, but their supporters responded to victory as if they had won the title, mocking Fergie's evident unhappiness. At Liverpool they were still very much aboard their perch, doing a conga on the Kop, chanting 'So now you're gonna believe us, you'll never win the League.' All Leeds had to do was retain their composure: the championship was handed to them. They took it by four clear points, Gordon Strachan wearing the most meaningful of grins as he lifted the trophy for them.

In the press there was a simple explanation: the manager lost it for United. Dithering with team selection, leaving out Kanchelskis the week after he had scored the winning goal at Southampton ('Andrei is my match-winner,' Ferguson said after that game, then promptly dropped him), leaving out Hughes against Forest when the manager's son Nigel Clough was plugging an injury crisis by playing centre back, going all defensive when he should have been attacking, confusing the team, communicating his nerves to the players. After the West Ham defeat he had looked a picture of shattered morale as he moaned on television about the Hammers 'obscene effort'. The players must have thought, He's gone. They knew how much he cared – too much perhaps – and they were terrified at his reaction should they fail. So terrified that they couldn't play any more.

'The modern media are so quick to blame the manager,' Ferguson once told me when I asked him if he was at fault for 1992. 'I can hand on heart say I was getting to a few players about performance in the middle of the season. But the latter part? Definitely not. If anything I laid off them. We lost because we had a lot of things against us. Four games in six days, you can't counter that.'

And indeed United did suffer from the FA's insistence on the season finishing early to allow England time to prepare for the summer's European Championships. Four games in six days was cruel and unusual punishment. But did Ferguson not compound the problem by fiddling with his team formations? He was the manager to whom the term 'tinkering' was affixed long before renowned tinkermen like Claudio Ranieri or Rafa Benítez were even on the horizon.

'No, no,' he said in his defence, 'because the pitch at Old Trafford was so bad I was caught in a dilemma of whether to start playing long forward passes. We toyed with the idea for maybe a couple of games, but then abandoned it. No, no, make no mistake about it. It was the run-in that did it.'

Even if the press did, the players did not blame the manager. Steve Bruce later talked about how Ferguson went out of his way to calm the collective nerves. And Hughes concurs. 'I don't remember him being nervous,' Hughes once told me. 'I think he thought we were very nervous. I remember him hiring a comedian for the pre-match meal before the Liverpool game to try to relax us. I felt sorry for the guy. We weren't exactly in the mood to laugh at his gags.'

Only Bryan Robson seemed to enjoy the man's act. But then his party piece was downing a pint in one.

After the Liverpool game that finally finished United's hopes Sharpe, Giggs and Ince, United's hip young praetorian guard, had been asked on their way out of the changing rooms for their autographs by a couple of Liverpool supporters. Despite their disappointment, all three took a moment to deliver their duty. When they had finished the fans ripped the sheets of paper up and threw them, cackling, back in the lads' faces, asking why on earth they thought they'd want the autographs of losers. Ferguson saw the incident and told the players to remember it for the rest of their lives and to make sure the next time they came back their performance would be the ultimate revenge.

'Now you know, it's us against the world, boys,' he said, as the coach made its way back to Manchester. 'Us against the world.'

But the fact was, however much he might seek to find ways to motivate them, as he approached his sixth anniversary in charge at United, Ferguson knew his team remained a work in progress. There was one element still required to transform it into the finished article.

16

THE FLASHY FOREIGNER

The late Emlyn Hughes was a man of many unusual qualities. His voice, for instance, was high-pitched enough to alarm dogs within a twenty-mile radius. He was renowned as fearlessly determined when faced with a physical opponent on the pitch, and fearlessly sycophantic when faced with a royal guest on *Question of Sport*. Clairvoyance, however, was not something of which anyone could accuse him. The day after Alex Ferguson signed Eric Cantona from Leeds United in November 1992, Hughes, then employed as a columnist at the *Daily Mirror*, opined that the deal would prove so disastrous it would be the manager's 'last gamble in charge of Manchester United'. Under the headline 'A Flashy Foreigner', Hughes, echoing the chant with which the Leeds followers had serenaded their hero, suggested that 'it will be oooh aargh Cantona' and that the Frenchman would so disrupt United's team that his arrival would signal the start of a further twenty-six years of League failure.

Short of the Presidential aide who assured Mrs Lincoln that her husband would love the play, it is hard to think of a prediction that events made more risible. That, though, is hindsight. At the time Hughes's view was not an unusual one. When Cantona came to Old Trafford, his career to that point had been a litany of terminated contracts and incendiary rows. Wherever he went, he didn't stay long. So temperamental was he, he had arrived in England from France the previous spring widely considered in his homeland to be unemployable. One of his previous coaches said that wherever he went he left the whiff of cordite. And this wasn't even the one he had called a bag of shite. His arrival at Elland Road towards the conclusion of the previous season may have provided the momentum that took Leeds to the championship at United's expense, but his manager, Howard Wilkinson, was always suspicious of him. He thought he was more interested in his own legend than in the good of the team. Unsettled by the Frenchman's cocksure self-confidence, he tried to bring him down a peg or two by dropping him. Cantona couldn't believe it. He simply could not fathom how he could be out and Lee Chapman remain in the side. So he went to see the manager.

'He told me he didn't care who was in the team as long as he was,' Wilkinson snorted. 'To my mind, that's not a team player.'

Obviously they were right in France, Wilkinson decided. Better to get some money for him when he could. So when he got the Leeds chairman Bill Fotherby to phone Martin Edwards to ask if Denis Irwin was available and the United chairman said no, but Alex Ferguson wondered if Cantona might be, Wilkinson was thrilled. He sold the player with the relief of someone passing on a dodgy motor. When it came to making the deal, Fotherby didn't even hold out for the £1.6 million he originally asked for. In the end Cantona cost United £1 million, £250,000 less than they had paid for Garry Birtles fourteen years before.

'I know,' says Martin Edwards, grinning widely fifteen years on. 'Ridiculous.'

Edwards admits the signing was one born of serendipity. Not wholly good fortune either. If Ferguson's summer signing Dion

Dublin hadn't snapped his leg in a game against Crystal Palace earlier in the season, the manager would not have been on the look-out for a new striker. For poor Dublin, his injury turned out to be United's lucky break.

Cantona was twenty-six when he arrived at Old Trafford, the same age George Best had been when he walked out. Best was satisfied he had achieved everything; Cantona knew he hadn't even started. For a footballer who considered himself the world's finest there was some work to do to prove it.

From the moment he strolled on to the Old Trafford pitch for his debut against Manchester City on 5 December 1992, coming on as a substitute for Ryan Giggs, he looked impatient to make his mark. He showed none of the nerves that had debilitated other gilded imports to the club. In his first six matches he scored four goals. But he was about a lot more than goalscoring. Big, powerful, born if not with speed, then acceleration, the thing Cantona was most blessed with on a football pitch was time. In the harem-scarem of English football, events seemed to stop around him, allowing him to move about untrammelled and unmolested; he seemed to operate under a different law of physics. The result was passes that set his colleagues free. It had been a long time since Old Trafford had seen anyone like him.

'He infected the place' is how Ferguson describes Cantona's influence. 'Stuck his chest out, put his collar up and said, look at me.'

His self-belief proved contagious, flooding the dressing room and turning colleagues – whose will had crumpled at the last in the previous year's championship run-in – into a bunch of winners. Mark Hughes recalls that just looking at him before games provided inspiration.

'I think we'd all been very nervous the season before,' says Hughes. 'But nervous is not something you'd call Eric. He was just so calm, so relaxed, so focused.'

And if they admired him, the feeling was mutual. Cantona liked the look of everything he found at Old Trafford. He loved the stadium, the fans, the history. He said he could feel when he went out on to the pitch the ghosts of the previous players reaching out and accepting him. Unlike at Leeds where he couldn't get on with many of them, he liked his colleagues, too, fearless flyers like Giggs and Kanchelskis who moved with such pace to his promptings and old bruisers like Hughes who took so much of the physical heat on his behalf. And Ince and Bruce and Pallister: none of whom gave any quarter in a scrap. With clever Brian McClair and Paul Parker and Denis Irwin, there was skill everywhere in this team. Not forgetting the angry, red-nosed Schmeichel, with whom he could play backgammon on away trips and who would always come out on the training pitch after official sessions had finished and try – how he'd try – to stop Cantona's practice free-kicks.

Most unexpected of all, he found he got on with the manager. Here, at last, was a coach on the same wavelength. Alex Ferguson appeared not remotely threatened by Cantona's extravagant self-will. He could be as self-important as he liked as long as he did the business on the field for Manchester United, because that was all Ferguson was interested in. And Ferguson managed Cantona brilliantly: he never dropped him and tweaked some of his strict rules – on dress and time-keeping – to make sure the new man stayed happy.

What the Boss liked about his new signing was that he understood. Whatever his drawbacks – arrogance, intolerance, madness – he knew all about the cause: it had been him against the world since he was a youth in Auxerre and had taken out seven players of the opposition single-handedly in a car park after the game. Howard Wilkinson had completely misread him. Cantona was not a dilettante, he was a worker. His authority problems were not of the oh-bugger-it-I-can't-be-arsed-this-morning variety. First on, last off the training ground was his modus operandi. His problems came because he cared too much, hated losing, was wound up by injustice. He was in love with the game and the possibilities it gave him for self-expression. For Ferguson, that was the perfect pro.

'Winning without pleasure I wasn't interested in,' Cantona said when I interviewed him about a series of photographs taken for the *Manchester United Opus*. 'But then you can't enjoy football if you lose every game. Winning with enjoyment, I love that. It's very difficult to find that balance, but I think I found it with Manchester. Some clubs they have it in the philosophy. At Manchester it has always been like this.'

So profound was his affection for the club, at times when Cantona describes his relationship with United he sounds as if he has been scripted by *The Fast Show*'s Swiss Tony. 'I cannot explain it,' he said to me. 'And I don't want to explain it. It's like love. You know when you are in love, you don't need to explain how you feel or why you feel like that. I think if you want to explain what was going on between me and the United fans, it would take six months. Sometimes it's better not to explain.'

If this was a marriage, its timing could not have been bettered. Cantona arrived at Old Trafford in the first season of the new Premier League. A breakaway by the top clubs, this was the dawn of a new era of football prosperity. Rupert Murdoch's Sky television paid £303 million for the rights to broadcast Premiership games live. United's finances were transformed, as their playing personnel would soon be. There was enough in the coffers to sign up the priciest of players, to shop in the world market. Cantona arrived on a contract worth an unheard-of £5400 a week, soon rising to £8000 as his performances blossomed. Twenty years before, the entire United squad would not have got that between them.

Murdoch bought football to push his pay television service; the Premiership became what marketeers call 'content'. Sky's breathless advertising promised a 'whole new ball game'. Not that there was anything much new on the pitch, here games still involved twenty-two players, a ball and a couple of red-faced blokes yelling on the touchline. It was off it that things changed. Football, so recently considered a pursuit about as commercially attractive as bear-baiting, was to be sold like never before. Murdoch used his newspapers, particularly the *Sun*, relentlessly to promote the product. Make football an inescapable, unmissable facet of life, was the thinking, then everyone will just have to buy a subscription to watch it. Every match was sold as a drama, every incident part of the plot. Conflict was central to the sales pitch: manager against manager, player against player, Grand Slam Sunday and Decision Day Saturday. It was football as pantomime, with heroes to swoon over and villains to hiss. Everything was good or bad, black or white, there was to be no grey in this new ball game. And there was Eric Cantona, the Premiership's perfect first star, a character you couldn't take your eyes off, hero and villain in one. Mr Look-At-Me, a character, best of all, right at the heart of the country's biggest football tale: Manchester United.

Although Ferguson did not think much of the new Premier League idea ('A piece of nonsense' he called it at the time), Murdoch's mission had not gone unnoticed elsewhere in the Old Trafford corridors. For twenty years Sandy Busby ran United's small souvenir shop in the forecourt in front of the stadium. Here, from within a glass-topped counter, you could take your pick of enamel badges, rosettes and nylon club scarves. Plus the odd mug with a player's face on the front. When Busby's lease ran out, Edwards did not renew it. Instead, after studying the Tottenham way to make money out of the game, he invited the Spurs marketing manager Edward Freedman up to Manchester to take over United's merchandising operation. Freedman was a bit like Jedd Clampett in the opening credits of *The Beverly Hillbillies*. He fired his shotgun into the pavement around Old Trafford and up bubbled red, white and black gold. Within weeks of opening a United superstore at the ground, hugely increasing the amount of United-endorsed stock available and starting up a mail order department, Freedman was making money for the club like no one had done before in football. He was soon clearing £250,000 a week; within two years his annual turnover was nearing £20 million.

'Sometimes,' he once told me, 'me and the chairman come down and look at the queues outside the superstore and we just smile at each other.'

His idea was simple: he gave the United diaspora the opportunity to express their affection by buying things. Lots of things. Fans in Swansea could wear the new Umbro home shirt when they went down the pub; supporters in Tunbridge Wells could sleep under a Ryan Giggs duvet; reds in Devon, who might never be able to get to a game, could nonetheless demonstrate their affiliation by decorating the spare room in United wallpaper. The shop became an attraction in itself, the centre of United's grand day out.

'By Christ do they see us coming,' Martin O'Neill, not the former Celtic manager but a United fan from Ireland, once told me. 'I reckon we spend about ten times more in that superstore than anyone local. I come here with a list of things as long as your arm for folk in Cork and you can bet United know I do.'

As the wallets opened, Giggs was the biggest sales weapon. Closely followed by Cantona. 'Eric was on T-shirts, sweat shirts – whatever I could do with him,' Freedman tells Mihir Bose in *Manchester DisUnited*. 'We did books, calendars, magazines. I sent someone over to spend a whole weekend with him in France taking photos. With Cantona I made every possible product.'

Not quite every product. Over the years United have been offered the idea of branded toilet paper, branded tampons, branded condoms, too. They always turn them down.

At Leeds Cantona had been a cult hero, a man whose face appeared on street vendors' T-shirts. At Manchester United he became an accountant's hero, a man whose image bolstered the plc's bottom line. He was the player who carried the game into new and lucrative territory. His appeal crossed class, gender and intellectual boundaries, a proposition that alerted the big corporations. Soon after his arrival at Old Trafford, Cantona was signed up to front commercials by Nike. The American training shoe manufacturer wanted to break into English football and he turned out to be the high-octane fuel that propelled their assault. He was what those in the business call a brand builder. They transformed his apparent haughty disdain of image into a brilliantly constructed icon. It was very different from the standard cool and sexy that was being applied to his young colleagues Giggs and Sharpe. Cantona, under Nike's tutelage, was promoted as unfathomable, elusive, football's misunderstood maverick. With his public utterances restricted to their campaigns, he became the first sportsman in Britain to be scripted by advertising copywriter. Cunningly the company played on his disciplinary problems, presenting them as evidence of a lack of convention that they claimed mirrored their own anti-establishment identity. Suggesting one of the largest corporations in the world was the choice of free-thinking rebels: it was a subtle, cynical, compelling way to sell trainers to the young and impressionable. If George Best had been football's first pop star, his exploitation had been haphazard and piecemeal. Here was Eric Cantona, football's first corporate marketing tool, his exploitation relentless, thought-through and determined.

And while United had the biggest star in the new drama, they determined to have a stage fit for him to perform on. 'We reached the conclusion you couldn't have a stadium empty and unused for thirteen days a fortnight,' says Edwards. 'We had to turn Old Trafford into a seven-day-a-week operation.'

So, as the wrecking ball moved in to remove the terraces, in their place came a very different new building. Lord Justice Taylor had stated in his report on the Hillsborough disaster that football clubs should not use his legal requirement on all-seater stadiums as an opportunity to raise admission prices. United were but one of many who regarded that as advice not instruction. Beneath the new Stretford End bloomed bars, hospitality suites, restaurants. In the middle of the stand were located a swathe of corporate seats: soft backed, a bit more legroom and twice the cost. Ticket prices rose as more was offered; it was no longer simple admission to the ground, you bought a package. A club museum was opened, tours round the stadium instituted. Old Trafford was turned from football ground into tourist destination, a sporting theme park. The

Theatre of Dreams Bobby Charlton called it. And the plc board immediately put a copyright symbol after it. And with that came a rapid change in the demographics of the place. A report in *Charles Buchan's Football Monthly* in March 1969 stated that 'more than 70 per cent of the Stretford End mob is made up of youngsters between 11 and 18'. By 1995 the new all-seater stand was beginning to fill up with older, more affluent, less boisterous football followers – probably the same people as Charlie Buchan had spotted, but now grown up. Alex Ferguson wrote in *Six Years at United* that he worried the new stand would 'rip the heart out of Old Trafford'. Time would be the judge of that. But it certainly muted the vocal chords.

All of this opened the eyes of City of London institutions. Whereas when shares in United were first offered they looked down their noses at the idea of football as a business, once they saw the money pouring in, they started to buy them up. The romantic notion on floatation that United would be owned by its supporters soon disappeared. Small investors were bought out by big agglomerates, anxious for a share of those profits. The BBC staff pension fund bought 10 per cent. Thus in the very success of Edwards's merchandising revolution were sown the seeds of the destruction of public ownership.

However, none of this, not the widening bottom line, not the burgeoning profits, not the rush of institutional shareholders, none of it would have happened if Ferguson's United team had not been successful. Triumph on the pitch was the lubricant that oiled the merchandise machine. Nobody in Belfast wanted duvet covers decorated with the faces of losers. Nobody in Basildon wanted the replica shirt of a second-rater. No Soho advertising executive was prepared to pay three times the price of an ordinary seat to invite his clients along to watch dull 0-0 draws. It was victory – handsomely achieved – that sold. Nothing else would do.

And Ferguson, Cantona, Giggs and the new United provided it.

Mind, it is easy to characterise United's first title in twenty-six years as a cake walk, a doddle, an inevitability. But all that waiting, all that yearning, all that anxiety did not come to an end without tension. The truth is, the squeaky bum made its seasonal return.

It is an indication of how much things were to change in football over the next decade that the first ever Premier League championship was a three-horse race between United, Aston Villa and Norwich City. Both the other teams had at the heart of their effort personal reason to want to pip United. Villa were managed by Big Ron – how he would like to prove Edwards wrong to let him go. Norwich had Mark Robins scoring their goals. After the hero of Nottingham had been sold for £800,000, how he would like to show Ferguson he was worthy of regular first-team football at Old Trafford. And both Norwich and Villa were still there, objects looking sizeable in the rear-view mirror, after a nervy March in which United accrued but three points from four games.

April, though, was a very gentle month for United. They finally finished off Norwich's challenge by winning 3 1 at Carrow Road. It was a game in which the pace of their counter-attack, with Giggs, Kanchelskis, Ince and Sharpe galloping forward to Cantona's promptings, spoke of a tactical approach as thrilling in its way as anything served up by Law, Best and Charlton. Villa, though, remained still there at Easter. Again, like the previous season, the title was Ferguson's to lose over the holiday weekend. On Easter Saturday his team appeared determined to do just that. Even with Cantona in their number, at home to Sheffield Wednesday they were nervy, disjointed, a jittery parody of the team who so recently had eviscerated Norwich. Wednesday were leading with seven minutes to go, before Steve Bruce, the captain in Robson's increasing absence, scored an equaliser. To the huge amusement of the crowd (some habits could not be eradicated by gentrification), the referee had collapsed with a pulled muscle earlier in the game. Seven minutes were added to compensate for the time it took to replace him. In the sixth of those Bruce scored his second. Ferguson and Kidd were caught by the Sky cameras cavorting on the pitch like overexcited tribal warriors dancing for rain. Kidd was on his knees, thumping at the grass, shrieking his delight to the skies. It was a compelling image. One that spoke of relief as much as joy.

Under Sky's management, from this season matches no longer kicked off at the same time every Saturday. Important fixtures the company wanted to transmit were switched across the days of the week. Thus United were not playing when Villa took on Oldham in a game they had to win to keep breathing down the reds' lace-up Umbro collars. Ferguson decided not to watch the live broadcast. He was playing golf at Mottram Hall with his son Mark when a man came running across the fairway shouting at him. Normally, Ferguson would have railed against such an interruption to his game. But the man brought the news that Oldham had won. United were champions. This time he kissed the intruder. He then ran to a Japanese golfer wearing a top emblazoned with the logo of Sharp, United's sponsors. Assuming him to be a fan he embraced him as well. The man looked at Ferguson as if he were unhinged: he had no idea what was going on.

There was a party at Bruce's place that night at which the management's strict rule about no alcohol while in training may well have been flouted. In the streets around Old Trafford it was like Rio when Brazil had won the World Cup. There were cars, horns, flags, delirium. In the final home game of the season against Blackburn, as Bruce and Robson held up the giant, garish new Premiership trophy with its crown-like lid, the cameras caught Matt Busby in the directors' box. He looked dewy-eyed, proud, fulfilled. In the hospitality areas Best, Law, Charlton, Crerand, Stiles, Stepney and the rest who had been there twenty-six years before moved among the well-heeled fans, sharing the pleasure, taking the congratulations. Busby and Ferguson hugged. And as the two great Scotsmen did so, in that moment, it was as if twenty-six years had never happened, as if their two eras had merged, as if the endless seasons of frustration and disappointment in between were but unhappy illusion. United were back. And this time it would be for good.

*

As if to prove his intent, that summer Ferguson bought a young midfielder from Nottingham Forest called Roy Keane. This was a player who, in time, was to be almost as significant in his influence over the way that United thought of themselves as Cantona. Unlike the Frenchman, Keane was not handed over on a plate. Ferguson and Edwards had to scrap to secure his signature. The manager had identified the tough, combative hard man as the perfect replacement for an ageing Bryan Robson, a player Keane had put on his backside when the two teams met the previous season, a player who, on his debut at Anfield, had astonished John Barnes by asking him what the fuck he was looking at. But he was not alone in his admiration. Blackburn, flush with money from Jack Walker, who had sold his steel business and used the windfall to subsidise a lifelong affection for the club, were suddenly movers in the transfer market. Their manager Kenny Dalglish, who had led Liverpool to three League titles and two FA Cups while Ferguson was finding his feet at Old Trafford, thought he had landed Keane. They had a verbal agreement that he was to join. But Ferguson, deftly using United's greater historical cachet to appeal to Keane's ambition, hijacked the deal. Dalglish was apoplectic, accusing Ferguson of breaking every non-written code in the managerial rulebook. Ferguson didn't care. He had a prize worth any amount of accusations of back-sliding and double-dealing. In the end United paid £3.75 million, an English record. It was to prove an investment as good as any Ferguson ever made. With it, he sent an important signal out both to his rivals and to his own dressing room: he was not satisfied with winning the title just the once. This was a manager hungry for more, a man in thrall to victory addiction. He was determined not to fall into the trap of assuming the future would take care of itself, the crime of so many of those previously in charge at United. He summed up his attitude in the little homily he gave his players at the start of the season. He told them United was a bus, moving ever forward. They could stay aboard and enjoy the ride, or they could get off and leave; there were dozens of players eager to take up their seat. Whatever happened, with or without them, the bus was moving on.

As United prepared to defend their title, as the hordes attracted by the new way of football arrived at the Cliff every day to seek out the signatures of Giggs and Sharpe, things had rapidly changed in the way they were perceived in the country. Suddenly they were everywhere, promoted with a ruthlessness never before experienced in the game. Whereas Liverpool had won everything for fifteen years and nobody beyond football's boundaries had really noticed, United were a story that stretched far and wide, its tentacles creeping into every aspect of life. For those without affection for the club, their every mention, all the accompanying talk of destiny and achievement, of history and fulfilment was like nails being dragged down a blackboard. Thus when the backlash against football's new commercialisation came – and it came with surprising rapidity – it was United, the most rampantly organised aspect of it, that became the manifestation of all that was bad about the game. With their sour, angry manager, with their arrogant, French centre forward, with their rampant merchandising operation – targeting, Edward Freedman once told me, the pound in the pocket of every football fan in every part of the country and beyond – they were cast as the devil incarnate. Even politicians used the issue to gain themselves easy popularity points.

'Less than a month after thousands of youngsters pulled on their favourite club jersey at Christmas, the men who run the club ordered the Red Devils to trot out in blue at Southampton,' said Tony Blair, a fresh-faced Labour front bench spokesman in 1994. 'Loyalty doesn't seem to be enough any more. Rather it is exploited to make us pay more.'

On the television shows springing up to exploit football's new fashionableness, United and their rampant commercialism were mocked ceaselessly. To show affection for them, reckoned David Baddiel, Nick Hancock and the rest, was somehow to miss the point about the game. In 1993 the Irish broadcaster Des Cahill started a club called Anyone But United. It was, he says, a reaction

'Aye and I'll always be here.' Law lurks against West Ham, 1971 (PA Photos/TopFoto).

Foot soldiers of Doc's Red Army occupy the Old Trafford pitch but fail to stop their team sinking to Division Two, April 1974 (Colorsport).

Kevin Moran is invited to take the long, lonely walk of shame, Wembley, 18 May 1985 (Colorsport).

Easily mistaken for a commissionaire, Michael Knighton plays keepy-uppy in front of the Stretford End, August 1989 (PA Photos/TopFoto).

'Just give it to Robbo, he'll win it for you':
Captain Marvel, Bryan Robson finally lifts
the title, May 1993 (PA Photos/TopFoto).

Martin Edwards in 1994, shortly before the
words Football and Club were deemed
superfluous on the club crest (UPP/TopFoto).

Paul Ince (front) is a little
late in the tackle as United
celebrate their first double,
May 1994 (UPP/TopFoto).

Eric Cantona takes a detour to the Selhurst Park dressing room, January 1995 (Andrew Cowie/Colorsport).

United fans at Wembley, May 1996, remind a former Liverpool favourite of his punditry (Colorsport).

'When I saw the cup I thought, I'm having that': David May hijacks the photoshoot, Camp Nou, Barcelona, 26 May 1999 (Colorsport).

Deansgate turns red as the
treble winners parade their
spoils, May 1999
(PA Photos/TopFoto).

The team Sir Alex thought
would see him into retirement
in 2002 by conquering
Europe. They didn't win. And
he didn't retire (Colorsport).

Paul Scholes, the ginger
genius, on his way to winning
the title for United, 2003
(ProSport/TopFoto).

United without boundaries: the manager meets the fans in Los Angeles, 2003
(ProSport/TopFoto).

The global marketeers: United's players train at Nike HQ in Oregon, 2003
(PA Photos/TopFoto).

The white Pélé: Wayne Rooney
(PA Photos/TopFoto).

127 YEARS
GLAZER = NOT IN
A MILLION YEARS

American predators not welcome, 2005
(Colorsport).

A corner of Moscow that is forever red, outside the Luzhniki Stadium, 21 May 2008 (ProSport/TopFoto).

John Terry, without whom this would have been a very different story (Colorsport).

Wayne Rooney lifts the biggest of all football trophies, Moscow, 21 May 2008 (ProSport/TopFoto).

He always looked good in a red shirt. Cristiano Ronaldo's finest hour as a United player, 21 May 2008 (Colorsport).

to the United fans coming out of every bit of Irish woodwork the moment the title was won. And the membership took off: within months every ground in the country – including Wembley during England matches – was echoing to the ABU national anthem: 'Stand up if you hate Man U.' Man U: the very diminutive that so infuriates old-time United fans. During one televised game at Chelsea the chairman Ken Bates was seen cheerfully rising to his feet to join in. And his team wasn't even playing United.

Publicly, Ferguson scratched his head about this burgeoning ill-will. 'There is a terrible amount of jealousy towards this club,' he said back then. 'I don't know why.'

Privately, however, he thrived on it, drawing energy from the loathing. Here was evidence of what he had always maintained in the dressing room: it is us against the world (at one point he claimed United were up against 'Mars, the Universe, everything'). Look at them, he would tell his players, they want you to lose, they want nothing more than to see you fail. Remember those auto graph hunters at Liverpool? They are all like that, everyone is out to get you. Go out and show them. The universal them.

To prove they were out there, he identified enemies at every turn. He banned journalists who wrote negatively from contact with the club, he railed against television pundits who criticised his team, he claimed conspiracy among officials when decisions went against him. He stalked the touchline pointing at his watch to remind referees of their duty. Most tellingly of all, when one of his players misbehaved on the pitch, he blamed someone else, describing any attempt to expose wrongdoing as a facet of an anti-United agenda.

This was most often seen with Eric Cantona. In his second season at United Cantona was targeted by opposition defenders in the not wholly unjustified belief that by stopping the Frenchman you could stop United. Cantona was easily riled. Several times, sensing that the referee was not going to protect him, he dispensed unilateral justice. On one occasion, during a Cup tie against Norwich, the referee didn't spot his off-the-ball stamp on John

Polston. Up in the television gantry, Jimmy Hill did. He called the Frenchman despicable. When he heard the description, Ferguson was quick to reply: 'Jimmy Hill is verbal when it suits him. If there's a prat going round, he's the prat. I'm not interested in Jimmy Hill. Four years ago he wrote us off in the warm-up, that's how much he knows about the game. The BBC are dying for us to lose. Everyone is from Liverpool with a Liverpool supporter's flag. They'll be here every time until we lose, that mob – Barry, Bob, Hansen, the lot of them. Liverpool Supporters Association.'

It was a brilliant manoeuvre. Instead of the papers focusing on Cantona, they were filled with attacks on the United manager and his inability to accept that his players might be in the wrong. Ferguson called it 'diversionary tactics'. The idea was, in times of crisis or indiscipline, to focus attention on himself. Not because he wanted to buff up his own ego, but to draw it away from the players. It didn't make him an attractive public figure, but the players knew, whatever he might say in the privacy of his office, that he would not publicly humiliate them. Among the knife-edge egos of his dressing room, such knowledge bred absolute respect. They knew he was on their side. Soon every manager was at it: Arsène Wenger and José Mourinho both later won the Premiership title using man-management techniques borrowed from the originator.

It was, however, a vicious circle. Ferguson's constant refusal to condemn his players in public created an ever more stinging media response. After he had defended another Cantona transgression – this time a stamp on Swindon's John Moncur – saying it was impossible to challenge a player's competitive instincts, Martin Samuel in the *Daily Express* made weighty comparison in order to sum up the outside view.

'Ferguson has turned his side into an arrogant rabble. When he discusses the misconduct of United players, he should remember that Sir Matt Busby never offered an excuse and certainly not Ferguson's absurd euphemism . . . "You can't stop players being competitive." Not even on another player's chest?'

Thus was United's public image changing. No longer was it the romantic upholder of sporting morality as epitomised by Matt Busby. It had become the cynical, manipulative agglomeration of sordid self-interest as epitomised by Alex Ferguson. And as they defended their title there were many who wanted United to fail. But through his skilled man-management, Ferguson had made his players stronger than ever, mentally as much as physically. Everywhere their muscular, aggressive, pacy football gave them an edge. At times Cantona played on another planet. Everywhere they were in the ascendant.

Everywhere that is except in Europe. Ferguson seemed particularly disturbed by a UEFA ruling restricting teams to only three foreign players. UEFA rules counted Irish, Scots and Welsh as foreign, meaning that in addition to Cantona, Kanchelskis and Schmeichel, Giggs, Hughes, Irwin, Keane, McClair, even the manager's own son, the young reserve Darren, came under the restriction. A half-strength European Cup campaign ended in November 1993 in chaotic scenes in Istanbul against Galatasaray, with Cantona sent off, dozens of United fans in prison, and the police hitting out at the visiting players with truncheons as they left the pitch.

At home, though, able to select his best line-up, a new thought began to grow in Ferguson's mind: so strong were his team, a domestic double to match the one he had won with Aberdeen ten years previously was in his crosshairs. Actually, more than that, he might be up for a clean sweep, the first ever treble in English football.

As always football's attendant Sky-endorsed PR machine cranked up the drama. As always Cantona was at the heart of it. Sent off twice in the early spring, he was identified in the popular press as the very characterisation of all that was wrong with the rapidly changing modern game. Commentators sought his deportation. Editorials raged against his devious foreign wiles. Watching from the other side of the Channel, *L'Equipe*'s headline 'L'Angleterre contre Cantona' seemed to sum up the mood.

Ferguson, though, was not against him. He was right behind

him, mocking the press obsession, claiming it was but lazy journalism that every story focused on Cantona and United. Perhaps reporters might look elsewhere for a headline, he suggested.

'We're like Christmas every day for youse guys,' he said.

Ferguson's loyalty was born from the same source as Martin Edwards's had been for him back in 1989. He could see what none of Cantona's detractors could: how hard the player was working away from the pitch. It turned out the flashy foreigner of Emlyn Hughes's dismissive phrase was the epitome of the work ethic. As his captain Steve Bruce recalls: 'We used to say after training, "Hey Eric, coming for a game of snooker" or whatever, but he'd just want to be out there, practising. That's where his success came from. It didn't arrive by chance.'

Ferguson agrees. In his autobiography, he notes this of the player: 'While he was with the club nothing he did in matches meant more than the way he opened my eyes to the indispensability of practice.'

It happened that Cantona's arrival coincided with the graduation into the first-team pool of the finest crop of young talent since the Busby Babes. In 1992 Eric Harrison's boys had won the club's first FA Youth Cup since the days when George Best was a teenager. Ryan Giggs was their talisman, but this was a side alive with talent, not least in the person of a short, red-haired lad from Langley, in Salford, a player whose very name brings a tear to Harrison's eye even today.

'Scholesy,' says Harrison, his voice drifting off wistfully. 'Robson, Bruce, Pally used to come and watch the kids training whenever they could and they loved him. They went to see the Youth Cup games, too. Saturday mornings at the Cliff there were big, big crowds for their games. And everyone's biggest favourite, always, was Paul Scholes. I never, ever worried about anything to do with him. I never taught him anything, Scholesy. He was as close to football perfection as it came.'

Had David Beckham, the Neville brothers, Nicky Butt and the ginger genius himself arrived at fruition five years earlier, their professional role models would have been McGrath and Whiteside, cheeky chappies whose goal was getting one over on the gaffer and whose afternoons were about getting bladdered. Instead, they shared training with a football addict. Cantona's favoured afternoon activity was rounding up a group of the youngsters and taking them out to help him with extra work. It became the habit of the whole club.

'I don't know about the other players, but if Eric was in the dressing room, I'd find myself watching him, checking out what he was doing, trying to work out exactly how he prepared for a game,' recalls Beckham. 'If he was there, I hardly seemed to notice anything else that was going on.'

As spring approached the only pause in the red assault on football domination was the death at eighty-three of Matt Busby on 20 January 1994. The Old Man died peacefully, content that his Manchester United were back in the ascendant. A sea of tributes – scarves, shirts, memorabilia – spread across the Old Trafford forecourt as news of his death was announced. Fans came from across the globe to add their contribution. A statue was commissioned, its body hollow and to be stuffed with the gifts of those leaving their respects. He now stands in the front of Old Trafford, perched high up at the stadium's front, looking down at the thousands arriving for games, hand on hip, ball under arm, apparently ready to answer the call at any moment. The master of all he surveys.

Before Ferguson sorted it out, the great manager was a living indictment in the Old Trafford corridors: a still eye of achievement, restraint and calm in a maelstrom of greed, inadequacy and panic. Physically, in the latter years, he appeared to age very little; he was always there, an unchanging reminder of the days when it seemed so easy to do things properly. So when finally Ferguson had achieved the title and the twenty-six-year gap was bridged, Busby's presence became a celebration.

'You remember the pictures of him the night against Blackburn after we won the title,' Ferguson said shortly after his death. 'His eyes were completely lit up. He was delighted. All the more so because I think it was achieved in a style he would have recognised and appreciated. The players were at last capturing some of the standards he set. Everyone was inspired by him, by the challenge he set for Manchester United. Right till the end he was in every day, with his cheese and his soup and his pipe, with a quiet word for everybody. I used to watch the players when he came on the bus to away matches, they'd nudge each other and go, "Hey that's Sir Matt".'

For Ferguson's United, meanwhile, success lay tantalisingly, teasingly ahead.

'The treble?' said Ferguson of his three-pronged assault on glory. 'It's never been done before. Why should we be any different?'

Well, he was right there. Defeat by Aston Villa in the Coca-Cola Cup, managed by – who else? – Big Ron made all hopes of unprecedented achievement go flat. But in the League and the FA Cup United were in cruise control, led by Cantona.

'Cantona the Conductor in United Cantata' was the headline in the *Independent* after one extravagant display. Until, that was, the Frenchman was sent off twice in successive games.

'Eric Cantona is a cry baby who hides when the going gets tough,' George Graham, Arsenal's manager, decided. You could see his point. In a foretaste of what lay ahead, Cantona's suspension knocked his team off kilter in the run-in. Without him United lost twice in the League, and watched Blackburn whittle their lead down from fourteen points to just three. If Cantona was casting himself as the player who made a difference, it was hard to do that sitting in the stand. His absence was most noticeable in the FA Cup semi-final, when Dion Dublin stood in for him and United played a sterile long-ball game against Oldham, coming within a whisker of being defeated. But Mark Hughes rescued them, securing a replay in the last moments of normal time with a stunning goal. Bryan Robson scored the winner in the replay, diverting the ball into the net from a yard out via his groin. It was his last significant touch in a red shirt. That summer the old warhorse left to manage Middlesbrough; his every return to United with his team greeted to the echo.

Once more available, Cantona demonstrated his value by scoring three goals in April as the championship was retained, comfortably by eight points from second-placed Blackburn Rovers. Asked what he had missed in the Frenchman's absence, Ferguson simply replied: 'His goals.'

But there was more to it than that. It was the way he set about his task without fear. It was the certainty he brought. This time, with him at the heart of the dressing room, there were no collective jitters. The panic of 1992 was a thing of the past.

'What nobody realised was that we'd learned,' Paul Ince said at the time. 'We'd learned how to win. You have to do it. You don't win titles by chance. Liverpool once did it. Now we have.'

United had developed into a steely operation, with teak-tough characters at every turn, their experience forged in disappointment, now refusing to buckle whatever the outside pressure. Plus there was their leader, Cantona. He scored two penalties in the Wembley rain as Chelsea were brushed aside 4-0 in the FA Cup final. The team Ferguson sent out that day – Schmeichel; Parker, Bruce, Pallister, Irwin; Kanchelskis, Keane, Ince, Giggs; Cantona, Hughes – only played together twelve times. But they won every game, scored twenty-four goals and conceded three. Statistically they are the best in the manager's long, long reign. And – following an injury to Parker – they were never to play together again. That day his best ever team secured Ferguson United's first ever double.

The treble remained but a distant dream.

17

THE KING IN EXILE

Nobody could accuse the *Sun* of underplaying what had happened. The headline on the front page two days after the event was 'I'll Never Forget His Evil Eyes'. Below it was a panel: 'The Shame of Cantona: Full story Pages 2, 3, 4, 5, 6, 22, 43, 44, 45, 46, 47 & 48.' On page forty-six, under the headline 'John Sadler on the Curse of Cantona', the pundit wrote, 'We have seen the best of him. Now we have to see the back of him.'

Two nights before, on the evening of 25 January 1995, when playing Crystal Palace at Selhurst Park, Cantona had been sent off for the fifth time in United's myriad colours. He had been kicked by the home centre back Richard Shaw and spent several minutes seeking retribution. When he found it on Shaw's shins, he was within feet of the referee, who had no option but to show him the red card. As Cantona approached his manager, Alex Ferguson stared straight past him, as if he no longer existed. For a moment United's number seven looked like a little boy, told off once too often. Then he pulled up his collar, thrust out his chest and made his way to the dressing room. As he walked alongside the crowd, something attracted his attention. It was a Palace fan called Matthew Simmons, running down the steps of the stand to unload some abuse in his direction. He had heard it all before. Many times, at Leeds, at Maine Road, at Anfield. But this time it was different.

'Provocation we always had,' he told me a dozen years later when I spoke to him for the *United Opus*. 'Millions of times people say these things, and then one day you don't accept it. Why? It's not about words. It's about how you feel at that moment. One day you react, but the words are exactly the same as those you have heard a million times, so it is impossible to say why you react.'

How he reacted this time was to launch himself at Simmons, leaping over the advertising hoarding, kicking him in the chest, then swinging a couple of haymakers in his direction. The cameras had an unobstructed view across the pitch of what he did. The images they caught played out across the British media in a continuous loop for a week. From merely a famous footballer, the kick elevated Cantona into the most notorious sportsman this country has ever seen. For days nobody, anywhere, talked of anything other than his Kung Fu assault. Newspapers were full of it. Roy Hattersley said it was the most disgraceful thing that had ever happened at a British football ground (the families of the Hillsborough victims probably disagreed). Brian Clough gave his sober view that Cantona should be castrated.

Charged with actual bodily harm, he appeared later that week at Croydon Magistrate's Court, where Mrs Jean Pearch sent him to prison for a fortnight. On immediate appeal, the sentence was reduced to community service. After the judgement Cantona faced a press conference, where he was asked for a comment. He had prepared what he was going to say with United's legal man, Maurice Watkins, working through the precise English wording. Taking a sip of water, he stared at the cameras whirring in front of him and said: 'When seagulls follow the trawler it is because they hope sardines will be thrown into the sea.'

Then he got up and left the room.

It became the most celebrated utterance made by a footballer, the title of books and radio series. Its meaning was picked over by pundits, analysed by academics, raged at by rivals. The comedian Nick Hancock, when asked for a comment about it for the television adaptation of Colin Schindler's memoir *Manchester United Ruined My Life*, kept up a stream of anti-Cantona invective for half an hour. As it happens, Hancock should have approved: in its depiction of the parasitic relationship between media and celebrity the line was intended to have a humorous edge.

'Yeah, I played that moment,' Cantona admitted. 'It was a drama and I was an actor.'

But if Cantona recognised the absurdity of his position, his colleagues were plunged into crisis. That night at Selhurst was one of only two occasions Ferguson lost his temper with the Frenchman. As Fergie raged in the dressing room, Cantona just sat there, silent and ashamed. It got worse when the manager finally returned home and watched a video recording his son had made of television footage. He knew this time he could not condone his favourite's behaviour. There was no justification. Several directors thought a line had been crossed and Cantona should be dismissed (were he not so vital to United's efforts, a cynic might suggest, he would have been). In the end they banned him from playing until the end of the season and fined him two weeks' wages. The FA extended the sanction until the following October, adding a further £10,000 fine. It was largely assumed in the papers that we had seen the last of the player. He would return to France, was the media consensus, tail between his legs.

United's hard core of fans rallied to his support. They, too, were alarmed that he might go. Their effort was to make him realise they understood, this was us against them. The fanzine *Red Issue* led the defence and, via radio phone-in and the newly arrived internet, its contributors excoriated all his detractors. On television Tony Wilson supported him with an absurdist flourish.

'The deification of Cantona was a fiercely Mancunian thing,' he once told me. 'Nobody played like him and nobody could have worshipped him like we did. The relationship he had with us fans was unique in the history of football.'

What is unquestionable is that in his absence that season United won nothing. They came close. Mighty close. But they were second all round. In the League the new signing Andy, later Andrew, Cole – snatched, amid much local wailing, from Newcastle – scored twelve goals, including five in a record 9-0 mauling of Ipswich (a victory Ferguson described as being so good 'it could have been set to music'). But when it mattered Cole couldn't seem to find the net. Needing a win in the last game against West Ham, the ball just wouldn't land for him, or indeed for anyone else. And the players – including the teenagers Paul Scholes and Gary Neville – trudged off the pitch at the end, socks round their ankles, heads bowed, looking as if they had just been relegated, not pipped to the title by one point. There was to be no consolation in the FA Cup final the following week, no lift to morale compromised from the moment Cantona launched his kick. They reached Wembley after a semi-final against Palace which was again laced with the sort of unhappy drama that was becoming associated with Ferguson's United. Before the drawn first game, a Palace supporter was run over by a car and killed after a street altercation with United followers. Remarks about Cantona were said to have been at the root of the disturbance. At the replay everyone was supposed to be on their best behaviour: football, the pundits decided, needed to heal itself. So it was probably not a good idea for Roy Keane to stamp all over Palace's Gareth Southgate and get himself sent off. The BBC's Alan Green called Keane a lout and Ferguson sought him out after the game, remonstrating with the commentator so angrily at one point he grabbed him by the throat. Five Live became his least favourite media outlet, all contact with them banned from there on. Even poor, meek John Motson felt the full fire of the hairdryer, cowering in the Villa Park tunnel after being verbally assaulted for asking a legitimate question about Keane for *Match of the Day*. It was United against the world all right. And none of the world seemed too unhappy to see Everton win a dull final.

That summer, with no trophies to add to his collection, was the least restful of Ferguson's United career. At the end of the season it was announced that Mark Hughes, Andrei Kanchelskis and Paul Ince were all to leave the club. No explanation was given, and no replacements were to be bought. With Cantona's future still by no means secure, to the fans watching at a distance it seemed an act of vandalism, the pointless destruction of a side that came within a couple of kicks of winning its second double. The sense of bewilderment was exacerbated when Ince briefed a couple of members of the newly formed Independent Manchester United Supporters' Association, telling them he was being eased out against his will. The news was immediately leaked. The papers loved it. And the *Manchester Evening News* ran a poll of readers asking whether they wished Ferguson to remain as manager. Hijacked by mischievous City supporters it may have been, but it concluded that 53 per cent wanted him out.

As was increasingly to become the case with United, that summer rumour, speculation and received wisdom became media currency. With Ferguson and Martin Edwards making no official comment, newspapers, radio and Sky's twenty-four-hour rolling news station filled in the gaps by quotes and information sought from fanzine writers and supporters' representatives. Although they didn't know what was going on either, they were happy to provide what they could, even if it was generally coloured by their own agenda. With United the most significant source of sporting news, anything and everything was seized upon, any snippet became a headline, its accuracy less important than its immediacy. And the consensus was, Ferguson had gone bonkers, that crazed with power he was acting vindictively, personally.

It was only later, when the manager published his autobiography and Michael Crick examined the issues for his magnificent biography of Ferguson, *The Boss*, that the facts became clear. They turned out to be significantly different from the assumption that summer.

Hughes, then thirty-one, was going to be sold to Everton when Cole signed. In Cantona's forced absence, he was kept on and Ferguson even offered him a new contract. But sensing he was not likely to be first choice when the Frenchman returned he didn't sign it and headed off to Chelsea, a free agent. The fans were distraught. Hughes himself departed with a wistful look over his shoulder.

'What I felt about United was: This is my club. I think the fans tuned into that,' he says. 'They could sense that I had a great feeling for the club.'

Kanchelskis felt less of an attachment. He had for some time been agitating for a move – and the injection of capital from a signing-on fee would certainly be handy. He left for Everton for £5 million, and a peripatetic career that never matched his time at Old Trafford; he was last seen turning out for Manchester City, his once formidable turn of speed slowed by what appeared to be the largest tongues ever seen on a pair of football boots.

As for Ince, Ferguson had been worried for some time that the self-styled 'Guvnor' was no longer effective. At half-time during United's ignominious 4-0 defeat at the Camp Nou in the Champions League the previous autumn, he had furiously denounced the midfielder as 'a fucking bottler'. So extreme was the row, the pair had to be separated. Taking the hint that he was no longer regarded, the midfielder had instructed his agent to encourage overtures from Internazionale. Indeed, he appeared ready to sign for them even before the Cup final. However, not wishing to be again vilified by supporters in the manner he had when he left West Ham for United, he had filled the summer information vacuum with the implication that his was an unwilling departure. This wasn't desertion, he insisted. He wanted to stay. Ultimately, his PR campaign failed. When he signed for Liverpool later in his career he became the only former player of the modern era to be booed on his return to Old Trafford.

What was going on here was different from the rows Busby had with his players. It was not about money. For a start Ferguson did not negotiate salaries, that was done by Martin Edwards, so he was in no position to dictate their conditions as his predecessor had been. Besides, although not in the top league of European payers, United were no longer the parsimonious outfit of old. The growing influence from agents had altered the balance of financial power. Players were beginning to do very well at Old Trafford, where the top earners were soon on £8000 a week, rising to £23,000 by the end of the century.

In fact the one person who felt undervalued for much of this time was Ferguson himself. As the vital cog at the heart of the money-spinning machine he was convinced he was not getting just reward. Here were United making more money than ever before in football history, with shirts and television and executive boxes spewing the stuff out, yet, never mind Cantona earning far more than him, he discovered he was on half what George Graham was getting at Arsenal. He was incandescent and threatened all sorts of go-slows and strikes. But Edwards and the plc chairman Roland Smith were canny. They knew Ferguson was addicted to United and whatever the offers to go and manage elsewhere – from England, the Republic of Ireland, Internazionale – he was welded to his seat in the Old Trafford dug-out. In salary negotiations they generally called his bluff.

Thus did money come to matter to him. It dominated his conversation. When he discovered that the photographer Paul Massey had maintained the rights to a photo shoot with Ryan Giggs, which he had sold on round the world, Ferguson cornered him one day after he spotted him at the club. 'I tell you what,' he said to the snapper. 'When I die, I'm coming back as a fucking photographer. You guys are making a fortune out of this club.'

He was convinced everyone was – Edwards, the players, the media. Everyone except him, the progenitor of it all.

'I had a conversation with him for about an hour once,' recalls the financial PR David Bick, who worked on several projects for the club. 'His sole topic of conversation was money – who was earning what and how to make more. Beyond the normal this was. I'd say he was obsessed.'

However obsessed, money had nothing to do with why he was happy to see three of his stalwarts leave. Underpinning all of Ferguson's manoeuvres was a faith in the young players Eric Harrison had developed at the Cliff. The manager had become convinced, after blooding several of them in the first team – particularly, to widespread criticism from the media, in League Cup ties – that these represented the real deal. He was hugely impressed by their attitude, the way they took their position and responsibility so seriously. According to Ben Thornley, a member of the 1992 Youth Cup-winning team whose chances of advancement were hamstrung by injury, the likes of Gary Neville and David Beckham were so dedicated to the cause, never mind matches, they wouldn't even hit the town the night before training. Their only social venture was to go out on a Wednesday, before they attended college on a Thursday morning. And even then it was for a meal in a quiet restaurant on Deansgate. No alcohol passed any lips.

Once they signed as pros, they were earning good money. Unlike the Babes, theirs was no life of digs and canasta. They were driving fast cars and buying sleek clothes; Giggs had his first architect-designed house (complete with atrium and enormous games room) built for him before he was twenty-one. When they went into Manchester's bars and clubs they were recognised, their behaviour monitored by locals as either 'sound' or 'snide'. Over the years some United youngsters would come to falter, dazzled by their own celebrity, imbibing too deeply of the opportunities that fame brought them. Kieron Richardson, Danny Simpson: two who were spotted as giving it too large. But the class of 1992 seemed singularly focused. They were all trained in media awareness, given financial advice, occasionally George Best was even brought in to lecture them on how not to blow it. Most of all Harrison, Ferguson and Kidd indoctrinated them in the mantra that you haven't seen anything yet. Work hard and the rewards will be immense. As Ferguson said of Giggs: 'I have never known anyone so determined to realise the genius within them.'

Now they were all turning twenty, the manager wanted to remove the blockage ahead of this dedicated bunch of achievers, and give them the space to develop.

'That season was the making of all of us,' David Beckham was later to say in his autobiography. 'Thanks to a Boss who believed in us before we even believed in ourselves.'

Plus, there may have been a romantic edge to Ferguson's reasoning: were he ever genuinely to stand comparison with Busby, then he had to do it with his own, with those from within the family.

'A Manchester United player has to want the ball, have the courage to want it,' he said at the time. 'He's a player with imagination. Someone who sees the bigger picture.'

Brought up in the United manner, these young players had it all right. It would be a gamble. But Ferguson had never been shy of a bet. It began on 19 August 1995, at Villa Park. In the starting line-up were five Harrison graduates – Scholes, Nicky Butt, Gary and Phil Neville and the now veteran Giggs – plus two who came on from the bench, Beckham and John O'Kane. With Keane just turned twenty-four and Cole only twenty-three, it was an astonishingly youthful team Ferguson fielded that day. Recklessly so, according to some tastes.

'The trick is always to buy when you are strong, so he needs to buy players,' said Alan Hansen, advising Ferguson after highlights of his callow team's 3-1 defeat were shown on *Match of the Day*. 'You can't win anything with kids.'

Events were to conspire never to allow Hansen to forget those words. But at the time many felt he had a point, especially when a naive United lost in the first round of the UEFA Cup to Rotor Volgograd, Peter Schmeichel preserving a long undefeated home record in Europe by scoring the equaliser in the final minute of a disappointing home leg (disappointing in every way, like many a European game in the early nineties, the crowd was dipping towards the thirty thousand mark).

Sure, everyone recognised the youthful new-look reds could

play – after a 3-0 demolition of Bolton in September, Keith Kent, the Old Trafford groundsman, noted that it had taken him 'an hour to get the scorch marks off the turf'. But what they needed was something more. They needed certainty.

The moment that turned potential into something altogether historic came in the game against Liverpool on 1 October. This marked the appearance back in the side of a wizened, ancient, gnarled twenty-nine-year-old Eric Cantona.

'I have been punished for my mistakes' read the accompanying announcement from his publicity manipulators at Nike. 'Now it's somebody else's turn.'

Many fans had assumed it would never happen. During his 248-day enforced absence he had several times threatened to walk from Old Trafford. Ferguson had once even been obliged to dash to France to persuade him not to join Internazionale, who were promising him five times what he was earning at United. A new contract stilled the wanderlust. And back he came, inevitably scoring a penalty in his first match. This time, however, he was different.

'I play with passion and fire,' he once said of himself. 'I have to accept that sometimes the fire does harm. But I cannot be who I am without these other sides to my character.'

With the world expecting an imminent explosion, Cantona managed to play that season as if his veins were filled with ice. In what was the most exciting championship race for years, United hauled back an exuberant Newcastle at the top of the table with a ruthlessness that was at times chilling. Made captain by Ferguson, Cantona's contribution was immense. During the title run-in, thirteen matches were decided by Cantona winners or equalisers. There was an inevitability about him that season, an almost surreal insistence that he would achieve.

Others played their part, too, Keane, Beckham, Butt, the wonderful Scholes. And most notably Schmeichel, whose performance at St James's Park was of a kind that breaks opponents' resolve. In many ways Newcastle slaughtered United that February evening.

But managed to lose 1-0 (Cantona – who else? – scored the only goal). The reason was Schmeichel. His saves from Newcastle's centre forward Les Ferdinand defied belief, never mind goalkeeping geometry. It was no wonder that the Geordies' manager Kevin Keegan found it hard to maintain his equilibrium faced with such indomitable opposition. With the pressure brewing and bubbling over the Easter holiday, Keegan unravelled on live television, ranting and raging, jabbing his finger, complaining about something Ferguson had said and shrieking about how he'd 'love it if we beat them, love it'. At that point everyone – including the Newcastle players – knew United, Cantona and Ferguson had the title in the bag. And Ferguson's ability to manipulate his rivals came to be regarded as being as significant as anything that happened on the pitch. The press had a new concept to play with. Managerial mind games were born.

There was still room for one comical stutter. On 13 April United played at Southampton. To avoid a colour clash, they trotted out in ugly grey change shirts. Three-nil down at half-time, they re-emerged for the second period in blue and white stripes. After the game Ferguson explained they had lost because the players found it difficult picking each other out from the crowd in those grey shirts. It was a lame excuse. But it seemed to mark a watershed in the ferocious merchandising drive emanating from Edward Freedman's superstore. The grey shirts had been specifically designed by Umbro as leisure items, to look good with jeans. They weren't sports kit, they were a mass-market fashion item. Now they were, apparently, interfering with the team's efficiency. It did not look good. But then neither did the shirt.

Grey was never worn again. And after securing Ferguson the title with an away victory at Middlesbrough wearing blue and white, United arrived at Wembley for their third attempt on the double in three seasons where fashion once more played a part. Their opponents were Liverpool. Before Ferguson lit his charge under Old Trafford, Liverpool were the ones who won title after title while dilettante United seemed content to win the odd cup.

The 1996 Cup final indicated how far the roles had reversed. Liverpool's players arrived at Wembley that day in suits designed by Giorgio Armani in an indelicate shade of cream. Robbie Fowler, Steve McManaman, David James, Stan Collymore and Neil Ruddock, the self-styled Spice Boys, strode across the turf looking like ice-cream salesmen. By contrast, in their sober black garb, Ferguson's kids looked focused, clean-cut, professional. One group of players were dressed for a bit of light relief. The other for business.

As it turned out the game was not as memorable as the pre-match fashion show. Deep into the second half of a turgid, scrappy, goalless game, David Beckham took a corner, James punched the ball to the edge of the area, where Cantona was lurking. He met the clearance with a screamer, bending his body to send the ball past half a dozen defenders into the back of the net. His shot originated from a plane of skill far higher than the game deserved. His celebration was ecstatic, running to the United supporters flapping the front of his shirt, demonstrating his attachment to the badge. Thanks to that strike, he became the first ever captain raised outside the British Isles to lift the oldest trophy in world football; the first flashy foreigner to pick up the FA Cup.

Earlier that week he had been at the football writers' annual dinner. The moment he went up on stage to collect the award as Footballer of the Year, with the nation's football writing fraternity standing as one to applaud him, represented Cantona's high water mark. As he acknowledged the acclaim of so many who had doubted and criticised, he appeared to be incapable of a wrong move. His legend was complete.

For United fans he personified what they thought of as the essence of their club: independent, aloof, superior, he was United. He was proclaimed the successor to Denis Law as the King of the Stretford End. But the affection for him went even further than with the Lawman. When United paraded their two trophies back to Trafford Town Hall in Stretford the day after the Cup final, there were as many French tricolours in the crowd as United flags. His name rang out continuously. This wasn't mere fandom. It was an act of worship.

That summer Ferguson tried to strengthen his team by buying Alan Shearer, the Blackburn striker who had enjoyed a fruitful Euro 96 on home soil. The player seemed willing – he even struck an agreement with the manager to let him wear the number-nine shirt – but his chairman was not.

'Jack Walker would never have let him come,' says Martin Edwards. 'He hated United. Hated us. There was no way he could ever have come here.'

So Shearer went to Newcastle for a British record fee of £15 million. And Ferguson spent the money instead on five new signings. All were from overseas. UEFA's ruling on foreigners had been lifted in February 1996 following a court case brought by the Belgian player Jean-Marc Bosman. Ferguson wanted some Euro experience to help him fulfil his one outstanding goal: the European Cup, the trophy that now dominated his ambition.

'I knew I would never be judged a great manager until I had won the European Cup,' he admitted.

To that end in came Jordi Cruyff, Karel Poborsky, Ronnie Johnsen, Raimond van der Gouw and a pixie-faced young striker from Norway called Ole Gunnar Solskjær. But it was one of his homegrown players who made the first mark on the 1996–97 season. At Selhurst Park, the place Cantona had trod so recently, a very different kick elevated David Beckham into renown. Receiving the ball in his own half, he spotted Wimbledon's goalie Neil Sullivan off his line. From more than forty yards, he chipped the keeper, leaving Sullivan floundering like a landed cod in the back of his net. Beckham turned to the crowd, arms extended and nodded his head, as if he was expecting it. His life changed that day. It was his Best-in-a-sombrero moment. Good-looking, dedicated, skilful, with a touch of the showman, he was everything the rapacious commercial circus attaching itself to football could want in a figurehead. What's more, unlike Giggs who was always a reluctant pin-up, Beckham craved attention. He was more than willing to sit for as many photo shoots as were required. Later that season he was to start dating the Spice Girl Victoria Adams, after he met her at Old Trafford where she was Martin Edwards's lunch guest and drew the numbers in the half-time draw (the crowd roundly booed her efforts). He was attracted to her from the off, he admits in his autobiography, not just because of her legs, her eyes, her pout. But also because of 'the recognition in the public eye' that came from her success. The boy was addicted to fame. And he was in the right place to find it.

United won the title again that year, with Solskjær proving himself a brilliant find, scoring nineteen goals. There were the usual stumbles along the way. One sequence involved consecutive defeats of 5-0 at Newcastle and 6-3 at Southampton, an autumnal blip that, not for the last time, had many a newspaper pundit predicting Ferguson's imminent demise. But from there it was another demonstration of resolve. Wimbledon's Vinnie Jones, not normally known for his perspicacity, noted something about United after they had beaten his team en route to the title: 'People go on about the great skill in United's side,' he said in the spring of 1997, 'but the most important thing is their team spirit. They give off a warmth to each other that you can almost touch.'

In Europe, however, skill, spirit and the manager's investment in fresh experience did not pay off as well as it had domestically. Qualification from the group stage of the Champions League was not convincing, only achieved despite looking horribly exposed in home and away defeats against Juventus, and losing the proud record of home invincibility to Fenerbahçe. In the quarter-finals a rousing 4-0 victory over Porto seemed for many United fans as if justice had been done. In the away leg in Portugal the seven thousand visiting supporters had been attacked outside the ground by riot police, who fired rubber bullets, injuring several. The win raised expectations, particularly when the team was drawn against Borussia Dortmund in the last four. This was the year, everyone in the Old Trafford stands predicted. But the Germans proved too clever, too experienced, too strong, easily outmanoeuvring United. Most disappointing was Cantona's performance. He seemed cowed, heavy-legged, as if he could not raise his game for the big one. It was a sense that lingered through much of the finale of the season. And when he went to lift the Premiership trophy at the season's end he looked uneasy, distracted, as if no longer interested.

We were soon to learn why. A week later he announced his retirement, publicly terminating the romance with Manchester United. In every way his departure was typical of him: enigmatic, dramatic, out at the top without a backward glance. He gave no explanation.

United fans were left to consider what he had achieved at Old Trafford. Perhaps the most significant thing was that not once after he returned from his suspension was he in trouble with authority. Not even a yellow card. For those eighteen months he managed to control his demons, casting himself as the peacemaker on the pitch, the wise old head, mother-henning the kids, never once succumbing to his weakness for retaliation. So how did he manage to play without the fire that he once said was fundamental to him?

'I'm sure if I'd played more, I would have been booked, redcarded,' he told me. 'I worked hard to be like that for one and a half years. But I hadn't changed. Something would have happened. Nine months without football, you prepare yourself, you tell yourself when you come back, people will provoke you because they know you have a short fuse, so ignore it. But you know, when you say play without fire, I wasn't as passionate in the last year I played. When you are not passionate, you don't get so wound up. You don't respond to the provocation.'

And this was the crucial point. It didn't come out at the time, largely because Ferguson persuaded him not to go public with his worries, but Cantona left United because of the organisation's growing infatuation with commerce. It had compromised his love of the game.

'I gave up early because I don't want to do anything without passion. For me that is part of the emptiness. When I felt I had lost the passion, I couldn't do it any more. I had to stop.'

United, he added, had treated him like a commodity, a merchandising opportunity: 'When the business is more important than the football, I don't care. I just gave up.'

This fervently anti-commercialist philosophy surprised those who had engaged with him on financial matters. He had willingly done several promotional activities with Freedman, had participated on an autobiography, was later to demand over £90,000 to play in the Munich families' testimonial at Old Trafford. He liked his cash all right.

The public image he maintained, however, tallied with one that was growing among United fans in the nineties. Just as Freedman's merchandising was putting a shirt on the back of thousands, many a United fan decided to show their affiliation by eschewing all merchandising. True fans, they believed, would not buy a replica shirt if their life depended on it. Let the day trippers and the tourists buy if they wished – it would pay the players' wages after all – but they wanted none of it. A good number of United fans would fork out only a season ticket from the club and nothing more.

'About that time there became two Uniteds,' reckons Andy Walsh. 'The people you went with were United, the relationship you had with the players on the pitch, that was United. But Martin Edwards had a different vision of what United was. You had to block out all the embarrassment and the shit, the shirt changes, the corporate boxes, the money-making. If you didn't you'd have to defend it and it was indefensible. What you defended was your experience of going to United with your friends and family. It was the sense of belonging, of being part of the Man United movement that was what United was.'

And Edwards was always wary of the other United. When he became the chair of IMUSA, Walsh was constantly trying to set up meetings with the chairman. He would write to him asking for face to face discussions or to invite him to come and sit among the fans to hear their grievances on ticket price increases or the way that certain policemen in the Scoreboard End were routinely unpleasant and disrespectful. Edwards always declined.

'He was very polite and always made a point of writing back promptly,' recalls Walsh. 'But it was always a no.'

Edwards admits his caution was a mistake. 'Yes, not engaging with the fans' groups didn't do me any good,' he says. 'Maybe I should have explained the case. But at the time I really couldn't see the purpose. I don't think you can run a football club as a committee. It has to be one person making the right choices for the well-being of the club. I was acutely aware that the fans were part of Manchester United. But they were only one part. As chairman I had to balance so many interests, the manager, the players, the shareholders, ground development. And who were the fans' groups representing anyway? The executive fans wanted something different from the fans on the terraces. No, actually, that's not strictly true. They all wanted the same thing: Cup final tickets. And I could never get enough of those to satisfy everyone.'

Not that everyone took the Walsh line. Tony Wilson would never have it that Edwards undermined United's core values. For Wilson, Edwards was always the hero of the piece. 'Listen,' he once told me. 'When you're a kid you think it's all about the players. Then you grow up a bit and think it's all to do with the manager. But when you finally mature into a sentient human being, you realise it is the chairman who is the only one who matters. And let me tell you, Martin Edwards is the best there is. Be warned, all you whingeing moaners, you will mourn him when he's gone.'

Before that, however, it was Cantona who was to go, driven out, he says, by the Edwards machine. More than a decade after his last season, when their team play at Arsenal, or Liverpool or anywhere else, United followers chant his name longer and louder than that of many a contemporary player; The Twelve Days of Cantona is still Old Trafford's Christmas carol of choice. And in a recent poll carried out by a United fanzine, his name came up as the man most fans would like to see follow Ferguson into the dug-out.

'I would enjoy it,' he said of the idea. 'If I want to do it, it is because I can create something as a manager, I want to be an artist. I'm not certain it would work, but I think I could create something. I don't want to learn coaching, go on courses, it is not for me. I want to do it as an artist. And we'll see. There are a lot of things to try in life. To be strong enough to try, brave enough. I'm sure there are a lot of managers who have their own ideas but they are not crazy enough to try. But I am. Yes, it would be crazy.'

Imagine Eric Cantona as manager of Manchester United. It would be the final act of madness.

18

IT'S NEVER OVER

The essence of tragedy, as defined by Sophocles, is this: 'No man can be called happy until he has died in peace.'

If it sounds rather alarming, that's the point. The Greek playwright's thesis was that at any time something catastrophic might happen that can utterly change our opinion of a man. Or an institution. Any second now, bang, the sky might fall in. This is what makes for real drama, he reckoned: it is never over until it's over. Even when the fat lady is clearing her throat there is always still time.

It is a certainty of life those who persist in writing off Alex Ferguson and his Manchester United might care to commit to heart. There were plenty, for instance, who thought the Fergie era was over in the summer of 1998. United won nothing in the year after Cantona, finishing behind Arsenal in the League and faltering badly in Europe, losing to Monaco in the quarter-finals of the Champions League. Teddy Sheringham, the thirty-one-year-old striker bought from Spurs for £3.5 million, had manifestly failed to fill Cantona's role. He had gone to Old Trafford, he said at the time, to win things. His ambition was roundly mocked, uniting even Spurs and Arsenal fans in a common chant: 'Oh Teddy, Teddy, he went to Man United and he won fuck all.'

What's more, David Beckham, United's dead ball maestro, had been sent off in the World Cup in France and had returned home vilified, blamed for England's early exit, public enemy number-one.

'Ten Lions and One Spoiled Brat' was the headline in the *Daily Mirror* after England's defeat to Argentina. Outside one pub in London's East End, chirpy cockney regulars had lynched his effigy. Wherever he played this season, the consensus went, he would be under such pressure he would crumble, taking the United edifice with him.

Not that there was much of an edifice. The previous year United had been comprehensively outwitted by Arsenal, who won a League and Cup double. The Highbury club had recently come under the management of Arsène Wenger, a French coach who before moving to Japan had been in charge of Monaco in the days when Glenn Hoddle and Mark Hateley had played. At Arsenal he transformed the beery culture he inherited, manifestly improving the game of a rugged, hedonistic team by introducing sensible preparation and dietary habits. Plus, in the way he motivated them; his grasp of psychology appeared to be on a new level. Stooped and angular, the bespectacled Wenger gave off a professorial air; his image was of a man who thought rather than raged. With his scientific methodology he made the likes of Alex Ferguson look old school. The press loved Wenger, eulogising his intelligence, enjoying his willingness to answer any press conference question without looking as if he might chin the questioner, spotting in his methods an approach missing from English kick and rush. In the era of millionaire players, he was talked up as the future. Nobody could shout and bully like Fergie any more. Wouldn't work. The hairdryer was over.

Ferguson felt particularly irked by the comparison. Not only did he not take to the man, he chafed at the idea that Wenger was more rounded than he. As it turned out, for all his manifest intelligence, the Frenchman was a one-dimensional football obsessive: his idea of a good night was watching videos of German Second Division matches. Ferguson, on the other hand, was relaxing into a growing hinterland. He liked wine, cooking, playing the piano. He was learning French, he enjoyed travel, had close friends in business and politics. He had – though he might come to regret this – a significant interest in horse racing. None of this seemed to be reflected in the press comparisons between the two men that summer. In the media profiles he was the Tyrannosaurus of managerial dinosaurs, outwitted at every turn by the French philosopher. It was so frequently implied that time had been called for Ferguson, for once he felt moved to respond.

'I intend to stay as manager,' he said. 'I say that because there has been another round of speculation about when I might retire, which frankly bugs me. I'm fifty-six, feel as fit as I ever did and have a lot more to achieve. I intend to work into my sixties because Manchester United is my life.'

To show his intent, he spruced up his squad with another round of expensive signings. In came Jaap Stam, PSV Eindhoven's commanding centre back, Jesper Blomqvist, the Swedish winger from Parma, and Dwight Yorke, the toothsome Trinidad and Tobago striker. Yorke was bought from Aston Villa for an eye-watering £12.6 million, an outlay that rather challenged Ferguson's view that the plc was parsimonious in releasing transfer funds. But that was what he had maintained over the previous couple of seasons as he pursued the likes of Gabriel Batistuta, Marcelo Salas, Louis Figo and the Brazilian forward Ronaldo. He landed none of them and blamed the club's financial structure for his failure. The fans accepted his analysis: Martin Edwards's tight control over the purse strings prevented him from buying in players of the stature this club deserved, they believed. Whether that is the case is another matter. The fact is, such players may not have come whoever was in charge, however much they were offered. Manchester is not as easy a sell internationally as Barcelona, Milan or London.

In early September 1998, however, it looked as if United's ownership was about to change and Ferguson's tetchy relationship with the plc would become a thing of the past. Rupert Murdoch's BSkyB television operation offered 240 pence per share to buy out existing stock-holders and take control of United. It valued the club at £623.4 million. Martin Edwards – and most of the directors – were keen to accept.

Many fans, however, were less enthusiastic. Sure, Murdoch was a powerful operator. But so were the supporters of Manchester United, who detested the idea of the club becoming a corporate plaything, to be used as a vehicle to deliver the business ambitions of someone without any history of affection for the object of their faith. Thus was the most sophisticated fan campaign ever seen in British football launched with a public meeting at the Bridgewater Hall, the new concert venue in Manchester city centre. This was not a case of demonstrating outside the ground chanting 'Sack the board'. Nor, despite a proposal at the meeting, was there reckoned much purpose in smashing all the windows at Edwards's house. In fact, throughout the campaign, very little obvious restlessness was visible at Old Trafford. Unlike when their predecessor George Greenhough led a fans' movement in 1931, what was being served up on the pitch was hardly conducive to complaint. Most fans, the campaigners realised, really didn't care who owned the club as long as it was winning. But that was no reason to do nothing.

Skilfully coordinated by Andy Walsh of IMUSA and Michael Crick of Shareholders United, the anti-Murdoch campaign was a reflection of the reds' huge range of support. There were bankers and trade unionists, political lobbyists and media men, accountants and actuaries working shoulder to shoulder with warehousemen, firemen, dustmen and students. All were bound by their love of the great intangible: Manchester United Football Club. Sky's representatives badly underestimated their opponents ('They admitted later they thought we were just a bunch of ragged-arsed hooligans,' says

Walsh) and found themselves outflanked continuously. Every City institution seemed to have a United fan at its heart, leaking information back to the campaigners.

'The speed with which information came out, even from the most secret of meetings, was astonishing,' says the financial PR David Bick. 'The campaign had moles everywhere.'

Walsh, though, says the part played by fans without inside influence was as crucial. 'What was put in by ordinary people was a real turner,' he says. 'People would show up at our house, which was campaign HQ, and say, "I've got a morning off work, is there anything I can do?"'

Such dedication paid off. After intensive lobbying, in October 1998 Peter Mandelson, the Trade and Industry Secretary, referred the takeover to the Monopolies and Mergers Commission. MPs pored over its details, before reporting to Mandelson's successor Stephen Byers. In April 1999, to everyone's evident astonishment, particularly Murdoch's, Byers announced that the bid could not go ahead. Sky withdrew, having acquired just over 9 per cent of the club's shares. Edwards was not to bank the £84 million he had anticipated. A bit of a downer, you would have thought.

'Actually, I was indifferent as to whether the bid succeeded or not,' he says now. 'But I was obliged to accept whatever was in the best interests of shareholders. And that bid would have delivered maximum value. When it didn't happen, it didn't happen. You move on.'

For the fans' groups it was a stunning victory. They were, however, well served by circumstance. There was a young Labour government in power, many of whose members were hugely antipathetic to Murdoch, remembering the manner in which he had broken the print unions in the 1980s. Many of them had bitten their tongues as Tony Blair's administration proved itself far less radical than they hoped. But Blair had no interest in the bid and was happy to throw the rottweilers on his back bench a bone he considered meaningless, especially if he could do it in exchange for support on more contentious issues. So he stood back as his colleagues took on the bid. Ultimately, Sky's plans were derailed by the politics of revenge.

Some of the United campaigners, however, believed their methodology was the sole cause of victory. An assumption took root that a large shareholding by fans would insulate the club against future takeover. It was later to prove over-optimistic.

Ferguson's own role in the putative takeover was mute. Publicly he talked only about his team and its chances. At one point Sky's negotiating team suggested paying him up to £2 million to support the bid in the media. Edwards reacted in horror to the idea. So the manager, the public face of the club, was left on the outside, entirely peripheral. Walsh spoke to him on the telephone throughout the campaign and recalls him being privately supportive of the campaigners' efforts. Michael Crick suggests he might even have tried – through his banker son Mark – to raise funds for a takeover himself. It never came to anything. But it shows the degree to which Ferguson had drifted away from his one-time principal supporter, Edwards. They no longer trusted one another. The manager had become increasingly disillusioned with his reward. He thought of himself as the wellspring of all the money spewing out of Old Trafford, yet it was the chairman who seemed to be trousering the lion's share of it. Worse, Edwards was then denying Ferguson his just return. As a result two distinct centres of power had developed: Edwards and the money men in their offices at the ever-growing Old Trafford, Ferguson at the Cliff. In the past they spoke every day, now the two men were barely able to hold a conversation, each considering the other secondary to the important issues at hand.

For Ferguson, those were developing rapidly on the pitch. What the manager had assembled here was the best squad of his career. Dwight Yorke bonded immediately with the moody Andy Cole and helped him flourish. Cole's relationship with his strike partner Sheringham the previous season had been brittle to the point where, like the club's manager and chairman, they didn't speak. So Ferguson rearranged his forwards and established a pattern among those attempting to win the Premier League by having at his disposal two pairs of razor-sharp strikers. If Yorke and Cole faltered or tired, Sheringham and Solskjær were there, ready. The Norwegian, in particular, was always ready, no matter how late into a game he was introduced. He showed his ability to maintain concentration on the bench by scoring four times in the final fourteen minutes after coming on against Nottingham Forest.

In midfield Roy Keane, now captain, ran every game. The previous season he had been largely absent after injuring himself fouling Alf-Inge Haaland at Leeds. It was a bitter moment: he had been drinking the night before the game, he subsequently admitted, and chasing Haaland across Elland Road had ruptured his knee ligaments. Haaland, fuming, had stood over him as he writhed in agony, accusing him of faking it to distract the referee's attention from his assault. Now Keane was back, and his economy in possession, his intelligent passing and above all his ferocious will to win secured him a position as the fan's new, post-Cantona favourite. Alongside him, Paul Scholes, Ryan Giggs, Nicky Butt and Beckham were a home-produced quartet of expansive ability. Just as Cantona had before him, Beckham confounded those who assumed he would crack under the strain of being pilloried and mocked. From the first kick of the season, the United fans lauded him. He became a symbol of their antipathy towards the national side: if England fans hated him, then he must be a good thing. Sure, he was a cockney, never the Mancunians' favourite type of footballer. But his Stakhanovite work ethic, his goals from free-kicks and his long-standing United affiliation (his dad was a lifelong cockney red who had persuaded him to sign for Ferguson when every team in London wanted him) were enough for them to back him through his little difficulty. It was us against the world once more. Just as it had been with Eric. Just as it would later be with others.

Behind Beckham and his midfield colleagues, Stam and Ronnie Johnsen, plus Henning Berg, the bright defender bought from Blackburn, provided reassurance on a Pallister/Bruce scale. With young Wes Brown, who Ferguson reckoned would eventually be the finest defender of his time, Gary and Phil Neville and the wise old head of Denis Irwin filling the full back positions, this was some defence. The final point of resistance was the colossus Peter Schmeichel, yelling incessantly, never accepting anything could be his fault, performing as well as he ever had in what he insisted was to be his valedictory year at Old Trafford.

Together they cut a swathe through English football, totally undermining any suggestion of Arsenal hegemony. It was a season in which wonderful games arrived as if by conveyor belt. Sophoclean drama was served up almost weekly. In the FA Cup Ferguson's team gave a pointer to their never-say-die spirit in a fourth round tie at home to Liverpool. The visitors led from the third minute and looked to be heading through to the next round before Yorke equalised with just a few seconds of normal time left. With everyone preparing themselves for a replay, the sub Solskjær scored the winner well into injury time.

To the tune of 'Skip-to-my Lou', the Stretford Enders chanted their new favourite tune: 'Who put the ball in the Scousers net? Ole Gunnar Solskjær.'

In Europe, too, horizons were opening up. UEFA, in a bid to head off the big clubs forming their own competition, had extended the Champions League to take in the League runners-up from the major nations. Ferguson, the unrepentant traditionalist, said he had considered not accepting the invitation to participate on the grounds this was the Champions Cup and his team were not champions. 'I thought about it,' he said, 'for about a millisecond.'

Without the benefit of seeding, England's runners-up had a tough draw. In their group were Barcelona and Bayern Munich. They drew all four games with their illustrious rivals, including a 3-3 tie in the Camp Nou, which did much to erase the memory of the 4-0 drubbing there earlier in the nineties. That was not the end of tough games. They drew Inter in the quarter-finals, beating them at home, then, after Berg produced a tackle on Ronaldo the equal of Bobby Moore's famous dispossession of Jairzinho in the 1970 World Cup, drawing in the San Siro. Scholes's equaliser came – there's a pattern emerging here – in the eighty-eighth minute.

'It was our coming of age in Europe,' said Ferguson.

It may have been, but at every stage of his assault on three competitions you assumed his team would falter. Not through any demonstrable weakness, but simply because the luck surely had to go against them eventually. The moment of disappointment appeared to have arrived with barely three minutes left of the FA Cup semi-final replay against Arsenal at Villa Park. The semi had been set up in the media as the old way against the new, the incumbent against the pretender, the Glaswegian streetfighter against the French sophisticate. With the scores at 1-1, Phil Neville tripped Ray Parlour in the penalty area. Up stepped Denis Bergkamp, Arsenal's Dutch lynchpin. This was it, the Sophoclean moment, the sudden, unforeseen catastrophe. United appeared to be eliminated, defeated at the last. There could be no way back from this. Especially with Keane, his unfussy prompting at its most insistent, sent off earlier in the game. Especially as Bergkamp hit his penalty well. But Schmeichel guessed his intention, dived prodigiously to his left, got his hand to the ball and saved. It was a save to rank with those he made a couple of years previously at Newcastle, the kind of save that wins things.

Then, midway through extra time, Giggs intercepted a pass from Patrick Vieira in his own half and ran at the Arsenal defence. It was what Matt Busby had told Bobby Charlton to do: run at a defence at pace. The Old Man would have loved it. Here was the most celebrated back line in English football history cleaving to Giggs's advance, allowing him to run unchecked, untrammelled, untouched. After skipping past five of them, from the edge of the six-yard box he thwacked the ball past David Seaman for the winner. It was a goal of skill, of cunning and above all of adventure. To attempt it in the circumstances was extraordinary. Giggs peeled off his shirt and, windmilling it above his head, ran back whence he came, chest hair pressed back by the breeze, his team-mates no more able to catch him up to celebrate than his opponents had been to stop him. Giggs was just twenty-five when he scored that goal. But he had been central to the Manchester United story for so long he had become part of the furniture, some-times barely noticed. Now, when it mattered, he had delivered something as exceptional as anything dreamed up by Best, Law or Charlton, Edwards, Colman or Robson. After the game hundreds of United fans invaded the pitch and lifted him shoulder-high. It was a moment of communion, a moment sharing a sense of what this club meant.

'Yeah,' said Giggs. 'I suppose it was the best goal I've ever scored.'

He was the rescuer in the European semi too. In the first leg against Juventus, the Italian side, with a midfield of Zinedine Zidane, Didier Deschamps and Edgar Davids as powerful as any ever assembled in Europe, were leading 1-0 for much of the game at Old Trafford. The Welshman got an equaliser with – can you believe it? – only a couple of minutes to spare. It was a scrappy toe poke, not in the same league as his creation of beauty at Villa Park. Once more, with Manchester United, it was too soon to make con-clusions about their demise.

The away game in Turin's wind-swirled Stadio delle Alpi was a performance to rank with the club's finest European escapades: the 1957 quarter-final against Bilbao, the 1968 semi-final against Real, the 1984 Cup Winners' Cup quarter against Barcelona. It shared so many qualities with those achievements – the persistence, the indomitable spirit, the refusal to be intimidated by misfortune – that you can only conclude there is something in the water at Old Trafford. Four different generations. Four sets of players who never knew or worked with each other. Yet four almost identikit achievements.

'They have a saying at United,' says Eric Harrison. 'Paul McGuinness [Wilf's son, who works in the youth set-up] came up with it. It's called "the thread". It's there. It's in the air: the history envelops you, it absorbs you, it draws you into the place. If you like, it's in the DNA of the club.'

Just like those other grand United Euro performances, the 1999 team had to dig themselves out of a hole. Juve were 2-0 up within eleven minutes. But Roy Keane, giving his singular most determined performance in a red shirt, was not to be cowed. Driving the team on, he got a goal back with a header from a corner. Then Dwight Yorke, who had been racially abused from the home stands throughout (a banner in the Juve end read 'Yorke is my dog') scored the equaliser. Juve, the most fearsome machine in Italian football, seemed nonplussed by the response, as if they could not control this force of nature. United were through on the away goals rule, but Cole scored a winner anyway, to record the club's first ever victory on Italian soil. Even the stunned home supporters applauded United's players off the field: it was a victory of such unusual quality.

Mind, it was a victory that did not come without consequence. In the ferocious midfield competition, Keane and Scholes were booked, meaning both would miss the final. It was in the very same stadium where nine years before Paul Gascoigne had been carded in the midst of another tumultuous semi-final. Had England not lost that World Cup encounter on penalties, he too would have been unavailable for the final. When he realised this, Gazza cried his eyes out, floods of self-pity that launched him on to the national stage. In the same circumstances Keane and Scholes remained dry-eyed. Disappointed for sure, but this was their job, one of those things. When Keane later was asked to comment on the immensity of his showing, he replied that he thought he had done 'all right'. Ferguson was more effusive: 'That was the greatest performance by any team under my management,' he said in the glow of the after-match press conference. Five years previously he had said that a treble of League championship, FA and League Cup was a footballing impossibility. Now he had a much more significant threesome in his sights.

The only surprise in all this was that it was done without Brian

Kidd. Ferguson's assistant left to manage Blackburn in November 1998. The good cop to Fergie's bad, Kidd had been hugely influential in the development of the young players at the heart of United's endeavours. He was the players' friend, the kindly voice in the dressing room, the arm round the shoulder. When he went to Ewood Park, Ferguson initially said little to suggest he had a problem with the move. But when his autobiography was published the following year, the manager was intemperate in his attacks on Kidd, calling him weak, venal and disloyal. It was an unhappy end for a United hero. Kidd was said to be distraught by his former friend's behaviour, refusing all invitations – including one by this book – to talk about it. But it indicated Ferguson's central obsession had grown ever stronger. Nothing mattered to him now except his vision of Manchester United. No one could be more important than the entity itself. And anyone who challenged it, as far as he was concerned, could depart; they no longer existed. It was a chilling portent of things to come.

With Steve McClaren, his new assistant signed from Derby, by his side, Ferguson faced his most challenging period as a manager: in a space of ten days the treble was up for negotiation. First Spurs came to Old Trafford in the final League game and victory secured him his fifth title. At Wembley Sheringham and Scholes saw off a disappointing Newcastle to give him his third double. It was an achievement extraordinary enough given the manner in which the manager and his methods had been so comprehensively dismissed the previous summer. But it was almost forgotten in the anticipation of what lay ahead.

The one that had grown to take on much greater significance – in Ferguson's mind as much as anywhere else – arrived the following Wednesday. United were to play Bayern Munich in the Champions League final at the Camp Nou.

'Two Cup finals in a week,' said Beckham, immediately sensing the important things in this the rush of major fixtures. 'I was happy, of course, as it meant two new suits.'

United and Bayern had drawn twice in the competition's group stages, so on the pitch the balance of power was delicate. Off it, however, was a different story. On 26 May 1999, forty thousand Bayern fans were said to be in Barcelona. You wouldn't have noticed. Catalunya was red that day. There were so many United supporters in town that hotels were full within a two-hour drive of the city and Barcelona's airport reported its busiest ever day – as did those in Reus to the south and Girona an hour north. Officially, United were allocated thirty-eight thousand tickets. But at least fifty-five thousand supporters turned up, many paying up to £600 for a ticket from the Manc touts patrolling Las Ramblas.

The players were stationed along the coast in a beachside hotel in Sitges. Ferguson did his best to relax them, not changing his standard preparation, hoping to convince them this was nothing more than an away game at Bolton. For some of the players, it didn't work. However hard the manager tried, Jesper Blomqvist remembers being consumed by nerves.

'I was very nervous before the game,' recalls the Swede, who played in thirty-eight games that season. 'I sat in the hotel writing a list: "You can do it . . . You are faster than the rest." I was trying to convince myself that I would have a good game. Being tense is not a bad thing, but I was too nervous for my own good.'

The nerves spilled out across the town. Everywhere heaved with United fans, trying to stifle their anticipation with alcohol. The sense of belonging that day was tangible. In every bar and every restaurant there were people bound by affection for the reds. They came from all backgrounds and income groups, people who in normal circumstances would never have shared oxygen. There were Sloanes and lads, posh and poor, Mancs and southerners. People of all races, several sexes and a huge variety of sizes. There was the crowd of old Labour union activists congregating in a bar owned by a workers' collective, drinking cava, 'the people's champagne'. There was a group of Muslim lads on the metro, trying to sober up their friend, 'What if his dad sees him like this?' Alongside them were a bunch of barristers singing a song in German at a group of Munich fans about how their lederhosen were about to be pulled down. At every turn were supporters who hadn't seen each other for years hugging and kissing and wiping away the tears of rediscovery, revelling in the combined sense of being red.

Of the tens of thousands of Manchester supporters there, maybe about half a dozen approached the Camp Nou sober. But this was a very different fan response to the seventies and eighties. This was nothing like the violent excesses of United fans in Turin in the mid-eighties described in Bill Buford's *Among the Thugs*. Regular European travellers, these fans were drunk but not disorderly, loud but not disrespectful, boisterous but not confrontational. It was an invasion now legendary in the Catalan capital, with stories retold to this day. Like the United fan asleep on the tram as it sped past the stadium – ten minutes into the game. Or the photo of a dozing fan surrounded by beer cans in a Plaça Catalunya fountain. The next morning the Catalan daily *La Vanguardia* wrote of United fans: 'They are ugly, but they are good people.'

It was an astonishing wave of humanity that left the Munich fans dumbfounded: they appreciated they could never match this. In the ground, however, their players matched United's. Ferguson, shorn of Keane and Scholes, played Butt and Beckham in central midfield, with Blomqvist on the left and Giggs on the right. After the power and energy of their midfield performances all season, with three players out of position this was the reds' most muted showing. Bayern led at half-time and Ferguson needed all his motivational skills to rouse the team from an uninspired, un-United display. Unlike the time he had shouted at Nicky Butt for giving away possession in this very same stadium ('You've fucking lost me the European Cup, Butt. Are you happy?'), he was measured, calm, to the point. He remembered something his former Aberdeen player Steve Archibald had told him about the awful emptiness of losing a European Cup with Barcelona.

'If you lose, you'll go up to collect losers' medals and you'll be six feet away from the European Cup. But you won't be able to touch it,' he said as the players prepared themselves for the second half. 'I want you to think about the fact you'll have been so close to it and for many of you that will be the closest you'll ever get. And you will hate the thought for the rest of your lives. So just make sure you don't lose.'

Like many of the reporters covering the game, with eighty-five minutes gone and United still behind I had all but completed a piece for the first edition of the *Guardian* which lamented that the treble was an impossible dream, talked about the players' exhaustion and blamed Ferguson for the defeat because of his poor team selection. It was never printed. Other media Mystic Megs were not so fortunate, and it is said Ferguson keeps a selection of the negative first editions in his office, as a handy aide-memoire of those who slighted him. It was not just the media, however, who assumed it was over. At that point George Best had left the stadium looking for a bar, unwilling to watch his team lose. And Lennart Johansson, UEFA's president, had headed down to the pitch side ready to present the trophy to Bayern.

We should have all known. Sophocles told us two and a half thousand years ago. It is not over till it's over. As Clive Tyldesley put it on the ITV commentary: 'United have to score. They always score.'

By the time Johansson came out of the tunnel to take up his position, the score was 1-1. Teddy Sheringham, on for Yorke, scrambled the ball home from close in. Johansson turned to make his way back upstairs for extra time. On the bench McClaren was yelling at the manager to rearrange the team, get them back into shape for extra time. But Ferguson wasn't listening. He was watching Irwin hump the ball forward where it span off a Bayern player for another corner. Beckham took it. Sheringham flicked it on. And Solskjær, reacting ahead of his dumb-founded, traumatised, statuesque Bayern markers, stuck out his right leg to prod the ball into the roof of the net. Johansson missed that goal, too.

'Name on the trophy,' yelled Tyldesley.

'Who put the ball in the Germans' net?' demanded those United fans who were capable of coherent thought. 'Ole Gunnar Solskjær.' Solskjær slid across the turf in joyful celebration, an act that damaged his ligaments and ultimately precipitated his retirement from the game.

Down on the pitch Sammy Kuffour, Bayern's Ghanaian centre back, pounded the grass with his fists in despair and disappointment. Up on the edge of the press enclosure, meanwhile, as I prepared completely to rewrite my story, a United fan leapt at me from the corporate seating alongside, punched my laptop to the ground and shouted: 'Now what you going to write, you bastard?'

It was hard to know where to start.

After the game, the players spent an hour on the pitch delirious with joy, led by David May, the substitute who gatecrashed the celebrations with shameless abandon. 'I'd signed from Blackburn in 1995,' he recalls. 'And David Batty rang me up shouting "Scum, scum, scum" down the phone all morning. But I'd made my mind up to go. You only get one chance to join United. Nor do you miss your chance to get hold of the European Cup. I always thought that if I got near the trophy then I'd be in the pictures. I saw it on a chair and thought, I'm having that.'

May was there, too, at the club's official victory party in the ballroom of the Arts, Barcelona's swankiest hotel. I know he was because I saw him there. I just walked in with a friend. We were in the room for fifteen minutes, watching the players grinning and high-fiving, cherishing their victory, cradling the cup with reverence, as Ferguson had told them only winners can. We stood in line for the buffet behind Ronnie Johnsen and Henning Berg and listened to them discussing the merits of coleslaw with Trevor Lea, United's nutritionalist. There we were, enjoying the sight and sound of fulfilment, when we were spotted by Ned Kelly, United's head of security. We probably would have got away with staying longer if he hadn't noticed my friend shoving half a dozen of the banquet menus down the front of her trousers.

'Those are the property of Manchester United plc,' Kelly said, humourlessly, as he peeled them off her and showed us the door.

On the way out we bumped into Alex Ferguson coming in. I have never seen anyone look so happy. Ever. We both hugged him and he chuckled and blushed and said, 'Football, eh, fucking hell.'

He had clearly been saying it to everyone. It was, in slightly more sober language, to be the phrase of the treble, repeated in headline and profile, on television and video compilation, a phrase that summed up the mad unpredictability of it, the way in which the odds had been so comprehensively bundled on their head. Just as 1968 had been the final glorious distillation of Busby's 'Just go out and play', so was this the endpiece of Ferguson's more rugged philosophy of never give up, never say die and, above all, never let the bastards grind you down. As we stood there with the man who had made it all possible, it was tempting to believe that nothing he could ever do now would come close to matching these moments in the ballroom of a Barcelona hotel. Surely nothing could beat this.

Sophocles, however, would caution against such certainty.

19

I WON'T BE MAKING A COMEBACK LIKE SINGERS DO

Normally Alex Ferguson looks a picture of control when facing the press. His eyes will scan the room busily for those who have recently slighted him. He will conduct things on his terms, steer the content in his direction, lambast anyone who tries to ask anything inconvenient. He has been known to leave the podium and confront pressmen who say things he doesn't like. He is in charge.

But in the press conference called in November 1999 to announce that Manchester United would not be defending the FA Cup in 2000, he looked edgy, unhappy, as if he had lost control. In a sense he had: United were now embroiled in politics on a level way beyond anything one man could corral, a level that reflected the game's growing prominence, the way it had become perceived as an engine for wider economic growth. He didn't say anything, leaving it to Martin Edwards and David Davies of the FA to explain that, as holders of the Champions League, United had been invited to represent Europe in FIFA's new world club competition, involving the champions from each continent. It was to be

held the following January in Brazil, coinciding with the FA Cup
fourth round. Rather than play a weakened team, or rearrange fixtures, it had been decided that United would withdraw from
domestic chores and go to Rio instead.

While Edwards and Davies carried on as if the announcement
was of no more import than a slight change in the fixture list,
Ferguson looked pained. He knew what it meant to be the only
club in the history of the world's oldest football competition not to
defend its trophy. He looked guilty. More to the point, he looked as
if he knew what was coming.

The announcement caused outrage. The press coverage
reflected the opinion of United widely held beyond the confines of
Old Trafford. The *Mirror*, edited by the Arsenal fan and arch ABU
Piers Morgan, led the assault. United, the paper exploded, were
now out of kilter, a body dedicated to self-interest, sneering at tradition and romance. It began a campaign to 'save the FA Cup'.

When, at one of his weekly press briefings, Ferguson later
countered that the club had been leaned on by the FA and the
government who were both anxious that they accept FIFA's
promptings because it might help England's chances of landing
the 2006 World Cup, it did not stem the complaints. In fact it
heightened them: the papers decided United and the FA were in
cosy conspiracy to undermine the country's finest sporting competition. They were trying to get away with it once more.

The more the press condemned the decision, the more tetchy
Ferguson became. He was particularly unhappy at the way the
government and FA, after pressuring the club behind the scenes,
did little to support them publicly. What a contrast this was with
1956, when the football authorities had been so reluctant to sanction a move abroad. Now they were happy to compromise their
own competition in order to facilitate the innovations of others,
or rather in a doomed attempt to land the World Cup. As was his
habit, Ferguson articulated his frustration by exploding at individual newsmen. At a League Cup tie at Aston Villa, one foolhardy
reporter (it might have been me) asked the manager why he could

not field a youth team in the FA Cup as he just had in the lesser competition that evening.

'Have you seen our fixture list?' he bellowed, getting up and walking out of the Villa Park press room. 'If you had you wouldn't even ask that question. You have no idea. No idea at all. That's it, it's over, you can all fuck off, the lot of you.'

A moment later he reappeared at the door.

'And that's all off the record. None of this better appear in the fucking papers.'

Anyone who thought Ferguson had mellowed in the fourteen years he had been at the club, or had changed after receiving his knighthood from the Queen that summer, or even, having won the lot the previous year, had just run out of steam (usually coming out of his ears), clearly did not encounter him often in the autumn of 1999. As far as he was concerned it was still United against the world. Those who questioned him, even in the normal course of journalistic inquiry, were working against him. He issued banning edicts with abandon. Individual reporters, anyone from the *Daily Mail*, the *Mirror*, at one point even the club's own propaganda division MUTV, all had their spells in exile. Some are still there. The BBC, for instance, after screening Alex Millar's documentary about Ferguson's transfer dealings involving agent son, Jason, have never been – and you sense will never be – admitted again into his inner sanctum. And – no matter how much Gary Lineker bemoans the fact on *Match of the Day* – you suspect Ferguson will never talk to them again.

'I don't hold grudges,' Fergie told Sir David Frost in a television interview. 'All the BBC need to do is apologise. But they never do.' As for Lineker, Ferguson dismissed his complaints as 'childish'.

United's fans didn't care. As long as the team was winning they saw no problem in the manager sparring with newspapers and television. They had all heard the stories of his kindness to individual supporters – the hospital visits, the time he paid for an unemployed lad's season ticket, the genial winks and hair ruffles when he met kids in the street – they knew the real man. Besides, didn't the press deserve its berating? Most United fans were convinced the media was institutionally biased against them in the first place. At least Fergie stood up to them.

But media memories are almost as long as Ferguson's own. His enemies within it, those who had been snubbed, sworn at or threatened, those whose outlets had been banned, had long relished the chance for revenge in moments like the Brazil escapade. The reporting at times was way out of proportion. It was as if Ferguson and United had committed mass murder, not merely let slip a football trophy. But that was the modern way with United: they were at the heart of the pantomime.

One thing is for sure, the regular media tit for tat spats like this coloured the wider view of the club. To casual inspection, it all looked snappy and undignified. There was a lack of the graciousness Busby brought. And there were those within the corridors of Old Trafford who believed that now the club was a major international business brand, a more benign image might be productive. Embarrassed by the exclusions and bannings, an idea began to form in certain minds that a less abrasive public face might benefit the plc bottom line.

Not that the club's own PR was a model of sophistication. As Ferguson's team prepared to head to Brazil in January 2000, a letter was sent to fans warning them not to travel to Rio – one of the world's great tourist destinations – as it was too dangerous (the four hundred fans who ignored this nonsense had a great time). Consternation among United's hosts was a cue for more bellowing headlines. Things weren't helped when the *Mirror* men following the tournament happened across Martin Edwards in a nightclub enjoying the company of a woman who looked like she might have been paid for the assistance she was giving in his acclimatisation. Or by the fact that while Real Madrid held open-door training sessions that the kids from the favellas flooded to watch, United trained behind closed doors.

Then, to add fuel to the growing consensus that United thought they could operate above the rules, David Beckham was sent off in the competition's first match for a tetchy stamp. No, as United failed to reach its final stages, the trip to Brazil was not a success.

Except in this one regard. Relaxed and refreshed by a two-week break from the debilitations of the English winter, United returned to storm the Premiership. By May they had won it by eighteen points from Arsenal. The ninety-one points accrued was a record in the era of three points for a win. And it was the highest proportion of points taken since Preston's Invincibles won the first League season of 1888–89.

Being Ferguson's United it did not happen without controversy, without mockery, without drawback. First there were his issues with goalkeepers. The Australian Mark Bosnich, who had been at United as a youngster before leaving because of work permit troubles, later resurfacing at Villa, was a patchy, flaky replacement for the now retired Peter Schmeichel. He was unpopular with his team-mates, too, who thought him insufferably arrogant. At times his shot-stopping was marvellous. But he was a terrible kicker, his clearances slicing off his toes with a regularity that made Old Trafford regulars wonder if he wore clown's boots. Though they were not as comical as those sported by Massimo Taibi, who suffered humiliation in games against Chelsea and Southampton – in the latter he let a weak shot through his legs. A player evidently not made of the right United stuff, the Italian was shunted to the reserves, mocked by the nickname 'The Blind Venetian', the several million he cost to recruit from Venezia quietly written off.

Then there was the David Beckham conundrum. Beckham had in the summer after the treble wed his Spice Girl. The ceremony was the celebrity event of the year, attended by three hundred of the couple's closest personal friends. The pictures sold for millions. The details – the Irish castle setting, the matching thrones, the purple outfits all the guests had to wear – became material for many a stand-up comic. It was reckoned in the press the ultimate in extravagant bad taste. Once players were paid like dustmen. Now they were paid like kings and behaved like Romans. Roy

Keane, meanwhile, didn't go. The idea of being told what to wear to a wedding made him laugh.

Ferguson felt much the same as his captain. He was worried about Beckham. This was not a Bestie problem. Beckham was sober, a diligent trainer, someone who consistently did his bit. It was more about focus: the manager thought the player was losing his. He fretted about the growing absurdity of Beckham's lifestyle, about the 160-mile distance his newly built Hertfordshire mansion (dubbed Beckingham Palace) was from the training ground, about the rumours that Posh wanted him to play somewhere more convenient for her favoured shops. So when Beckham missed a training session because his son was feeling ill and Ferguson saw pictures of Mrs B attending a celebrity function that very same evening, the response was not a sympathetic one. This was proof of what he had long suspected: the pop star wife was undermining his player's resolve. His priorities were out of kilter. Everyone at the club had to buy into this one certainty: in all their lives Manchester United came first. Remember that flag in the Stretford End? 'United, Kids, Wife: in that order', it read. Nothing articulated Fergie's philosophy as neatly. There was a truth in it too: the owner of the flag, offered a 'United or me' ultimatum by his first wife, had chosen United.

When he saw Beckham the next day, the manager exploded as only he could. A row on the training field was caught by a paparazzo hiding in a bush. The pictures made all the papers. Posh got her PR people to brief journalists; many a piece appeared applauding Beckham's priorities and lambasting Ferguson's archaic approach to modern parenting. This was a new kind of row for Ferguson, one that was to be played out in the gossip columns as much as the back pages. But he wasn't going to lose it. Beckham was dropped for a game. In the scheme of things it made little difference, United won the League. But the close relationship between manager and player that had been nurtured over the previous decade, the one that both had described as like a father and a son, had been critically damaged.

As for Europe, after the high of Barcelona, the champions were back to the nearly weres. Far from the treble precipitating a period of Continental domination, United were eased out at the quarter-finals by Real Madrid. Keane, on a personal crusade to make the final after missing out the year before, started the slide in the home defeat to the Spaniards by scoring an own goal. Ferguson was dismayed by the speed of their exit. After all, even Nottingham Forest had managed to defend the trophy.

So he determined to strengthen his team. Convinced that Dwight Yorke, too, was descending into celebrity (he was dating the pneumatic model Jordan), the manager bought the Dutch striker Ruud van Nistelrooy from PSV Eindhoven for £18 million. He had been alerted to the player by his son Darren, who had encountered him when out on loan in the Netherlands. Strong, mobile and a Law-like goal predator, the twenty-three-year-old Van Nistelrooy was reckoned to be the new Marco van Basten. But on the day the player was supposed to sign for United, he never showed at his unveiling press conference. He had failed a medical. There was trouble with his knee. He went back to Holland to recuperate. A couple of days later, filmed training with PSV, he was seen to fall to the ground, clutching his knee and squealing in agony. That, it was widely thought, was that.

Not for Ferguson it wasn't. His persistence has always been extraordinary. As is his innate understanding of a player's psychology. He kept in touch with Van Nistelrooy, ringing him constantly with encouraging tales about how Keane and Wes Brown had overcome similar injuries, telling him he, too, would be fine and how he still wanted him at United. Thus encouraged, Van Nistelrooy flourished in his rehabilitation. PSV, however, who had continued to pay him as he recuperated for a year, were less happy about the idea that United would seize him the moment his fitness returned. Their president Harry van Raaj said of Ferguson when Van Nistelrooy finally signed for the reds in June 2001: 'He has overstepped the bounds of good manners. He must really think he is the king of football.'

The player, meantime, was effusive about the United way. 'He showed me such warmth,' he said of the manager. Given what was later to happen between the two men, it was a remark laced with irony.

For a season the United bus rolled on without the Dutchman, though Ferguson got himself a goalkeeper when he bought the French World Cup winner Fabien Barthez from Marseille. Barthez arrived as fundamental changes were being made to the way of doing things at United. That summer of 2000 the club's long-standing axis shifted to the new training complex at Carrington. With the finest in manicured pitches, a full-sized indoor AstroTurf, gyms, steam rooms, weight rooms, endless medical facilities, conference rooms, press areas, offices for the managerial staff, the place has everything the modern football club needs. With expensive mechanical engineering parked between low-rise steel and glass pavilions it looks like a cross between the headquarters of a Silicon Valley software company and a pharmaceutical multinational's secret laboratory. That is if you ever get to see it. It lies down a nondescript lane in semi-rural Cheshire, just past an oil refinery, a power station and a lorry park. It is hard to locate and harder to get to: there is no public transport within two miles of the place. Which is no coincidence. Ferguson felt the Cliff, for all its historic resonance and cosy tradition, had become way too open, too accessible. While it might have been part of the dialogue between players and fans, he believed the conversation was becoming entirely one way. Latterly, after training the more helpful players, Ole Gunnar Solskjær for instance, could spend an hour, easily, in the Cliff car park signing autographs, on items that would often end up on eBay. And those who demurred were chastised in the fanzines as stuck up and unaware of who paid their wages. Now at Carrington everything is protected behind security barriers and twenty-four-hour patrols. Instead of thousands turning up for training sessions as they used to in the early nineties, now the only hint of the great United fanbase outside is half a dozen Japanese tourists hanging around the entrance gate, hoping the players will ignore the discreet notice prohibiting the signing of autographs.

'The journalists call this place Colditz,' Ferguson said as he sat in the press room at Carrington at the end of the 2007-08 season. 'That's right. And that's just the way we like it.'

The Cliff was kept on for the youth players and today hums with shrill voices as the under-tens are groomed in the United way. It is one of the paradoxes of Ferguson's management that his youth system is a pioneer in child-centred learning. Coaches stand aside and let the young players get on with their small-sided games. There is no adult shouting, no overbearing imposition of systems. No one is on the touchline pointing at their watch. Under Les Kershaw, the Academy director, and René Meulensteen, the skills coach, the idea is to have fun first and worry about the result later. And this, at a place presided over by the world's most competitive football man. It is one of the many ways in which United confound assumption at every turn.

Certainly, as the boys go about their cheery business, the Cliff can be a lot noisier than Old Trafford. On 8 November 2000, for instance, United just about beat Dynamo Kiev 1-0 in a Champions League tie that was played in a reverential hush, broken by the occasional catcall and tutted complaint at a misplaced pass. Afterwards the captain Roy Keane, who was becoming increasingly prepared to voice his concerns about everything to do with United, had this to say: 'Away from home our fans are fantastic, but at home they have a few drinks and probably their prawn sandwiches and they don't realise what's going on out on the pitch. These people want fantasy football but they should be out in the real world.'

After Eric Cantona's sardines, this was another fishy metaphor by a United skipper to make the headlines. It led to much mockery from rival fans and the press. But as with most Keane challenges, the hard core of United fans loved it. It was what they had been saying for years about the growing corporatisation of their home ground: it would end not so much in tears as silence.

It had come about because, with costs spiralling upwards, United's directors needed to unlock ever more revenue streams. Since the traditional, old school United supporters wanted no more when they turned up at the ground than what Danny McGregor, United's former commercial manager, once described as 'the three Ps' (a pint, a pie and a piss), the accountants needed to look elsewhere. Hence the huge increase in corporate entertaining sections. As the ground expanded in stages, from a capacity of 44,000 to 55,000 to 67,000, eventually to 76,000, the new seats were disproportionately ones that came complete with match-day entertainment possibilities. These were the areas that generated the revenue that would eventually meet Keane's demands for a sizeable contract hike. But they did not create noise. Here were gathered the kind of supporters who sat back and waited to be entertained. They were no more likely to participate in communal singing than they would chant Gordon Ramsey's name when they'd paid to eat in one of his places. What they would expect there was a good meal. And at Old Trafford what they expected was good football.

This was how the character of the match experience at United had changed as the new century began: where thirty years before the Stretford End had been an intimidating cauldron of youthful noise, now it was a civilised, restrained repository of corporate expectation. Old Trafford was growing ever quieter, frustrating the hard core, mocked by away fans and now noted by the captain. As for prawn sandwiches, the catering manager was quick to point out none were available anywhere in the ground. No, his menu was a lot more sophisticated than prawn sandwiches.

Everyone, however, chanters and corporates alike, got what they wanted that season: another title. Within recent memory, the club had not won the championship in twenty-six years, now they had done it seven times in nine years. That season they won it earlier than any of their previous titles, too, wrapping things up before Easter. Although effectively everything was theirs on 25 February, when they beat their nearest challengers, Arsène Wenger's clever, modern Arsenal, 6-1. Or as their fans would no doubt put it: 1 6 to the Arsenal.

The Achilles heel of Ferguson's United remained Europe. Here, Bayern Munich administered revenge for 1999 by winning in the quarter-final. United appeared to be in a curious limbo: too good domestically, not up to Europe. Keane, typically, articulated the frustration: 'Maybe it is the end of the road for this team,' he said. 'Maybe it is time to move on. We have given our all and we're just not good enough. You have to face facts.'

If not the end of the road for the team, the summer of 2000 appeared to mark the conclusion for the two men who had been the architects of United's ascent both on and off the pitch. The first to go was Martin Edwards. Although only fifty-five, he relinquished the role of chief executive and chairman of the football side of the business, handing things over to Peter Kenyon, a busy former Umbro executive. Edwards had ambition to become the plc chairman, but his previous role as chief executive plus the eye-opening details of his odd private life hopelessly compromised him as a candidate. He accepted his fate, sold his remaining shares to an investor called Harry Dobson (he had already offloaded £40 million worth in 1999), and retired to his office with a view, to be known from now on by the title of life president.

At the same time – and for the fans far more significantly – Alex Ferguson, also approaching his sixties, decided he too would call time on United. He made his intentions clear to the board that spring: he would retire in May 2002. By an exquisite piece of serendipity, the Champions League final was to be held in his home city of Glasgow, surely the most appropriate way to sign off. He had other things to do with his life now, not least his part share of a racehorse called Rock of Gibraltar that was winning everything in sight. After a campaign by fans groups, including a twenty-one-minute rendition of 'Every single one of us loves Alex Ferguson' aired during the away game at Spurs, not to mention a substantial offer from Kenyon, he decided he would not, as he initially threatened, sever all ties with the club. He was to become a roving ambassador, paid £1 million a year. Privately, Edwards seethed at the news. He had been around when Busby had left. He didn't want the same to happen again. He advised the other directors (he remained an active board member until November 2002) that it would be best to bid teary farewell when Ferguson retired, let him disappear to the racecourse. The hanging on, his presence lurking in the corridors, his shadow lengthening over the training pitches, could only cause problems. It happened before. They would be mad even to risk letting it happen again. But Edwards was no longer in charge of his train set. And Kenyon believed the madness would be to relinquish Ferguson's renown. So he made his offer and in the process upped the manager's salary for his last year to £3 million, briefly more than any of his players.

The new chief executive's presence could be seen in the transfer market, too. That summer, in addition to finally bringing in Ruud van Nistelrooy, United paid Lazio a British record £28 million for the Argentina captain Juan Sebastián Verón. Ferguson was thrilled. He reckoned this his most significant signing: it sent a signal to everyone else that United were buying at the top. Now he had a team that would surely mark his reign with the most glittering of full stops: a second Champions League win.

Edwards, meanwhile, was deeply unhappy about Verón. Or rather, about the amount Kenyon agreed to pay the South American: £80,000 a week. Edwards had always prided himself on the tightness of his financial control. Now here was his successor breaking with his precedent and paying what he thought were vanity wages. So alarmed was he, he went to see Roland Smith, the plc chairman, pleading for a rethink.

'Roland told me he'd always backed me, now he was backing Peter,' says Edwards. 'So that was that. But as soon as word got out what Verón was on, they were all lining up outside Peter's office: Keane, Beckham, Giggs, Scholes. Or at least their agents were. And what could he say? It wasn't as if Verón was pulling up trees.'

There was one more change to Ferguson's team. And it was an unexpected one. In September, just as the League was once more underway, it was suddenly announced that Jaap Stam was being sold to Lazio for £18 million. Stam was stunned: he thought he was at United for the long term, his wife had just bought a new kitchen, for God's sake. Unfortunately, in order to pay for it, he had just published his autobiography. Worse, it had been serialised in the *Mirror*, never Ferguson's favourite paper. Never mind that the book was overwhelmingly positive about United, a few disparaging remarks about his team-mates (the Nevilles were a 'busy pair of cunts') and the claim that Ferguson had tapped him up when he was at PSV made the headlines. A week later he was gone. Sold. History.

Though he was much later to admit selling the player was a mistake, at the time, Ferguson was anxious to defend his decision. He said immediately it was a footballing issue. Stam was non-communicative, not helping Wes Brown and the Nevilles develop as they might. Plus he'd slowed up a bit since an injury. He wasn't the future. In his place the manager brought in Laurent Blanc, the veteran French World Cup winner (a man who Ferguson was later to try to persuade to become his assistant manager), whose future, many observed, was a long way behind him. Blanc's purpose was to educate the boys. Stam's book, Ferguson said, had nothing to do with it. But everyone thought it did. Mind, if the book had been the cause, then you wonder how Roy Keane got away with his autobiography. A masterful read from Busby's biographer Eamon Dunphy, it was full of tales of getting pissed, brawling, behaving badly, all on Ferguson's watch. Keane revealed that widescale drinking had only stopped in the United squad with the elevation of the class of 1992 and the greater influx of foreigners; he and the others were at it long after Whiteside and McGrath; Keane himself was still boozing heavily right up until publication. Plus, there was a little snippet about his tackle on Alf-Inge Haaland that had earned him a red card during the Manchester derby in April 2001. Everyone who was at Old Trafford when he launched his assault three years after he had injured himself fouling Haaland could see it was motivated by revenge. You could spot that from the very top of the third tier of the North Stand. Now came confirmation: 'He had the ball on the far touchline. Alfie was taking the piss. I'd waited long enough. Take that you cunt. And don't ever stand over me again sneering about fake injuries. I didn't wait for Mr Elleray to show the card. I turned and walked to the dressing room.'

Keane was not like most players who never even bother to read their own life story. He went through Dunphy's manuscript carefully, suggesting seventeen changes. But he never for a moment thought the Haaland passage was contentious. Nor did United's press department, who had a glance at it pre-publication. The FA did, though: Keane was given a record fine and banned for four matches.

It was later watered down for the paperback, but still the tone was evident. This was not what might be expected from the captain of Manchester United. It wasn't what Sir Bobby might write. But far from criticising it, Ferguson called the book a great read and said he loved it (as did most United fans). For him his captain could do no wrong. He was his voice on the pitch, the conduit for his values, his alter ego.

'When I look at Roy Keane I often see myself,' he said. 'He cares, he's a born winner.'

Not that Keane could do much about his mentor's final season. Verón appeared to be wearing someone else's boots, Blanc proved himself no Stam, Barthez was even flakier and by Christmas United had lost six times in the League. In the press the reason was obvious: Ferguson had become a lame duck manager. There were rumours that his players were no longer scared of him now he was off. There was talk that the dressing room was more concerned about jockeying for position ready for the new man than winning matches.

Internally, other explanations for the slump were mooted. In the autumn of 2000 Steve McClaren had gone to be manager at Middlesbrough, with Ferguson's blessing. The Boss reckoned since a new man would bring in his own backroom staff, he could not stand in his assistant's way. For the same reason he did not think it right to recruit an outsider, so promoted Jim Ryan, one of his coaches. Ryan was not liked. The players found him uninspiring, his training sessions dull. One told him to his face he was a prat. Like Busby thirty years before, in his admirable attempt to organise a staged retreat, Ferguson appeared to have undermined the whole enterprise. Not that it altered his resolve.

'I'm absolutely going,' he said on Boxing Day 2001. 'I won't be making a comeback like singers do. It's a decision me and the family have made.'

The rumours swirled about his successor. Martin O'Neill was much favoured. Fabio Capello was mentioned. There were some who suggested Roy Keane might get it. But within the offices of Old Trafford there was only one preferred candidate. For Peter Kenyon Sven-Göran Eriksson was media friendly, not prone to explosions, an easy, genial man round the place (provided you locked up all the secretaries). He would be a perfect, trouble-free, smooth, bland figurehead for the modern entertainment corporation. The deal, taking him away from England duties after the World Cup that summer, was as good as done.

Maybe it was a hint of that which changed Ferguson's mind. Edwards was worried about him exercising control over his successor, and maybe this was what he was doing. Michael Crick believes Ferguson became obsessed by who would succeed him. He didn't want Edwards's choice of David O'Leary and Brian Kidd from Leeds (though Edwards denies this. 'O'Leary was always a little noisy wasn't he?'). He certainly didn't want Sven. In fact he was alarmed at the prospect of anyone taking over his team and winning things with it. And there was only one sure way to make sure that couldn't happen.

Gary Neville says it happened when he was casually surveying the fixture list in the dressing room one day and said, 'Boss, you've only got twelve more games.' Others reckoned it was when UEFA announced that the Champions League final would be held at Old Trafford in 2003. Ferguson himself claims it was his wife who persuaded him. She didn't want him mooching round the house, getting under her feet. Whatever the cause, on 5 February 2002 he announced he was revoking his intention to retire. Kenyon immediately rewarded him with a new contract. It was for three years.

'I have absolutely no intention of staying beyond 2005,' he said. A few days later, at the Valley for the League game with Charlton, three thousand relieved United fans made it clear who they thought was responsible for the change of mind. 'Every single one of us,' they sang, 'loves Cathy Ferguson.'

It was as well he did decide to stay on, because had he left his final year would have been no epitaph: it was his most disappointing in a decade. United came third in the League, nowhere in the FA Cup and worse, when history seemed to be opening up for them, they lost to Bayer Leverkusen in the Champions League semifinal. It was the European equivalent of losing to Norwich in the Cup. While Ruud van Nistelrooy had been an immediate success, banging in goals at every turn, Blanc and especially Verón looked expensive misfits. Not that the captain saw it that way. Now established as the most cogent critic of his own team, he reckoned it the fault of his colleagues' ever more elevated lifestyles.

'Blame Seba? Too easy, wrong,' he said. 'Glory, believing the publicity has cost us. Rolex watches, garages full of cars, fucking mansions, set up for life, forget about the game, lost the hunger that got you the Rolex, the cars, the mansions.'

Ferguson, as always, seemed to agree. That summer he made changes. He brought in Carlos Queiroz, the Portuguese coach who had latterly been manager of the South African national side, as his assistant. He made his old favourite Brian McClair head of the youth academy. And most tellingly of all, he bought Rio Ferdinand from Leeds for a record £29.3 million. Well, someone had to do some defending.

None of it seemed to work. Ferguson faced his worst autumn since 1989. As United fell behind Liverpool and Arsenal, Verón was fitful, Keane, Ferdinand and Beckham all absent injured. As was traditional at that time of year Ferguson was written off by his detractors in the media. Now, they reckoned, it was a mistake to stay on. He was too old for the job. Too tired. Des Kelly in the *Mirror* summed up the consensus: 'United's dynasty is crumbling and Fergie's end is nigh.'

The nadir was reached in the last ever derby at Maine Road. City were about to move to their new tax-payer-funded home, the stadium built to host Manchester's Commonwealth Games, later to be dubbed The Council House by United fans. To celebrate their departure, the Blues won the game 3-1, with Shaun Goater, a former United youth-team player who was never considered good enough at the Cliff to make it, scoring twice. After the game Ferguson threatened to allow the angry United fans into the dressing room, so the players could explain to them directly why they had put up such a pitiable show. He screamed that he would have to rebuild the team again. Ship out the lot of them. No one safe, whatever their reputation or celebrity. All that mattered was restoring United to the top. Nothing else counted. Gary Neville – horribly, abjectly, crassly at fault for at least one of the goals – says he has never seen his manager that angry.

A few days later Ferguson undertook his least favourite duty. He never liked the idea of the club being a plc, now he had to go to the AGM. The reason he didn't like being there, in front of the shareholders, was evident from almost the first question.

'This season', said a shareholder called Peter Brody standing up near the back of the huge function room under the North Stand at Old Trafford, 'you've come out wearing Rock of Gibraltar's blinkers. You need to go back to the stable and have a clear out. Start with the biggest carthorse of the lot, Juan Sebastián Verón.'

Ferguson's reaction was terse: 'I'm not responding to that,' he said. 'He's an idiot.'

Brody had hit a nerve. Though little did he realise quite what a role the Rock was to play in the future of the institution of which he was a part-owner.

20

GALLOPING ON, ON, ON

It became a familiar sight in the Old Trafford dug-out as the new century got underway: Sir Alex Ferguson doing a little charade. Before, we knew what he did in the technical area. He'd engage in lengthy debate with the fourth official, point at his watch, ask Gary Neville if he wouldn't mind awfully just tracking back. But from the spring of 2002 we would occasionally see him prance around, fist up near his chest, whipping his backside, looking not unlike the horse-free knights in *Monty Python and the Holy Grail*. His mime was picked up by the television commentators, who wondered what on earth it meant. Its significance was pored over, too, by many an Old Trafford Kremlinologist looking for clues about the seemingly endless contract negotiations with one of his star players: was he trying to whip Roy Keane into submission? Or was it something he wanted to do to Mrs Beckham? It turned out he was signalling to an old ally in the press box, hoping to get news of how his horse was faring in a race that afternoon. Or at least he thought it was his horse.

Rock of Gibraltar came into Ferguson's life as a result of meeting the Irish racing don, John Magnier, at the 1997 Cheltenham Festival. The pair struck up an immediate rapport: though they both loved racing, neither of them much fancied the tweedy snoots who dominated the sport, and found each other convivial company. Ferguson had dabbled a bit in ownership, running nags in places like Yarmouth and Ayr. But his friendship with Magnier lifted him to the top table. This was a man right at the very peak of the turf. So when he suggested that Ferguson might fancy running a horse from the Coolmore stables in his colours, it was a bit like being asked if he wanted to sign Ronaldinho on a free transfer. He wasn't going to say no.

Born in the midst of the treble rush in March 1999, Rock of Gibraltar is the offspring of two excellent beasts, Danehill and Offshore Boom. From the moment it was conceived Magnier was convinced the horse would provide a bit of an offshore boom for his stables. He was right: through the flat seasons of 2001 and 2002, the Rock didn't stop winning. Usually ridden by Mick Kinane, he was first past the post in ten of the thirteen races he entered. This included a world record seven consecutive Group One wins. The Rock's favoured method of running was to linger near the back, then surge through the field to the tape as the line approached. Ferguson liked that in the horse. It mirrored his way of operating.

'I time my teams to be at their peak in March and April,' he once said.

Unlike Sir Alex's team that season, however, the Rock even conquered Europe, being named European Horse of the Year in 2002. It was a nice consolation for the Boss as Arsène Wenger's Arsenal won the double, thus quickly disabusing everyone of the notion that United had it all too easy domestically.

For the manager and the Irish stock man the partnership was a marriage, if not made in heaven, then consummated in the final furlong of Longchamps. Sure, Magnier provided the four legs. But Sir Alex brought plenty to the party. The horse's association with the most famous name in British sport made it far better known than any ordinary pony. People whose knowledge of racing ended with putting a quid each way on the favourite at the Grand National, knew Rock of Gibraltar. It was the red horse, running in Sir Alex's colours. And the pair's relationship seemed to become further entwined as Magnier, with his business partner the horse owner and professional gambler J. P. McManus, started buying United shares through their company Cubic Expression. Long-term red watchers saw this as entirely positive: Fergie's mates were buying into the club and would surely install him as chairman when he retired from management. This was continuity in the offing.

The Rock's main purpose in life was not to win races – though that was a bonus – it was to produce lots of little Rocks, Pebbles perhaps we should call them. That's what he went off to do in the autumn of 2002, he retired to stud. Such were the prices a horse of the Rock's achievement could attract for making a bit of whoopy in the stalls, the racing press estimated his half share could net Sir Alex £3 million a year for a good ten years. It was some pension. Tax free, too, as the horse was stabled in Ireland where the racing industry rises above little conventions like engaging with the Exchequer. There was just a slight problem. Although the horse raced in his colours, although everyone thought he had a half share, although everyone assumed the beast was as good as his, there was nothing that proved he owned a piece of it. After increasingly frantic efforts to establish ownership, on 14 February 2003 he was told by Magnier that, as legally not a fetlock of the horse was his, he would be getting nothing at all from the Rock's amorous adventures. It was not quite the Valentine he was hoping for.

The next day United played Arsenal in the fifth round of the FA Cup. Arsène Wenger, now Ferguson's least favourite person in football, had said before things kicked off that year that his double winners would go through the season undefeated. Now they arrived at Old Trafford and won 2-0. No amount of carefully targeted mind games could swing that one. That appeared to be the main significance of the result: in the endless spat between Fergie and Wenger, it was another round to the Frenchman. Until, that is, the *Sun* appeared on the Monday morning. Under the headline 'Fergie Decks Becks', the paper's Neil Custis revealed how the manager had been so incensed at defeat, in the dressing room afterwards he had kicked a boot in the direction of David Beckham, which had struck the player and cut him above the eye. The pair subsequently squared up to one another and were separated by half the squad, while the other half got on their mobiles – as Fabien Barthez did to Thierry Henry – to text the details to their mates. It was only a matter of time (about five hours) before the press found out. Ferguson, who had always insisted on the dressing room door remaining locked to outsiders, had just seen it blown off its hinges.

Beckham, as was now his wont, played the incident as high drama, his every move choreographed by image advisers. He allowed himself to be photographed with his luxuriant locks raked back by an alice band, giving full view of the plaster on his eyebrow. He looked grave. He looked the hurt party. His people briefed journalists about Ferguson's subsequent half-hearted apology. The man had gone too far, was the press consensus, assaulting a national treasure. Even Madame Tussauds got in on the fun, applying a sticking plaster to their Becks waxwork. And despite Ferguson's attempt to joke the issue away at a Champions League press conference that week – it must have been an accident, did you ever see me shoot for goal? – everyone knew this marked the end at Old Trafford for the world's most visible footballer.

Still, at least it took the headlines from Roy Keane for a while. The Ireland captain had returned from the World Cup the previous summer before a ball had been kicked in anger. His departure had been of his own volition after a team meeting in which he had spent eight minutes calling his international manager Mick McCarthy virtually any name he could think of. Though not Mick.

United had sent a private plane to facilitate the player's return from Japan. And he arrived into a maelstrom. One Irishman of my acquaintance told me that summer that Keane divided his homeland like no other issue before or since. What, I said, more than civil war, more than abortion, more than paedophile clergy, more than divorce, more than the euro? Seriously, he said, it was black or white, you were either for him or against him and the gap between the two camps was filled with bile. Keane's autobiography became the number-two bestselling book in Irish publishing history. Behind the Bible. As his home in Hale was surrounded by paparazzi, Keane didn't hide. He would walk his dog. It must have been the fittest hound in the northern hemisphere: he would be out three times a day, pursued by half the snappers in Fleet Street. Such was Keano's prominence that year, the headteacher at his kids' school had to send a letter to other parents asking them not to bother him in the playground. Mr Keane, apparently, wished to retain his privacy.

You would have thought, what with Becks, Keano, the Rock and Wenger, Ferguson might be somewhat distracted from his day job. But instead, across a glorious season of League achievement, he masterminded the most dramatic act of catch-up since his feat against Newcastle in 1996. In his battle with Wenger, Ferguson proved himself the master of timing a Rock-like surge. From a position way down the table, from Boxing Day his team put together a run accruing fifty-one points out of fifty-seven. The breath was never off Wenger's players' necks. Every time they slipped, they looked to see United hadn't. When the title was eventually won – probably with a draw at Highbury, which the United manager celebrated by doing a little jig on the turf after the final whistle – Ferguson called it his most satisfying since the breakthrough in 1993. With good reason: it made him the most successful manager of all time in English football, his eight League titles more than Bob Paisley at Liverpool. His total of fifteen trophies was more than every other United manager combined (Mangnall won three, Busby eight, Docherty one and Atkinson two). Asked of everything he had done what his greatest achievement was, he said, 'Knocking Liverpool off their fucking perch.' Naturally.

Ruud van Nistelrooy was huge in the victory. There was no difficult second season for the Dutchman. He scored forty-four goals, one in every one and a quarter appearances, the most prolific return ever for a United player. Young John O'Shea had a dream season at left back. Keane had his moments, too. His performance away at Arsenal, when he was returning from a hip operation everybody assumed would slow him terminally, was so prodigious, Sir Bobby Charlton was heard to remark that 'as a player and a competitor, [Keane is] the nearest I've seen in my lifetime to Duncan Edwards'.

But ask Martin Edwards how Ferguson did it and he will give you a one word answer: 'Scholes,' he says. 'He won it for us that year, no question.'

The little guy was a giant: the ginger general. Twenty goals he scored from midfield. But it was his intelligence, his use of space, his refusal to cede possession that marked him out. The temperamental opposite of Beckham, he kept out of the sun (and the *Sun*), lived quietly, had only one commercial deal, signed his contract within a couple of days of being presented with it. All he was interested in, he said, was football and his family: United, kids and wife. Discussing the rumour that season that they might be soon joined by an Englishman, the galacticos in the Real Madrid dressing room apparently decided among themselves that they wished it might be Scholes.

Scholes – together with the Nevilles, Giggs and Butt – was the beating heart of the team, local lads shot through with a passion for the club no outsider could match. The 2003 season was their peak, the year a team of Manchester men made Manchester proud.

But however well they performed domestically, United couldn't crack Europe. For a moment it seemed they might. With Ryan Giggs playing his best ever game for the reds and earning himself an unprecedented nine in *Gazzetta dello Sport*'s player ratings, they beat Juventus 3-0 away in the preliminary stages. With the final to be played on their home turf (if that is not too elevated a term for Old Trafford's ever-ragged surface), it seemed as if, finally, this was to be the year for the world's richest football club. But Real Madrid – with Raul masterful in the first leg – did for such romance. The quarter-final second leg in Manchester was a game in which David Beckham's ability to control the media agenda around a football match was at its most apparent. He was dropped for the game in favour of Juan Sebastián Verón. All eyes, all lenses were on him on the bench. Nothing could divert their gaze. Not Ronaldo's hat-trick, not even the manner in which the buck-toothed Brazilian was acknowledged by a standing ovation from the United crowd. Nothing could pull the cameras away. Everything was about Beckham. And, with the sense of destiny that seems to attach itself to him, he duly almost did it, scoring twice in a 4-3 victory that was agonisingly close to propelling United forward. Beckham reckoned it was probably the reaction on the manager's face when he missed a tricky chance to win the tie that spoke loudest of all: he looked furious. With that glance, Beckham knew his days were numbered. After the whistle sounded the Madrid players crowded round him asking if he were going to join them in Spain. As did some United players in the final game of the season, when they picked up the Premiership trophy at Goodison Park and paraded it with the now traditional supporting cast of wives and children. Much to Des Lynam's amusement on ITV's *The Premiership*, Gary Neville was seen to ask, 'Are you going then, David?' To which the response was: 'There have been talks.'

That's what talent on a level of Beckham did: they held talks. And went on PR expeditions. After a comical private promotional tour of the US, during which Beckham showed his intention by wearing white throughout, after a phantom bid from Barcelona, after enough headlines and speculation to fill a good-sized skip, the player finally signed for Madrid for £24.5 million in July 2003. It was the largest amount ever received for a United player. Though there were those who reckoned it not enough.

'Manchester United lost 50 per cent of their brand value the day Beckham left,' said Rolf Beisswanger, the chief executive of Madrid's sponsors Siemens.

And that was how football was being viewed in the summer of 2003: through a prism of cash. When the *Sunday Times* published its annual wealth supplement there were eight United players in the Young Rich List, rubbing shoulders with the internet entrepreneurs and media magnates: Giggs, Ferdinand, Verón, Butt, Neville, Scholes, Solskjær and Van Nistelrooy. Even Phil Neville was in there. Keane and Beckham were a bit more grown up. They were in the main list, with Becks, thanks to his portfolio of commercial deals, estimated to be peeling in £10 million a year. Ferguson, meanwhile, was joint 976th alongside Annie Lennox, Pete Townshend and Carl Fogarty, reckoned to be worth £30 million.

That, though, was as nothing compared to the wealth of the bloke who had just bought Chelsea from Ken Bates. Roman Abramovich left that sort of money as a tip. And proved it by poaching United's Peter Kenyon for a player's wage to be his chief executive. Unlike those days when Michael Knighton couldn't get a loan to buy United, everyone with cash seemed to be buying into football. At United, John de Mol, the man behind television's hit of the moment, *Big Brother*, picked up 2.9 per cent of the action, Dermot Desmond, owner of Celtic, bought 2 per cent, and so did an unknown American, the owner of the Tampa Bay Buccaneers, a sports entrepreneur called Malcolm Glazer.

But the biggest buyers were Cubic. By August of 2003, as it became clear that a row was fomenting between Ferguson and Magnier that made his spat with Wenger look like a love-in, Cubic were buying shares in a frenzy. Suddenly the idea of Irish ownership seemed a little less benevolent. The United board began to worry that this could turn into the most hostile of takeovers.

Ferguson, meanwhile, carried on as normal. With the Beckham circus having pitched its big top elsewhere and with the rest of his midfield ageing rapidly together, he made his most substantial foray into the transfer market in an age. After offloading Verón and his wages to the newly flush Chelsea, he went shopping. Two of the young international players he bought would turn out to be as duff as any he signed. But who cares about Kleberson and Eric Djemba-Djemba (so bad they named him twice), when you can have Cristiano Ronaldo? Ferguson was alerted by his players to the prodigy from Madeira during a friendly against Sporting Club of Portugal in Lisbon. Wow, was the gist of the scouting report from the likes of Giggs, Butt and the poor sap obliged to mark him, John O'Shea. You must sign this player, they insisted. He cost £12.6 million. It is a sum that seems a steal now, but at the time was regarded as the most sizeable of the manager's summer gambles. Ferguson showed his faith in the boy – who spoke no English and was so shy he barely said anything – by gifting him Beckham's old number-seven shirt. And the kid with the acne and the bad hair responded by making a debut against Bolton that was so extravagant it had United fans of more nostalgic inclination on the edge of their seats wondering if this were a reincarnation of George Best. Perhaps there was one too many step-overs, maybe he could have reduced the number of lollipops, and few could argue he might have stayed on his feet a bit more. But even so, he appeared to have talent oozing from every rather enlarged pore.

'David Who?' was the inevitable headline in the *Sun*. Ferguson seemed convinced by what he had seen. 'He is going to be the best player in the world,' the manager said. Big, strong, powerful, quick, skilful and blessed with an extravagant self-confidence, a self-certainty that extended way beyond mere arrogance: it was hard to argue that the kid had no chance of fulfilling that prophecy.

But that September, just as Ferguson girded his loins for the challenge from Arsenal with his new players bedding in, Rio Ferdinand missed a routine drugs test at Carrington. Despite the stories spinning round the internet chat rooms suggesting he was avoiding the test to disguise everything from a personal disease to a pregnancy, it seemed it was a genuine case of forgetfulness. After all, the modern footballer has so much to remember – the time of the next celebrity photo shoot, where he left his bank paying-in book, picking up his new 4×4 – it is hard to keep track. Rio offered to go in any time for another test. He wasn't trying to hide anything, he said. Come on, he said, give us a break, it's just a missed appointment. We players never keep them. We're above the strictures of ordinary life. But the authorities were not impressed: missing a test is as bad as testing positive for illicit substances. Despite Ferguson's furious defence (including a four-letter-word-fuelled phone call to the head of the FA drug compliance unit), the defender was banned for nine months and consequently missed Euro 2004.

Ferdinand's story – not least the fact that he continued to pick up his sizeable wage packet while he twiddled his thumbs – was noted by those circling the club. Despite advice from friends who pointed out that Magnier had not arrived at a position of wealth and power by being easily steamrollered, that autumn Ferguson issued a writ against the stable owner demanding his share of Rock of Gibraltar's burgeoning profits. His sons Jason and Mark were particularly anxious that the family should get what it was owed from the horse's stud activity. As if to prove he was an altogether more elevated opponent than Ferguson was used to, as the legal correspondence flew, so Magnier and Cubic bought up more shares. By November they had picked up Murdoch's stake and now owned 21 per cent of the club. At the AGM that month David Gill, by now Kenyon's replacement as chief executive, made a bullish speech about the club not needing 'sugar daddies'. He had a point. Debt-free and raking in the profits, this was a hugely successful operation, regularly coming out top of the Deloitte rankings as the world's richest club. But Cubic's intention didn't seem to be about ownership. Rather it was more personal. They issued what they called ninety-nine questions about the governance of United. Their PR people said this was motivated by a desire to see the place maximise investor value. But those looking from the outside couldn't help noticing how many of the questions concerned Ferguson's conduct. The Cubic team seemed to have paid special attention to the revelations in Michael Crick's biography of the manager about the close relationship between the club and his son Jason's football agency. One question read: 'Please identify on behalf of the company who conducted the negotiations with agents in the purchase or sale of the above players.'

The players concerned were Verón, Ferdinand, Diego Forlan, Stam, Tim Howard, Kleberson, Ronaldo, Roy Carroll, Blanc, David Bellion, Jonathan Greening, Mark Wilson and Taibi. In other words virtually every bit of recent business. Another question was about transparency in players' wages. Another concerned Ferguson's new contract, though it couldn't bear to mention him by name: 'Can you inform us whether you have complemented legal advice with medical advice in the light of the executive's recent health concerns and his age,' it read.

The health concerns referred to Ferguson's diagnosis with a heart murmur the previous year. He joked at the time that the real scare had been for his players: they were astonished at the news that he possessed a heart after all.

For Gill this was a huge embarrassment. His principal employee was at war with his biggest shareholder and he was stuck in the middle. Ferguson may have been ill-advised to pursue the case, but for Gill, Cubic were, frankly, a pain. If this was the way they behaved when they owned 21 per cent of the club, imagine what they would be like if they snapped up the whole thing? For a start there was no way they would keep Ferguson on. Indeed it was hard to see the purchase motivated by anything other than the grandest of revenge. Quietly Gill encouraged some of the other new investors to start picking up shares, to act as a block to the Irish. Particularly the American Glazer, who seemed increasingly interested in extending his portfolio. By November Glazer had 14 per cent.

Meanwhile, the fans showed whose side they were on in the war of the Rock. A group called United 4 Action issued a statement accusing Cubic of 'bullying our manager and destabilising our football club' and threatened to picket the next Cheltenham Festival in protest. A bunch calling itself the Manchester Education

Committee took direct action, disrupting a meeting at Hereford where a Coolmore horse was running and daubing the walls of the stables in Ireland in graffiti. And Shareholders United encouraged United fans to buy up as many shares as they could, to act as a block to anyone getting too big a hold. But few fans had the sort of money Cubic and Glazer were investing. Though the group insisted they could call on over 30 per cent of shares held in individual portfolios, that was the most optimistic of guesswork. Some observers put their actual controllable holding at closer to 1 per cent.

One thing is for certain. None of those circling Manchester United knew what on earth they were buying into. Sure, they had studied the figures, yes they were alert to the bottom line, they were proper businessmen, they would have done their due diligence. But they had no inkling of the club's meaning, of its culture, of its character. None of them had ever seen a game live at Old Trafford, never mind tested the very elasticity of their overdraft buying a black market ticket for an oversubscribed Cup tie. None of them had chanted Cantona's name long into the night in a bar in some foreign city. None of them had argued United's value with an ABU at work who mocked their every tenet of faith. None of them really knew.

United had grown into a thriving multinational business to the point where it was now coveted by investors and arbitrageurs, hoping for a nice little profit. It had arrived at such a position via the pockets of its fans. They were the ones clacking through the turnstiles, they were the ones buying beers in the stadium's secondary spend opportunities, they were the ones filing out of the Megastore with the new Nike home shirt in XXL size with Ronaldo printed on the back. As Gill had said, there had never been a sugar daddy at Old Trafford underwriting the place. This was an institution built on love, on hope, on faith. And suddenly those who had done the construction work felt horribly compromised. Violated even.

Worse, as the dispute between Ferguson and Magnier dragged

on into the following spring, it appeared to suck the energy from the whole of Manchester United. Everyone seemed distracted. Rumours shot daily round the United blogosphere of imminent takeovers and subsequent sackings. Fans worried about the future of the club began to harden their resolve. There were internal disputes in supporters' organisations about the best action to take. Andy Walsh, who was trying to take a back seat in IMUSA after the time he had expended over the Murdoch battle, warned David Gill that he was daily being assailed by furious reds, demanding serious action. The Manchester Education Committee staged ever more vigorous protests. The board became increasingly twitchy. Meanwhile, as Ferguson insisted he was in the right (hadn't his name appeared as co-owner on all the Rock's race paperwork?), as Magnier built up his stake in the reds to over 28 per cent, as Glazer began to up his position to nearly 19 per cent, Arsenal were annexing the title. They weren't doing it quietly either. A year before Arsène Wenger had been much mocked when he said his side could go through a season unbeaten. It turned out he was just a little premature. Now they were doing just that, refusing to lose, noisily lauded by a press who could not get enough of their high-speed passing and movement, of their slick front man Thierry Henry, of the fact they weren't United.

It was only when news emerged on 6 March 2004 that Ferguson had finally ended his dispute with Magnier that United seemed to snap back into action. The settlement was done privately, without recourse to a court case. It centred around a one-off payment in lieu of stud fees reckoned to be close to £2.5 million.

'We have all decided to move on, it's over now,' said Ferguson as the news was released. 'This has been a tough time for all the families of those involved. While we were working this out, I spoke personally to John Magnier and that helped. I am glad that it has been an amicable settlement. Though it has been a difficult time, I believe I have dealt with everything that has happened. How do I do that? You don't read the papers, don't socialise with players and keep your own counsel.'

An amicable settlement? Well, that was one way of putting it. What was certain was that – whatever his reasons in building up his stockholding – Magnier remained the most significant figure in deciding United's future ownership. Meanwhile, Ferguson's team were all that stood in the way of Arsenal emulating Preston in 1888–89 and winning the double without losing a game. After a win at Old Trafford the League was already as good as in the possession of the Gunners. But they had to play the reds in the FA Cup semi-final. Given that the other semi was between Sunderland and Millwall, two Championship sides, this was Ferguson's only realistic hope of stopping Wenger making history. At Villa Park United had to build a road block to Arsenal destiny. Producing by far their most accomplished performance of the season, with Paul Scholes once more the orchestrator, with the fans singing non-stop in full-throated celebration of the underdog (for that was what United had become), they did it. They went on to beat Millwall 3-0 in the final at the Millennium Stadium (Ronaldo marking his first appearance in an English set-piece game with a goal, Van Nistelrooy getting the other two.) It was as one-sided a game as any in recent Cup history, not even the buzz of Millwall's player-manager Dennis Wise put United off their stride. It all felt a little anticlimactic, as if the real action was going on somewhere else.

Ferguson encountered a more significant figure than Wise during yet another stalled Champions League campaign. In the quarter-final his team was drawn against Porto. After losing 2-1 away, they were 1-0 ahead in the home leg when Scholes supplied the finish to a smart passing move. But the linesman wrongly ruled him to be offside. The goal did not stand. A few moments later Porto scored. And their manager celebrated on the touchline, running out of his technical area and jigging with joy, soiling the knees of his sharply cut suit as he slid across the turf. It carried echoes of Ferguson's own reaction to Steve Bruce's goals against Sheffield Wednesday ten years before. Porto went on to win the trophy, and their manager accepted Roman Abramovich's well-funded offer to come to Chelsea. However, it is not fanciful to suggest that José Mourinho's subsequent career, and the nuisance he caused Ferguson, would have never unfolded as it did if Scholes's goal had stood. Such is the consequence of a wrongly raised linesman's flag.

As Mourinho – calling himself a Special One – came to London to set about engaging with Abramovich's current account, England had a new hero. Wayne Rooney, Everton's teenaged forward, was the country's best player in the European Championships in Portugal. Until he broke a metatarsal in the quarter-final, his precocious talent hinted that England might actually go all the way; the moment he left the field, it was finished. For many observers, for the feature-writers in the papers eulogising this pugnacious kid from the Liverpool badlands, for the gossip columnists delving into the lives of him and his girlfriend Colleen, Rooney was a revelation. But Ferguson had known about him for some time.

'I remember watching a United under-eighteens game against Everton at Altrincham,' says Eric Harrison. 'Rooney came on. He was just fourteen at the time. I turned to Jim Ryan after five minutes and I said, "What are we watching?" Colin Harvey, who was a good friend of mine from my Everton days, was in charge of them, and afterwards he was very cagey about him. We said, "Who was that?" He said, "Him? Oh no one". He didn't want anyone to know because they'd all be after him. And he was right. Jim said he was going to see the manager first thing next day and tell him about this Rooney. So he did. The manager couldn't wait to see him. From that day really, we wanted Rooney. The manager made him his absolute priority.'

Ferguson had to move earlier than he anticipated to secure what he described as the best English youth prospect in thirty years. He intended to try and sign him in the summer of 2005. But an offer from Newcastle propelled him to action. It also propelled the price into the stratosphere. An initial down payment of £23 million was required to secure the young Scouser's signature, rising to £31 million. Rooney, who had once sported a T-shirt in a Merseyside derby bearing the legend 'Once a blue always a blue', was now a red. Any doubts about his loyalty, however, were dispelled from the moment he made his belated debut after recovering from the Euro injury. Against Fenerbahçe on 28 September 2004 he scored a hat-trick. Not just any hat-trick either, but a threesome of such power, such daring, such joie de vivre, it took the breath away. A month later he scored the second goal in a 2-0 win over Arsenal that ended the club's forty-nine-game run without defeat. Wenger's team did not react well to the bruising tactics Ferguson had employed to stall their charge on history. In an altercation outside the dressing rooms, Wenger's players chucked half the after-match buffet at the United manager. 'Pizzagate' it was called. Ferguson didn't mind. He laughed about it. After all, he said, he had been to many a Glasgow wedding. Besides, he now had in his possession the finest young talent in the country. And with Rooney playing alongside Ruud and Ronaldo, United fans began to day-dream about their three Rs, the new heroic trilogy of Old Trafford.

As it happened, Rooney was the plc's last significant outlay. Quietly, without notice or fanfare, Malcolm Glazer was upping his shareholding in the club. The man who had been targeted by Gill as a blocking mechanism to protect the plc against assault from the Irish had decided that he would like to own outright what he termed as 'the franchise'. Within four months of Magnier and Ferguson coming to their agreement, the roles had been reversed. Now, suddenly, it was Cubic who held the plc's independence in their gift. Glazer was accumulating so many shares, many of them from those who had rushed into ownership in the previous year or so, the Irish were soon the only people preventing him from having sufficient number to trigger a total takeover. The trouble was, the Irish had little sympathy for Manchester United or its fans. Now that their principal motive of embarrassing Ferguson no longer obtained, it was all about money. If they stalled on selling, it was simply to up the price.

The fan groups acted quickly. 'Not for Sale' became the mantra. The MEC burned an American flag during a pitch invasion at a televised reserve match. It was the manner of Malcolm Glazer's intentions that worried them. Glazer was no Abramovich. He wasn't going to pour cash into the club as the Russian had at Chelsea. He was going to borrow big. And his collateral was the asset he was buying. In other words he was going to mortgage United to the very hilt in order to buy it. A club that had enjoyed a debt-free existence was suddenly about to be plunged into monumental hock, not to build, not to develop, but just so someone who had no idea of its heritage could take control, his purchase effectively guaranteed by the labours of those who had gone before.

'It's called a leveraged buyout,' says David Bick. 'You put in as little of your own money as you can get away with and borrow the rest. Then, as the asset increases in value, the debt remains static and the profit is all yours.'

Unlike with the Murdoch attempt, there was no wider, political dimension to Glazer's takeover. He was doing nothing illegal. There was nothing to stop anyone buying a plc provided there was no conflict of interest involved. And since Glazer's other businesses were American sport, there wasn't any. However much the fans battled and manoeuvred, the future independence of the club depended on this: would the Irish sell?

A City of London banker and United sympathiser called Keith Harris took a more proactive approach. Harris – who had advised the Sky team during their attempted takeover – moved to put together a rival bid. Backed by the financial services group Nomura, it was seriously funded. He intended to secure the club for the fans, turn it into a trust. And his resolve hardened when word reached him – allegedly through one of the fortuitously placed United supporters – that there was a gaping hole in the Glazer bid. The hedge funds from whom he was looking to borrow money were insisting that there was to be a continuity of management. Gill and Ferguson had to stay in place. Although Gill had privately told the secretary of Shareholders United that 'if I wasn't where I am now I would be behind the barricades', he would not take Harris's calls. So Harris approached Andy Walsh and explained the situation. If Walsh could persuade Ferguson to walk out of Old Trafford, the Glazer bid would be dead in the middle of the Atlantic. If he put his name behind the Nomura bid, the manager could walk back in to his office the next day and head up a fan-friendly, benevolent ownership. Walsh made the call.

'I said to Alex I'm sorry to put you in this position,' says Walsh. 'But you are our last hope. He listened to me in silence, which was unusual for him. I explained the bid, explained how he was crucial to saving the club from debt. When I finished, he said he understood what I was saying but that he needed to take advice from his sons. He said he'd get back to me. He never did.'

Ferguson stayed put, later explaining that he had to consider the well-being of his staff. He had, he said, dozens of people dependent on him; defending their livelihood was his priority. Nomura withdrew its support and the Harris bid withered away. The end came when the Irish – suddenly and unexpectedly – sold to Glazer in May 2005, making a handy profit of some £30 million for their brief involvement in Manchester United. By now the American was within a whisker from his scraggly beard of owning sufficient shares to trigger a takeover. The fans protests became ever more desperate: an effigy was burned outside Old Trafford, graffiti sprung up everywhere, the United chat rooms fizzed with rage. The final, forlorn act of resistance was at the FA Cup final against Arsenal. For once this was not about doubles for either club. Chelsea, under the shrewd stewardship of Mourinho, had won the League – the minimum requirement for Abramovich's investment. The Portuguese manager was the media's new favourite, his intelligence and scheming providing an intriguing counterbalance to the old tale of Ferguson v Wenger. So, with Chelsea in the ascendant, at the Millennium Stadium the two old hands were playing for the consolation prizes. United's fans wore black in symbolic protest at the Glazer bid. The Arsenal supporters, smugly ignoring the wider significance of the takeover, mocked the Manc discomfort, chanting 'USA' and waving wads of photocopied dollars. Black was the appropriate colour for

United's chances, too. The game was as disappointing as United's boardroom manoeuvres. Arsenal were negative and twitchy. United had all the possession, but couldn't score. After 120 minutes of goalless sterility, Arsenal won on penalties, after Scholes missed his. Scholesy – the last man you would ever back to miss a spot kick – looked distraught, like he was the man who had dropped the FA Cup. Outside the ground after the game as the rain fell insistently, United's black-clad fans chanted their defiance: 'Not for sale,' they sang. Like Scholes's penalty, it was a claim woefully off-target.

On 12 May 2005 Malcolm Glazer acquired a controlling interest in Manchester United through his investment vehicle Red Football Ltd, in a takeover valuing the club at approximately £800 million. On 16 May he increased his share to the 75 per cent necessary to de-list the club from the Stock Exchange, making it private again. Small shareholders like me had no choice about selling. We received a cheque in the post and, whether we cashed it or not, our shares were now worthless. So much for a Manchester club to make Manchester proud. On 8 June Glazer, now in sole control, appointed his several sons and daughter to the board as non-executive directors. He was the new owner of Manchester United.

Or rather the banks were. Glazer put up no more than £200 million of the necessary collateral. The rest came from loans, money borrowed at punitive interest. Estimates reckoned he would need to find profits of around £60 million a year just to meet the annual payments. Mind, the Glazers' timing had been shrewd; albeit fiendishly expensive, this was a real asset they were getting their hands on. Old Trafford had been completely redeveloped and was now easily the largest ground in the country. With capacity at seventy-five thousand, its match-day takings were around £3 million. A further quarter of a million was spent every home game in the megastore. New television deals had been signed supplying ever more money. But that wasn't enough for a debt this big. The Glazers immediately got to work. Insiders spoke of every aspect of the club being chivvied up. If the club had seemed the apex of foot-ball money-making under Martin Edwards and Edward Freedman, that was as nothing. Now cash became the single over-riding motivation.

'All we ever hear is "Get more",' says one Old Trafford employee. 'More sponsorship, more corporate tickets, more, more, more.' Another says, 'If there's a grand to be had, they'll take it.'

And the first target of the new regime was the ticket prices. While the hospitality areas of Old Trafford were pricey, general tickets had been traditionally among the cheapest in the top flight. In 1991 a League Match Ticket Book cost £110.50. By the end of the 1994 season, with the move to an all-seater stadium, they had gone up to £266. The Glazer regime, despite assuring government fig-ures during the takeover that they were not going to, remorselessly raised prices to the point that in 2009 a season ticket cost £750. Plus, from 2007–08, season ticket holders were obliged to buy Cup tickets whether they wanted to go to the additional games or not, the money debited from their credit cards without debate.

'I think that's their big mistake,' says Martin Edwards. 'We always kept ticket prices affordable. It was important to remember that the club served the whole of Manchester.'

Glazer, however, applied American levels of supply-side eco-nomics: if some people don't like it, there are always others to take their place. That was certainly how the club reacted to the most significant fans' protest. Soon after the Glazer takeover became official, distraught supporters announced the most desperate of measures: divorce. A breakaway club, modelled on AFC Wimble-don – who had fractured from their host club five years earlier – was to be formed. FC United of Manchester it was to be called. It would start its journey at the bottom of the League pyramid, it would be owned entirely by the fans and it would provide a cheap alternative for those excluded from Old Trafford by the debt-driven cash steamroller.

'The idea had been circulated during the Murdoch fight,' says Andy Walsh, who became FC's first chairman. 'Initially I was against it. I wanted to stay on and fight from within. But my personal belief that things could be improved by dialogue had been whittled away over the years. And besides, what was it we were fighting for? It was our friends, our family, our shared love of the game. We could take that with us to a new place without any of the shit.'

FC immediately drew sizeable crowds of United refuseniks to their games at Bury's Gigg Lane. Here the regulars found much that had been long lost at Old Trafford: great atmosphere, the chance to stand with mates, endless comedy chanting. For the thirty- and forty-something supporter it was like going back in a time machine to the carefree days of Doc's Red Army. With prices to match, this was Nostalgia United. In their first season, buoyed by way the biggest crowds in the division, FC won the Moore & Co. Solicitors North West Counties League Division Two; they were only eight more promotions away from competing in the same league as United.

At first there was much sympathy from those who chose to stay on at Old Trafford to the FC effort. Many people went to both sets of games. Some still do. But the split soon grew rancorous and fetid. FC regulars accused Old Trafford goers of being sell-outs to the Americans, those who stayed on called the FC bunch Judases.

'I don't like FC because I think they allowed the Glazers an easy win, they left when we needed them most,' says Stephen Armstrong, a lifelong red from Moston, who decided not to break away. 'I couldn't do that. I look at United in the same way my dog looks at me. No matter what I do he loves me. It's totally unconditional. However disillusioned you get, I'm afraid keeping the faith is a characteristic that has to come out on top. Keeping faith has got United through drama on the pitch and the most tragic thing to happen to a club off the pitch. I'm glad I was able to. I'm glad I was strong enough in my own mind to ignore that religious cult-like brainwashing and stay true to what was right. Going to Old Trafford. To see United.'

The bean counters at Old Trafford say that the FC United revolt made no difference to their bottom line. The two thousand or so season tickets that were relinquished were snapped up by those on the waiting list. As for Sir Alex Ferguson, he was in no doubt about the FC betrayal, bristling at every mention of the word. 'These people think they are the conscience of this club, the independent supporters' associations, FC United, when they are not, they are not the conscience of this club,' he once said. 'No way are they. No way.'

21

NEVER, EVER WRITE HIM OFF

At the end of a supreme performance in the chucking rain of a Mancunian spring, a game in which United dispatched Aston Villa with a flourish that made anyone watching on television reach for the remote control just so they could slow it down sufficiently to see how it was done, Wayne Rooney paid his team-mates this compliment: 'Growing up, I used to love watching Brazil and I think the football we play is similar to the way Brazil play,' he said. 'It's an honour to play in this team and I love it.'

A couple of days before, Rooney had looked tetchy and distracted in a laboured England friendly in Paris. Now here he was, playing with a grin, exchanging frisky one-twos with the diminutive Argentinian Carlos Tevez, engaging in passing movements of eye-watering precision with Paul Scholes, Ryan Giggs and the Geordie Michael Carrick (bought from Spurs in the summer of 2006), watching Cristiano Ronaldo score with a back heel from almost the exact spot Denis Law had done for Manchester City in less propitious times three decades before. Rooney was having fun. And so was Old Trafford. The noise emanating from the stands was close to purring. For older observers, though, never mind Brazil, the performance was reminiscent of something much closer to their hearts: it was just like watching United. This team were playing exactly how United teams should, with adventure, with panache, with a spirit that refused to be cowed by circumstance. Winning football played the right way. The way Cantona, Best, Charlton and Edwards played it. Somehow players who had no connection with the past (Anderson, the young substitute that day, wasn't even born when Sir Alex Ferguson arrived at the club) had fitted right into the template of passionate, attacking football that has so long been the ambition of the club and its supporters. This was continuity. This was the DNA in full flow. And it was led by a couple of players who slipped directly into United heritage: Rooney and Ronaldo, irresistible, irrepressible and for now at least entirely, 100 per cent red.

No wonder the manager looked so pleased in the dug out. As United eased in on the tenth title of his reign, taking them to within one of Liverpool's record total, the years seemed to fall away from his face. He was now sixty-six, older than any other manager in football, older than any in United's history. Yet he appeared to have gone into chronological reverse, rejuvenating with every new victory.

'I'm getting beyond the future now,' he said on his birthday. 'I still have a lot of passion. I'm still happy. You cannot put a time limit on it. Saying I was leaving was the biggest mistake I made.'

Watching him in the dug-out, grinning widely at a piece of Ronaldo impudence, doing his dodgy little arhythmical jig of delight when the hugely popular Rooney scored his second goal, it was hard to imagine Manchester United without him. He had become synonymous with the place, his moods the club's moods, his spirit the club's spirit, his belief in attacking football central to the blueprint of what made the place unique. No wonder the new owners loved him. Such was the product he delivered, he was the man who put muscle into their bottom line.

It was, however, almost impossible to reconcile Ferguson's demeanour that afternoon in March 2008 with the figure he cut but two years before. Back then it looked all over for him. Back then he looked shrivelled and defeated. Back then – whisper it – he looked old.

The year 2005–06 was among Ferguson's worst at Old Trafford, right down there with 1989. After settling his battle with outsiders now he found himself at war with those on the inside, old allies, old mates, old supporters. And in the case of one spat, with his own alter ego.

The 2005–06 season started under a cloud. It was cast by the death of George Best. The great chancer's luck had finally run out. Fatally addicted to drink, he never gave his freshly transplanted liver a hope. Told after the operation a couple of years previously that any return to the bottle would kill him, he chose death over abstinence. His passing before he had even reached sixty, filled Old Trafford with particular sadness. A sense of glorious past detaching itself from what at the time seemed a less than illustrious present pervaded the stadium on the day his demise was marked with a minute's silence.

The pessimism at the great hero's sad end flowed forward into the present predicament. José Mourinho and Chelsea were in the ascendant. With more spending money than Victoria Beckham, Mourinho had refreshed his championship-winning side from the previous season and stood ready to begin what he believed was a lengthy annexation of the title. In the press he was the big story. It was his mind games, his little disputes with rival managers, his strops with referees that made the news. He was the story; Ferguson was beginning to look like yesterday's man and United yesterday's team.

Ferguson has been written off many a time through many a groggy autumn. But this autumn it really did seem as if the final drum roll was beating a tattoo on the side of the dug-out.

This autumn was a shocker and long-term United watchers began to wonder if the manager had the energy to turn it round. Much of the problem stemmed from Roy Keane. Or rather his absence. Now slowed beyond repair by hip trouble, he was more often injured than not. But Ferguson had failed adequately to replace him. It was not through want of trying. Kleberson and Eric Djemba-Djemba were disastrous buys. Juan Verón almost as bad. Liam Miller came in from Celtic and disappeared from view just as quickly. For much of the season, with Paul Scholes also missing, Ferguson was obliged to play Ryan Giggs in central midfield where Keane should be, alongside one of either John O'Shea, moved from full back, or Alan Smith, a converted striker he had bought from Leeds with little immediate effect.

Keane, obsessive, fixated, neurotic, watched from a distance, growling. He was in Dubai, attempting to recuperate, when he caught televised coverage of the team losing 4-1 away at Middlesbrough in a bar. What he saw did not help his recovery. On his return from the break he was still fuming. After training the players found him one day waiting for them in the dressing room. His verbal ambush was unrestrained. His mood had not been helped when he heard the young winger Kieron Richardson had recently ordered himself a Bentley. That was a red rag to the Keano loathing of bull. The kid had achieved nothing, but was awash with the trappings of success. This was the very thing that made him fume, Richardson – who announced to the dressing room on the return from the close season that from now on he should be addressed as Rico – the very symptom of everything that was going wrong.

But if the players thought the storm had abated after their ear-bashing, they were wrong. Keane was booked as the studio guest for MUTV's show *Play the Pundit*. Keane played the pundit all right.

'There are no characters in this team any more,' he thundered. 'The players have been asked questions and are just not coming up with answers. I'm sick of having to say it and they are sick of listening.'

He then named six players he felt were not pulling their weight. The list included the new goalkeeper Edwin van der Sar; of Darren Fletcher – much admired by Fergie – he said, 'I know they think a lot of him in Scotland but I can't see it'; of the limited but willing Smith, he said, 'What is he doing there? He is wandering around as if he is lost. He doesn't know what he's doing.'

In an instant the wheels fell off the propaganda vehicle. Fortunately for the producers, the show was pre-recorded. Sensing controversy, they sent a tape to David Gill. The chief executive ordered it not to be aired. Except in the United dressing room. After word had leaked of its content and hints and rumours spun across the headlines, Ferguson arranged for Keane to show the tape to his team-mates. When it had finished, some of the players – Rio Ferdinand for instance – thought it nothing like as bad as the papers had suggested. Ferguson, however, was not so relaxed. He may have ordered its screening as a cunning ploy to do his bollocking by proxy, but from the moment it started, steam began to emerge from his ears. When it was over he accused Keane of ranting, of no longer thinking like the leader of Manchester United, of losing the key to the dressing room door. Keane – never one to sit back and let complaint wash over him – responded with reference to Rock of Gibraltar. Carlos Queiroz intervened with a plea for loyalty. Keane accused him of being 'a fucking waste of space' and told him that he was hardly in a position to preach loyalty having gone to Real Madrid without a second thought, only to return with his tail between his legs when he was fired.

Ferguson knew that was it. It was Keane or everyone else. And since the skipper was now almost permanently walking wounded, there could only be one conclusion. On Friday 19 November 2005 a meeting was held in Ferguson's Carrington office with the manager, Keane and the player's solicitor. Keane had already taken the precaution of clearing his locker. Captain and manager shook hands, wished each other well in the future and at 9.20 a.m., the man who embodied the spirit of United every time he pulled on a red shirt, left Carrington for the last time. He went first to Celtic and later to manage Sunderland (where – oddly – he bought several of the players he had criticised in his MUTV rant, including Richardson and Miller) before settling, after yet another walk-out, in East Anglia, at Ipswich. Few bet on his staying long.

The speed of Keane's exclusion was evidence that Ferguson's ruthlessness was still in full working order. To cut the player from his squad must have been like conducting open-heart surgery on himself. For the United fans who chanted his name non-stop over the next few months, however, it was clear evidence of Ferguson's decline. For them Keano was United, just as Cantona and Best had been before. This was the man who, as the television cameras rolled in the tunnel before a game at Highbury, was seen to tell Patrick Vieira that he would 'see him out there'. This was the man who yelled and cajoled. This was the leader. This was the keeper of the conscience.

And without him how United drifted. Everything he said in his MUTV critique seemed to pan out on the pitch. In December they lost to Benfica in a Champions League qualifier they had to win. For only the second time since the competition became a league, they were out before the knock-out stage; worse, since they came bottom of group they didn't even qualify for the consolation of the UEFA Cup. With at least £20 million disappearing south, there were plenty in the press assuming the owners would soon act. Ferguson himself appeared to think the same. Coming back from Lisbon, several journalists noted that the manager's fingernails were chewed to the root.

As usual, in his insecurity Ferguson blamed the media, refusing to continue with even his very modest contact, no longer attending after-match press conferences. Now, though, it wasn't just his traditional enemies; he was losing the support of those who had always stood behind him. The fanzine *Red Issue* printed a list of ten reasons why Sir Alex must go. Not least among them was his refusal to speak out against the new ownership.

As Chelsea moved clear in the League, if he hoped for consolation in the FA Cup, there was to be none. After scraping through following a replay against non-League Burton in the third round, the fifth brought an away game at Anfield. Always spiky, the atmosphere that day was vile. Instead of merely taking the piss, the home supporters filled cups with urine and dropped them on the heads of their visitors in the lower sections of the Anfield Road stand. And when Smith broke his leg horribly in an accidental collision, the home crowd crowed and cackled in a manner that mocked the club's tradition for good sportsmanship. Outside the ground the ambulance arriving to take him to hospital was attacked.

But it was Ferguson who came in for particular opprobrium. Liverpool's success in the Champions League the previous season, in the first term of new manager Rafael Benítez, brought his continued Continental failure into stark focus. And how the local fans rubbed it in. They unveiled a banner in the Kop that made ironic reference to his most famous rallying call: 'Look, Alex, back on our *****ng perch'. Each asterisk was picked out in gold, to signify the number of European Cups the club had won. Against such weight of evidence, defeat that day was apparently preordained. United were out.

The following week Ferguson's team won the final of the League Cup, 4-0 against Wigan. It was a victory, it was silverware, but for many at Old Trafford it was something of an embarrassment. The Cup arrived at the Millennium Stadium protected by members of the Royal Welsh Regiment. It seemed an extreme precaution: for the previous ten years Ferguson wouldn't have picked it up had it been left lying unattended on the turf. This was the competition he had always treated with disdain, fielding youthful teams in the early rounds hoping for a quick exit. How times had changed. This time it was his only hope of success. Ferguson's season was effectively over in February. There was no squeaky bum time this year. All that was left to do was to get his players to form a guard of honour when Chelsea, the champions, came to play at Old Trafford. As John Terry and his team made their way through the applause from their principal rivals it looked like a handover of power, the changing of the guard.

Sure, United came second. Sure, they won a trophy. Sure, it would have been enough twenty years previously to save the manager's job. But times were different. Expectations had been ratcheted up. And for the fans there was time for one more dispiriting piece of news from their worst season in a generation. At the Carling Cup final Ferguson had preferred Louis Saha, the oft-absent striker reckoned in one fanzine to be constructed of balsa wood so frequently was he injured, to Ruud van Nistelrooy. The centre forward was left looking furious on the bench. As is the wont of Dutch players, he did not take his exclusion well and made it clear what he thought of training, of Queiroz, of Ronaldo. When he made the young pretender burst into tears one morning at Carrington, that was it. He was gone. He was sold to Real Madrid with Ferguson barely acknowledging the contribution he had made over the years. For the manager team spirit was all (and Ronaldo not far behind). And he simply could not countenance an old pro scowling in the corner.

For those who had stayed loyal to United in part because of the promise of the three Rs these were grim times. And the mood was not helped that summer when the two remaining Rs were involved in a spat during the World Cup quarter-final. Ronaldo's intervention with the referee helped get Rooney sent off, his little wink at the bench when he concluded his conversation was replayed endlessly on British television. After Beckham in 1998, after Phil Neville, who gave away a crucial penalty at Euro 2000, here was another United player blamed for England's demise. And the widely held view in the papers was that Rooney and Ronaldo could never again play together.

Thus as United gathered for the 2006–07 season, it was almost universally thought they were gearing up to be also-rans. They had not won the title in four years and Europe was still way beyond them. Surely at last time was up for Ferguson. The manager, as was his way, came out for the new season fighting, picking a couple of new scraps along the way. In his official diary of the season, for instance, he made dismissive reference to the breakaway club at FC United. 'When the club became a plc, that was the time to challenge,' he wrote, perhaps temporarily forgetting how many fans argued against the move at the time. 'I wonder how big a United supporter they are. They seem to be promoting or projecting themselves a wee bit. It says more about them than about us.'

He also, in a move calculated to undermine the anti-Glazer resistance, talked of how he was enjoying his working relationship with the new owners: 'In the main the Glazers have been far more flexible and easier to deal with than the plc in that respect because so far anything I have asked for they have said fine. They have been great.'

Within Old Trafford there are those who will provide explanation for the relationship. Since the Glazers know little about football, they have deferred to Ferguson on everything. He is allowed to run things entirely unquestioned. Which for him is manna. No wonder he calls them 'good as gold'. Never mind that – in the words of one insider – had United remained a plc it would now be 'drowning in money instead of up to its neck in debt', Ferguson was officially in love with the new ownership.

Mind, his transfer business seems to have entered a new phase of success under the Glazer regime. After the touch-and-go buys of the latter end of the plc, every player he has brought in under the Americans has delivered something to the party. Patrice Evra, Nemanja Vidic, Michael Carrick, Park Ji-Sung, Tomasz Kuszczak, Carlos Tevez, Anderson, Nani and Owen Hargreaves: practically a whole team, almost a full roster of excellence, every one of them making a mark, bringing something to the party. Now he had a squad, now he was able to rotate without fear of suddenly weakening the enterprise. Not that the Glazers have funded the buys. Not a penny has come from their pockets. As they scour the markets for cheaper sources of credit to underpin their giant mortgage, as always it has been the fans who have paid for it: ticket prices have risen exponentially.

Still, those prepared to fork out ever more for their season passes have had something back. Something grand, something joyful and in truth something unexpected. Ferguson's recovery in the 2006–07 season was not just yet further reproof against anyone writing the man off, it was one of the great stories in sport. Against better-funded, younger, more media-friendly rivals he proved that no one could match his hunger, his desire, his all-consuming need for success. What was more, he did it by sticking to the principles that have governed Manchester United since Matt Busby became manager in 1945. He did not wrestle back the title from the all-conquering Chelsea by employing pragmatic football, by scraping out 1-0 wins and shutting up shop. He did it expansively, by encouraging his players to be fluid, to express themselves on the pitch. He recovered from the loss of his on-pitch leader and chief goalscorer (though he himself did not consider Van Nistelrooy's departure 'a big decision'; 'we were glad to get rid of him, from the moment Real Madrid came in for him, him and his agent were wanting away: good') to refashion a side full of resilience, full of goals, full of charm. Such was the total lack of cynicism at their core, for the first time in fifteen years in the battle for domestic supremacy they became the neutrals' favourite. Compared to the west London juggernaut, his United were light of touch, subtle. Above all entertainers.

He had, he said, seen the possibilities of recovery in the gloomiest moments of the previous season. 'Even when we got knocked out against Benfica I felt that if we stuck together we would develop into a really good team,' he said. Spirit, he added, was at the centre of it. United spirit.

And develop they did. With a proper goalkeeper, with the best defence of his tenure, with Ronaldo and Rooney confounding post-World Cup assumption and forging a coruscating attacking partnership, it was a really good team all right. Plus the manager was blessed by the most golden of autumns from Giggs and Paul Scholes. Now in their thirties, the two remaining stalwarts of the class of 1992 (Butt and Phil Neville had, like Beckham, left, while Gary Neville succumbed to an injury that put his future in doubt), they gave the team a vital grounding.

The culmination of it all came at home in the Champions League against Roma on 10 April. The visitors were a good side, marshalled by Francesco Totti, the Italian Beckham. But United murdered them that night, hammered them. The final score was 7-1, but it could, seriously, have been ten. It was a game that most who saw it immediately slotted into their top three all-time United performances and it hinted, in its fluidity and power, of another treble.

Milan put paid to such thoughts – and to the chances of a meeting with Liverpool in the final – by blitzing United in the semi. And Chelsea were to prevent the double in an FA Cup final that was supposed to open the new Wembley with a flourish, but instead was mired in sterility, the stodgy new pitch destroying any attempts at good football.

But, against all expectation, the League was Ferguson's. For the manager and United's travelling support the highlight had come the week before the Cup final, in the penultimate game of the season at Stamford Bridge. The fixture that was supposed to decide the League was instead a coronation. This time it was the turn of Chelsea's players to form a guard of honour and Ferguson rubbed salt in the wound by sending out a team of reserves and youth-teamers. The look on Terry's face could have been framed and hung in the National Gallery. The Chelsea captain chivvied his players into position to do the decent thing, then was obliged to clap on to the pitch what appeared to be a bunch of ball boys.

Meanwhile, the United fans loved it. For over twenty minutes in the first half, they gave non-stop airing to their favoured new ditty:

'Mourinho are you listening/ You'd better keep that trophy glistening/ We'll be back in May/ To take it away/ Walking in a Fergie wonderland.' In the dug-out Ferguson appeared relaxed, wreathed in smiles, master of all he surveyed. By contrast Mourinho looked tetchy, edgy, beaten. At one point he unleashed such a torrent of invective at the referee Graham Poll (referring, apparently, to sexual activity with Ferguson) that he sent himself to the stands in the assumption he had been red-carded. A moment or two later, having discovered Poll had not excluded him, he slunk back, humiliated, to the bench.

What was going on along the Stamford Bridge touchline that night was completely at odds with what had happened but a year before. Back then, no one could have believed Ferguson and his United would ever again see off a rival. So unexpected was the change in the order of things that Mourinho himself was soon to become victim of Chelsea's Borgia-like internal politics and was sacked in September 2007, leaving the way open to the old guard to take the title once more.

When he first came to Manchester, Ferguson's chief rivals were George Graham, Brian Clough and Bob Paisley. England have had nine managers in the time he has been at Old Trafford, Manchester City twelve; two men have even done both jobs during his watch. He has outwitted, outfoxed and outlasted the lot. He is the great eternal of English football. United without him is almost unthinkable. How could the place be shorn of his gum-chewing, spiky, all-consuming presence? A City-supporting friend of mine suggests the old boy is so determined to stay on and on, he will still be managing the club via a séance. It is a point of view. Chronology, however, stands in the way even of legend. Time dictates there will eventually be a conclusion. When it happens, it will be done capriciously, deliberately timed just to catch everyone out. Then there will be someone else. There always is. The fans would prefer it to be a figure of their collective past, someone imbued in the United ethic, Keane, Mark Hughes, Ole Gunnar Solskjær or Eric Cantona. The reality is it will probably be someone with European experience, Frank Rijkaard, Carlo Ancelotti, perhaps Mourinho. Or maybe it will be the manager's own son, Darren, who has celebrated promotion in successive years in his first managerial job at Peterborough. Keep it in the family: now that would be a story.

Whoever it is, though, he will find himself to be, like Ferguson, just the custodian. As George Best, Norman Whiteside, Paul Ince, Jaap Stam, David Beckham, Ruud van Nistelrooy, even Keano himself have demonstrated, this is a club that has never been a one-man operation. Ferguson has always insisted as much: Old Trafford is bigger than any individual. Individuals are expendable. One day even he will demonstrate that reality.

Coming away from the ground on the spring day after Villa had been trounced, listening to the excited chatter of the supporters calculating how close another title was to their grasp, looking at the smiles, soaking up the happy expectation, it became clear Ferguson was right. No one man, not even him, can outgrow this place.

Whatever the rain – I was wet enough already – I decided to walk from the ground back into Manchester, through the Salford quays, along the Rochdale canal, up past Deansgate towards the centre of town. These days the city looks once again spectacular in its beguiling mix of Victorian and modern, of brick and steel, of gothic and glass. Central station has become an exhibition centre, the old cotton exchange a huge bar and entertainment complex, the former generators of wealth turned into modern factories of retail. Yet there is nothing twee about the new Manchester. The aesthetics remain true to the place's heart: gritty, unpolished, rough-hewn.

And that applies also to United. This is an institution transformed, one that has become a multinational corporation, owned by Americans and employing out on the pitch a polyglot of Argentinians, Brazilians, Serbs, Portuguese, Poles, South Koreans, French and Dutchmen. Yet – though its current owners will never understand this – the purpose at its core remains as Matt Busby once insisted it must be. It is there to shine a light on the heart of its supporters, to give them something nothing else in their lives ever could. It is a place that is all about the unique relationship between those who provide the entertainment and those who sustain it. And that will continue whoever is in charge. The chant echoing across a damp and glistening St Peter's Square that evening, being sung by a bedraggled bunch of three young lads standing on the platform waiting for a tram, summed it up: 'Man United', they shouted in cheery defiance, 'will never die.'

22

A MAY DAY IN MOSCOW

It was approaching two o'clock on the morning of Thursday 22 May 2008 and the weather in Moscow was familiar to anyone who has ever taken a summer holiday in the Lake District. For the previous hour it had sheeted it down, the rain suddenly illuminated as it fell out of the inky gloom and into the Luzhniki Stadium lights. The rumour circulating the stadium press room was that the deluge had come on the orders of the mayor of Moscow. Normally, the story went, when his city is about to host a major outdoor event, he dispatches the Russian air force to seed incoming storm clouds, to encourage them to drop their loads long before they near Moscow's suburbs. This time, though, he had let nature take its course, in the hope the spirits of the English hordes fetching up for the Champions League final might be dampened. That was the welcome the visitors got. That and the biggest troop deployment hereabouts since the invasion of Czechoslovakia.

Down below me the pitch, freshened by the continuing torrent, gleamed so green it just didn't look a natural colour. Which was right: it wasn't. According to those who walked across it before kick-off it had been painted, the bare patches greened up with a lick of gloss, to ensure it shone on the television pictures beamed round the world. What with the pitch, the rain and the six thousand troops ringing the stadium, not a lot was being left to chance here. Except for the result of the game. We were approaching the climax of club football's most significant match of the season, the Champions League final. And it was being decided by the enduring lottery that is the penalty shoot-out.

Across to my left, in the far goalmouth, Manchester United's Edwin van der Sar stood, his legs apart, his arms outstretched, his outfit almost as green as the turf. On the halfway line, the players of both United and their opponents Chelsea lined up in two sodden groups, their arms round each other's shoulders in solidarity, their soaked hair flat against their heads, their faces – picked up by the cameras and projected on to the screens at each end of the stadium – riven with anxiety. From the blue line, a figure broke away and approached the penalty area, his eyes down at the turf, not looking at the keeper ahead. The United fans banked in the stand behind Van der Sar's goal booed his every step from the moment they recognised who it was: the former Arsenal, Liverpool and City man, Nicolas Anelka. The referee had already put the ball on the penalty spot as he approached. As the official backed away to give him room, Anelka stood over the ball and looked momentarily at the goal. As he did so, Van der Sar pointed with his left index finger up to the top left-hand corner of the net. Anelka ignored him and took two or three quick paces back. Then, with a little skip forward, he ran at the ball and clipped it in the opposite direction to Van der Sar's instruction. But almost from the second he hit it – not quite hard enough, not quite high enough, not quite with sufficient conviction – you could see that Van der Sar, pitching his enormous frame rightwards, was going to reach it. You could see, even from a distance of some two hundred yards, that the Dutchman was smiling as he dived rightwards, smiling wide even before he got his right hand to the ball. As he pushed it away from the net, so that it clattered into the advertising hoardings behind him, as Anelka froze, momentarily replaying the kick in his mental cinema hoping desperately for a different conclusion, the big man was already laughing. Laughing in sheer bloody relief at it all.

Like most Muscovite architecture, the Luzhniki is a monumental stadium, solid and muscular, nothing shy or delicate about it. Its roof is held up by more steel than Sheffield once produced in a year. Which is just as well: the noise that erupted as the big keeper scooped that shot away would have threatened anything less substantial with instant demolition. As one, twenty-five thousand United fans roared their delight into the Russian air. Van der Sar stood for a moment, his arms outstretched, his fists clenched, shrieking over and again the single word 'Yes' as his team-mates ran at him from the halfway line and leapt on to him, forming a pyramid of delight, Rio Ferdinand at its peak. They were almost immediately joined by the back room staff, the substitutes and the substituted, players in suits who had not been involved, all dashing in delirium from the bench. From the stands the sound grew, a rolling roar of triumph. And there, as the other players whelped and danced and hugged, lying in the centre circle with his face in the turf and his shoulders jerking as involuntary sobs racked through him, lay Cristiano Ronaldo. At that moment the world's finest footballer knew how close he had been to ignominy, how close he had been to undermining the whole enterprise. He had missed his penalty earlier in the shoot-out. Now his colleague had rescued him and he would not be the villain of the piece after all. The headlines being prepared in newsrooms across the globe would not now be published. The anticipated *schadenfreude* would not be employed. His exhausted tears of relief were eloquent testimony to how close it had been. How fine was the margin between the history man and the fall guy.

Six days earlier, Ronaldo had been in the ballroom of a London hotel to receive the Football Writers' Association's Footballer of the

Year trophy for the second season on the bounce. His was an overwhelming triumph, he polled more than five times the votes of the rest of the candidates combined. He added it to the PFA Footballer of the Year award, a rare double he had greeted with suitable economy by giving the same acceptance speech at both ceremonies ('This award is very nice for me, but is very nice to play in nice team,' the gist of it.) As he stood there, being handed the trophy by Sir Bobby Charlton, as the appreciation of those whose job it is to watch every single second he spends on a football pitch echoed round the room, there was no doubt about it: 2008 was Ronaldo's season. He scored forty-two goals, easily eclipsing George Best's forty-year record for a United winger. He scored with his left, he scored with his right and none of them were shite. He scored them, too, with his head. Like the one against Roma in the Olympic Stadium in the Champions League quarter-final when he dashed forty yards to meet a ball chipped – with beauty and precision – by Paul Scholes. He headed it with such power the Roma defence was breached before it had even realised he was in the vicinity. Joe Jordan in his pomp could not have bettered its amalgam of artistry and muscularity. As Simon Barnes suggested in *The Times* of Ronaldo, 'He'd be a pretty useful goal scorer even if he couldn't kick a ball.' But kick a ball he could. Throughout the year he had kicked it in ways few before him had ever dared try. He jinked, he shimmied, he dummied. He danced, he sprinted, he back-heeled. And he hit free-kicks of blinding force and dip, like one against Portsmouth in a Premier League fixture at Old Trafford, its flight so inexplicable it left a keeper as canny as David James flat-footed, rooted to his line, looking perplexed at its passage into the top corner of his net.

Yet still his detractors claimed that Ronaldo was a player incapable of performing on the biggest stage. It became the cliché central to many a newspaper preview of every big game United played in 2008. But time and again Ronaldo proved he was no flat-track bully, a spinner of magic only against the weak. He was entirely democratic about who he scored against: big teams, little teams, those in between were equally treated to his attentions. For instance, in eleven Champions League games, against the toughest opponents on the Continent, he scored eight goals, including one in the final. As was suggested by the pictures of that goal, as he soared above anyone else to meet the ball with his forehead and plant it in the corner of the Chelsea net, he was a man more than capable of rising to the occasion.

Mind, Ronaldo was assisted hugely in his endeavours by a team he calls 'nice', an outfit which Sir Alex Ferguson was to announce at the season's end was the finest he had constructed in his twenty-two years at Old Trafford. Fans might argue the toss between 1958, 1967, 1994, 1999 and 2008, but of this there was no doubt: it was the deepest squad ever assembled in British football.

In the summer of 2007, Ferguson had spent heavily. In came Anderson and Nani – two players whose recruitment showed the growing influence of his Portuguese assistant Carlos Queiroz, a man whose eye for detail and penchant for preparation neatly dovetailed with Ferguson's own. The pair announced their arrival by making the front page of the *News of the World* after joining with Ronaldo in being serviced by some of Manchester's less discreet call girls, whose first instinct on netting clients of such renown was to sell the tale to the highest bidder. Owen Hargreaves, the energetic Canadian of Welsh descent who had somehow managed to engineer an international career with England, had a less noisy introduction. The Argentina international Carlos Tevez also arrived from West Ham, his paperwork trailing the cloud of obfuscation that reflected the growing South American model of player ownership. None of them were cheap. But what they represented was a prodigious fattening up of resources ready to defend the championship won the previous year.

It began quietly for United. By Christmas, Arsenal were streaking ahead in the Premier League and, after beating Milan away, looked good for the Champions League, too. Chelsea, having sacked José Mourinho, replaced him with Avram Grant, an unhappy-looking Israeli who had by coincidence gained experience for his coaching badges at Carrington. Grant's first game was a 2-0 defeat at Old Trafford in which his side looked disorganised, uninspired, uninterested, missing the charismatic command of the man who had constructed it.

Looks, though, can be deceptive. And by February, both United and Grant's Chelsea were in Arsenal's rearview mirror at the top of the domestic table ('They are the favourites, no question of that,' said Ferguson of the leaders. 'But if they slip, we'll be there. That's our job.') United, however, were temporarily inconvenienced at home by first defeat to City in the game that marked the emotional fiftieth anniversary of the Munich crash and then to Portsmouth in the FA Cup.

In Europe, though, there was no faltering. Showing the growing power of the English game, half the quarter-finalists in the Champions League hailed from the Premier League. United played Roma for the second time in the season and demonstrated that any sense of inferiority about the Italian game was a thing of the past by winning 2-0 at the Olympic Stadium. Outside the ground, a round of stabbing and buttock-slicing depressingly familiar to these Anglo-Italian encounters took place. This time three United fans ended up in a local prison. According to those who were there, the red supporters who had gathered on the notorious Ponte Milvio behind the stadium were happy to indulge any local desire for a scrap. These were no innocent bystanders. None the less the United communications director Phil Townsend, a former civil servant at the Department of Culture, Media and Sport, used his influence to persuade Andy Burnham, the minister there, to look into the jailed trio's case. The core of Burnham's response on doing so was 'Have you seen the evidence against these guys?'

Perhaps more significant to United's season was Arsenal's result at this stage. They lost, easily and surprisingly, to Liverpool at the start of a woeful spell in which their early season dominance evaporated. It was proof of what Ferguson had learned in the past five years: the demands of English football had grown to the point where it was now a game involving numbers far higher than eleven against eleven. Arsenal's first choice was good. But when Mathieu Flamini and Alexander Hleb were injured, and their central fulcrum Cesc Fabregas tired, they had no one comparable to bring in. In contrast, United's midfield was bristling with possibility. Ferguson had Michael Carrick, Hargreaves, Nani, Anderson, Darren Fletcher and Park Ji-Sung, not to mention the golden oldies of Paul Scholes and Ryan Giggs. Perming any three from that roster, he could rest and recover whomsoever he needed. Suspensions crippled Arsène Wenger; Ferguson could brush them off with disdain. When first United then Chelsea beat them in the League, Arsenal were out of it, finished, done, their season collapsing in acrimony, the press largely concluding it was the fault of their captain William Gallas, whose tetchy self-obsession led to him being described by the Gunner cheerleader Piers Morgan as 'a great big French blouson'.

At United such attitudes would never be tolerated. Here, there was a growing singularity of purpose. They may have possessed the game's biggest star, but players like Wayne Rooney, Rio Ferdinand, Wes Brown and Nemanja Vidic personified a work ethic in which the collective was always more important than the individual. In the Champions League semi-final played in April in the Camp Nou, for instance, Rooney was deployed as auxiliary right back without demur, happy to relinquish personal glory in pursuit of the greater good. He ran himself to the point of exhaustion, blocking and harrying and denying Barcelona's expansive forward line the room in which to move. It was the game Ferguson – always ready with a dig at his domestic rivals – reckoned 'the natural final, the one everyone wants'. Had it been, you assume he would have had his team playing with greater fluency than they did in the first-leg goalless draw. The country's most attractive, attacking side had countered Barcelona's threat with disciplined, determined defence. It wasn't pretty, it wasn't romantic, but it worked. Mind, it might have been very different had

Ronaldo not missed a penalty in the second minute, his first – though not last – spot-kick error of the season. And it meant the reds remained unbeaten in every away game in Europe across the season: a symptom of a team closing in on fulfilment.

In the other semi-final, Liverpool took on Chelsea, a tie that might appear to have represented the trickiest of choices for United followers were their team to ease past Barcelona. Who would they most prefer to meet in Moscow, their long-standing rivals down the road or the financially bloated upstarts from London? Actually, there was no dilemma here. For true United fans, the thought of losing to Liverpool, the thought of the crowing and the commemorative banners, the very idea of 'We've won it five times' becoming six was too awful. Sure, losing to Chelsea would hurt. But in time, it would be one of those things. Liverpool were of a different order altogether: defeat would never diminish. And the red pessimists got their wish as the Londoners, in the kind of rain that was a harbinger of Moscow, eased past Liverpool, Avram Grant greeting the victory by falling to his knees in thanks.

For United, it was just a matter of beating Barcelona. Which they did after Scholes – the mighty, the evergreen – smacked in an astonishing thirty-yard half volley. Ronaldo had looked as if he were carrying the effects of one too many player-of-the-season awards that game, but, as was the way of this United, others came to the fore. Brown was magnificent, Ferdinand dogged, Carrick's precision in possession reflective of a growing authority. And, in the absence of the injured Rooney, little Tevez gave a masterclass in defending from the front. In a night of unrelenting tension, during which Barcelona could have, in any one moment, scored the goal that would have sent them through on away goals, Tevez tore and harried, niggled and hassled, snapping at ankles with the energy of a terrier puppy that had just gorged on the household supply of Pro-Plus. In the 96th minute, as the added time stretched the nerves of everyone crammed inside Old Trafford, he was still doing it, still tearing across the halfway line, still, in David Pleat's odd little malapropism on the television coverage, 'dogging it'. He is only five feet seven, but you suspect he started off at over six foot and wore his legs down with all the endless running around.

So United were in Moscow for the final, their third in the competition's long history and its first ever all-English affair. Before the fans could worry about tickets, or visas, or hotels, there was the small matter of the Premier League to be decided. Arsenal were out of it, but Chelsea were still there, fighting every step, beating United in a game at Stamford Bridge to set up the closest final day since 1995. United were due to play away at Wigan, Chelsea at home to Bolton. They were equal on points. United's superior goal difference, however, meant Chelsea had to better their result to take the title. United's advantage was recognised by the Premier League: they had dispatched their trophy to Wigan and sent a replica to Stamford Bridge. In a crazy example of how United-haters everywhere think that there is a conspiracy abroad designed solely to assist the reds at every turn, my City-supporting mate texted to say there was no need for such precaution: it was obviously United's. Wigan were managed by Steve Bruce, he pointed out, just as Blackburn were by Mark Hughes (now at City), Sunderland by Roy Keane and Birmingham by Alex McLeish. As far as he was concerned, since Ferguson had been in the game so long, it was only a matter of time before every other team in the League would be managed by one of his ex-players, ensuring he would always get a result in crucial games. As if having one of the finest collections of players ever assembled in England isn't enough to facilitate victory. Chelsea drew and United, thanks to a goal from – who else – Ronaldo and a second, nerve-soothing finish from Giggs, landed the trophy. 'He's won it ten times, that boy Giggsy, he's won it ten times,' chanted the happy Mancunian masses, taking over Wigan for the day. It was Giggs's 758th appearance for United. It equalled Bobby Charlton's longevity, demonstrating the kind of loyalty thought obsolete in an era in which Andy Cole and Nicolas Anelka have between them played for nearly twenty clubs. Soon after his coruscating performance in Turin in 2003, Giggs was offered a name-your-own-figure contract by Juventus. Whatever he wanted was his, they insisted. He never considered it for a moment. United flowed in his blood. He was as big a fan of the institution as the lads who had chanted his name for the last seventeen years. You could tell what he thought when he was asked after the Wigan game to name his finest achievement. Was it winning ten titles, winning more trophies than anyone else in the game or equalling Charlton's record?

'None of them,' he said. 'My finest moment was my first appearance for the first team. Nothing has beaten that feeling and nothing ever will.'

When United last made it to the Champions League final, all of those I used to stand with at Old Trafford as a teenager journeyed to Barcelona. The whole gang of us, the lads who had grown up on the Scoreboard Paddock. Nine years later, only I made it to Moscow and that was through work. Too far, too difficult, above all too pricey was the others' reasoning. The cost of the trip to Russia was roughly the same as a season ticket and none of them can justify forking out for both. They were not alone. For the first time in living memory, United failed to sell out their full allocation for a big game. Tickets were on open sale the day before.

It was, then, less than half the size of the invasion of Catalunya in 1999. The diehards were there, mind, the United long-marchers, who found whatever way they could to reduce costs. With direct flights priced at upwards of £700, people took budget airlines to Riga, St Petersburg and Helsinki, then got the train from there. One bunch flew to Warsaw then spent twenty-two hours on what they described as the 'rattler'. It was clear by their grey-faced demeanour the level of comfort that had entailed. Ferguson called them 'true supporters'. And they came from all over – Australia, Singapore, Ireland. Plus Manchester, every corner of the city was represented. From none of them was there a hint of trouble. For a start, not many got close to a drink. Red Square, the principal gathering place of fans, was an alcohol-free zone. Here United and

Chelsea mixed in cheery sobriety, turning the place purple. These did not look, or act, like the English hooligans the Russian media had been fearing since the semis. This was an entirely friendly invasion, keen to avoid any trouble. Indeed, I met a red in Red Square who told me of his minor altercation with some locals the night before.

'We was in a bar and some young CSKA lads – teenagers really – come in and started on us,' he explained. 'They was giving it all fists up and shouting "Fighty fucky fighty". I says to 'em, never mind fighty fucky fighty, I'm nearly fucking fifty.'

It was an older crowd, men with the time and resources to spend three days and several thousand pounds on their obsession. These were hard-core United, people whose lives had been marked and measured by the fortunes of their club, men who had been there long before Ronaldo was born, and would still be there long after he disappeared westwards.

Unlike in 1999, nobody came without a ticket, though they were easy enough to get hold of, changing hands at face value in most Moscow hotel lobbies. Those who made the journey had just about enough cash left over for the favoured souvenir: a furry Russian hat, with a Soviet-style metal badge on the front. They cost about a tenner, and St Basil's cathedral, the Gum shopping mall, the enviably efficient Moscow underground, were full of them, bobbing around in anticipation. Though on the underground it was largely a bob of confusion. The local authorities had not put up any special signage to direct the forty-five thousand visiting English folk and everywhere you looked, there were confused United and Chelsea fans failing to make sense of the Cyrillic alphabet.

Once they got there, on the approaches to the stadium, through the underpasses, beyond the ranks of armoured vehicles lined up across the road from the entrance, past the giant statue of Lenin, the talk was all of destiny. What better way to mark the memories of those who died fifty years ago than to win the very trophy they had perished pursuing? Aware of the moment, United ensured all the surviving participants in the Munich crash were in the

Luzhniki: Sir Bobby, Bill Foulkes, Albert Scanlon, Harry Gregg and Kenny Morgans were all there, VIPs in a drama for which, half a century on, they still craved a very different narrative. But Chelsea felt a sense of destiny of their own. The game was being played in the home town of their benefactor, Roman Abramovich. Someone assured me on the tube on the way to the game that he was not going to spend £500 million chasing this dream to see his lads come second.

Inside the ground the fears of empty seats seemed largely unfounded. It was packed in there, loud and excited. After a pre-match pageant featuring several hundred caped acrobats apparently kitted out in costumes borrowed from one of Rick Wakeman's ice spectaculars, the teams came out on to the pitch. The United end greeting their arrival by holding up a huge mosaic which spelled out the single word 'Believe'. Believe in destiny, believe in history, believe in the spirit of United. It was a powerful image, one that must have set pulses racing across the globe as millions hunkered down to watch on television, including my old Stretford Paddock mates in the Railway, a pub in south Manchester. This was a swelling throng of United lovers who were not suffering from the same alcohol deficit as those in Moscow.

Without injury or – unlike 1999 – suspension to detain him, Ferguson chose what was his strongest team: Van der Sar, Brown, Evra, Ferdinand, Vidic, Hargreaves, Carrick, Scholes, Ronaldo, Tevez and Rooney. Giggs was on the bench, as were Anderson and Nani. There were six Englishmen in there, two more than in 1999, only one fewer than in 1968. And it was two of them who fashioned United's goal. Brown and Scholes played a one-two on the touchline, Brown delivering a sumptuous cross which Ronaldo leapt at to score. It was a Manchester goal fashioned by Manchester men, finished by the man of the moment, the man who was later to compromise his place in United legend through his behaviour during a protracted transfer saga to Real Madrid. And for ten minutes following it, United played as if possessed by the spirit of every lost great who had ever trod the pitch at Old Trafford. Meredith, Mitten, Edwards, Best: they seemed all to be there in every quick-fire pass, every jink, every stepover. It was mesmerising football, everything you could have wished for and the occasion craved. Tevez could have scored twice, Carrick was denied by an incredible save by Chelsea's Petr Cech. But the score remained 1-0.

And you sensed as the game progressed that United might pay for not taking advantage of their dominance. It was a sense exacerbated when Frank Lampard equalised, then made flesh as Chelsea took control of the second half. United enjoyed good fortune for the next forty-five minutes ('We were lucky,' Ferguson admitted afterwards. 'You need luck at this level and we had it'). But as the game accelerated into extra time, as two magnificent teams exchanged blows like tiring championship fighters, exhaustion and cramp democratised things. It was equal: Lampard hit the post, Giggs (who replaced the injured Scholes) had an effort cleared off the line by John Terry, Tevez almost got his studs to a Rooney cross. It was pulsating, astonishing, speed and technique in one magnificent amalgam, the perfect advertisement for the English club game. Then came perhaps the decisive moment. As the game neared its end, as the managers sent on substitutes specifically to participate in the penalty shoot-out, Chelsea's Didier Drogba, in a childish flash of petulance, gave Vidic a girly slap right in front of the referee. He was sent off no more than five minutes from the critical shoot-out.

When it came down to the twelve-yard roulette, then, Chelsea's leading striker was missing. Ferguson had never won a competitive round of penalties in his time as a manager. The last had been lost when Scholes missed against Arsenal in the 2005 FA Cup final. But Scholes was no longer on the pitch. He had broken his nose in a challenge with Claude Makelele and now it was down to the new generation of reds: Anderson, Nani, Hargreaves, Carrick, Evra and Tevez. Plus Ronaldo. He stepped up at two penalties each. And, giving huge joy to United haters everywhere, put the ball too close to Cech. Everyone else scored, which meant when John Terry walked forward, the destination of the Cup was in his gift. Many a red – in the Luzhniki, in the Railway, in bars and front rooms across the world – could not watch. Terry was Mr Chelsea, a one-club man, a singular cockney presence. It was the first of many apparently scripted potential conclusions to this drama. But miss he did, slipping as he addressed the ball, ballooning it harmlessly wide. From there, the momentum was all United's. Anderson – perhaps hitting the ball harder than anyone can have done before – and – gloriously – Giggs scored in sudden death. So did Salomon Kalou for Chelsea. Then came Anelka.

United were led up to receive the trophy by Sir Bobby Charlton, soaked to the skin through his neat, blue mac and grey suit. It was an inspired piece of casting. Here was the living link between the lads who perished in 1958 and the glory boys who stand on their shoulders. Here was the right man to take them to their appointment with the trophy that has always been at the heart of the red endeavour. Sir Bobby, the embodiment of United, the quiet, dignified personification of everything the red flag stands for. The holder of a flame kept alive by men like Paul Scholes who, five minutes before, even as his team-mates danced and hugged and grinned, went round every single Chelsea player, to shake their hand and commiserate. Scholes knows on what a fine edge does glory balance, brought up as he is on the dictum of Matt Busby: 'There should be no despair in defeat and no conceit in victory.'

After Giggs and Ferdinand had lifted the trophy, outside the Railway men who should have known better danced on the bonnets of cars. At Old Trafford, the forecourt was soon filled with jabberingly excited crowds. In Moscow some were so exhausted they could hardly stand: not the players, the fans, their nerves mangled by 150 minutes of relentless excitement. But they managed to find a second wind and filled the Luzhniki with chanting for a good hour after the presentations, before making their way off into the rain to attempt to connect with their flights or trains home.

The players were given a party at their city centre hotel, the Crowne Plaza, no more than a meaty Van der Sar clearance from the spot outside the Duma where Boris Yeltsin had once stood on a tank and faced down a coup. They arrived there at about 3.30 a.m. and, after a swift change of clothes, didn't stop. What followed was a triumphant seven-hour knees-up, involving dancing, drinking and Rio Ferdinand serenading fans with an impromptu chant of 'Manchester, la la la'. Plus that most traditional of post-match celebrations: a team singalong to French tribal house DJ Laurent Wolf's 'No Stress' ('I don't wanna work today/Just take it easy cause there is no stress'). It was not entirely clear if Sir Bobby joined in.

When it finally finished in the middle of that morning, the hotel's function room was awash with champagne corks, empty bottles of Veuve Clicquot Ponsardin Brut and an abandoned stick of Chanel lipstick in a vibrant shade of magenta. After breakfast (the hero Van der Sar ate two small packets of Coco Pops and a banana) the team bus made its way to the airport, sent on its way by a gathering of fans singing their new favourite:

'Viva John Terry/You could have won the Cup but you fucked it up/Viva John Terry.' Except Daniel Welbeck, then an untried seventeen-year-old member of the United youth team, was not on board. Exhausted by the morning's exertions, he had gone back to his room, slept through his alarm and missed it. He had to scramble his way into a cab to meet up with the rest of the party at the airport. Soon after the return to England, Welbeck was invited to Ferguson's office in Carrington to explain. At Manchester United it never stops. Ever.

EPILOGUE

At least Danny Welbeck made it out of bed for the FA Cup semi-final nine months later. The leggy, speedy, spirited young forward was picked by Sir Alex Ferguson to play against Everton in the game at Wembley Stadium. But then even the average student might have managed to be up and about by the 1 p.m. kick off. On a Sunday. The FA Cup semi-final between representatives of Merseyside and Manchester was played in the capital on public transport's day of rest at a time when the last train north disappeared from Euston long before the final whistle. No thought to Villa Park or Hillsborough or somewhere convenient for the match-going fan. Not when the deepening financial hole that is the national stadium had to be filled directly from the supporters' wallet, not when a Sunday tea-time broadcast offered beleaguered, advertising-bereft television companies a bumper audience. Such was the game's ever-increasing distance from its root and heart.

As for Welbeck, history might suggest it was something of a speedy elevation – from being ticked off for lying in to member of the starting line-up in the penultimate round of the world's oldest football competition – but there was sound reason for it. Reason that extended beyond the fact the eighteen-year-old Mancunian had proved himself to be so useful in his debut season that Ferguson cheekily informed the England manager Fabio Capello that he would be picking the lad for the 2010 World Cup. Together with the seventeen-year-old Italian Federico Macheda and the likes of Darron Gibson, Jonny Evans, Ben Foster and Rafael da Silva, Welbeck had been asked to play at Wembley so as to rest more senior limbs for scraps ahead.

Embroiled in the most claustrophobic fixture crush in United's competitive history, Ferguson was obliged to use his resources in a manner even he had never done before. Once, Sir Matt Busby made do with fielding no more than fourteen players in a season. Now the back page of the United match-day programme listing Ferguson's squad contained as many names as the Manchester phone book. And the manager used almost all of them in the course of his longest ever campaign.

Now, with the World Club Championship and the Carling Cup already on the sideboard, United were, at the point of the FA Cup encounter with Liverpool's blue half, pursuing silverware in no fewer than five competitions. Never mind the treble, from Christmas the talk in Manchester was all of the quintuple. 'Five' became the word in the stands at Old Trafford. The phone-ins and chat rooms were alive with five. The nap hand was everywhere. Except, that is, in media interviews by players and management. Here, when even to mention the possibility was reckoned to court ill fortune, they insisted that the focus remained on taking each game as it came.

'I know it's a cliché, but that's all we can do,' said Rio Ferdinand, in the midst of his most convincing run of form in his time at the club. 'You can't look beyond the next opponent.'

Yeah, sure Rio. The idea of making history and simultaneously being required to build an extension at Ferdinand Towers to house all the medals never entered the mind.

Such was the crush of fixtures, with a Premier League game against Portsmouth just three days after the FA Cup semi, that Ferguson decided to field his young squad members at Wembley. Naturally, this being United and it being Ferguson in charge, his choice of team caused outrage and uproar in equal measure. Back pages were cleared to announce that he was disrespecting the great competition. Worse, he was treating paying customers, inconvenienced as they were by the FA and television schedulers, with contempt; fancy driving 150 miles on a Sunday to watch the reserves. As always, Ferguson didn't listen. He was doing what was best for Manchester United, he insisted. And as it happened, his young players performed sufficiently well to match an organised Everton at every turn, in perhaps the dullest semi in the Cup's long history, a game stifled by the appalling Wembley pitch, a surface so sticky and spongy it could act as a brake to Lewis Hamilton. It was a game that, within moments of kick-off, you knew was heading to penalties. And when they came, United's young keeper Foster, who had saved the crucial spot kick at the end of an equally inconclusive Carling Cup final against Spurs, got nowhere near the Everton efforts. As the winning Everton penalty hit the back of the net, the entire blues team ran as one in hectic pursuit of the scorer Phil Jagielka. Except that is, their skipper. Phil Neville looked so distressed it was as if, rather than leading his team to the club's first final since 1995, he had just learned that his brother Gary had undergone surgery for sexual realignment. Once a red, always a red.

Ferguson had no complaint about the outcome, mind. Yes, he had lost the chance for yet another double. Yes, the silverware targets were now down to the mere four. But he knew what he had just seen: a young, vibrant and largely homegrown team that spoke of the future. 'They'll do for me,' he said of his boys after the game.

In fact, it was possible for much of the season to see the next great Ferguson team taking shape even as the last one was competing on every front. At times during the 2008-09 campaign it was like peeking through the scaffolding at a new building being constructed behind the façade of an old one. It was regeneration on the hoof, something that had proved impossible for Ferguson's eminent predecessor Busby, a trick which suggested this was a manager at the very height of his powers. Reaching sixty-seven years old, there seemed no diminution in his ability to look ahead.

Players like Welbeck, Evans and Macheda – who announced his arrival with a sumptuous goal against Villa that topped a comeback impressive even by United's long history of reversing fortune – were being blooded to serve long after he had retired. It was, in a sense, the most selfless of managerial acts, putting in place a legacy he was unlikely to enjoy except by proxy.

His rebuilding was in marked contrast to that undertaken by Arsène Wenger at Arsenal. The Frenchman spent much of the season watching in mute frustration as the skilled but fragile youngsters, in whom he had placed great faith, wilted under the requirements of an English campaign. Nowhere was the contrast between Ferguson's condition and that of his old rival clearer than when their teams met in the Champions League semi-final. Before the first leg at Old Trafford, the number of medals accrued by the United starting eleven was totted up: it was over a hundred. The Arsenal players had thirteen between them. And eight of those had been earned by Mikaël Silvestre during his time in Manchester. United's ensuing 1-0 victory was so comprehensive, the post-match analysis concluded that Arsenal had been gifted a stay of execution.

It was not to last. The game plan of Wenger's youngsters simply fell apart in the second leg at the Emirates. The Gunners' callowness was exposed time and again by United's quicksilver counter-attacks. For the home side, there was no cohesion, no defence, no leadership. Wenger was introducing young players into a team bereft of experience; Ferguson, by contrast, was blooding his next generation even as the last maintained possession of the shirt. For Evans, what could be a better tutelage than playing alongside Ferdinand or Nemanja Vidić? For Gibson, who better to train alongside than Paul Scholes and Ryan Giggs? And if Welbeck wanted reminding to set his alarm, who was more likely to insist he did than Gary Neville? While Wenger had allowed his older players to head off for pay days new, Ferguson had kept a core in place, there to tutor the next generation in the spirit and understanding of United. Every day, in every game, with every kick, they were learning the rules of the club. His club.

And how Ferguson needed those youngsters to be raised in the traditions he held dear. In the new English footballing reality, loyalty was increasingly a matter between a player and his current account. The thought that one of the new mercenaries of the game would ever match Ryan Giggs's 800-odd appearances for one club was laughable. As if to demonstrate the new order, on 11 June 2009 came the news everyone had been expecting for almost a year. The board had accepted a world record offer from Real Madrid of £80 million for Cristiano Ronaldo. The player was keen to go. No wonder, with a contract worth £9.5 million a year, rising by 25 per cent every season. Thus came to an end the most protracted, unsavoury, debilitating transfer saga in red history.

It had begun soon after that victory in Moscow. In the summer recess of 2008, Madrid put in a bid for the man who was to be named European and World Player of the Year for his *annus mirabilis*. Ferguson rejected it immediately and accused the Spanish team of serial unscrupulousness in their transfer dealings. The man suspected by PSV, Bayern Munich, Tottenham and so many others of tapping-up, railed against Real for unsettling his player. He dismissed their chances of buying the footballer who now, more than any other, was identified with United in the memorable observation, 'I would not sell a virus to that mob'.

But as Ferguson dug in his heels in the summer of 2008 so Ronaldo revealed he had a pair of his own (possibly of stiletto shape and almost certainly of glittery detailing). Like many a youngster growing up in the Iberian peninsula, for him Madrid was the apex of footballing ambition. To play for them was something he had fantasised about since he was five. Now, since he had everything else he wanted in life, he couldn't understand why he was not being allowed this, the fulfilment of a youthful dream. He pouted and moaned in the Portuguese press, conducting a lengthy PR campaign to secure release. At times it was comical, as during the European Championships in Switzerland when turning out in Portugal's change strip he told watching reporters he always looked better in white. At times it was pathetic, as when he agreed with the absurd observation of Sepp Blatter that he was a modern-day slave. You can just imagine the thousands of Filipinas working in Dubai for subsistence wages must have immediately extended their hearts to the poor lad, earning as he was no more than £120,000 a week for running around for 90 minutes at a time while 75,000 adoring fans chanted his name. William Wilberforce's grave must have been awash with anxiety at his plight.

Whatever his insistence, as the summer drifted into autumn, it appeared as if Ferguson had won: Ronaldo would be remaining a United player. Especially when the transfer deadline passed and, instead of seeing his squad substantially depleted, the manager added to it by signing the urbane and languid Dimitar Berbatov from Tottenham for some £30 million.

'We're building something great here,' Ferguson said at the Bulgarian's unveiling at Old Trafford in early September 2008. 'Cristiano knows that. Why would he want to go anywhere else? This is the place where his best interests lie.'

The manager added that never once in his twenty-two years at United had he let go a player he didn't want to leave. Paul Ince, Jaap Stam, David Beckham, Ruud van Nistelrooy, Roy Keane: tough as their departures might have been, they had all gone on his terms. He was not going to change that habit for anyone. Especially not to sell them to a club like Madrid, whose actions he likened to the mafia and whose historic affiliation with the fascist regime of General Franco he raised at every opportunity. No, there was nothing personal about it, he claimed. This was football business. Personal football business.

Despite Ferguson's bullish certainty, rumours soon began to spin out from within the club that a deal had been done. The manager had agreed with the player that if he stayed for one more year, and still felt like going, he could do so with Fergie's blessing. The Scot was convinced, during that time, that he could employ his renowned powers of persuasion. After all, why would Ronaldo want to go? United were now the centre of the game. It was in Manchester that he was winning every trophy known to man. It was at Carrington that his career had been nurtured and developed. Surely, there could be nowhere better for the man who now, without a hint of self-doubt, considered himself the finest in the world, if not the finest that had ever been.

But, even after he returned to United action following an ankle operation, the issue would not die. At every press conference, in every interview, the prospect of his imminent departure southwards was raised. Ferguson may have broiled, Ronaldo may have remained enigmatic, but the question kept on coming. In such an atmosphere, something changed. The United fans were not inclined to forgive Ronaldo for his spoilt summer of wanderlust. This was someone for whom they had shown unconditional love, a player whose name had been chanted more than any other, whom they had lifted, without equivocation, into the Old Trafford pantheon. And here he was belittling them by claiming he was desperate to leave, as if to escape the chains of their affection. They began to view him as the rest of the footballing community had long done: as a conceited brat. When he tumbled to the ground in theatrical flights of fancy, the grumbles emanating from the stands grew ever louder: 'Get up and get on with it' is the United way. When he pouted and preened, moaning his way through the season apparently in the belief that the world was conspiring against him, the regulars rolled their eyes. When he berated colleagues if a pass was not pinpoint accurate, red observers grew weary at his reckless disregard for team spirit. They warm to scrappers at Old Trafford. Their heroes are those who battle for the cause. Pouters, preeners and prima donnas have never endeared themselves to the Mancunian psyche.

As evidence that the love affair had cooled, the Ronaldo chant, which had soundtracked the Moscow season, was heard much less frequently. More often it was in the parody version celebrating the Chelsea captain's role in the European Cup win: 'Viva John Terry/You could have won the Cup, but you fucked it up/Viva

John Terry.' The hardcore away fans refused to sing it at all, preferring to serenade new heroes: Carlos Tevez, the whole-hearted Rooney, and, establishing himself as the senior defensive midfielder after Owen Hargreaves suffered a career-threatening knee complaint, Darren Fletcher, once the butt of jokes, now the source of admiration.

But still there was a dichotomy at the heart of the United fans' relationship with Ronaldo. Personally, he may have been intolerable, his gloating self-regard insufferable. As a player, though, he remained invaluable. Of this there was never any doubt: Ronaldo scored goals. In five years at Old Trafford, 116 of them, 42 in one year. Goals that won games. Goals that made the difference. In the 2008–09 Premier League season Liverpool lost on two fewer occasions than United and beat the reds home and away. Yet they finished second, trailing the champions by four points. Why? Because they drew seven matches at Anfield. Liverpool drew with Stoke, with Sunderland, with City. United beat them all. And it was Ronaldo who got the goals that dispatched them, week after week.

He did it too in the big games. Against Arsenal in that Champions League semi his second was a thing of beauty, a goal that summed up Ferguson's towering faith in counter-attack. Tearing alongside Rooney and Ji-Sung Park, he ran sixty yards in six seconds to connect with Rooney's sumptuous invitation to score. In that moment United seemed unbeatable, impregnable, irresistible. So good were they, those few Arsenal fans who remained to hear the final whistle sound on a 3-1 slaughter, applauded them to the echo.

That victory, coupled with Andres Iniesta's last-minute equaliser at Chelsea in the other semi, served up the Champions League final red fans had long craved: United against Barcelona. This was European football as it should be, a clash between aristocrats who shared a common belief in the primacy of skill.

But before that much anticipated date in Rome, there was the matter of closing in on the Premier League title. Liverpool, led by the muscular forward pair of Steven Gerrard and Fernando Torres, who between them destroyed United in the Old Trafford League game, had incentive to ensure the trophy did not find its way to Manchester. Their club's primacy in League titles was under threat. Back in 1990, when Alex Ferguson faced his stickiest time as manager at Old Trafford, Liverpool had won the title to extend their lead over United to an apparently unassailable eleven championships. Slowly, in the eighteen years that followed, Ferguson had nibbled at the lead, until the point where in 2008, his United stood just one behind their old rivals. In a reversal of fortune that would have any clairvoyant laughed out of the Psychics' Circle had they predicted it back in the days of Lee Martin, Mike Phelan and Clayton Blackmore, another Premier League win for the reds would put United level. As a mark of the hegemony established under the great Scot it could not be more clear.

There were dips, there were stumbles, there were moments when Rafa Benitez – whose rant against Ferguson in January 2009 was one of the season's comedy highlights – could announce it as a fact that Liverpool would win. But Ferguson's unsurpassed ability to time a campaign saw results ground out at Middlesbrough, at Wigan and at Spurs. Eyes gimlet-like on the prize, there was no reduction in ruthlessness. By the time of the Manchester derby at Old Trafford in early May, United were almost there, almost on the top of the podium, their toes beginning to brush those of Hansen, Dalglish, Rush at the pinnacle of the English club game. The perch was in sight.

City, though, were a different entity from what they had been just twelve months before. A summer takeover by the Abu Dhabi royal family had turned them overnight into the wealthiest club in the world. Mark Hughes, their manager, was gifted the riches of if not Croesus then half the oil revenues of the Middle East to turn City into world beaters. He had begun to assemble quite a side, including the mercurial Brazilian Robinho and the Welshman Craig Bellamy. The minimum expectation of his new employers was that he would match the neighbours. But Ferguson, slyly pointing out to his erstwhile player that there is more to accumulating a proper football team than flourishing the cheque book, was not prepared to be overtaken.

Within an hour of the game starting, United were in a comfortable lead and with fixtures piling up like jets over Heathrow, the manager decided to preserve the energies of his best player for battles ahead. He ordered the number seven to be illuminated on the substitute's board and readied a rested Rooney to come on. When Ronaldo saw he was to be taken off, however, he looked visibly appalled. He stood there, arms held out as if subject of the most appalling miscarriage of justice. Realising his manager was serious, he stormed off the pitch, snatched a tracksuit offered by United's kit man and flung it to the ground. He then sat in the home dug-out shaking his head in an extended, unabashed and public sulk. Apparently, his mother was in attendance that day and he wanted her to see him play. Ferguson tends not to place the desire to please a player's mum above the needs of his team. Generally, Ferguson requires his players to subsume themselves in the team ethic. He had made much accommodation for the Ronaldo ego, but in that moment everyone in the ground joined together in a sharp intake of breath. A line had been crossed. And it wasn't the touchline.

Still, Ronaldo was there celebrating on the podium when United lifted the Premier League trophy at Hull in the last weekend of the season. With the title already secured following a draw with Arsenal in his last home game, Ferguson risked the wrath of Hull's rivals for relegation by fielding a team so young the combined total of their shirt numbers exceeded two hundred. No matter, they won, and, despite not playing, Ronaldo took his place bouncing around in the champagne spume, chanting out about United's eighteenth title as if he understood its full meaning.

'My heart is in Manchester,' he said after the game. 'Ever since I joined United this manager has been like a second father. This is my true home now. But I think even when I say my heart is here people are going to speak against me and make things up. But this is where I want to be, Manchester United is my home.'

Alongside Ronaldo, winning his eleventh championship medal, Ryan Giggs looked almost subdued by comparison. 'We'll have a couple of drinks to celebrate tonight,' he said. 'But then we'll think about the next challenge. At this club there's always a next challenge.'

This time the next challenge was a substantial one: Barcelona. And for most United fans it was a challenge getting a ticket to Rome. A Liverpool-supporting acquaintance who had secured two through the UEFA website, offered them to me for £400 each. I offered him £500 for the pair. He came back insisting he would take nothing less than £500 each.

'You started at £400,' I pointed out.

'Scouse bargaining,' he countered.

I should have bought them even at that price. On the Manchester black market they were fetching a grand apiece. Instead, I found myself unable to join the Manc exodus, the fulfilment of the old song about being there if the reds should play in Rome or Mandalay, and joined nearly four hundred other United supporters in a London pub. And there, collectively, we all awaited what was surely going to be the greatest final of them all. The Barcelona of Xavi, Iniesta and Messi against the United of Ronaldo, Rooney and Giggs. And the consensus in the room, as pints were sunk and sweat dribbled down the walls in the minutes before kick-off, was that United would do it. The presiding opinion was 2-1. Even without Fletcher, sent off in the last moments of the semi, and cruelly denied his place in the final, United's busy midfielders would constrict the room in which Barca's gilded trio roamed, leaving them vulnerable to the breakaways of the red's own gifted trinity. Everyone remembered what Chelsea had done to Barca in the semi, squeezing the pips almost to the final moment. They remembered too what United had done to Arsenal, shredding them on the break. The combination was irresistible: the rapier emerging from behind the smothering blanket. United would become the first team since the European Cup transmogrified into the Champions League to retain the trophy. Now, having levelled with Liverpool domestically, they would be within one European Cup of matching them. That would end all argument. United were poised on the lip of immortality.

Ninety minutes later a dull silence had descended over the room. United had been taken apart. Everything on which red fans relied had proved a chimera. The defence, which set a world record during the course of the season for remaining unbreached, twice proved culpable. First failing to deal with a run by Samuel Eto'o, then, early in the second half, allowing Lionel Messi, the smallest man on the pitch, to rise between two static, statuesque six-footers and head home unmolested.

But it was Xavi and Iniesta who most confounded expectation. Instead of being harried into submission, they passed United to distraction. Players who could find acres of room in a Tokyo tube train during rush hour, they exercised such dominance of the ball, you could only stand back and admire. Which is roughly what the United midfield did. A moment late in the game exemplified the contribution of Iniesta, the man Wayne Rooney rightly identified as the finest midfielder in the world: four United players formed a tight rectangle blocking the advance of Sylvinho on the Barcelona left. As if from nowhere Iniesta appeared bang in the middle of the foursome to receive a pass from his full back. He then threaded the ball through to Xavi inside him. With one sprint and swivel he took out four opponents, making them look about as mobile and effective as training ground cones.

It was extraordinary to watch, a masterclass of skill. By the end, as the Catalans went up to receive their medals, all the red players could do was applaud. Ferguson, usually so animated in the technical area, was reduced to sitting in his dug-out chair bearing the look of a man who has just read his own obituary. Outplayed? United were hammered.

Most disappointingly of all, while Barca's big name players flourished, Ronaldo was dire. Spending the game consumed in a personal spat with Barca's Carlos Puyol, a man who has little time for Madrid or those who admire them, he was at his most frustratingly self-absorbed, apparently incapable of adapting to team orders. While his opponents passed endlessly, and accurately, Ronaldo appeared to have no faith in his team-mates, preferring the aimless dribble or the distant pot shot. On the rare occasions that Ferguson rose from his seat it was to rail against his pouting superstar, the one hope he had of redemption.

It was a performance that spoke of imminent divorce. And indeed it came no more than a month later. And, in the end, it was Ferguson's choice. Despite the conspiracy theorists gathering outside Old Trafford on the day that it had been announced United had accepted Madrid's bid, despite those who muttered darkly about the Glazer family snatching at the offer in the urgent requirement of using the transfer fee to pay off some of their gargantuan debt, they had, in fact, left the decision to the manager. He finally decided he could no longer keep the player focused on the cause. The ego had grown too big. Ronaldo wanted greater freedom to pursue image rights, he wanted to exploit his position as the world's best player, he wanted to become an international brand. Ferguson wanted him to remain a Manchester United player. When the manager realised such a requirement was beyond the player, he decided to cut their ties. No man is bigger than United has long been the driving philosophy at the club. Ronaldo presented its most fundamental challenge. He had to go. So Ferguson acceded to his wish. And the boy disappeared to Los Angeles to celebrate with Paris Hilton (someone whose worldwide popularity – unlike Ronaldo's – was significantly boosted by a video replay).

'I've had my time at United,' he said. 'Now I can look forward to Madrid.'

For Ferguson, too, it was time to look forward. To a time of Macheda and Evans, of the da Silva twins and Ben Foster. Look ahead to the era of Danny Welbeck. Because at United the bus stops for no man. Not even Cristiano Ronaldo.

SELECTED RECORDS

Eleven youngest players in United history

1 David Gaskell, goalkeeper, made his debut on 24.10.1956 v Manchester City (Charity Shield); aged 16 years 19 days
2 Jeff Whitefoot, full back, 15.04.1950 v Portsmouth (Football League); 16y 105d
3= Sammy McIlroy, midfield, 21.01.1971 v Bohemians (Friendly); 16y 172d
   Ian Moir, forward, 05.04.1960 v Shamrock Rovers (Friendly); 16y 172d
5 Duncan Edwards, half-back, 04.04.1953 v Cardiff City (FL); 16y 185d
6 Roy Morton, forward, 18.05.1972 v Real Mallorca (Friendly); 16y 202d
7 Willie Anderson, winger, 28.12.1963 v Burnley (FL); 16y 338d
8 Norman Whiteside, midfield, 24.04.1982 v Brighton (FL); 16y 352d
9 Alex Dawson, forward, 22.04.1957 v Burnley (FL); 17y 60d; scored
10 Peter Coyne, forward, 24.04.1976 v Leicester City (FL); 17y 162d; scored
11 Jimmy Nicholson, half-back, 24.08.1960 v Everton (FL); 17y 177d

Eleven oldest reds

1   Billy Meredith, forward, 46 years 281 days; 1921
2   Raimond van der Gouw, goalkeeper, 39y 48d; 2002
3   Frank Mann, midfield, 38y 240d; 1929
4   Jack Warner, midfield, 38y 213d; 1950
5   Laurent Blanc, defender, 38y 169d; 2003
6   Thomas Jones, defender, 38y 5d; 1937
7   Teddy Partridge, forward, 37y 323d; 1929
8   George Livingstone, forward, 37y 313d; 1914
9   Clarence Hilditch, midfield, 37y 243d; 1932
10   Bill Foulkes, defender, 37y 223d; 1969
11   Edwin van der Sar, goalkeeper, 37y 204d; 2008

Most successful League seasons

	Season	P	W	D	L	F	A	Pts	%
1	1999–00	38	28	7	3	97	45	63	82.8
2	2008–09	38	28	6	4	68	24	62	81.5
3	2006–07	38	28	5	5	83	27	61	80.26
4	2007–08	38	27	6	5	80	22	60	78.95
5	1993–94	42	27	11	4	80	38	65	77.3
6	2002–03	38	25	8	5	74	34	58	76.3
7	1956–57	42	28	8	6	103	54	64	76.1
8	1998–99	38	22	13	3	80	37	57	75.0
9	1995–96	38	25	7	6	73	35	57	75.0
10	2000–01	38	24	8	6	79	31	56	73.6

This table is devised using the old system of two points for a League win. Rankings are according to the total percentage of points gained. Goal difference is used to separate seasons.

Greatest victories

1   10-0 v Anderlecht (h), European Cup, September 1956
2   10-1 v Wolves (h), Division One, October 1892
3=   9-0 v Ipswich (h), Premiership, March 1995

9-0 v Walsall Town Swifts (h), Division Two, April 1895

9-0 v Darwen (h), Division Two, December 1898

6 8-0 v Yeovil Town (h), FA Cup, February 1949

7 8-1 v Nottingham Forest (a), Premiership, February 1999

8 8-2 v Northampton Town (a), FA Cup, January 1970

9 7-0 v Grimsby Town (a), Division Two, December 1899

10 7-1 v AS Roma 7-1 (h), Champions League, April 2007

Worst defeats

1= 0-7 v Blackburn Rovers (a), Division One, April 1926

0-7 v Aston Villa (a), Division One, December 1930

0-7 v Wolves (a), Division Two, December 1931

4= 0-6 v Leicester City (a), Division One, March 1961

0-6 v Ipswich Town (a), Division One, March 1980

0-6 v Aston Villa (h), Division One, March 1914

0-6 v Huddersfield Town (h), Division One, September 1930

8= 1-7 v Burnley (a), FA Cup, February 1901

1-7 v Newcastle United (h), Division One, September 1927

10 2-7 v Sheffield Wednesday (h), FA Cup, February 1961

Red heavyweights

1 Peter Schmeichel, goalkeeper (1991–99), 15st 13lbs

2= Gary Pallister, defender (1989–98), 14st 13lbs

Gary Walsh, goalkeeper (1986–95), 14st 13lbs

4 Caesar August Llewelyn Jenkins, defender (1896–98), 14st 4lbs

5 Jaap Stam, defender (1998–2001), 14st 1lbs

6 Gary Bailey, goalkeeper (1978–86), 13st 12lbs

7 Eric Cantona, god (1992–97), 13st 11lbs

8 Gordon Clayton, goalkeeper (1956–57), 13st 9lbs

9 Les Sealey, goalkeeper (1989–90), 13 lb 8lbs

10 Mark Bosnich, goalkeeper (1989–91 & 1999–2000), 13st 7lbs

One-appearance wonders

1   Tony Hawksworth. A lance-corporal in the Tank Regiment, he received a call at work asking him to play in goal for United at Blackpool that very afternoon in October 1956. United drew 2-2.

2   Harold Bratt. He played in front of the lowest post-war United crowd (see low crowds list) as Bradford City beat the reds 2-1 in 1960's inaugural League Cup.

3   Denis Walker. The first black player to wear red, the Northwich-born forward played in a weakened pre-FA Cup final team against Forest in May 1963. United lost 3-2.

4   Jonathan Clark. Waited three years for his debut and when it came he gave the ball away with one of his first touches against Sunderland at Old Trafford in October 1976. The Mackems equalised.

5   'Anto' Whelan. A Dubliner who covered for injured compatriot Kevin Moran in a home game against Southampton in 1980.

6   Peter Beardsley. A £250,000 signing from Vancouver Whitecaps, the future Newcastle, Liverpool and England forward wore red for forty-five minutes in a 1982 League Cup tie against Bournemouth.

7   Colin McKee. A member of the 1992 FA Youth Cup-winning side, the Glaswegian winger played seventy-five minutes in the celebratory final game of the 1993–94 season.

8   Pat McGibbon. Not only was his only game the 3-0 home defeat to York City in 1995, but the Ulsterman also had the ignominy of being sent off.

9   Nick Culkin. The man with the shortest first-team career in United history, the goalkeeper replaced Raimond van der Gouw for the final eighty seconds in a 2-1 victory at Arsenal in 1999.

10   Jimmy Davis. The talented winger played in the 4-0 League Cup defeat at Arsenal in 2001. He then spent two years on loan at Swindon and Watford. Davis died in a car accident on the M40 in 2003.

Tallest reds

1   Edwin van der Sar, goalkeeper (2005–), 6ft 5.5in.
2   Peter Fletcher, forward (1972–73), 6ft 5in.
3= Peter Schmeichel, goalkeeper (1991–99), 6ft 4in.
    Gary Pallister, defender (1989–98), 6ft 4in.
    Gordon McQueen, defender (1978–85), 6ft 4in.
6= Laurent Blanc, defender (2001–03), 6ft 3in.
    Gary Walsh, goalkeeper (1986–95), 6ft 3in.
    Henry Moger, goalkeeper (1903–12), 6ft 3in.
9= Rio Ferdinand, defender (2002–), 6ft 2.5in.
    Michael Carrick, midfielder (2006–), 6ft 2.5in

*Despite the terrace song that exaggerated his height, 'big' Jim Holton was actually 6ft 1in.

Shortest reds

1= Terry Gibson, forward (1985–87), 5ft 4in.
    Ernie Taylor, forward (1957–59), 5ft 4in.
3= Danny Wallace, forward (1989–93), 5ft 5in.
    Herbert Burgess, defender (1906–10), 5ft 5in.
    Henry Cockburn, midfield (1946–54), 5ft 5in.
6   Gordon Strachan, midfield (1984–89), 5ft 5.5in.
7= Carlos Tevez, forward (2007–), 5ft 6in.
    Steve Coppell, forward (1975–83), 5ft 6in.
    Jesper Olsen, forward (1984–89), 5ft 6in.
    Nobby Stiles, midfield (1960–71), 5ft 6in.
    Johnny Giles, midfield (1959–63), 5ft 6in.

Biggest United attendances, excluding Cup finals

1   135,000 Real Madrid (a), April 1957
2   125,000 Real Madrid (a), May 1968
3   114,432 Barcelona (a), November 1994
4   105,000 Gornik Zabreze (a), March 1968
5   82,771 Bradford Park Avenue (h), January 1949
6   81,962 Arsenal (h), January 1948

7   81,565 Yeovil Town (h), February 1949
8   80,000 AC Milan (a), May 1958
9   80,000 AC Milan (a), April 1969
10   76,098 Blackburn (h), March 2007

United's lowest League top scorers

1=   1972–73, Bobby Charlton, 6 goals
     1973–74, Sammy McIlroy, 6
3   1920–21, Three players on 7
4=   1933–34, Neil Dewar, 8
     1893–94, Alf Farman, 8
6   1914–15, George Anderson, 10
7=   1978–79, Steve Coppell and Jimmy Greenhoff, 11
     1932–33, Bill Ridding, 11
     1906–07, George Wall, 11
     1902–03, Jack Peddie, 11
     1901–02, Steve Preston, 11
     1903–04, Three players on 11

Record English transfer fees paid by United

1   Albert Quixall   £45,000, Sheffield Wednesday,
                           September 1958
2   Denis Law   £115,000, Torino, August 1962
3   Willie Morgan   £117,000, Burnley, August 1968
4   Gordon McQueen   £450,000, Leeds United,
                           February 1978
5   Bryan Robson   £1,500,000, West Bromwich Albion,
                           October 1981
6   Gary Pallister   £2,300,000, Middlesbrough,
                           August 1989
7   Roy Keane   £3,750,000, Nottingham Forest,
                           July 1993
8   Andy Cole   £7,000,000, Newcastle United,
                           January 1995

9	Ruud van Nistelrooy	£19,000,000, PSV Eindhoven, July 2001
10	Juan Sebastian Veron	£28,100,000, Lazio, July 2001
11	Rio Ferdinand	£29,000,000, Leeds United, July 2002

Eleven striking seasons

1 Denis Law, 1963–64: 46 goals
2 Ruud van Nistelrooy, 2002–03: 44
3 Cristiano Ronaldo, 2007–08: 42
4 Denis Law, 1964–65: 39
5 Ruud van Nistelrooy, 2001–02: 36
6 Tommy Taylor, 1956–57: 34
7= Billy Whelan, 1956–57: 33
    David Herd, 1965–66: 33
9= Dennis Viollet, 1959–60: 32
    George Best, 1967–68: 32

Championship-winning red captains

1 Charlie Roberts, 1908, 1911
2 Johnny Carey, 1952
3 Roger Byrne, 1956, 1957
4 Denis Law, 1965
5 Bobby Charlton, 1967
6 Steve Bruce, 1993, 1994, 1996
7 Eric Cantona, 1997
8 Roy Keane, 1999, 2000, 2001, 2003
9 Gary Neville, 2007, 2009
10 Ryan Giggs/Rio Ferdinand, 2008

INDEX